Montana: A History of Two Centuries

MONTANA

A HISTORY OF TWO CENTURIES

Revised Edition

Michael P. Malone,
Richard B. Roeder,
and William L. Lang

UNIVERSITY OF WASHINGTON PRESS

Seattle and London

Library of Congress Cataloging-in-Publication Data
Malone, Michael P.
  Montana: a history of two centuries / Michael P. Malone, Richard B. Roeder, and
William L. Lang – Rev. Ed.
      p. cm.
  Includes bibliographical references and index.
  ISBN 0-295-97129-0 (pbk.)
  1. Montana—History. I. Roeder, Richard B. II. Lang, William L. III. Title.
F731. M339   1991   91-21742
978.6—dc20   CIP

Cover photo: "View of the Bear Paw Mountains from Fort McKenzie" by Karl Bodmer
(courtesy of the Joslyn Art Museum, Omaha, Nebraska)

TO OUR PARENTS, *Dolores F. Malone Chard and the late John A. Malone, Herman H. Roeder and Mary E. Roeder, and William J. Lang and Norma K. Lang*

Contents

Illustrations

PHOTOGRAPHS

Note: All photographs, unless otherwise credited in the captions, are courtesy of the Montana Historical Society, Helena

Preface to the Second Edition

Montana: A History of Two Centuries first appeared in 1976. In this thoroughgoing revision, William L. Lang has joined the two original authors in drawing on the great outpouring of scholarship that has appeared during the past fifteen years both to revise the earlier volume and to carry forward the narrative to 1990. Fully 20 percent of the text is new or revised, the bibliography has been updated and expanded, new maps have been drawn, and new photographs have been selected.

Like its predecessor, this volume is meant to be a general, interpretive history of Montana for the mature reader. The book is based on our teaching and researching this general subject over many years. We have endeavored to focus here, as before, on those historical trends, events, and personalities that proved most vital to the shaping of present-day Montana. In practice, this has meant the avoidance of such "Wild West" and romanticized perennials as Calamity Jane, Liver-Eating Johnson, and Kid Curry. Instead, the emphasis is on the serious economic, social, political, and cultural threads in the main fabric of the state's history. Without denigrating Montana's frontier heritage, we have attempted again to develop further the traditionally neglected years since the 1920s.

In both the first edition and in this revision, many friends, colleagues, and fellow Montanans have graciously helped us in preparing these volumes. They include Jon Axline, Edward Barry, E. J. Bell Jr., Harry Billings, Doc Bowler, Charles Bradley, Dorothy Bradley, Robert E. Burke, Merrill Burlingame, Brian Cockhill, Gail Cramer, Jeff Cuniff, Ivan Doig, Robert Dunbar, Jeanne Eder, Harry Fritz, H. Duane Hampton, Roy Huffman, Mark Hufstetler, Chuck Johnson, Dale Johnson, William Kittridge, Richard McConnen, Laurie Mercier, John Montagne, Pierce Mullen, John Munsell, Rex Myers, Vivian Paladin, Thomas Payne,

xiv   *Preface*

Robert Peterson, Paula Petrik, Richard Ruetten, Ken Ryan, Jeffrey Safford, David Schwab, Ted Shwinden, Richard Stroup, Robert Taylor, Myles Watts, Thomas Wessel, Tom Wigal, and Lester Zeihen. Harriet Meloy of the Montana Historical Society and Minnie Paugh and Ilah Shriver of the Montana State University Archives gave us invaluable aid in gathering source materials. Lory Morrow, Photograph Curator at the Montana Historical Society, gave us exceptional help in selecting photographs, and David Walter, MHS Reference Librarian, provided essential guidance to the Society's holdings. Diane Arnold, Stan James, Diane Jones, Dianne Ostermiller, and Ellen Sanford assisted in the physical preparation of the manuscript.

Finally, we owe special thanks to Marianne Keddington for superb copyediting, and to Julidta Tarver, our highly capable editor at the University of Washington Press and a native Montanan, who saw the manuscript through production. We alone are responsible, of course, for the judgments here expressed and for the accuracy of what we have written.

MPM, RBR, WLL
January 1991

Montana: A History of Two Centuries

CHAPTER 1

Montana in Prehistory

THE recorded history of Montana covers only a fragment of the more than twelve thousand years that humans have resided on this landscape. We know some of that earlier history from Native American oral tradition, but most of it is beyond our reach. The identity of the first whites to visit Montana is open to conjecture—possibly French or Spanish adventurers looking for better fur-trapping regions. The first recorded descriptions of Montana and its indigenous people were written by members of the Lewis and Clark Expedition, which traversed the area in 1805-6. What Lewis and Clark described was a land of dramatic landscapes, practically the image of what later Americans would call wilderness. The harshness and beauty of the region impressed the explorers, who remarked on the impressive Native American cultures they encountered and the richness of natural resources they saw. The portrait of this country, drawn on maps and described in exploration journals nearly two centuries ago, has undergone massive revision, but its expansiveness and stark beauty continue to characterize Montana.

THE ENVIRONMENT

Montana is a place of broad dimensions and sharp contrasts. In its sheer immensity, the state overwhelms its visitor. The "Treasure State" contains 147,138 square miles. It averages 535 miles from east to west and 275 miles from north to south and is considerably larger than Italy or Greece. Yet Montana's population in 1990 stood at only slightly more than eight hundred thousand, about half the population of metropolitan Seattle. It is a classic "acreage state," with lots of land and few people. In many other ways, too, Montana is a collection of contrasts. Its altitude,

3

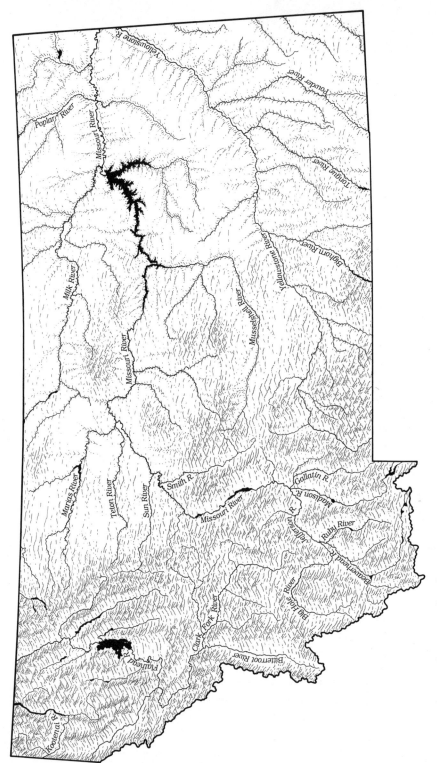

Map 1. *Physiographic diagram (map by Barbara Lien)*

averaging 3,400 feet above sea level, ranges from a high of 12,850 feet at Granite Peak to a low of 1,800 feet where the Kootenai River flows into northern Idaho near Troy. Temperatures vary from the very hottest, occasionally over 110 degrees in the far eastern section, to a low of nearly 70 degrees below zero at Rogers Pass near Helena in 1954, the lowest recorded temperature in the contiguous United States.

Montana's topography presents the most striking contrasts of all, from the alpine peaks of Glacier National Park to the rolling plains near the Dakota state line. On all sides, but mainly in the far west, there is evidence of a sometimes turbulent geologic past. During a dramatic geologic period, culminating about sixty million years ago, the mountains of western Montana were formed by massive shifts of the earth's surface and the explosive spurting of lava through volcanoes and fissures. Ancient seas and lakes rose and fell, covering at various times all of today's Montana, leaving behind fascinating geologic formations and sedimentary deposits of limestone, phosphates, and many other compounds. Great swamps formed east of the mountains and were later buried to become coal and oil fields.

About eighty to one hundred million years ago, after the seas receded from the Montana region, dinosaurs roamed the plains east of the Rockies. Over the years, paleontologists have found some of the world's most impressive and important dinosaur fossils, including a *Tyrannosaurus* fossil north of Jordan in 1908. In the Judith Basin and the Bears Paw Mountains, and especially along the Rocky Mountain Front in the Two Medicine Formation, recent finds have made Montana a major center of attention for paleontologists. Jack Horner and his associates at Montana State University's Museum of the Rockies have made startling discoveries in the eroded hills near Choteau, including fossils of baby dinosaurs and colonies of the duckbilled *Maiasaura*. In the summer of 1990, Horner excavated what was reportedly the most complete *Tyrannosaurus* skeleton yet found in North America. The results of these discoveries have revolutionized how scientists interpret dinosaurs.

The dinosaurs died off around sixty to eighty million years ago at the dawn of the age of mammals, when Montana's landscape and environment went through another series of dramatic changes. During the Pleistocene era, beginning two million years ago, dropping temperatures periodically caused enormous glaciers to form across Canada. Four times, at least, these great ice sheets moved into the northern third of Montana, reaching as far south as present-day Great Falls and Glendive. They retreated again and again with spells of warm weather, the last time roughly twenty thousand years ago. The glaciers ground through the landscape, sculpting U-shaped valleys and damming huge lakes created by icemelt.

One such lake, Lake Missoula, flooded all of the valleys west of the Rockies to depths of eight hundred feet or more. In the mountainous areas, localized glaciers hollowed out and widened the valleys and created cirque lakes. The glaciers transformed the region's waterways, most notably the Missouri River, which flowed to the Arctic north of Hudson Bay until the ice sheets blocked and shifted it eastward and eventually southward to the Gulf of Mexico.

What emerged, of course, was the land as we know it today. Perhaps the most striking feature of Montana is its geographically split personality—its western one-third, which is ruggedly mountainous, and its eastern two-thirds, which breaks into clefted and undulating plains. These two geographical provinces were joined into one community, not by any geographical logic, but simply by the accidental occurrences of history. Eastern and western Montana have much in common: both are remote and rugged; both have a cold, semiarid climate. But the two regions also reveal many differences, both in environment and in human history.

When speaking of "western" Montana, we may mean either the western third of the state, which is mountainous, or that smaller, far northwestern sector that lies west of the Continental Divide. Western Montana embraces the major United States share of the Northern Rocky Mountains, a broad series of crosscutting and interlaced mountain chains generally running northwest to southeast. The main spine of the Rockies extends through today's Glacier National Park in a broken pattern southeastward into Yellowstone National Park in Wyoming. To the east and especially to the west of this main divide lie other ranges—for example, the Cabinet, Mission, Swan, Garnet, Ruby, and Tobacco Root mountains to the west, and the Big Belt, Little Belt, Snowy, Judith, Absaroka, Beartooth, and Big Horn mountains to the east. Especially prominent are the massive shoulders of the Bitterroot Range, whose summits form the boundary with Idaho. The Continental Divide follows the primary chains southward from Glacier National Park to Butte, where it bows westward to the Bitterroot crests like an inverted question mark, then turns southeastward again into Yellowstone Park, enclosing the Beaverhead Basin of southwestern Montana in the Atlantic drainage.

Two major tributaries of the mighty Columbia River drain northwestern Montana. Flowing out of Canada, the Kootenai River crosses the state's extreme northwestern corner and passes into the Idaho panhandle. Draining the larger portion of western Montana is the Clark Fork River, which gathers its headwaters near Butte-Anaconda, and then flows northwesterly through Hellgate Canyon east of Missoula. Three other tributaries enlarge the Clark Fork as it flows west through the Bitterroot Mountains into Idaho and Pend d'Oreille Lake. The Bitterroot River joins the Clark Fork from south of Missoula, the Big Blackfoot River drains the west slope of the Continental Divide to the north, and the Flathead River flows south from Flathead Lake, running into the Clark Fork west of present-day Plains.

In far southwestern Montana lies the bulge in the Continental Divide that is drained by the three streams that join at Three Forks to form the east-flowing Missouri: the Jefferson, the Madison, and the Gallatin rivers. Like the westward inclined lands to the north, this is also a region of fertile valleys and broken mountain chains. Western Montana's high mountain valleys, such as the Flathead, Bitterroot, Deer Lodge, and Gallatin, are some of the most beautiful landscapes in the United States.

In west-central Montana, the mountains give way to the Great Plains. At some points, especially in the north, the steep mountains break abruptly onto the plains. More generally, however, the Rockies slope into clefted foothills, steep valleys, plateaus, and mesas. The Shields River Valley and the Crazy Mountains north of Livingston are good examples of this terrain. So is the beautiful country around Great Falls, which artist Charlie Russell portrayed with such brilliant accuracy on canvas. Occasional isolated mountain ranges punctuate the hill country of central Montana; and in some choice locations, like the lush Judith Basin, they form fertile and lovely valleys between them. A. B. Guthrie Jr. called the region "These Thousand Hills," and they form a sort of twilight zone between mountains and prairies.

Waters from the east side of Glacier National Park flow out of the state in the St. Mary River, eventually to join the Saskatchewan River and finally Hudson Bay. Beyond the Rocky Mountain shadows, the true Great Plains expands to the east. There, the landscape broadens its contour and extends into eroded flatlands and coulees, where windblown grasses give an oceanic appearance. Through these dry plains flow the Missouri River and its tributaries. The upper Missouri and its principal branches, the Yellowstone and the Milk, cut meandering valleys through the Great Plains, where much of today's population and best croplands are located. Because the Rockies trap most of the moisture from Pacific air masses, eastern Montana is drier than the west. In that arid land, water means everything, and civilization clings to the vital waterways.

The mighty Missouri heads at Three Forks in southwestern Montana. It flows northward, breaking suddenly out of the mountains upstream and south of its Great Falls. Then, below the falls, the Missouri bends eastward toward Dakota, en route to its rendezvous with the Mississippi. Major northern tributaries of the Missouri include the Sun, the Teton-Marias, and the Milk rivers. From the south come the Judith, the Musselshell, and, just beyond the Dakota line, the Yellowstone. The Yellowstone, which begins in Wyoming and drains southeastern Montana, is the last major free-flowing river in the continental United States. Forming Yellowstone Lake and falling spectacularly out of today's Yellowstone National Park, the river flows to the northeast and receives its major tributaries from the south: the Clark's Fork (of the Yellowstone), the Big Horn, the Tongue, and the Powder rivers.

EARLY IMMIGRANTS

Authorities have argued for many years over how and when prehistoric peoples migrated to North America, but they overwhelmingly agree as to the route. Climatic changes many thousands of years ago caused the formation of glaciers, with the obvious result of falling sea levels. This, in turn, caused a large land bridge to appear across the Bering Strait, connecting Asian Siberia to Alaska. Recent archaeological discoveries indicate that Asiatic peoples probably crossed the Bering land bridge at least as early as fifteen to twenty thousand years ago, and perhaps much earlier, probably in pursuit of large Pleistocene animals that were migrating to the New World. Traditional origin stories told by Montana Indians, the descendants of the earliest people in the region, tend to support this early date. But the origin stories include no mention of the land bridge or the trek to the New World. They portray the ancestral people as having always been part of this continent.

The immigrant peoples headed eastward through the interior of Alaska, then southward, mainly down the eastern slopes of the Rocky Mountains. Along this route, sometimes called the "Great North Trail," they pushed to the south, many of them passing through east-central Montana, and eventually to the American Southwest and South America. Archaeologists have found evidence of prehistoric habitation in Montana as early as thirteen thousand years ago. These earliest prehistoric peoples lived on the plains and in the mountain foothills. As the climate and environment changed, they adapted successfully, relying on a variety of hunting and gathering techniques.

During the earliest period, these peoples hunted the ancient bison and mammoth and gathered plant foods. Living in groups of a dozen or more, they moved as many as fifty or a hundred times a year within a hundred-mile range, following the seasonal migrations of game animals. Hunters killed their prey with large spear points that were attached to heavy shafts. Sometimes the spears were flung as darts with great accuracy and force using an *atlatl*.

Archaeological evidence of early prehistoric life in Montana has been discovered at several sites in the Yellowstone River Valley, some of them

Ulm Pishkun State Park. For thousands of years, Native American hunters used their collective efforts to kill bison by stampeding them off cliffs such as these. (Photo by John Smart)

dating back thirteen thousand years. Other locations in southeastern Montana, and one especially important Folsom-era site near Helena, indicate that Montana's prehistoric hunter-gatherers lived a relatively sophisticated communal life. Today, we can see evidence of their lives in stone circles—so-called tipi rings—that probably held down the edges of skin lodges or braced larger structures; they may even have served religious purposes.

Beginning about eight thousand years ago, a major change in climate began to dry up the Great Plains, decreasing the numbers of animals and pushing them to higher elevations. Hunters and gatherers, forced to adapt to the new conditions, moved off the plains and began living more on plants and smaller animals. Soon, they began to stalk the modern bison or buffalo, and they eventually developed communal hunting techniques by chasing the animals into corrals and over cliffs. At so-called buffalo jumps, prehistoric and later Indians drove bison over steep drops, killing or crippling them. By the time of Christ's birth, these hunters had developed bows and were using finely crafted points on slender arrow shafts.

The Plains Indian lifeways that Europeans first encountered in the late eighteenth century developed directly from these prehistoric cultures. Late prehistoric peoples perfected their pursuit of buffalo in seasonal rounds, made increasingly sophisticated stone tools, and created vast trading networks that carried goods back and forth across North America. The lattices of prehistoric trails that archaeologists have discovered across Montana testify to the long distances these peoples traveled in pursuit of game and trade.

Nearly five hundred years ago, when Europeans first invaded North America, over five million Native Americans lived in a variety of cultural groups throughout what is now the United States. The coming of the whites, with their advanced technologies and especially their diseases, disrupted these Indian civilizations: many Indians died from disease or were killed, and most lost their lands. As early as the sixteenth century, European diseases, particularly smallpox, devastated tribes in eastern North America. After the first encounters between eastern tribes and Europeans, the results of the white invasion affected Indians to the west long before they actually saw the invaders. Like ripples spreading outward from a stone thrown into a pond, the shock waves of the whites' intrusion spread rapidly across the continent. The shocks came both from the Spanish colonies to the south in Mexico and New Mexico and from French and English frontiers far to the east.

The Europeans destroyed some of the tribes, pushed others off their lands, and traded and allied with still others. The net effect was extreme dislocation. Eastern Indians, armed with firearms and iron weapons obtained from whites, set upon poorer armed tribes farther west, forcing them to abandon their lands and retreat toward the west. It became a process of falling dominoes, as tribe after tribe, hit by better armed peoples from the east, fell upon weaker neighbors to the west. Throughout the seventeenth and eighteenth centuries, wave upon wave of Indians, pushed ahead of the advancing European frontier, moved westward across the Mississippi, beyond the woodlands, out upon the Great Plains to the Rockies. Several of the retreating tribes had found a homeland in Montana by the mid-seventeenth century.

During the seventeenth and eighteenth centuries, Indians acquired two of the whites' most valuable possessions—horses and guns—and the Indian cultures were transformed. Ironically, horses had originated in North America during prehistoric times; but after spreading to Eurasia, they had become extinct on this continent. It was the European invasion that brought horses within reach of Native Americans. The Indians of the West first acquired horses from the Spanish colony in New Mexico, especially after a revolt of Pueblo Indians in 1680 made sizable herds available for the taking. Native Americans adapted to horses rapidly and successfully, and a new horse culture spread northward up both the western and eastern flanks of the Rockies.

By the late seventeenth century, the Shoshoni Indians, who inhabited the desert-mountain regions south and west of Montana, had acquired horses from their southern neighbors, the Utes. The Shoshonis, mounted and wearing leather armor in imitation of the Spaniards, fell upon their enemies to the north and east. Terrorizing their foes, they swept over most of Montana, driving the Flatheads from the plains into the northwest mountains and pressing northward into Blackfeet territory and the Canadian prairies. Two factors finally stopped them: other tribes soon got horses of their own and learned to breed them, and Indians migrating from east to west brought smooth-bore trade guns with them that allowed warriors on foot to bring down mounted Shoshonis. The horse culture, moving out of the southwest, met the gun frontier advancing from the east, there on the Canadian-American plains.

By the late eighteenth century, a successful Plains Indian culture had been established throughout present-day Montana east of the Rockies. Although each tribe lived by distinct traditions, all Plains Indian societies relied on a hunting and gathering economy that centered on the bison. Their civilization might be better described as an Indian-horse-buffalo culture characterized by great mobility, mounted warriors and hunters, and ownership of horses as a measure of wealth. With the acquisition of guns, horses, and trade goods, Montana's Indians had more power and wealth than their ancestors could have imagined. It was a dramatic change, comparable to similar cultural revolutions in European history. In contrast to the simple characterization of Indian cultures as "primitive," we should understand them as highly adaptive and complex societies.

Plains Indians continued the pattern of seasonal travels that their prehistoric ancestors had followed, but with horses they extended their range, more than doubling the distances they could travel in a day and greatly enlarging their stores of household goods. The hunt became a chase on horseback, and the hunters bred and trained their horses to run down the buffalo. After acquiring European trade goods, Plains Indians discarded stone spears and armed themselves with iron-tipped arrows. The long bows of unmounted hunters gave way to shorter bows that could be wielded with remarkable accuracy and power from horseback. The hunt thus became more individualized, and hunters could strike their prey at greater distances from camp. A band of a dozen hunters could kill nearly a thousand buffalo in a single season.

With horses, Plains Indians could move their camps with ease, using *travois*—horse-drawn platforms riding on two dragging poles—to transport their belongings and large buffalo-hide tipis. Horses also extended and changed the Indians' trading relationships, and the expansion of hunting territories escalated intertribal conflict and warfare. Both to meet their needs and to increase their personal wealth, warriors pursued horse-stealing raids. Possession of horses meant wealth and distinctions of class and power that were not prevalent during earlier times. More important, perhaps, the conduct of war changed from relatively static standoffs between tribes to dynamic and bloodier confrontations that emphasized individual acts of courage. Indian warriors, astride swift horses and carrying quivers full of arrows, became some of the world's greatest cavalry forces.

Indians of the plains lived and traveled as extended families, loosely organized into larger tribal groups. The division of labor cleaved roughly along sexual lines. Women fashioned and owned the tipis and tended to domestic tasks, and men did most of the hunting and fighting. In some tribes—the Crows, for example—women had equal involvement in social, religious, and artistic life. They followed the hunters, dressing out the downed buffalo in the field and later preparing the hides and fashioning clothing and domestic articles from the carcasses. As the acquisition of horses and iron tools increased the kills—and the processing of hides— women's labor became more occupied with meat and hide preparation, diminishing their roles from the pre-horse days when they had played a larger role in the hunt.

Indian bands and tribes gathered in larger groups for communal buffalo hunts and for religious ceremonies. Religion lay at the heart of their existence. Recognizing supernatural powers all about them in nature, they appealed to these spirits for aid and protection in a harsh environment. Both men and women played key roles in their ceremonies, including the all-important Sun Dance that brought numerous bands together in summer. An appeal to the powerful and life-giving spirit of the sun and its transcendent powers, the Sun Dance extended over several days and included fasting, the building of a medicine lodge, and self-torture. In this and other ceremonies, the Indians' strong belief in personal communication with the spirits made dreams and visions the conduit for individual strength and group protection.

While the Plains culture dominated the eastern portions of Montana, the Plateau culture prevailed in the western mountains. The Plateau Indians lived throughout the basins of the Columbia and Fraser rivers in the interior Pacific Northwest. The easternmost of these tribes occupied the Rockies in Montana. Generally speaking, the Plateau Indians lived more by fishing and gathering plants, especially camas roots, than by hunting buffalo. They moved their camps less often and within a smaller territory than did the Plains Indians, and some traveled extensively by canoe. But Plateau Indians living in or near the Rockies, such as the Flatheads, also adopted many aspects of the Plains culture. Although they used tipis and seasonally hunted buffalo on the plains, they also lived in long lodges, especially during the winter, and they manufactured household goods and clothing from bark and fibers. They borrowed clothing and decoration fashions from both the Plains and Columbia River tribes, and their religious dances and ceremonies reflected a similar melding of cultures.

Plateau and Plains Indians in Montana lived as part of the natural world, and their view of that world is reflected in a spectacular artistic tradition. In stunningly beautiful ways, they decorated nearly every piece of clothing, implement of war, utensil, or incidental article, making all of them works of art. Their aesthetics emphasized color and symmetry, geometric designs, and a range of materials from wood and fur to glass beads and dyed quills. Always, they sought to express their oneness with nature. The continuation of this tradition, which has remained vital throughout the history of the region, is a key part of the evolving legacy of Indian Montana.

THE MONTANA TRIBES

The only Indians who lived in Montana before 1600 were the tribes in the western mountains—the Plateau Indians—and perhaps the Crows in the Yellowstone Valley, who may have migrated there as early as the mid-sixteenth century. The best known of the Plateau Indians were the Flat-

Earthlodge, Mandan Villages, North Dakota. Carl Bodmer sketched this scene during his travels in the American West with Prince Maximilian of Wied-Neuwied in 1833. (Smithsonian Institution)

heads. Archaeological evidence indicates that Indians lived in the Flathead Lake area as early as nine thousand years ago, but the Salishan-speaking Flatheads probably did not migrate to the area until just prior to 1700. The Flatheads, who prefer to be called Salish, were the eastern-most of all the Salishan tribes, whose territory ranged across the Columbia Plateau and north well into British Columbia. Prior to the invasions of eastern Indians after 1600, the Salish lived in the Three Forks area and ranged as far eastward as the Big Horn Mountains. Beginning before 1700, the arrival first of Shoshonis from the south and then of Blackfeet from the northeast forced them to retreat westward into the mountains. By the time Lewis and Clark encountered the Salish in 1805, their homeland centered in the beautiful Bitterroot Valley.

The Salish combined in roughly equal parts the cultures of the Plains and the Plateau peoples. They joined forces once or twice a year with their allies, the Nez Perces of Idaho, to hunt buffalo on the plains. Like the other mountain tribes, they lived in constant fear of, and war with, the fierce Blackfeet of north-central Montana. Whites found the Salish "peaceful," friendly, and interested in Christianity. This friendliness likely stemmed not from any special meekness on their part, but from their need for allies, even white allies, against the better armed and more numerous Blackfeet.

Closely related to the Salish were the Pend d'Oreille or Kalispel Indians, who were also of Salishan linguistic origin. The Lower Pend d'Oreille lived mainly along the Clark Fork River and around Pend d'Oreille Lake in Idaho. The Upper Pend d'Oreille were located generally to the south of Flathead Lake and for a time even occupied the Sun River Valley east of the Continental Divide. These Indians intermingled and allied with their Salishan cousins, the Salish and Spokans, but they absorbed less of the Plains culture than did the Salish. Instead, like most Plateau people, they depended heavily on plants and fish for food. After the invasion of the eastern Plains Indians, the Pend d'Oreilles joined the Salish in their westward retreat and also welcomed the whites and their religion.

In the far northwest corner of Montana lived the Kutenai Indians. Their ancestry is uncertain, and their language is apparently unrelated to that of any other tribe. Although they were not Salishan, the Kutenai had become friends of the Salish and Pend d'Oreilles by 1800, and today they live on the same reservation. Like the Salish, they merged the ways of the Plains and the Plateau tribes. Until the Shoshonis and Blackfeet drove them out, the Plains Kutenai traveled the prairies above and below the Canadian boundary. The Upper and Lower Kutenai lived for the most part in the rugged Kootenai Valley of southeastern British Columbia, in northwestern Montana, and in the Idaho panhandle. Later, many

Kutenais moved southward to the Flathead Lake area. The first British and American explorers found these people isolated in their remote mountain valleys, too poor in horses to contest the invaders from the plains. They had only limited contact with the whites until later in the nineteenth century.

Beyond the mountains lived the invaders from the east, the Plains Indians who by 1800 had driven the Salish and the Kutenai from their buffalo lands. The most fierce and powerful of these were the Blackfeet, who belonged to the Algonquian language group. The Blackfeet were very numerous, probably totaling fifteen thousand people by 1780. Three separate tribes made up the Blackfeet Nation: the Blackfeet proper, or Siksika, to the far north; the Kainah, or Bloods, south of them; and the Piegans, or "Poor Robes," to the far south. The earliest white explorers found them prior to 1650 on the central plains of Canada, already migrating westward under pressure from eastern neighbors like the Cree. The Piegans led the Blackfeet advance, and they collided with the Shoshonis on the Canada-Montana plains. After acquiring horses, the Blackfeet drove the Shoshonis south and west, and by 1800 they lived on the eastern slopes of the Rockies and ranged well into southern Montana.

At the time of Lewis and Clark, early in the nineteenth century, the Piegan Blackfeet controlled north-central Montana east of the mountains. Their war parties patrolled from the Saskatchewan plains to the Yellowstone River. They drove the Shoshonis out of the Three Forks area, making that region an unclaimed terrain where Blackfeet clashed with other tribes for valuable game.

Only the Piegans were true Montana Blackfeet, for the Bloods and Siksikas remained largely to the north in Canada. The Piegans, immortalized in the paintings of Charlie Russell, were classic plains people and among the most fierce and feared of all American Indians. Among the males, status depended almost exclusively on a man's role as a warrior. Those men who did not belong to military societies had to join the women in their work. Accustomed to Canadian trading methods and goods, and perhaps urged on by Canadian traders, the Blackfeet became mortal enemies of American fur traders, and they kept the white invaders at bay until disease struck the Piegans down during the late 1830s.

To the south and east of the Blackfeet, mainly in the Yellowstone Valley of south-central Montana, lived the Piegans' hated enemies, the Crows, or Apsaalooke—the "Big-Bird-People." The Crows, a handsome people of Siouan linguistic background, were among the earliest Indians to enter Montana from the east. Along with their close relatives, the Hidatsas, the Crows left their homeland on the Canadian plains in the sixteenth century and migrated west, perhaps drawn by better opportunities or pushed by other tribes. They paused on their western journey at the Missouri River in present-day North Dakota, where they lived with the Mandans and turned to horticulture for a time. Pressured by the aggressive Sioux and Cheyennes, the Crows separated from the Hidatsas sometime before 1600 and headed west again.

By the time the whites encountered the Crows in the Yellowstone Valley, they had divided into River Crows, who lived north of the Yellowstone River, especially in the Musselshell and Judith basins, and the Mountain Crows, who hunted south of the Yellowstone, primarily in the Absaroka and Big Horn mountains. Although they still maintained clan societies acquired in the East, which most of their plains neighbors had abandoned, all of the Crows had become nomadic plainsmen by 1800. The white American invaders discovered the Crows to be quite friendly and "peaceful." Such labels were misleading, however, because the Crows were as warlike as most Plains Indians. Surrounded by hostile Blackfeet and Sioux, they welcomed the whites because they badly needed allies, especially allies with guns. The Crows were famous travelers and horse thieves, and they traded with other tribes from eastern Dakota to the Rockies.

Two smaller Indian groups lived beyond the Blackfeet in northeastern Montana: the Atsinas and the Assiniboines. The Atsinas, who spoke an Algonquian language, were very close relatives of the Arapaho, who had earlier moved southward into Wyoming and Colorado. Misunderstanding sign language, as they so often did, French traders named them the "Gros Ventres," meaning "big bellies." This was doubly unfortunate, because the Atsinas had ordinary stomachs and because the Hidatsas of Dakota also became known as "Gros Ventres," leading to much confusion. The Atsinas migrated out of the Minnesota region onto the Canadian plains, in close proximity to the Blackfeet; they eventually settled directly to the east of the Blackfeet between the Missouri and Saskatchewan rivers. The Atsinas became close allies of the Piegans, so much so that whites often mistook them for Blackfeet. Like their Piegan allies, the Atsinas were extremely warlike and hostile to the Americans.

The Assiniboine Indians lived on the Canadian-American plains, with their southernmost flank extending into northeastern Montana. They were Siouan in linguistic ancestry and at one time belonged to the Yanktonai branch of the Sioux Nation. Evidently, the Assiniboines formerly lived in the Mississippi headwaters area. Pressured by the Chippewas, Crees, and even the Sioux, with whom they became bitter enemies after their break from the Yanktonai, the Assiniboines migrated northward and westward onto the plains. Like other tribes of the upper Missouri, they would be hard hit by the smallpox epidemic of the late 1830s.

Carl Bodmer's sketch of a Crow Indian he met at Mandan in 1833 is one of the best sources of the appearance and dress of Plains Indians in the nineteenth century. (Smithsonian Institution)

The Indians' hunting lands had general boundaries, and they freely invaded one another's territory. So the place we call "Montana" was often visited by neighboring tribes from all points of the compass. Later, well after the white invasion, some of these visitors came to Montana to stay.

From the west, plateau neighbors of the Flatheads and Pend d'Oreilles frequently crossed over the Bitterroot passes and ventured onto the plains to hunt buffalo. These tribes, particularly the Spokans and Nez Perces, had to exercise considerable caution on their journeys, for Plains Indians jealously guarded their hunting lands. The Nez Perces, for example, entered Montana over the Salmon River trail or Lolo Pass, which dropped down into the Bitterroot Valley. Often with their Flathead friends, they would head through Hellgate Canyon into Blackfeet country, or they would pass southeastward into the lands of the more friendly Crows.

Indians of Shoshonian stock flanked Montana on the south and southwest. They included the Shoshonis, the Bannocks, and the horseless Sheepeaters. The Shoshonian peoples were desert and mountain dwellers from the Great Basin country of Utah, Nevada, and southern Idaho; their easternmost lands extended into west-central Wyoming. Although the Shoshonis had conquered much of today's Montana during the eighteenth century, by 1800 the Blackfeet had driven them into what is now the state's southwestern corner. Lewis and Clark met them along the Idaho-Montana line near Lemhi Pass, without guns and no longer in control of the plains.

Neither the Shoshonis nor the Bannocks became "legal" Montana residents during the nineteenth century, but they entered its southwestern extremities to hunt. Peculiarly, even though these Indians no longer lived in Montana, Congress entertained the idea of giving the name "Shoshoni" to the territory in 1864. Prominent Montana pioneer Granville Stuart thought an ideal name for the new territory would be "To yabe-Shock up," the Shoshoni expression for mountainous country. Stuart's brainstorm, not surprisingly, failed to arouse much enthusiasm.

Eastward from present-day Montana, the great Sioux or Dakota Nation controlled the vast plains area north of Nebraska's Platte River. Prior to the mid-seventeenth century, the Sioux lived along the western edges of the Great Lakes and in the upper Mississippi woodlands. Invasions by well-armed enemies, like the Chippewas, crowded them westward until, by the later nineteenth century, they controlled an area reaching from western Minnesota across the Northern Plains into the easternmost fringes of Montana and Wyoming. The westernmost Sioux tribes of the

Yanktonai and Teton groups edged into Montana, and today there are Sioux living with the Assiniboines on Montana's Fort Peck Indian Reservation. Although the center of Sioux power lay well to the east of Montana, these Indians would figure largely in the state's frontier history, most spectacularly with their defeat of Custer in 1876.

The Northern Cheyenne Indians intermingled with the Sioux and became their friends and allies. The Cheyennes belong to the Algonquian language group. Like the Sioux, they were elbowed from their traditional homeland in the Minnesota region. The Cheyennes paused for a time along the lower Missouri River and practiced agriculture until mounting pressure from the east forced them farther west. They crossed the Dakota plains, and by the time of Lewis and Clark they had reached the Black Hills. In the process, they adapted well to the nomadic ways of the Plains Indians. Their warriors became outstanding cavalry: the Cheyenne Dog Soldiers were among the most respected of Indian fighting men.

After reaching the Black Hills, the tribe divided, with the more numerous Southern Cheyennes heading toward Colorado and Oklahoma and the Northern Cheyennes proceeding to the northwest. By the 1820s and 1830s, the Northern Cheyennes lived among the Sioux in the area where the state lines of Montana, Wyoming, and South Dakota meet. These late-arriving Indians would join the Sioux during the 1860s and 1870s to fight against American military forces. Eventually, they received a small reservation on the Tongue River in southeastern Montana.

The last of Montana's Indian residents to enter the state were bands of Chippewas, Crees, and Metis who began filtering across the Canadian and North Dakota borders later in the nineteenth century. Some of these scattered bands and families were refugees from the unsuccessful rebellion that Louis Riel led against the Canadian government in 1885. Others, like the band of Chief Little Shell, came in from North Dakota, abandoning the squalor of their reservations. The Montana Crees and Chippewas are only splinters of much larger Indian groups. Of Algonquian heritage, the numerous Crees came originally from the frozen forests and plains of Canada. The Chippewas (Ojibwas) were Athabaskan-speaking people from both north and south of the Great Lakes. A large proportion of these latecomers consisted of the Metis, a mixed-blood people of Cree, Assiniboine, Chippewa, and French backgrounds who had begun to see themselves as a unique group. From their origins on the French fur-trade frontier in Canada, the Metis spoke Michif, a creole language of their own, and they brought a new culture with them to Montana.

These refugee Indians presented a problem to state and federal officials, who did not know how to treat them. Known as "Landless Indians," they moved about from town to town and became familiar figures at

Havre, Chinook, and even Butte. Their settlement in Great Falls, "Hill 57," became a byword for urban Indian poverty. Finally, in 1916, after much delay, the federal government carved a tiny reservation for the Chippewa-Cree and Metis from the large Fort Assinniboine Military Reserve south of Havre. The Rocky Boy's Indian Reservation is named for the famous Chippewa Chief Stone Child, whose noble title was changed and debased by the whites to "Rocky Boy." The last of Montana's seven Indian reservations had been shaped.

Montana's aboriginal peoples, the descendants of prehistoric hunters, had developed rich and enduring cultures by the time whites first encountered them early in the nineteenth century. Significantly, however, those Indians first seen by Lewis and Clark and by other white explorers had been in this region for no more than three centuries, and many were late arrivals. The Cheyennes, Chippewas, and Crees did not reside within Montana's boundaries until late in the nineteenth century. Before that time, Montana was truly the eye of a cultural hurricane, where Indians migrating from all directions, each with their own centuries-old traditions, met and created new societies. They shared a common fate, as Americans and Canadians drove them from their lands; reduced them by disease, war, and alcohol; and sought to destroy their native cultures. Their descendants live today on seven Indian reservations and in cities and towns throughout Montana.

CHAPTER 2

Exploration and the Rivalry of Empires

THE exploration of the Great Northwest produced some of the most heroic figures in our history. Meriwether Lewis and William Clark, Alexander Mackenzie, David Thompson, and Simon Fraser were the first whites to describe and chart the region. By placing geographic descriptions and names on their maps, they registered claims to the territory; and this was, in fact, one of the chief purposes of exploration—to claim these new lands for distant, imperial governments. With little or no respect for the rights of the native inhabitants, four nations—France, England, Spain, and the United States—competed for mastery of the interior of North America. Usually hunting for furs, sometimes searching for the long-imagined "Northwest Passage" through the continent, the agents of these nations raced and sometimes fought one another for advantage. To a large extent, their activities determined which nation or nations would ultimately possess the new territories.

THE RIVALRY OF FRANCE AND BRITAIN

During the century that followed the discovery of the Americas by Columbus, three of the great nations of Europe began the work of colonizing this continent. Spain based its North American empire on the fabulously rich gold and silver mines of Mexico. Early in the seventeenth century, the Spanish frontier pushed northward into New Mexico, carrying the flag of that nation onto the soil of today's United States. Meanwhile, French explorers moved up the St. Lawrence River toward the Great Lakes, planting the seed of French Canada. And British imperialists, beginning with Sir Humphrey Gilbert and Sir Walter Raleigh, attempted to establish permanent settlements on the Atlantic seaboard.

22

The French and British empires in North America grew apace during the 150 years following 1600, and they collided in a series of wars that would eventually decide the mastery of the continent. Beginning at Jamestown in 1607 and at the Plymouth Colony in 1620, the English settlements grew steadily until by the mid-eighteenth century they reached from New England in the north to the borders of Spanish Florida in the south, and from the Atlantic Coast westward to the crests of the Appalachian Mountains. The English colonies prospered and swelled in population. They would soon grow restive at the restraints placed on them by the mother country.

France, in the meantime, forged an empire to the north and west that was smaller in population but larger in area. The builders of New France thrust up the St. Lawrence River and centered their operations at Montreal and Quebec. The bountiful trade in furs formed the lifeblood of New France, and the unending quest for new fur-trapping areas drew French frontiersmen irresistibly westward, into and beyond the Great Lakes region. They pressed beyond the Great Lakes to the upper Mississippi, southward into the Ohio Valley, and inevitably down the great Mississippi toward the Gulf of Mexico.

In one of the epic journeys of North American exploration, Robert Cavelier, Sieur de La Salle, traveled in 1682 down the Mississippi River to its mouth, where he claimed the entire drainage of the mighty river for King Louis XIV. In his monarch's honor, La Salle named this vast and little known province "Louisiana," which included all of the Mississippi-Missouri Basin and the major portion of present-day Montana. The sweep of French explorers and traders southward from the Great Lakes set them on an inevitable course toward collision with the English. During the decades following La Salle's journey, French traders moved up the Ohio River toward the westward slopes of the Appalachians, into the shadow of the advancing English frontier. Eventually, a major war would determine who would have the inviting lands between the Mississippi and the Appalachian divide.

The Anglo-French rivalry, meanwhile, flared up in another area, far to the north of New France. In 1670, the English crown granted a charter to a syndicate of traders that was destined to become one of the great corporations in world history, the "Governor and Company of Adventurers of England Trading into Hudson's Bay." The Hudson's Bay Company was given exclusive control over the lands draining into Hudson Bay and exclusive rights to the fur-bearing animals they contained. The firm erected posts on the west shore of Hudson Bay and soon had the Indians of the interior bringing in furs for trade. Enormous profits resulted. The leaders of New France now faced English competition from another direction.

In order to retain command of the fur trade, the French had to cut into the Indian traffic that funnelled furs from the interior to Hudson Bay. They had to advance northward and westward from the Great Lakes into the heartland of present-day Canada. The French, in their movement west, were seeking more than just furs. They also longed to find the legendary "Northwest Passage," the mythical waterway through the continent that promised a short trade route to Asia.

The Northwest Passage assumed different forms in the European imagination as geographic knowledge slowly expanded. Some speculated that it was a simple waterway from sea to sea, joining the Pacific perhaps to Hudson Bay or the Great Lakes. Others thought it might be the "River of the West," a great west-flowing river that must head near the upper Mississippi. Still others saw the possibility of the long-imagined "Western Sea," from which rivers supposedly radiated to both the Atlantic and Pacific oceans. This was a geography of fantasy, of course, but the imperialist nations pursued the passage feverishly because it could bring them a monopoly of trade with the Orient. The idea fired the passions of many, including the Baron de Lahontan, who wrote a popular account in 1703 of his "Nouveaux Voyages" in the interior of North America. Lahontan claimed to have ascended the Mississippi and wintered on a great stream, the "River Longue," which flowed from the far west, where fascinating natives lived. The "River Longue" was a variant of the Northwest Passage myth, and it helped keep the myth alive.

Thus, several motives—the quest for a Northwest Passage, the urgent need to expand the fur trade, the patriotic urge to beat the British—drew the French westward. The leader of their advance was Pierre Gaultier de Varennes, Sieur de La Verendrye, a dedicated soldier who had been wounded nine times serving his country. Having gained a trade monopoly over the areas west of Lake Nipigon-Lake Superior, Verendrye pressed steadily into the wilderness until by 1734 he had reached Lake Winnipeg, the great natural crossroads of central Canada. The French had entered the Great Plains, and they began to hear Indian accounts of a mighty River of the West that lay to the south.

Searching for this long-sought-after stream, Verendrye and his sons ventured southwestward in 1738 until they reached the villages of the Mandan Indians on the Missouri River in present-day North Dakota. Setbacks forced the aging Sieur de La Verendrye to return to France. But in 1742 he sent his sons, Louis-Joseph and Francois, to revisit the Mandans and to probe farther toward the west in search of a route to the Pacific. The Verendrye brothers crossed the Dakota plains, where they encountered numerous Indian tribes, which they called by such names as the "Horse People" or the "Bow People." The Bow People, possibly Cheyenne or Crow Indians, told them of mountains to the west, beyond which lay the sea. The Verendryes traveled westward with a war party until, in January 1743, they saw before them what they called the "Shining Mountains." The war party of Bow People turned back, and the Verendryes determined they could go no farther.

The brothers returned to the Missouri and eventually to Canada, bringing reports of the Shining Mountains, which "were for the most part well wooded with all kinds of timber, and appeared very high." These mountains may have been the Black Hills. More likely, they were the Big Horn Range of Wyoming; and, if so, the brothers may have been the first white men to enter Montana. Be this as it may, the Verendryes' journey signified the farthest thrust by the French into the American West below the present United States-Canada boundary. They had found no Northwest Passage, but they had found the eastern fringes of the Rocky Mountains, whose massive presence meant that there probably was no water passage to the Pacific. So the dream of the Sieur de La Verendrye ended in failure. The old man died in 1749, and the French empire in North America outlived him by little more than a dozen years.

The last and greatest struggle between the French and the British over mastery of North America erupted in 1754. This all-important contest—variously called the Seven Years' War, the French and Indian War, or the Great War for Empire—ended in the triumph of Great Britain and the loss by France of almost all its hard-won possessions in North America. In 1762, France saw the inevitability of defeat and ceded all of its territory west of the Mississippi to its ally, Spain. The war ended in 1763 with the signing of the Treaty of Paris, which surrendered almost all the rest of France's American possessions to Britain. The French domain in North America vanished, Louisiana belonged to Spain, and Canada and its rich fur trade passed into the control of Great Britain.

These defeats did not mean the end of French influence in North America. Far from it. Although French Canada came under British control, the French fur companies, based mainly at Montreal, continued their competition with the Hudson's Bay Company. British and Scottish merchants began moving in on Montreal, but French *coureurs de bois* ("wood runners," or trappers), riverboat men, and *voyageurs* (traveling agents and explorers) remained in the field. Between 1779 and 1787, these Montreal firms joined forces to create the loosely organized outfit that, reorganized several times, came to be known as the North West Company.

While the newborn United States was fighting to win its independence from England, the North West Company pushed out onto the plains of Canada and headed northwest toward the Arctic. The "Nor'Westers," as the firm's men were called, were determined to move rapidly into the interior in order to cut off the slow-moving and conservative Hudson's Bay Company. Stung by their competition, the Hudson's Bay Company thrust inland, too. Agents of both companies were soon advancing up the Saskatchewan River system toward the Rockies, and they quickly realized that the great distances to be traveled across the Canadian plains made a port of supply on the Pacific Coast especially desirable. The Nor'Westers desperately needed such a port, for supplying their men in the field from Montreal was much more difficult than the Hudson's Bay Company's system. So North West Company leaders Peter Pond and Alexander Mackenzie set out to find better supply routes.

Alexander Mackenzie, one of the truly great explorers in world history, made two incredible attempts to find a navigable river—a Northwest Passage—flowing to the western sea. In 1789, pursuing waterways to the west, he followed a large stream out of Great Slave Lake in northern Canada. To his understandable dismay, this stream that now bears his name led him far north to the Arctic Ocean, not west to the Pacific. He tried again in 1793, and this time succeeded in making the first northern crossing of the continent. His route to the Pacific, however, passed through the tortuous mountains of British Columbia and was too difficult for transportation use. Meanwhile, other agents of both the North West and Hudson's Bay companies were continuing their march into the Canadian West. In 1792, for instance, Peter Fidler of the Hudson's Bay Company pressed into the Blackfeet lands southwest of present-day Calgary. Fidler's trek brought the British advance, at that early date, to within a hundred miles of today's Montana-Canada boundary.

By the time of George Washington's presidency in the 1790s, the British-Canadian frontier was reaching into the Rockies and probing toward the Pacific Coast. In 1792, when the American Robert Gray rediscovered the mouth of the Columbia River, which Spanish explorer Bruno Hezeta had first identified in 1775, British-Canadian imperialists like Mackenzie reacted with predictable alarm, urging their government to move rapidly before the Americans could occupy the strategic waterway. Control of the Columbia meant control of the entire Northwest, and the shrewd Mackenzie pressed for negotiation of a Canadian-American boundary at the 45th parallel, a line that would have placed the Columbia—and almost all of Montana—within the realm of Canada. Had the British government not been distracted by war with France, it might have pursued Mackenzie's plans and won these borders for Canada. If it had, the following pages would tell a much different story.

Intelligent Americans like Thomas Jefferson, who became president in 1801, watched these British-Canadian maneuvers closely and suspiciously. One of Jefferson's prime motives in sending out the Lewis and Clark Expedition would be to counter the Canadian westward thrust and to strengthen the American claim to the Columbia River Basin. Lewis and Clark would carry a copy of Mackenzie's *Voyages from Montreal* with them to the Pacific. In addition, both England and the United States looked warily at the Russians' advance into present-day Alaska and their profits from the sea otter trade, which had begun as early as 1759 and had accelerated rapidly during the 1780s. The Russian-America Company, created in 1799 and led by the dynamic Alexander Baranov, had brought another imperial player into the region, whose designs and capabilities were unknown to both the British and the Americans. By the turn of the nineteenth century, therefore, the imperial vision of both British Canada and the United States was focused on the far Northwest, and both countries wanted hegemony.

SPAIN, LOUISIANA, AND THE MISSOURI RIVER

Spain was the first European power to found New World colonies. By the early 1600s, Spain's American empire blanketed Central and much of South America and extended northward along the Rio Grande to New Mexico. Spain added Louisiana to its holdings in 1762, when France broke up its American realm at the close of the French and Indian War. Spain held Louisiana for thirty-eight years, from 1762 until 1800. During that time, however, it did little to develop the vast, little-known province, valuing it mainly as an enormous buffer to insulate Mexico from approach by its enemies. The Spanish, like the French, based their activities at strategic New Orleans, which controlled the mouth of the Mississippi, and to a lesser extent at the village of St. Louis, near the confluence of the Missouri River with the Mississippi.

By the 1790s, several considerations began to draw Spain's attention toward upper Louisiana and the river that drained it, the muddy Missouri. The Spaniards knew that British Canadians were trading among the Indian tribes who lived north of the Platte River. They wished, naturally, to hold the loyalty of these natives, to open a fur trade with them, and to prevent any British inroads into Louisiana that might one day threaten Mexico. The Spaniards also realized that the wide Missouri offered the best remaining hope of a river route to the Pacific, a Northwest Passage.

In 1792, Jacques D'Eglise, a French trader in the service of Spain, traveled up the Missouri to the strategic villages of the Mandan Indians, which were situated on the great bend of the river near present-day Bismarck, North Dakota. The Mandan Villages, which the Verendryes had visited a half century earlier, was the key Indian trading center of the upper Missouri. There D'Eglise found plenty of evidence that the British had made inroads from Canada. He returned to St. Louis to warn his employers of British penetration into Spanish lands and to announce that the Missouri could be navigated far into its upper reaches. The Spanish authorities reacted to the news by establishing the "Missouri Company" to take over the upriver trade and forge a route to the Pacific Ocean.

The Missouri Company, made up of St. Louis fur men—mostly French and English—found little success. Sioux, Omaha, and Arikara Indians, who occupied the Missouri below the Mandans, were determined to keep white merchandise out of the hands of their enemies upstream, and they made passage up the river very difficult. But even though Indian resistance cut off trade and traffic, the St. Louis men still managed to break through occasionally and to pick up accounts of what lay beyond, to the north and west. Between 1793 and 1797, employees of the Missouri Company, such as D'Eglise, Jean Baptiste Truteau, James Mackay, and John Evans, worked the river between St. Louis and the Mandan Villages.

The Indians told Missouri Company traders about the upper river, and so did a few Canadians who had taken up residence among the natives. One of these was an intriguing fellow named Menard, or "Old Menard," a Frenchman who had lived with the Mandans since 1778. Menard and other informants spoke tantalizingly of the "Stony Mountains" rising in the faraway distance, of a great cataract on the upper river, of native peoples like the Atsinas, Assiniboines, Blackfeet, and Crows. The St. Louis traders heard for the first time of a great southern tributary of the upper Missouri called "La Roche Jaune," river of the Yellow Rock. Menard told Truteau in 1795 that he had traveled this area among the Crows and that "this river is navigable with pirogues more than one hundred and fifty leagues above its mouth, without meeting any falls or rapids." Menard may have been the first white on the Yellowstone River.

The Missouri Company failed and, so far as we know, the Spaniards and their employees never approached the headwaters of the long river. Yet they began to grasp, however vaguely, the outlines of northern Louisiana, an abundant land that stretched westward into a mighty range of mountains. Some geographers believed that these mountains were a singular range—a "pyramidal height of land"—which meant that the headwaters of the Missouri and Columbia rivers must lie very closely together. This was the old dream of the Northwest Passage in a new form.

As the eighteenth century closed, the Spaniards had reached northward to the bend of the Missouri. There they met the British Canadians, who, even farther west, had pressed to within a hundred miles of what would become the northern border of Montana. Neither the Spaniards nor the British, though, would win the race to the upper Missouri. The newly arrived United States would get there first, and in doing so it would solve forever the puzzle of the Northwest Passage.

THE UNITED STATES AND LOUISIANA

The United States of America had not even existed, as such, when Spain received Louisiana from France in 1762. This new nation, destined to bestride the continent, was born with its Declaration of Independence from Great Britain in 1776. Following a seven-year Revolutionary War, the United States confirmed its independence by signing the Treaty of Paris with Britain in 1783. Significantly, the Treaty of Paris allowed the United States generous boundaries, which reached northward to the Great Lakes and westward to the Mississippi. The new American republic now looked across the big river into Spanish Louisiana.

During the two decades following the 1783 treaty, increasing numbers of aggressive American pioneers crossed the Appalachian Mountains and dropped down into the valleys of the west-flowing Ohio and Tennessee rivers. They were farmers, primarily, and they relied on the Mississippi as their avenue to national and world markets. Navigation of the river inevitably became a pressing issue between the United States and Spain. The Spaniards at New Orleans could easily strangle the western commerce of the United States, either by closing the river to its vessels or by refusing them the "right of deposit" to use the city's docks for transferring cargoes to oceangoing ships. This issue, combined with American hunger for the Spanish lands in Florida and lower Louisiana, caused considerable tension between the two countries. The friction never led to war, however, in part because Spain lacked the strength to build up its holdings in Florida and Louisiana.

The situation took a sudden and momentous turn with the dawn of the nineteenth century. France, the founder of Louisiana, had been bargaining with the Spanish government for several years about regaining its lost colony. Louisiana held the promise of a reborn French empire in the New World, an empire based on sugar, cotton, and grains. In October 1800, Napoleon, now rising to the domination of France, wrung from Spain the secret Treaty of San Ildefonso, which ceded Louisiana back to its mother country. Rumors of the agreement soon reached America, and in the fall of 1802 Spanish officials in New Orleans received orders to make way for the French.

The rumors, and then the certainty of a French return to America, sent shock waves through the United States, especially through its western frontiers. Unlike Spain, Napoleonic France posed the threat of establishing real military might along the western borders and of closing off Mississippi commerce forever. President Thomas Jefferson, perhaps the most imperially inclined of all early American leaders, clearly understood the French threat. Of New Orleans in French hands, he wrote the famous words: "There is on the globe one single spot, the possessor of which is our natural and habitual enemy."

Jefferson moved shrewdly and decisively to meet this critical situation. He sent special envoy James Monroe to assist the United States Minister to France, Robert Livingston, in negotiating a possible agreement. Assuming wrongly that Napoleon had also obtained the Floridas from Spain, the president ordered his representatives to offer up to ten million dollars for both these areas and New Orleans. If the attempt failed, they were to bargain for river frontage or permanent access to the docks at New Orleans. And if all negotiations failed, Jefferson was even prepared to seek an alliance with Great Britain against France.

Good fortune intervened for the United States. Napoleon finally found, by the spring of 1803, that he was unable to pursue his plans for a new French empire in the western hemisphere. He had hoped all along to base his empire both in Louisiana and in the sugar-producing island of Santo Domingo in the Caribbean Sea. But native uprisings had forced Napoleon to send large armies into Santo Domingo, where the natives— assisted by a yellow fever epidemic—had killed over fifty thousand French troops. Even more important, Napoleon now faced a war with Great Britain. Because the British navy would probably continue to maintain its control of the Atlantic, France had little hope of defending Louisiana against the British, or against the Americans for that matter.

Simple logic forced Napoleon to sell Louisiana to the United States. On April 11, 1803, Foreign Minister Charles-Maurice de Talleyrand dumbfounded Livingston by raising the issue of selling all of Louisiana. The negotiators spent the rest of the month working out the details, and on April 30 they signed the agreement by which the United States paid fifteen million dollars for the entire province. No one knew precisely what this enormous land transfer entailed, but, generally speaking, Louisiana was understood to be the western drainage of the Mississippi River. Its eastern boundary was the Mississippi itself, and its western limit was probably the Continental Divide, wherever that was. The northern border of Louisiana with Canada and the southern border with the Spanish possessions remained to be defined.

The overwhelming significance of the Louisiana Purchase can scarcely be overstated. In one stroke the United States gained the midsection of the continent, including that far corner of Louisiana that would one day become Montana. This purchase, more than any other single action, transformed the United States into a true imperial power. Over the next

William Clark and Meriwether Lewis (Corcoran Gallery of Art) and Shahaka, Mandan chief (American Philosophical Society). Portraits by C. B. Févret de St. Mémin.

"Lewis and Clark Meeting Indians at Ross' Hole." Painting by Charles M. Russell.

forty-five years the Americans would extend their newly acquired dominion to the Pacific. Jefferson recognized the significance of the Louisiana
Purchase, and he moved quickly to find out what it contained.

THE JOURNEY OF LEWIS AND CLARK

Intelligent Americans readily saw the need to explore Louisiana, but the
necessity had special meaning to the president. Jefferson was a man of
many scientific and philosophical interests, and western exploration was
much on his mind even as early as the 1780s. In 1783, he proposed that
frontiersman and Revolutionary War hero George Rogers Clark take a
privately organized expedition into the West. Four years later, he gave
active encouragement to John Ledyard, a Connecticut adventurer who
proposed to cross Russia, sail to North America, and explore the Northwest. Then, in 1793, while Louisiana still belonged to Spain, Secretary of
State Jefferson acted as a representative of the American Philosophical
Society in sponsoring French botanist Andre Michaux to follow the Missouri River to its headwaters and to travel from there to the Pacific Ocean.
But Michaux's mission failed to materialize.

Jefferson continued to plan the exploration of Louisiana after his inauguration to the presidency in 1801. In January 1803, even before the
United States had gained possession of Louisiana, he secured twenty-five
hundred dollars from Congress to finance an overland journey of discovery via the Missouri and Columbia rivers to the Pacific. To lead the expedition Jefferson appointed his private secretary, Meriwether Lewis, a
young Virginian and a long-time acquaintance. At Lewis's suggestion,
William Clark, his old friend from their days together in the army, was
made co-captain. Clark, at age thirty-three, was four years older than
Lewis; he was also a Virginian and was the youngest brother of frontiersman George Rogers Clark. Although William Clark never received the
captain's commission that had been promised him and thus remained a
second lieutenant during the expedition, Lewis and the men recognized
him as an equal commander of the enterprise.

Much of the success of this amazing venture was due not just to the impressive abilities of Lewis and Clark, but also to the manner in which the
two men complemented one another. They almost always agreed, publicly and privately. Lewis was more reserved, more of an introvert, and
Clark was more gregarious and the more experienced frontiersman.
While they fully shared the tasks of leadership, Lewis specialized in col-
lecting scientific data and specimens and in navigating their route. Clark,
an experienced engineer, generally handled the boats, drew maps, and
proved to be an ingenious makeshift doctor. In their relations with Indi-

ans, Clark demonstrated greater patience and sensitivity than did Lewis, and he generally had better success at negotiations.

The success of the Lewis and Clark Expedition also reflected clearly the astute planning of President Jefferson. In a detailed letter to Lewis on June 20, 1803, Jefferson laid out his instructions with precision. The explorers were to follow the Missouri to its head and to pass from there down a west-flowing river, the Columbia, to the Pacific. Jefferson hoped that the Continental Divide would prove to be only a slight barrier, easily portaged, perhaps in less than a day's time, and that a Northwest Passage might yet be improvised. The president further instructed the captains to plot precise maps, to make extensive observations about the climate, and to collect specimens of soils, minerals, and plant and animal life. Well aware of the British thrust into northern Louisiana, Jefferson ordered Lewis to carefully assess the fur potential and to watch for signs of Canadian intrusion. With the interior fur trade in mind, the president also instructed the captains to take careful and detailed notes on the Native American tribes, their cultures and languages, and their relationships with other tribes. Jefferson cautioned the explorers to treat Indians diplomatically, to inform them of their new master—"the chief of seventeen fires"—and to enlist them as commercial allies. The president clearly aimed not only to thwart British influence in upper Louisiana, but also to beat the Canadian explorers into the Pacific Northwest, an area he was eager to gain for the United States.

The captains spent the winter of 1803-4 preparing for a spring departure. They gathered their personnel and encamped on the east bank of the Mississippi, opposite the mouth of the Missouri. The permanent exploring party consisted of the two captains, twenty-six regulars in the army, Clark's slave York, two French rivermen, and the highly valuable French interpreter George Drouillard, whose name usually appears in the Lewis and Clark journals as "Drewyer." Lewis and Clark divided their command into three squads, under Sergeant Charles Floyd, Sergeant John Ordway, and Sergeant Nathaniel Pryor. Throughout the winter, Clark spent much of his time drilling the men and preparing the fifty-foot keelboat and the two smaller vessels (pirogues) that would carry their cargo up the Missouri. Lewis concentrated on gathering information from French rivermen in St. Louis. An auxiliary crew of sixteen men would accompany them upstream as far as the Mandan Villages. In mid-May of 1804, the expedition departed, heading up the endless Missouri en route to the western sea.

Their destination for the first season of travel was the Mandan Villages, the already well-known Indian crossroads that lay sixteen hundred miles upriver. The group averaged ten miles per day by rowing, poling, or hauling the keelboat against the current. Late in October, after testing their mettle against the river and confronting the trade-wise Arikaras and the obstreperous Teton Sioux, the explorers reached the villages. The Corps of Discovery selected a site for their encampment, "Fort Mandan," and settled in for the winter with their Mandan and Hidatsa neighbors.

During the long Great Plains winter, Lewis and Clark worked on their field notes and filled their journals with ethnographic descriptions of the Indians. Struggling with the politics of the complicated intertribal trade network, the captains strenuously negotiated with Mandan and Hidatsa leaders Sheheke and Le Borgne, hoping to make them willing allies who would rely on American trade. More important, Lewis and Clark gathered considerable intelligence about western geography, which would prove vital to the expedition. They learned that the upper Missouri flowed northward out of the Rockies before bending eastward and that those mountains consisted of many interlocking chains, not just one. They also heard of the Great Falls, which lay just below the river's exit from the mountains, and of the primary tributaries of the Missouri, especially the large northern fork that the Indians called "the river which scolds at all others."

A number of British and French Canadians frequented these villages, and Lewis and Clark eyed them suspiciously, especially after Nor'Wester Toussaint Charbonneau told them that HBC traders had been scheming against the Americans. The captains distrusted Charbonneau—Lewis later called him a "man of no peculiar merit"—but they needed an interpreter for the westward journey, and he was well versed in Indian languages. With Charbonneau came his purchased wife, Sacagawea, a teenaged Shoshoni woman whom the Hidatsas had captured near the Three Forks of the Missouri four years earlier. Although her role in the expedition has been enormously exaggerated, Sacagawea did substantially aid the captains in their later relations with her own people, as well as in recognizing landmarks along the way. Because she had an infant son with her, Jean Baptiste, Indians who met the corps did not see it as a party of war.

Early in April 1805, the explorers broke camp. Corporal Richard Warfington and the auxiliary crew returned to St. Louis with the keelboat and the specimens the explorers had collected so far. Lewis and Clark headed upstream in the two pirogues and six canoes. They reached the mouth of the Yellowstone on April 25 and, recognizing its obvious strategic importance, they recommended this location as the site of a future fort. The expedition entered present-day northeastern Montana in blustery weather. Clark thought it "a verry extraodernary climate, to behold the trees Green & flowers spred on the plain, & Snow an inch deep." They marveled at the enormous herds of buffalo, elk, and antelope, and they began to encounter the feared grizzly bears. The landmarks seemed to bear out what the Indians had told them. They recognized the "river which scolds at all others" and named it the "Milk," from its color. They named two sizable southern forks of the river "Musselshell" and "Judith." Isolated mountain chains began to loom on the far horizon.

On June 2, they saw ahead of them "the entrance of a very considerable river" flowing in from the northwest. The explorers were surprised, for the Indians had made no mention of such a large river. The stream, which they eventually named "Maria's River," was swollen with late spring runoff, and it appeared large enough to be the main stem of the Missouri. Lewis and Clark spent several days examining each river and attempting to determine which was the Missouri proper.

It was a crucial decision. A wrong choice could mean a disastrous winter trapped in the mountains and the possible failure of the entire expedition. The men unanimously believed the northwest fork to be the main Missouri channel, but the captains shrewdly chose the southern fork instead, primarily because its rocky bed and its flow from the southwest indicated that it was a mountain stream. The explorers' decision proved correct, as they learned on June 13, when Lewis suddenly saw "spray arrise above the plain like a collumn of smoke." It had to be the Great Falls of the Missouri. Their all-important—and impressively intelligent—decision at the Marias River had been right.

The falls, which Lewis described as "the grandest sight I ever beheld," were a welcome landmark, but they were also a formidable barrier to progress upriver. The explorers had to portage their canoes and cargo eighteen miles around a series of cataracts, leaving the remainder of their equipment in caches below the falls. It took a month of backbreaking labor, hauling their loads on carts made by cutting wheels from cottonwood logs, to move around the Great Falls. Bedeviled by gumbo mud, prickly pear cactus, "Musquetores," and grizzly bears, the men nonetheless kept up their spirits. They celebrated the first Fourth of July in Montana by drinking the last of the "grog."

The expedition entered the Rockies. The captains fretted about the massive mountain ranges to the west as they headed southward up the Missouri. Haste was imperative, and they pressed ahead, hurrying to get through the mountains before winter. They had to find Sacagawea's people, the Shoshonis, to get horses that would ensure a speedy transit over the mountains. On July 25, 1805, in a state of fatigue, Clark finally reached the Three Forks of the Missouri, the river's headwaters; Lewis arrived with the main party two days later. The explorers recognized the Three Forks as "an essential point in the geography of this western part of

This Carl Bodmer painting, "Camp of the Gros Ventres of the Prairies," shows the upper Missouri River landscape and the style of boats used by explorers on the river during the early nineteenth century. (Joslyn Art Museum)

the Continent," and they named the three rivers that join to form the mighty Missouri after the three principal heads of state. The large west fork they named the Jefferson, the middle branch the Madison, after Secretary of State James Madison, and the smaller east fork the Gallatin, after Treasury Secretary Albert Gallatin.

As August warned of summer's passing, the party headed southwest up the Jefferson River, pulling their canoes against the strong current and clambering over the slippery rocks. Lewis pressed ahead of the main group, trying desperately to make contact with the elusive Shoshonis. He and his companions crossed the Continental Divide on August 12 and came down on the Lemhi, a fork of the west-flowing Salmon River. Finally, they found some Shoshonis, but the Indians had recently clashed with Atsinas and were suspicious. The Shoshonis remained wary, even after Lewis and his party offered their guns as a measure of goodwill. Lewis wrote worriedly in his journal that their fate depended "in great measure upon the caprice of a few savages who are ever as fickle as the wind." But when Clark arrived in camp with the main group, the situation immediately reversed itself. As Sacagawea came forward, Clark wrote in his journal, she "made signs to me [Clark] that they were her nation." More incredibly, the Shoshoni chief, Cameahwait, turned out to be her brother. By trading with the isolated Shoshonis, Lewis and Clark obtained the horses they so vitally needed. But they also learned that the wild Salmon River country was impassable and that they would have to skirt far to the north in order to cross the last, great Rocky Mountain range.

Guided by Pi-kee queen-ah, a Shoshoni whom the captains called "Old Toby," the party headed northward into Montana's Bitterroot Valley. They met the friendly Flathead Indians in Ross's Hole, an event immortalized in Charlie Russell's fine painting. Following the Indians' advice, they moved down the Bitterroot to the mouth of Lolo Creek, a spot they named "Traveler's Rest," and followed this creek westward, crossing over the Bitterroot summits. This autumn passage of the difficult Lolo Trail became an exhausting race against winter, made worse by the scarcity of game. It was the most desperate leg of the explorers' journey. By late September, the famished explorers had dropped down into the meadowlands of the beautiful Clearwater River in present-day Idaho. Friendly Nez Perce Indians helped them and kept their horses, and men of the expedition fashioned boats for their trip to the sea. Floating down the Clearwater, the Snake, and finally the great Columbia River, they reached their destination in rain and fog on November 7, 1805. Clark wrote that evening: "Great joy in camp we are in view of the Ocian, this great Pacific Octean which we been so long anxious to see."

The travelers first camped on the north bank of the Columbia, but later moved south of the river near the coast, naming the encampment Fort Clatsop after a local Indian tribe. It proved to be a long, wet, and dreary winter. Although British and American ships frequented the coast, the explorers never made contact with any of them. The captains occupied themselves during those long months by plotting their return journey, and Clark prepared a brilliant map of the land they had crossed. The men spent much of their time hunting and socializing with the natives, with the result that venereal disease became a problem. Lewis wrote on March 15, 1806:

> we were visited this afternoon by Delashelwilt a Chinnook Chief his wife and six women of his nation which the old baud his wife had brought for market. this was the same party that had communicated the venerial to so many of our party in November last, and of which they have finally recovered. I therefore gave the men a particular charge with rispect to them which they promised me to observe.

With the greening of spring, the Lewis and Clark Expedition headed back up the Columbia on March 23, 1806. Near the mouth of the Snake River, they traded for enough Indian horses to permit them to abandon their canoes and traveled overland through the clefted hill country of present-day southeastern Washington. The men moved up the Snake to the Clearwater River, where they retrieved their horses from the Nez Perces. Snow in the high Bitterroots delayed their recrossing of the Lolo Trail, but finally, with two Nez Perce guides leading the way, they headed over the rugged Bitterroots in late June. On July 1, they reached Traveler's Rest once again.

Eager to survey the areas north and south of the Missouri, the captains divided their command. Lewis, along with a small party and the two Nez Perce scouts, headed down the Bitterroot River and northeastward toward the Great Falls. Clark took the larger segment of the party back up the Bitterroot, across the Continental Divide, and down the Jefferson drainage to the Three Forks of the Missouri. At the Three Forks, Clark divided his force. Sergeant Ordway and nine men headed down the Missouri, traveling in canoes they had stored the year before, to join Lewis at the Great Falls. Clark, with the remainder of the party and the horses, set out across the Gallatin Valley to explore the Yellowstone River, which lay to the east.

Clark met no serious mishaps on his journey. Sacagawea knew the country and recognized the brilliant white outcroppings that marked the strategic Bozeman Pass. On July 15, they reached the Yellowstone, the great southern fork of the upper Missouri. While the men were busily building dugout canoes to use in their descent of the river, Crow Indians deftly stole half their horses. So Clark took most of his party downriver by boat, leaving Sergeant Pryor and two men to drive the remaining horses overland to the Mandan Villages. Their float down the Yellowstone was peaceful and enjoyable, carrying them past the mouths of large southern tributaries, the Clark Fork, Big Horn, Tongue, and Powder. At the "remarkable rock" that he named "Pompey's Pillar" after Sacagawea's son, Clark paused to carve his name and the date. His party reached the Missouri on August 3. An embarrassed Sergeant Pryor joined Clark a few days later. The Crows, the most renowned horse thieves on the plains, had stolen all the remaining horses, and Pryor had been forced to bring his men down the Yellowstone in makeshift skinboats.

Lewis and his group faced greater challenges. The Nez Perces led the men up the Big Blackfoot River, which they knew as Cokahlarishkit, "river of the road to buffalo." The trail took them over the Divide by way of what is now Lewis and Clark Pass and down the Sun River to the Great Falls. Lewis reached the falls from Traveler's Rest in only one week. In the roundabout, reversed journey of the year before, it had taken fifty-eight days! Leaving Sergeant Gass and two men to help Ordway and his group move their boats and equipment around the falls, Lewis headed north with Drouillard and the Fields brothers to explore the Marias River. The Marias impressed Lewis as a highly strategic river. It seemed to offer a navigable passage northward into the Canadian fur areas on the Saskatchewan, and its upper extremities might push the boundaries of Louisiana above the 50th parallel.

The small party moved north and west up the Marias to its Cut Bank fork. Cloudy weather and a failure of their clock made it impossible to gauge their exact location, and, disappointed, they headed back toward the Missouri. In a rare lapse of judgment, Lewis agreed to make camp with a band of Blackfeet, even though the Flatheads and Nez Perces had warned them about these Indians. Worse, Lewis boasted to the Blackfeet that he had effected alliances with the Nez Perces, Atsinas, and Kutenais, an arrangement that would bring American weapons into the hands of Blackfeet enemies. During the night, the Blackfeet tried to seize the explorers' guns, and in the ensuing melee Reuben Field knifed and killed one Indian and Lewis shot another dead. The Indians fled, and the Americans raced from the scene, fearing retaliation. Using Indian horses, Lewis and his men rushed southward at a hectic pace, covering over a hundred miles by daybreak. In a Hollywood-style stroke of luck, they reached the Missouri just in time to meet the Ordway-Gass party coming downstream from the Great Falls.

With the Missouri's current in their favor, traveling was easy. Lewis's group floated leisurely downriver and joined Clark's force below the mouth of the Yellowstone on August 12. The joy of reunion was marred, however, when Clark learned that Lewis had been wounded by a gunshot in the thigh while hunting with a comrade. The explorers made good time returning to St. Louis and reached that city on September 23, 1806. The nation, which had given up the expedition for lost, accorded them a heroes' welcome.

The amazingly successful exploration of the Lewis and Clark Expedition bears great significance in the course of national and regional history. Aside from the obvious importance of its observations, mapping, and accumulation of scientific specimens, the expedition left other lasting marks as well. Except for the fracas with the Blackfeet, the expedition initiated generally friendly relations between white Americans and Indians of the Northwest. It countered the British-Canadian thrust into those regions and gave the United States a valuable claim to the Columbia River Valley. And the expedition ended, once and for all, the persistent hope for a "Northwest Passage."

Most important, Lewis and Clark revealed to the world the immensity, beauty, and wealth of the far Northwest and advertised its potential to the nation. The journals and reports of the expedition spoke with special enthusiasm about one lucrative resource—fur. The upper Missouri, they said categorically, "is richer in beaver and otter than any country on earth." These words would have an immediate and lasting impact on the lands crossed by Lewis and Clark. The restless Americans were about to enter yet another new frontier.

CHAPTER 3

The Era of the Fur Trade

T HE fur trade formed the cutting edge of the European frontiers that moved inexorably across the northern reaches of the North American continent after 1600. Traders and trappers were usually the first whites into the western wilderness. Their extractive business drew them deep into that country and attracted large investments by men of commerce who aspired to make huge profits. It turned out to be a risky trade, but, more than that, it thrust whites into a complicated set of relationships with Indians that altered the Native Americans' world forever. Indians and whites embraced the exchange and bargained shrewdly, each acquiring what they wanted—guns and manufactured items for Indians and valuable furs and hides for fur traders. For Native Americans, the results were cataclysmic, as disease, profound economic change, and political disruptions seriously compromised their cultures. For whites, the trade had important benefits that included more than wealth in furs and increased geographical knowledge. It also brought to a climax the rivalry between the Americans and the British for the far Northwest. And the trade created the first generation of American heroes from the Far West, characterized by the fantastic exploits of the "mountain men." Perhaps most strikingly, the fur trade began Montana's long and sad history of pillaging the environment, stripping the surface wealth, and returning little of the proceeds.

THE BRITISH IN MONTANA

The fur trade had been the mainstay of Canada ever since the beginnings of New France along the St. Lawrence River. For many years, the Canadian fur trade was dominated by the rivalry between the Hudson's Bay

Company and the French fur interests based at Montreal. The Hudson's Bay Company, holding a monopoly charter over the vast lands draining into the bay, advanced westward cautiously, funnelling a prosperous trade into its posts on the east-flowing rivers. Even after Canada fell under British rule in 1763, the French-Canadians were more expansive. Joined by enterprising Scots and Englishmen, they created the North West Company during the years prior to 1784, and they pressed steadily westward up the waterways beyond Lake Superior. The "Nor'Westers" were desperately eager to beat the Hudson's Bay Company into the Canadian interior and to secure a Pacific seaport on the Columbia River before either their British or American rivals could get there. By the time of Lewis and Clark, both companies had posts on the central Canadian plains, and the North West Company had men as far west as British Columbia and as far south as the Mandan Villages on the Missouri River.

The first of the Nor'Westers to enter present-day Montana came only months after Lewis and Clark. During their stay at the Mandan Villages in the winter of 1804-5, the American explorers had encountered a number of Canadian traders, one of whom was Francois Antoine Larocque. "Mr. La Rocke," as Clark called him, wanted to accompany the Americans; but, ever suspicious of the Canadians, they refused. So Larocque, along with two assistants, set out on his own during the summer of 1805, heading southward from the Assiniboine River to scout the upper Missouri. Traveling usually with Indians, the Canadians crossed the Little Missouri River into southeastern Montana and headed up the Powder River, which the Indians had named, according to Larocque, because of "a fine sand which obscures and dirties the water." According to Larocque's sketchy journal, the men ranged far enough southwest to see the Big Horn Mountains, crossed the Big Horn River, and then descended the Yellowstone on their return toward Canada. Larocque obtained many pelts and made good contacts with the Crow, Shoshoni, and Gros Ventre Indians. He promised them he would return for trade, but the North West Company failed to follow his lead into the lands south of the Missouri.

Instead of penetrating the upper Missouri and clearly into United States territory, the Nor'Westers moved westward up the Saskatchewan drainage into the Rocky Mountains in present-day Canada. They then headed southwest to the headwaters of the west-flowing Columbia, Kootenai, and Clark Fork rivers, into what is now northwestern Montana. The leader of this thrust into the upper Columbia Basin was David Thompson, one of the truly great geographers of all time. The son of Welsh parents, Thompson migrated to Canada in 1784 and served the Hudson's Bay Company until 1797, when he joined up with the North

"Conversing with Signs," Alfred J. Miller's depiction of the fur trade in the American West, illustrates how Indians and non-Indians conducted business. (Walters Art Gallery)

West Company. The shrewd leaders of this firm quickly recognized Thompson's genius as a surveyor. Well aware of American interest in the Columbia Basin, they ordered him to carry the fur trade into that region immediately.

In 1807, Thompson and his men penetrated the Canadian Rockies west of present-day Calgary. They built trading posts—or "houses," as they often called them—on the upper Columbia and Kootenai rivers. The Canadians entered Montana during the autumn of 1808, when Thompson sent his trusted lieutenant, Finan McDonald, with a crew of mixed-bloods down the Kootenai to trade with the Kutenai Indians. "Big Finan," a giant of a man, built a structure usually called "Kootenai Post" near present-day Libby, Montana, and spent the following year there. The post was relocated farther upstream three years later. Over the next few years, Thompson and his men crisscrossed the drainages of the Kootenai, Clark Fork, and Flathead rivers, opening a friendly and profitable commerce with the Salish and Kutenai tribes. In November 1809, Thompson established the most important of his Montana posts, "Saleesh House," on the Clark Fork near the present-day town of Thompson Falls.

These posts formed part of a network of North West Company houses that extended westward, beyond the Rockies into the lower Columbia River Basin. As trade prospered, Thompson pursued his first loves, travel and mapping. In mid-1811, pursuant to North West Company instructions, Thompson set out on what he called his "Voyage of a Summer Moon": "down the Columbia River to explore this river in order to open out a passage for the interior trade with the Pacific Ocean." At the strategic confluence of the Columbia and Snake rivers, he fastened a note to a pole bearing the solemn declaration "that this country is claimed by Great Britain as part of its territories." On July 15, 1811, Thompson arrived at Astoria, where Astor's Pacific Fur Company had just established the first American post on the Pacific Coast. Astor and the North West Company had struck a bargain earlier, so Thompson greeted potential partners at Astoria; but the North West Company also advised him to watch the Americans closely. It would not be long before the British and American traders would be vying for control of both the Columbia and Missouri river fur-trading regions.

Thompson was back at Saleesh House during the following winter. In the early months of 1812, he surveyed the upper Clark Fork. From atop the towering butte now called Mount Jumbo, he mapped the complex Missoula area. He continued up the Flathead River and along the shores of Flathead Lake, mapping all of that country with amazing accuracy. Thompson left the area that spring and would never return, but he left behind him an impressive record of exploration. More important, he left the North West Company in firm control of the fur trade of the upper Columbia.

During the decade following Thompson's departure, the North West Company extended its trapping activities in the Pacific Northwest. The War of 1812 disrupted the fur trade, but it also helped the British force Astor's American traders from the lower Columbia. Saleesh House, under the direction of James McMillan and Ross Cox, was renamed "Flathead Post" and remained the company's key base in the western Montana area. The fur trade in these high mountain valleys was profitable and secure. Friendly Indians, some of them trained as trappers by Iroquois from the east, reliably brought in the pelts year after year.

The Nor'Westers faced less danger from Indians or Americans than from their long-time rival, the Hudson's Bay Company. Stung by the success of the Nor'Westers, the venerable old corporation moved west with new vigor. In 1810, for instance, agents of the Hudson's Bay Company built a post with the unlikely name "Howes House" north of Flathead Lake. Competition between the two Canadian rivals became ever more fierce until by 1816, in the "Pemmican War," it erupted in violence when the Nor'Westers massacred the HBC governor and twenty-one settlers at the company's Red River Colony. The resulting public outrage in England drew Parliament's attention and led to a consolidation of the two companies in 1821, when the British crown granted the now enlarged Hudson's Bay Company a twenty-one-year monopoly in the Pacific Northwest trade. The company created the Columbia Department to expand its operations and incorporate the old North West Company apparatus west of the Divide.

Through its Columbia Department, the HBC proceeded rapidly during the early 1820s to solidify its control over the Columbia River Valley. The governments of the United States and Great Britain had agreed by now to a "joint occupation" of this vast, little-known region. "Joint occupation" meant, in effect, that whichever nation first occupied the Pacific Northwest would eventually own it. The Hudson's Bay Company built its headquarters, Fort Vancouver, on the lower Columbia in 1824-25 and placed it under the command of the amiable and shrewd Dr. John McLoughlin. McLoughlin had new posts built on the upper Columbia and its tributaries, and he sent large "brigades" of men to trap out the interior before the Americans could establish themselves there. Americans entering the Northwest joked that the initials "HBC," which seemed to appear everywhere, meant "Here Before Christ."

Present-day northwestern Montana, on the upper Clark Fork and Kootenai tributaries of the Columbia, lay on the far eastern fringe of the Hudson's Bay Company's Columbia Department. The HBC seldom pressed its activities far east of the Continental Divide. It continued to concentrate its trade in these valleys at the posts established earlier by the Nor'Westers—Flathead Post (Saleesh House) on the Clark Fork and Kootenai Post on the Kootenai. In 1846-47, HBC men Neil McArthur and Angus McDonald built the last of the major British posts, variously known as "Fort Connen" or "Connah" on Post Creek in the Flathead Valley. Fort Connah became the center of HBC operations in Montana during the twilight years of the fur trade and continued in business until 1871. Through these fixed posts, and because of their generally decent trading practices, the British won and held the loyalty of the western Montana Indians. The Americans entered the area only occasionally. In 1833, the Hudson's Bay Company signed an agreement with its great United States rival, the American Fur Company, whereby each agreed to stay out of the other's territory.

The HBC complemented its trading posts with the use of large trapping "brigades," which brought in large and profitable hauls of fur through intensive trapping. By stripping the outer reaches of the Columbia drainage of fur-bearing animals, the HBC hoped to keep the aggressive Americans at a distance. The North West Company sent out the first brigade under Donald McKenzie in 1818, and the Hudson's Bay Company continued the practice in a big way. Alexander Ross led the first of the major HBC trapping brigades, made up of fifty-five men, out of Saleesh House in early 1824. Ross's party followed a long, twisting arc to the south and west into the Salmon River country of present-day Idaho and returned to Saleesh House late in the year with an impressive haul of five thousand beaver skins.

Pleased by Ross's success, McLoughlin placed more emphasis on the brigade method and gave command of the brigades to Peter Skene Ogden, one of the most able of the British fur men and a major explorer of western America. Ogden amply possessed the qualities needed to succeed in the fur business—shrewdness, toughness, even viciousness. Legends of his violent disposition abound. In one fit of anger, he ordered one of his men to climb a tree and then set the tree afire, forcing the poor man to climb down through the flames. For six years, beginning in late 1824, Ogden led large trapping brigades through the Northern Rockies and intermountain regions. Ogden's trapping expeditions traveled northward to the Marias country, eastward to the Gallatin, and southward to the Great Salt Lake, the Nevada deserts, and far into California.

The Canadian fur frontier came to dominate the Pacific Northwest. While established houses such as Flathead Post and Fort Connah held the Indian trade, the profitable brigades harvested a bounty of pelts from the eastern and southern extremities of the Columbia watershed. The dream of Alexander Mackenzie and David Thompson—British control of the Columbia—seemed destined to come true.

THE AMERICANS

Even as David Thompson pressed the Canadian fur trade into the Columbia River Valley, American traders at St. Louis turned their attention northwestward toward the far reaches of the muddy Missouri River. The fur trade of the United States had been centered in the bountiful lands surrounding the Great Lakes and the Mississippi headwaters; but after the return of Lewis and Clark, the upper Missouri, Northern Rockies, and Columbia Basin beckoned as inviting new frontiers. St. Louis, located near the juncture of the Missouri with the Mississippi, was the natural gateway to these virgin lands. As Lewis and Clark's glowing assessment of the fur potential of the Northwest became known, St. Louis buzzed with excitement.

The first of the St. Louis traders to pursue the region upriver was Manuel Lisa. A Louisiana Spaniard by birth, Lisa was brave, tough, cunning, and, according to his many enemies, unscrupulous. Backed by two partners from Illinois, he led a sizable expedition out of St. Louis and up the Missouri in the spring of 1807. Lisa had with him a keelboat full of trade goods and a number of seasoned frontiersmen, including George Drouillard of the Lewis and Clark Expedition. At the mouth of the Platte River, Lisa's party met another Lewis and Clark veteran, John Colter, who had spent the previous year trapping on the Yellowstone. Colter agreed to hire on with Lisa and to return once again to the wilderness. No doubt following the advice of Colter and Drouillard, Lisa avoided the hostile Blackfeet of the upper Missouri and went up the Yellowstone instead. In November 1807, the group reached the strategic confluence of the Yellowstone and Big Horn rivers, where they built a trading post, the first permanent structure erected by whites in Montana. Lisa named the post Fort Remon after his son, but it was usually known as "Lisa's Fort," or "Fort Manuel."

During the winter of 1807-8, Lisa's men made many contacts with the Crows. The Crows, perennial foes of the Blackfeet and Sioux, needed American aid, and they generally cooperated with the fur traders. It was also during that winter that John Colter, with a thirty-pound pack on his back, made his fabulous winter journey, traveling hundreds of miles in search of Indian allies and, perhaps, Spanish settlements to the south. From Lisa's Fort, Colter explored southwestward beyond Jackson Hole and back, entering present-day Yellowstone National Park from the southwest, crossing the Yellowstone River near Tower Fall, and returning to the lower Yellowstone by way of the Shoshone River Valley. When he arrived back at the fort, Colter described hot springs near present-day Cody, Wyoming, which brought looks of disbelief from associates and the name "Colter's Hell" for the hydrothermal features he had seen.

Lisa returned to St. Louis in 1808, full of enthusiasm for the fur trade upriver. He gathered some of the foremost merchants of that city into a partnership that would finance trapping in the upstream lands on a major scale. These men included Pierre Menard and William Morrison, who were Lisa's partners the year before, Andrew Henry, William Clark, Reuben Lewis (Meriwether's brother), and Auguste and Pierre Chouteau, members of one of the oldest and most powerful families in St. Louis. In early 1809, they organized the "St. Louis Missouri Fur Company," which they capitalized at $40,000. The company, which became known as the Missouri Fur Company, would carry the first major thrust by the Americans into the Northern Plains and Rockies.

The aggressive Manuel Lisa dominated the organization. In June 1809, he took a party numbering at least one hundred fifty men, many of them French frontiersmen, up the Missouri. They traded profitably among the Crows during the next year, and in March 1810 Andrew Henry and Pierre Menard led a force of thirty-two men westward to the Three Forks of the Missouri. There the partners planned to establish their central base and open trade with the powerful Blackfeet, who controlled the best fur lands in the region. Henry's men built a trading post on the point of land between the converging Jefferson and Madison rivers and found excellent trapping. Angry at this invasion, the Blackfeet and their Gros Ventre allies quickly reacted with violence, and eight of Henry's party lost their lives. Among them was the invaluable George Drouillard, who died in ambush only two miles from the Three Forks post. Such losses were intolerable, and by the close of 1810 Henry had abandoned the Three Forks venture.

The Missouri Fur Company faced other problems, too. A fire destroyed nearly twenty thousand dollars worth of furs and robes, and the approach of war between the United States and Great Britain threatened to disrupt European fur markets and to allow the Canadians to move south and cut off American traffic on the upper Missouri. In 1811, Lisa and his partners vacated the post on the Big Horn and abandoned the upriver trade. Over the next few years, during and after the War of 1812, the Missouri Fur Company confined its activities to the lower course of the Big Muddy. The firm languished during this period, and most of the original partners left it.

In 1819, Lisa reorganized the old Missouri Fur Company and drew in such new and energetic partners as Joshua Pilcher, Andrew Drips, and

Robert Jones. By then, the United States and Britain had agreed to extend the 49th parallel boundary westward to the crest of the Rockies, and the Northern Plains and Rockies seemed more secure from Canadian inroads. Before he could re-establish his company on the upper Missouri, however, Lisa fell ill of an unknown disease and died in 1820. His untimely death removed the strongest of the early upriver traders, and Joshua Pilcher took his place. Once again, the Missouri Fur Company headed upstream.

With a large army of trappers, Pilcher established a post at the juncture of the Yellowstone and Big Horn rivers in 1821. The post took the name Fort Benton in honor of the influential Missouri senator and protector of the fur business, Thomas Hart Benton. During the following year, Robert Jones and Michael Immel brought a group of one hundred fifty men to Fort Benton. With roughly three hundred men in the area, the Missouri Fur Company enjoyed real success, sending $25,000 worth of furs to market that autumn. But once again, the lure of the Blackfeet lands proved irresistible—and fatal. In the spring of 1823, Jones and Immel led a sizable force to the Three Forks, where they trapped successfully on the Jefferson. In mid-May, they managed to meet with a band of Blackfeet, who seemed friendly and welcomed the idea of an American post in their territory. One of the Indians carried a letter bearing the inscription "God Save the King" that certified him as a friend of the whites.

But friends they were not. The Blackfeet secretly raised a large war party and stealthily pursued the Americans back into the Crow territory on the Yellowstone River. As the Jones-Immel party was climbing down through the rimrocks along the river, near present-day Billings, the Indians ambushed them. Jones, Immel, and five of their men died in the attack, and $15,000 worth of furs was lost. Some American traders blamed the Hudson's Bay Company, charging that it had incited the Indian attack to protect its near-monopoly over the Blackfeet trade from its posts on the Saskatchewan River. Although there is no evidence to support the Americans' suspicions, surely the HBC men were not displeased with these events and must have hoped that the Blackfeet would discourage their southern competitors. From the Indians' viewpoint, it may have been the Americans' trading methods that so provoked them. By using white and mixed-blood trappers, the Americans were competing with the Blackfeet, who sold their pelts directly to the British. Whatever the reason, the Blackfeet succeeded in driving out the intruders with severe losses. Pilcher and his associates gave up the effort to establish an upriver trade and confined their activities to the lower Missouri. The Missouri Fur Company lingered on for only a few more years; by 1830, it had folded.

Even as Pilcher was developing his operation on the Yellowstone

River, another organization began to take shape in St. Louis. In March 1822, an advertisement appeared in the *Missouri Republican*: "To enterprising young men. The subscriber wishes to engage one hundred young men to ascend the Missouri River to its source, there to be employed for one, two or three years." The "subscribers" were General William H. Ashley, a prominent Missouri businessman, politician, and militia leader, and Andrew Henry, Lisa's former partner and a well-known Missouri investor. The outfit the two men were assembling, which would later be known as the Rocky Mountain Fur Company, would play a key role in the exploration of the West. Several young men responded to the notice, and some, like Jim Bridger and Thomas Fitzpatrick, soon rose to prominence in the Rocky Mountain fur business.

Ashley and Henry hoped to trade with the Blackfeet from a fixed post at either the Three Forks or the Great Falls, but the treacherous river and the troublesome Indians en route forced a change of plans. Instead, they built a post at the mouth of the Yellowstone, and Henry located his men there during the winter of 1822-23. In the spring, Henry led his force up to the Great Falls, where, predictably, the Blackfeet hit them at once. The Piegans struck Henry's party, killing four men and wounding several others. When Henry returned to the mouth of the Yellowstone, he learned that Ashley had suffered severe losses from attacks by Arikara Indians downstream. Their plans badly disrupted, the partners were able to salvage something when Henry moved to the mouth of the Big Horn and set up a post among the Crows.

The combined dangers of the Blackfeet and the uncertainties of travel on the Big Muddy led Ashley and Henry to abandon their plans of commerce on the upper Missouri. They decided to divert their activities southward into the mountains drained by the Green, Snake, Wind, and Bear rivers of present-day Wyoming, Idaho, and Utah. The partners also abandoned the traditional method of relying on fixed posts and trading with the unpredictable Indians. Rather, they would turn their employees loose in the wilderness as "free trappers" or "mountain men," who would work on their own and sell their furs to the St. Louis-based partners at an annual trading fair in the mountains called "rendezvous."

Beginning in 1824, Ashley and his successors staged a rendezvous each year in early summer, usually along the upper Green, Snake, or Bear rivers. The St. Louis merchants' caravan carried trade goods, guns, ammunition, and flat casks of alcohol overland to the rendezvous site. There, the mountain men—and many Indians—congregated to sell the pelts from their spring and fall hunts. "We constituted quite a little town," trapper James Beckwourth wrote about the 1825 rendezvous, "numbering at least eight hundred souls, of whom one half were women and children. . . . All kinds of sports were indulged in with a heartiness that would astonish more civilized societies." They spent several days, and sometimes weeks, in camp at what Captain Benjamin de Bonneville called a "saturnalia among the mountains," punctuated with drinking, debauchery, mayhem, and sometimes even murder. Then the free trappers and their Indian cohorts returned to the wilderness for the fall hunt and a winter of cold and boredom. The mountain men, like Jedediah Smith, Kit Carson, and Hugh Glass, explored much of the Far West, and their exploits, usually exaggerated in the retelling, captured the nation's imagination. And the facts of Glass's encounter with a grizzly bear and Jed Smith's desert crossings into California were stranger than fiction. The mountain men introduced the Indians to the wilder side of white civilization, and sometimes the whites degenerated into savagery, like the fictional hero of A. B. Guthrie Jr.'s fine novel, *The Big Sky*.

The yearly rendezvous was one of the great spectacles in the history of the West, but the system returned little profit for the mountain men. Not surprisingly, the wealth from the trade passed into the hands of the investors who sent the caravans out from St. Louis. Ashley did so well at this that he was able to retire in 1826, a wealthy man. He sold out to three of his men, Jed Smith, David Jackson, and William Sublette. In 1830, they sold to yet another group of partners, Thomas Fitzpatrick, Baptiste Gervais, Jim Bridger, Milton Sublette, and Henry Fraeb. This last group was the first to officially use the name "Rocky Mountain Fur Company," but that name is often applied to the firm from the time of its inception in 1822.

Although the Rocky Mountain Fur Company centered its activities to the south of Montana, its partners and trappers often entered the state's present-day borders. In the fall hunt of 1830, for instance, Sublette, Fitzpatrick, and Bridger led a party of more than two hundred men on a northward sweep. They descended the Big Horn River, crossed to the Great Falls, and then followed the Missouri and Jefferson rivers on their southbound return. The size of the party kept the Blackfeet at a distance, and the result was a rich harvest of furs. A similar expedition in 1831, however, met frustration when the Crows ran off the trappers' horses. The company's rendezvous system thrived from the mid-1820s until the mid-1830s, always facing some competition from American rivals and from the Hudson's Bay Company. By the early 1830s, though, the Rocky Mountain Fur Company found itself face-to-face with a rival it could not match.

MONOPOLY: THE AMERICAN FUR COMPANY

The American Fur Company, incorporated in New York in 1808, grew to dominate the fur trade of the entire United States. The firm was com-

Fort McKenzie, at the mouth of the Marias River, was two years old in 1833, when Carl Bodmer made this sketch of the American Fur Company's trading post. The Blackfeet destroyed the fort ten years later in 1843. (Joslyn Art Museum)

pletely the creature of its powerful founder, John Jacob Astor. A German immigrant, Astor accumulated one of the great early American fortunes, first as a New York fur merchant and later as master of the fur business from the trapping stage to the marketing of finished products. As early as 1788, Astor had been doing business with Montreal fur men, particularly Alexander Henry, which led directly to his creation of the Pacific Fur Company in 1810. This enterprise, which resulted in the establishment of Astoria at the mouth of the Columbia River, would later give Americans a claim to the Northwest, but the labor and the original ideas came as much from Montreal as from New York. Even though Astor's gamble at Astoria did not pay off, he had taken a large step into the competitive fur trade of the Northwest. In creating the American Fur Company, Astor aimed to take over the Great Lakes trade from the Canadians, who were flagrantly stripping this United States territory of its fur-bearing animals. After the War of 1812, Astor succeeded in gaining control of this area and organized the Northern Department of the American Fur Company to manage the business of the Great Lakes-Upper Mississippi region.

By 1820, Astor had become the colossus of the American fur business. The dwindling animal population of the Old Northwest and the irresistible lure of new, untrammeled wilderness farther west drew him inevitably toward St. Louis and the Missouri. Fearing Astor's domination, the St. Louis merchants had kept him out of the old Missouri Fur Company. But they could not keep him out forever.

In 1822, the year that Ashley and Henry headed up the river, Astor formed the Western Department of his American Fur Company, centered at St. Louis under the tough-minded direction of his close associate Ramsay Crooks, who had earlier been part of the Astoria operation. Astor and Crooks contracted with local St. Louis businessmen to handle the work of the Western Department. The firm of Bernard Pratte and Company proved to be the most efficient, and in 1827 it took over the entire management of Astor's western operation. Pierre Chouteau Jr., one of Pratte's associates, was an exceptionally shrewd, third-generation member of St. Louis's best established family. Chouteau would soon rise to command the entire western operation of the American Fur Company.

Directed by such able men as Crooks and Chouteau, the American Fur Company pushed inexorably up the Big Muddy. Of the several small firms that lay across its path, the most formidable was the Columbia Fur Company. A number of hard-nosed ex-Nor'Westers, who had left Canada after that firm had been absorbed by the Hudson's Bay Company, ran the Columbia operation. They were making impressive profits and extending their system of posts far up the Missouri. When the Columbia Fur Company proved too tough a nut to crack, the American Fur Company simply bought it out. In 1827, through an agreement worked out by Crooks, it became the "Upper Missouri Outfit" of Astor's Western Department.

The path to the far upriver region now lay open to the American Fur Company. The company had a solid base of operations at St. Louis, and now the Upper Missouri Outfit provided the striking arm. Kenneth McKenzie, a tough, ruthless, red-faced Scot and a veteran of the Columbia organization, ran the Upper Missouri Outfit. In 1828, he sent a work force under James Kipp to build a large trading fort at that most strategic of locations, the mouth of the Yellowstone. Fort Floyd, which would soon become Fort Union, was located almost precisely on what would be the Montana-North Dakota state line. Well-situated and elaborate in construction, Fort Union became headquarters for Astor's Upper Missouri Outfit and was for years one of the major forts of the American West.

From St. Louis and now from Fort Union, the American Fur Company set out to monopolize the fur trade of the Northern Plains and Rockies. Beginning in 1829, the company sent its own trading caravans to the rendezvous; and by paying better prices for pelts, it put the squeeze on the Rocky Mountain Fur Company. The American Fur Company further harassed its competitor by sending parties of its own trappers to follow the Rocky Mountain men and find their best beaver streams. This practice, not surprisingly, sometimes led to violence. In 1832, for example, Bridger and Fitzpatrick lured one of McKenzie's best men, William Henry Vanderburgh, into a Blackfeet ambush that cost Vanderburgh his life.

For a time, the Rocky Mountain partners and other independent "opposition" outfits fought back against the encroachments of the American Fur Company. The rendezvous became scenes of vigorous bidding for pelts, and the free trappers did well. The rendezvous at Pierre's Hole in 1832 was the greatest gathering of them all. Two former Rocky Mountain men, William Sublette and Robert Campbell, even retaliated by building a post named Fort William in the shadow of Fort Union. With the backing of William H. Ashley, Sublette and Campbell posed a real threat to the company. But McKenzie drove them to the wall by underselling them and, probably, by turning the Indians against them. Sublette and Campbell soon ended up selling out to the company.

The simple fact was that no "opposition" outfit—the Rocky Mountain partners or anyone else—could match the awesome resources of the American Fur Company. The company had the financial power to get the best men and the most potent weapons. Two of those weapons proved to be especially critical—steamboats and a distillery. The steamboats, as Pierre Chouteau Jr. foresaw, were the key, for they could haul much larger cargoes upriver much faster than small, man-powered keelboats could. Specially built for navigating the treacherous upper Missouri, the first of these light-draft steamboats, the *Yellowstone*, reached Fort Union on the high waters of June 1832. Thereafter, the boats traveled regularly to Fort Union and became the lifeline of the Upper Missouri Outfit.

The distillery also had a sizable impact on the trade. Liquor had long been the most valuable of the fur man's trade goods, and also the most lethal in its effects on the Indians. Most traders ignored an 1832 federal law that specifically forbid the transport of liquor into "Indian Country." Instead of trying to smuggle large quantities past government inspectors, McKenzie had a small distillery secretly brought to Fort Union in 1833. With imported corn, his men began producing rotgut right on the spot. This ready supply of liquor gave McKenzie a formidable advantage over the competition.

Under such pressure, the Rocky Mountain Fur Company buckled and folded. The partners tried desperately to bargain with the American Fur Company for a division of the trade, but to no avail. In 1834, the Rocky Mountain owners sold out to their giant rival. Most of their holdings and many of their men passed into the company's employ. The American Fur Company continued the rendezvous for only a few more years, and the last of the colorful meetings, in 1840, drew only 120 participants. The day of the mountain men was coming to an end.

Even as Astor's giant company crushed its smaller American rivals, it turned its attention toward the prize that had eluded all of its predecessors—the Blackfeet lands of the far upper Missouri. The Blackfeet trade lay firmly in the grasp of the Hudson's Bay Company, operating out of its posts on the South Saskatchewan. Astor's foray up the Missouri was also another challenge to the British. Using Jacob Berger, a former Nor'Wester who knew many Blackfeet and understood their language, Kenneth McKenzie was able to make friendly contact with the Indians who had been so hostile to American traders. Along with a group of terrified companions, Berger traveled from Fort Union to the Marias River on a peace mission in 1830. He parleyed with the Piegans and persuaded a group of them to accompany him back to Fort Union for a conference with McKenzie. There, the Blackfeet appeared to be enthusiastic about having a post built on their lands, and they agreed to a full-scale trade with the Americans. During the following year, McKenzie played on the Indians' desire for guns, liquor, and trade items and won compliance from them, even including a treaty of peace with the Blackfeet's old enemies, the Assiniboines, who traded regularly at Fort Union.

The Upper Missouri Outfit had its foot in the door. In the summer of 1831, McKenzie sent James Kipp upriver with twenty-five men to open the Blackfeet trade. Near the mouth of the Marias, they built a structure that they named Fort Piegan. The Blackfeet responded with surprising enthusiasm, reportedly bringing in twenty-four hundred beaver pelts in the first ten days of business. According at least to American suspicions, the British were so alarmed at the Americans' success on the Marias that they incited the Blood tribe of Blackfeet to strike at Kipp's post. Kipp deflated their attack by feeding the Indians whiskey until they gave it up. In the spring of 1832, Kipp returned to Fort Union with an impressive cargo of furs. Because none of his men would agree to stay behind in Blackfeet lands, Fort Piegan was abandoned, and the angry Indians burned it.

Later that summer, another of McKenzie's men, David D. Mitchell, returned and built a new post a few miles upstream from Fort Piegan. Mitchell and his men worked in an atmosphere of incredible tension, watched by thousands of suspicious and unfriendly Blackfeet. For years, Fort McKenzie served as the depot where the great wealth of Blackfeet furs were brought to market. In the autumn of 1832, McKenzie's men built a similar post among the Crows, locating it at the traditional spot, near the mouth of the Big Horn. They named the post Fort Cass. Fort Cass and Fort McKenzie both served as subposts to Fort Union. Together, they cemented the hold of the American Fur Company on the entire upper Missouri region.

By the mid-1830s, the American Fur Company reigned supreme. It had destroyed its American competition and had beaten the Hudson's Bay Company by weaning the Blackfeet away from the Saskatchewan trade with superior goods ferried up the Missouri by steamboats. This was an advantage that the HBC, with its long supply lines, could not match. Nonetheless, J. J. Astor, aging but still astute, foresaw the decline of the fur trade, as silk garments and textiles were beginning to supplant furs. In 1834, he abandoned the business and sold his Western Department to its long-time managers, Pratte, Chouteau and Company. When Pratte retired in 1838, Chouteau took over, and the firm became Pierre Chouteau Jr. and Company. The changes meant little. The same individuals— mainly Chouteau—still ran things, and even after 1834 most people still called the organization the American Fur Company.

Kenneth McKenzie, the tough ruler of Fort Union and the Upper Missouri Outfit, soon left the scene. When the government learned of the distillery at Fort Union, McKenzie's superiors made him the scapegoat. The episode cost McKenzie his job, and it nearly cost the company its trading license. Alexander Culbertson took McKenzie's place at Fort Union. A tall, strong, and forceful man, Culbertson dominated the upper Missouri trade after 1840. His Blackfeet wife, Natawista Ixsana, aided him in his dealings with the Indians.

Under Culbertson, the company maintained its smooth control of the

region, but problems still arose. A major calamity occurred at Fort Mc-
Kenzie in 1843 when two company men of especially vicious character,
F. A. Chardon and Alexander Harvey, sought revenge against the Black-
feet for murdering Chardon's slave. Using a concealed cannon, the two
men slaughtered twenty-one unsuspecting Indians and wounded others.
Then they murdered the wounded and scalped all of the corpses. Too
frightened to remain, Chardon and his men soon abandoned Fort Mc-
Kenzie, and the enraged Indians burned it.

For awhile, this appalling incident disrupted the Blackfeet trade, but
Chouteau finally persuaded Culbertson to try again. In 1845, Culbertson
took a party of men up from Fort Union, past the site of Fort McKenzie,
and built a new post called Fort Lewis. The Blackfeet trusted Culbertson,
and they soon resumed trade with the company. Because they disliked
the location of Fort Lewis, Culbertson built an elaborate new post the following year, downstream at a more accessible spot on the Missouri. This
post, first called Fort Lewis, was later renamed to honor the company's
best friend in Congress, Senator Thomas Hart Benton. Built of adobe
brick, Fort Benton arose to become a major trading center. Its 250-foot-
perimeter walls enclosed an interior courtyard and several buildings. The
fort served as the company's base of operations on the upper Missouri
during the twilight years of the fur trade. It later became head of steamboat navigation on the river and a key transportation center during the
mining rushes.

The American Fur Company, under both Chouteau and later owners,
continued its operations from these and other posts for many years. Various "opposition" companies entered the field as competitors, but they
had little success. Culbertson ran the upriver trade from Fort Benton until his retirement in the late 1850s, when Andrew Dawson, another enterprising Scot, took his place. Dawson ably oversaw the operation until his
retirement in 1864. By then, buffalo hides were replacing beaver pelts in
the trade.

The fur trade had faded appreciably even before the mining rushes of
the 1860s. It left behind a mixed but generally negative legacy. The fur
frontier, in a positive sense, caused intensive exploration and widened
the horizon of geographical knowledge. As an instrument of empire, the
fur trade had far-reaching results. It solidified the American grip on most
of Montana and almost gained the Columbia River Valley for Great Britain. In 1846, the British government agreed to cede all lands below the
49th parallel to the United States. In general, however, the fur trade had
a negative impact on the region and its native peoples. It exploited a valuable resource, fur-bearing animals, without heed; and the consequent
profits passed only to a few, distant individuals.

Alexander Culbertson, photo-graphed with his Blackfeet wife, Natawista Ixsana, and son Joseph, was the American Fur Company's chief factor on the Missouri during the 1840s and 1850s.

Left: Pierre-Jean DeSmet, S. J. (Photo by Gustavus Sohon)

Perhaps the most important result of the fur trade was its irrevocable alteration of the Native Americans' world. The influx of trading goods immediately made commerce with the whites a major part of Indian life. The trade revolved upon the exchange of commodities, in which whites bargained with anything they had to acquire the best peltry, and the Indians demanded top quality merchandise. Native Americans approached these exchanges as they did intertribal trade, but for whites it was often a frustrating process. Trading took time and considerable effort, including gift-giving, extended negotiations, and personal commitment. Middlemen like Jim Beckwourth, Robert Meldrum, and Edward Rose overcame these difficulties by living with the Indians. But the most effective middlemen were Indians who deftly handled the negotiations and brought their tribes more and better goods in exchange for furs. By controlling access to goods and their distribution in the tribe, these men often achieved status and power that only war deeds could otherwise have brought. The trade, in effect, created a new status structure within the tribes and thereby changed Native American politics. Some Indian women also gained power by marrying white traders, who welcomed these unions in part as an advantage over other traders.

The fur trade also had a dark side. Early on, alcohol became a favored trade item, and it wrought great havoc, especially on those who became addicted. Disease became the most debilitating consequence of the fur trade. As early as 1780, epidemics spread from white traders on the Pacific Coast hundreds of miles inland, decimating the tribes. Smallpox struck the upper Missouri in the late 1830s, killing thousands of Plains Indians. In 1837, a smallpox pestilence carried by traders hit the Mandans with such fury that they disappeared as a people. The Assiniboines contracted the disease at Fort Union and died by the hundreds. The Crows fared better, because they heeded warnings and stayed away from Fort Cass; and the Gros Ventres escaped the worst of it, because they had been partially immunized during an earlier epidemic.

The Blackfeet suffered terribly. A keelboat brought the disease to Fort McKenzie. Culbertson tried to warn the Indians away, but his warnings only aroused their suspicions. They came, then left—ominously, they failed to return. Culbertson went out in the fall to find them. At the Three Forks, he discovered a major camp where only two people remained alive, amid the stench of dead bodies. "Hundreds of decaying forms of human beings, horses, and dogs," he reported, "lay scattered everywhere among the lodges." Half or maybe more of the Blackfeet died of smallpox, and their military supremacy was broken forever. It was a tragedy beyond description.

St. Mary's Mission in the Bitterroot Valley, shown here in 1884, was first established in 1841, abandoned in 1850, and re-established in 1866. (Photo by F. Jay Haynes)

THE INDIANS AND THE MISSIONARIES

The fur trade did bring to the Indians a glimpse of a generally more admirable side of white civilization, religion. Many of the Canadian fur men who came to western Montana after 1808 were French Roman Catholics. They brought with them a number of Iroquois Indians from the East. The Iroquois were experienced trappers, and the Canadians wanted them to teach their skills to the local tribes. According to one disgusted Nor'Wester, however, the Iroquois "preferred to feast and dance in the tents of the Flatheads than hunt for beaver."

The Iroquois told the Flatheads about the mysteries and powers of Christianity. The most influential of the Iroquois was Ignace La Mousse, or "Big Ignace." Ignace told the Flatheads, as Father Gregory Mengarini later learned, "of certain white men clothed in black whose practice it was to instruct people, bring them to know God and all good things, and enable them to live after death." The Flatheads reacted enthusiastically. They determined to find a "Black Robe" who would bring them religion and the "white man's Book of Heaven."

The Flatheads were remarkably persistent in their quest for Christianity. Along with their Nez Perce friends, they sent four different parties—in 1831, 1835, 1837, and 1839—on long and dangerous journeys through enemy territory to St. Louis in search of a missionary. The first group aroused the interest of Protestants, but their missionaries ended up in the Oregon Country, not the eastern Rockies. Big Ignace led the next two journeys, and on his second expedition he was killed by Indian enemies. Finally, the fourth effort brought results. Bishop Rosati of St. Louis received the Indians, led by Ignace's son, and he promised to send them a priest.

The priest he sent was a Jesuit named Pierre-Jean DeSmet, one of the truly remarkable missionaries in American history. A Belgian by birth, DeSmet, even though often in poor health, would prove himself to be one of the frontier's greatest travelers and one of the most patient and understanding friends the Indians would ever had. Along with young Ignace, he accompanied an American Fur Company caravan to the 1840 rendezvous at Green River. There, Flatheads, Nez Perces, and Shoshonis welcomed him and watched as he performed mass in French, English, and through an interpreter. "It was a spectacle truly moving for the heart of a missionary," DeSmet later wrote, "to behold an assembly composed of so many different nations, who all assisted at our holy mysteries with great satisfaction." Traveling with the Indians to the Three Forks area, DeSmet took leave of them in the Gallatin Valley, much impressed with their zeal and promising to return soon.

DeSmet spent the following winter raising funds for his project, and in the spring of 1841 he set out once again for the Rockies. He brought with him two other priests, Gregory Mengarini and Nicholas Point, and three lay brothers. They met the Flatheads at Fort Hall on the Oregon Trail and accompanied them to their favorite area, the Bitterroot Valley. There, in September 1841, they began building St. Mary's Mission, which Montanans have recognized ever since as one of the birthplaces of their history. While his comrades worked at the mission, DeSmet made one of his legendary treks, this time to the Columbia River and back, bringing seed wheat, potatoes, and oats for planting. This marked the real beginning of agriculture in Montana, and it enthralled the Indians, who watched the ripening plants with fascination.

For a few years, St. Mary's Mission seemed to be a remarkable success. DeSmet returned east in 1842 and went on to Europe, where he raised support for his endeavors. Meanwhile, other Jesuits traveled to St. Mary's, and some continued west to build more missions beyond the mountains. DeSmet returned to the mission in the spring of 1845, bringing with him the capable Italian Jesuit, Father Anthony Ravalli, a dedicated priest and a man of many skills. Largely through Ravalli's efforts, the priests put together crude flour and sawmills, and in 1846 they built a new and larger church.

All went well until 1846, when the Indians returned from their summer hunt, indifferent to Christianity and openly hostile to the priests. There were several probable reasons for the turnabout. DeSmet, whom the Indians liked, had left again for the East, leaving Mengarini, not a favorite of the Flatheads, in charge. Also, white trappers had settled near the mission and had been exerting a worldly influence on the Indians. But the main reason for the Flatheads' "apostacy" arose from DeSmet's effort in 1846 to take religion to the Blackfeet. To the Flatheads, this was near treason; the priest was sharing sacred "medicine" with the Flatheads' mortal enemies.

Relations became so bad between the clerics and the Indians that the priests closed their Bitterroot mission in 1850. They sold the property to Major John Owen, who converted the mission into a trading post that became a popular and important gathering place for early Montanans. The Jesuits' setback among the Flatheads, however, was temporary. For a few years, the priests focused their activities among the Indians to the west. Then, in 1854, the Jesuits returned to Montana under the leadership of Father Adrian Hoecken and located the St. Ignatius Mission in the country south of Flathead Lake. The Indians responded with surprising enthusiasm to this renewed missionary effort. Over a thousand Kutenais, Pend d'Oreilles, and Flatheads came to the Easter services at St. Ignatius in 1855, and hundreds were baptized.

Several years later, in 1866, Ravalli and Father Joseph Giorda returned to the Bitterroot and reopened St. Mary's Mission. Ravalli, whose name was given to the county embracing this area, remained among the Flatheads until 1884, beloved by both Indians and whites. The mission closed in 1891, when the Flatheads sadly left the Bitterroot Valley for the reservation to the north. At St. Ignatius, Hoecken and his colleagues continued to work among the Indians who were moving onto the reservation south of Flathead Lake. Some Sisters of Providence came from Canada to open a school there in 1864. The Catholics remained, helping Indians adjust to the new, closed world of the reservation.

The Catholics made the major missionary efforts in frontier Montana. Although the Methodists did some work among the Crows and the Fort Peck tribes, most Protestant ministers came with and stayed among the whites. The Catholics eventually expanded their activities throughout Montana. They established the St. Peter's and Holy Family missions among the Blackfeet, St. Paul's for the Indians at Fort Belknap, St. Xavier's on the Crow Indian Reservation, and a mission school on the Northern Cheyenne Indian Reservation. As in Oregon, California, and Arizona, missionaries played a significant role in "opening" Montana.

CHAPTER 4

The Mining Frontier

MONTANA'S foundation, like that of many other western states, stands on a golden cornerstone. The promise of gold first attracted significant numbers of whites to the area, and their coming laid the basis of a community. The initial gold rush to Montana was part of a population movement that crisscrossed much of the Mountain West. As happened in other areas, the movement lost its momentum in Montana within only a few years. As the easy diggings played out, some miners turned to more elaborate methods of extracting the ore, while others prospected for new deposits. The population shifted constantly as new goldfields were discovered, transportation routes were opened, and new mining technology was applied. New boomtowns appeared and old ones died. In Montana, as in Colorado, Nevada, and Idaho, gold soon gave way to silver, a metal much more difficult and expensive to extract. Eventually, silver mining would also fade. By the mid-1890s, copper would prove to be Montana's premier metal, its production centered at Butte, with gold and silver becoming mere byproducts.

GOLD: THE PLACER BOOM

The question of who first discovered gold in Montana has always been, and always will be, a matter of conjecture. Some credit Father DeSmet or John Owen on the Bitterroot; others argue, plausibly, that fur trappers, such as John Silverthorne or Francois Finlay, made the first find. The first recorded discovery occurred in the spring of 1858, when brothers James and Granville Stuart and Reece Anderson found placer gold deposits at Gold Creek east of present-day Drummond. By the summer of 1862, the Stuart brothers and other men were at work there. A small settlement called American Fork took hold at Gold Creek, but neither the diggings nor the town ever amounted to much.

By mid-1862, general conditions favored a major gold rush to what is now Montana. Earlier centers of gold-mining opportunity—California, Nevada, and Colorado—were in decline, and prospectors were combing the western slopes of the Rockies in Idaho, where new discoveries had just been made. The Mullan Road, which connected ports on the Missouri and Columbia rivers, had just opened, and steamboats were successfully plying the treacherous Missouri River all the way to Fort Benton, carrying miners who trekked eastward along the road to the Idaho mines. Not surprisingly, some Idaho-bound miners made their way into the southwestern portion of today's Montana as they attempted to find shortcuts through the Bitterroot Mountains. John White, a member of one Colorado-based party, touched off Montana's first major placer rush in the summer of 1862 when he uncovered sizable deposits of placer gold on Grasshopper Creek, a tributary of the Beaverhead (upper Jefferson) River. At the "Grasshopper Diggings," miners created Montana's first boomtown, a hell-for-leather burg named Bannack City.

By the fall of 1862, Bannack's population stood at four to five hundred people. As usual on mining frontiers, the early arrivals grabbed up the best-paying gold claims and the latecomers had to turn elsewhere. Prospectors fanned out through the upper Missouri drainage, and new discoveries came in rapid-fire succession. A cluster of claims appeared on Horse Prairie Creek, fifteen miles west of Bannack; other activity was fruitful on the Prickly Pear, far to the north. These smaller placers, however, paled in comparison to the deposits found at Alder Gulch, seventy miles east of Bannack.

In the spring of 1863, a prospecting party under the leadership of James Stuart left Bannack to prospect in the Yellowstone Valley. Several members of the group, including Bill Fairweather, Henry Edgar, and Barney Hughes, missed a rendezvous with the main party, which would encounter hostile Indians and end up traveling a circuitous sixteen hundred miles back to Bannack by way of the Oregon Trail. The smaller Fairweather-Edgar group, after running into Crow Indians, headed despondently back through the Gallatin and Madison valleys en route to Bannack. On the evening of May 26, 1863, after making camp on the Madison-Jefferson divide, Fairweather and Edgar decided to prospect for some tobacco money. Their first pan turned up $2.40. They knew at once that Alder Gulch, as they christened it, held great potential.

The opening of Alder Gulch would set off the greatest placer rush of Montana's history. Hundreds of miners, always on the lookout for prospectors who acted suspiciously, followed Fairweather and Edgar when

In addition to laboring for white miners, many Chinese worked their own claims. W. H. Jackson took this photograph of Chinese working a sluice at Alder Gulch in 1871.

they returned to Alder Gulch from Bannack. Within the next year and a half, at least ten thousand people crowded into the steep, rugged contours of the area. Mining districts named Fairweather, Summit, Highland, Pine Grove, and Junction blanketed the gulch. Several towns appeared, the best known being Virginia City and Nevada City, but population was so scattered that some contemporaries called the area "Fourteen-mile City."

Alder Gulch–Virginia City grew to become one of the great gold camps of the American West and the center of activity for early Montana. During its first five years, the gulch produced an estimated thirty to forty million dollars in gold. More important, the diggings attracted into the area several thousand prospectors who, arriving too late to cash in at Virginia City, ranged out in all directions looking for other bonanzas. Traveling in groups of from five to fifty men, they understood the miners' craft, and they could easily recognize gold-bearing terrain. Many were veterans of the rushes to California, Colorado, Nevada, or Idaho.

During the years following the Alder Gulch strike, miners enjoyed one new discovery after another. The most important was at Last Chance Gulch, located at the geographic center of Montana's mining region. A group of Virginia City prospectors on their way to the Kootenai country first found color there in the spring of 1864, but they continued on to the north, where they met no success. The four men, who would later be called the "Four Georgians," returned to what they would name, appropriately, Last Chance Gulch, and where, on July 14, 1864, they uncovered significant placer deposits. When two of the men returned to Virginia City for supplies, the usual horde of miners followed them back. They established the town of Helena in Last Chance Gulch. Well-situated on major transportation routes, well-supplied with foodstuffs from the nearby Prickly Pear Valley, and located close to other mining towns, such as Montana City and Jefferson City, Helena would survive and grow. Next to Alder Gulch, the Last Chance gold deposits proved to be the most extensive in Montana, producing an estimated nineteen million dollars within four years.

During that summer of 1864, miners opened Confederate Gulch, the third of the important Montana placer districts. The rush to the diggings, located about thirty miles east of Helena in the Big Belt Mountains, reached boom proportions in 1865. Confederate Gulch miners found gold deposits, such as Montana Bar and Diamond Bar, that were richer in terms of yield per acre than any others in the territory. At the crest of the boom, some ten thousand people lived in Confederate Gulch and its vicinity. Diamond City, the most spectacular of Montana's boom-and-bust gold towns, dominated the area and was the seat of Meagher County. Although there are no accurate records, the Confederate Gulch diggings produced roughly ten to thirty million dollars in gold.

Many other gold camps sprouted up throughout west-central Montana during the middle and late 1860s. Too numerous to mention, they were smaller than Confederate Gulch and Diamond City but similar in atmosphere and ethnic composition. These towns lay scattered over a huge, tangled area, from Emigrant on the upper Yellowstone River westward to Cedar Creek on the Clark Fork. Most of the gold deposits played out quickly. Only in favored places like Butte did gold mining lead to big-time industrial mining.

The movement of miners to Montana, sudden as it was, seemed less of a stampede than the rushes of "Forty-niners" to California or of "Fifty-niners" to Colorado. The sheer remoteness of the place limited the size of the miners' invasion, and so did the Civil War. Nevertheless, even by 1866, Montana had been catapulted into second place among United States gold producers; only California ranked higher. According to federal estimates, Montana's population peaked at roughly 28,000 in 1866 and then declined to 21,000-24,000 later in the decade. The 1870 census, Montana's first, listed the population as a mere 20,595.

The mining profession has always drawn together a diverse, cosmopolitan population, and the miners in Montana were no exception. Many miners and prospectors came from the Midwest and from border states like Missouri, but more drifted in directly from mining states and territories like California, Idaho, and Nevada. Because they moved about constantly, frontier prospectors and miners cared little about their neighbors' background or status. Even proper names had small meaning among casual acquaintances, and nicknames predominated. A typical roster of Montana miners might include Wild Goose Bill, Cayuse George, Nubbins, Roachy, Canary Bird, Old Badger, Frenchy, Dirty Ike, Jewsharp Jack, Whiskey Bill, and Black Jack. Such nicknames still abound in Butte, Montana's premier mining camp.

Most of the prospectors looked for placer gold. Erosion and other natural forces had created placer, or surface, gold deposits by disintegrating large veins of ore. In the slow process of geological time, flowing water and glacial ice had carried away the particulate gold and deposited it in the beds of ancient or still active streams, where it lay as dust, flakes, or nuggets. Placer gold, scattered about in its natural state, usually required no special processing. Such deposits were "poor man's diggings," and men of little wealth or special skill could work them easily. For this reason, new-found placers always attracted a sudden population of young men, motivated by little else than a get-rich-quick impulse. Placer towns, naturally enough, were jerry-built, ephemeral, and hectic places. The

Earl of Dunraven described Virginia City in the 1870s: "Good Lord!... A street of straggling shanties, a bank, a blacksmith's shop, a few dry good stores, and bar-rooms, constitute the main attractions of the 'city.'" When production began to decline in these mining boomtowns or when news arrived of new strikes elsewhere, the unattached population simply evaporated.

Placer miners, in Montana as elsewhere, stampeded easily. "There is no animal on earth," wrote pioneer Robert Vaughan, "that will stampede quicker, keep on going with the same stubbornness and determination, as a fortune hunter; they are worse than Texas cattle." A classic case of such lemming-like behavior occurred at Helena in the winter of 1866. When John McClellan, a prospector of exceptional reputation, left town for the Sun River country, hundreds of men immediately followed him, even though no one knew for sure the purpose of his trip. Many of them left in such a hurry that they made no preparations for winter travel. As a result of this misadventure, so many prospectors returned to Helena with frostbite that the residents of the town came to their aid by establishing a hospital.

In its simplest form, placer mining involved little more than scratching the surface. Using simple picks and shovels and usually working in small groups, miners dug up the gold-bearing dirt and then used water to flush the waste material. Small-scale washing could be done with a flat-bottomed wash pan, in which a sourdough dissolved and sloshed away the dirt while its gold content fell to the bottom of the pan. Panning was simple and cheap, but it allowed miners to work only small amounts of gold-bearing soils. So the frontiersmen most often used a pan to prospect and used other methods to work larger quantities of promising ground. In some places, like Alder Gulch, the prospectors first had to remove a heavy overburden in order to get at the gold. This meant digging shafts and tunnels and using hoists to carry gravel to the surface for washing. As Mary Ronan described Virginia City in 1863, "Every foot of earth in the gulches was being turned upside down." It was dangerous work, and some died in cave-ins.

In order to wash larger quantities of dirt, miners often worked in groups and used more elaborate methods and equipment. The simplest of these was the rocker, or cradle. Workmen simply filled the upper end of the rocker with soil, then rocked the device while pouring in water. As the material dissolved and floated out of the rocker, gold particles lodged in cleats along the bottom. With ample water and manpower, miners used a "tom" or "sluice" to supplant the rocker. Six or more men could wash large amounts of dirt using a tom, a long wooden trough with perforated sheet metal at the lower end. Sometimes a hundred and even a

"*Placer Mining, Jeffersen Bar,*" an F. Jay Haynes photograph of 1890, shows the power and ecological results of hydraulic mining, in which high pressure nozzles washed gold-bearing gravels out of hillsides.

Left: Heavy, rock-crushing stamps, such as these at the Battery-Algonquin Mill near Phillipsburg, pulverized mined ore in preparation for heat and chemical processes that separated precious from base metals.

thousand feet in length, the sluice employed the same principle of using water and gravity to trap the gold. Often, twenty or more men worked together on sluices in Montana; sometimes they added mercury to gather the gold by amalgamation.

With each of these steps beyond the simple wash pan, miners could afford to work lower and lower grades of ore. In some places, like Confederate Gulch, they turned to the ultimate form of placering, hydraulic mining. Hydraulicking, first developed in the "Mother Lode" country of California, involved the use of "little giants," high pressure hoses that could blast away whole stream banks and beds. The water separated earth from rocks and carried it through a long series of sluices. Some hydraulic outfits worked up to a hundred cubic yards of gravel per day. By the late 1860s, as Montana's placers were fading out, hydraulic mining became more and more popular. The 1870 census found 64 such operations employing 434 men in Montana, nearly half of them in Deer Lodge County. Hydraulic mining, like the floating dredges later used to tear up the Ruby River, involved high costs, both in capital and in environmental damage. Expensive ditches and flumes for transporting water to dry goldbeds required large investments, and local capitalists like Samuel T. Hauser and Conrad Kohrs provided them. Such operations played havoc with the environment, as they tore up the gulches, scattered rocks in all directions, and flushed huge amounts of silt into lower streams and rivers.

The surface mining of gold, whether by wash pan, sluice, or hydraulics, never lasted for long; it depended on isolated, eroded deposits, not the large and rich "mother lodes" imbedded in buried rock. These larger, "quartz" veins required heavy, expensive machinery for reduction. Mine owners built large mills that crushed the rock using enormous, steam-powered metal stamps. Workers operated the mills much like factories, while small armies of other men cut wood to feed the steam engines, worked as teamsters, and did the other jobs to keep the mills operating. All of this required a significant investment of money.

In Montana, the less expensive method of placering reached its peak as early as 1866, when the territory produced eighteen million dollars in precious metals. Although the booming Comstock Lode in Nevada dropped Montana from second to third place among mining regions, annual yields of over ten million dollars continued for several more years. By the close of the boom decade, however, prospectors were leaving Montana in droves. The 1870 census revealed only about six hundred placers, employing roughly three thousand men. Gold output continued to decline until 1883, when it amounted to only a million dollars; then it began to climb again, this time mainly as a byproduct of industrial silver and copper mining.

THE TRANSPORTATION FRONTIER

As mining began to boom in Montana, transportation routes quickly emerged to link the gold towns and connect them to the outside world. Before the gold bonanza, trappers and explorers had marked out and followed the favored trails of Indians and buffalo. One such route, even in the mid-1850s, ran from Fort Hall on the Oregon Trail northward into the Bitterroot, Beaverhead, and Deer Lodge valleys of southwestern Montana. This trail would later become the major freight and coach road into frontier Montana.

Montana's first really improved route of traffic, the Mullan Road, began to take shape in the late 1850s. In 1853, Governor Isaac I. Stevens, en route to his post in newly created Washington Territory, led a sizable expedition westward to lay out the course of a possible transcontinental railroad between Minnesota and the Northwest coast. One of Stevens's most valuable men was a young West Point graduate named Lieutenant John Mullan. While exploring the mountain mazes of the Northern Rockies, Mullan became enthusiastic about the idea of building a road to link Fort Benton on the upper Missouri with the Columbia River above its northward bend near Walla Walla, Washington. Mullan convinced Stevens of the feasibility of his plan; and after gaining election to Congress, Stevens pushed through a bill providing for construction of such a road in 1857.

Mullan, who was designated to build the road, arrived in Washington Territory from the East in the spring of 1858. Local Indian disorders delayed his plans for a year. Then, beginning early in 1859, the first season of construction extended the route across the hill country of eastern Washington, up the Coeur d'Alene River of Idaho, and over Sohon Pass to the St. Regis River in western Montana. During the following year, Mullan continued his road up the Clark Fork and Little Blackfoot rivers and over Mullan Pass to the vicinity of future Helena. The roadbuilders continued in a northeasterly direction, roughly paralleling the Missouri River, and reached Fort Benton on August 1, 1860. Crossing through such rugged, mountainous country, the Mullan Road never became a major thoroughfare. On large sections of its mountain crossings, it was really no more than a pack trail, too rough for consistent wagon use. Nevertheless, the road was significant to early Montana. It connected the local goldfields, however tenuously, to Idaho and the Columbia River, and it provided a link between Fort Benton and the gold camps lying to the south and west.

During the peak years of the fur trade, steamboats from St. Louis traveled no farther upriver than Fort Union, near the mouth of the Yellowstone. But Pierre Chouteau Jr. and his associates, eager to secure government contracts for carrying Indian goods and military supplies to the upper Missouri, saw the advantages of attempting to get the boats to Fort Benton on the floodwaters of early summer. In 1859, Chouteau dispatched the *Chippewa*, a steamboat designed especially for the shallower upstream channel, to carry Indian annuity cargoes to Fort Benton. A fuel shortage forced the *Chippewa* to unload its cargo fifteen miles short of its objective. During the following year, at Mullan's suggestion, the government contracted with Chouteau to transport Major George Blake and three hundred soldiers to Fort Benton. Two boats, the *Chippewa* and the *Key West*, arrived at the fort with the troops aboard in early July. Eager to prove the utility of his road, Mullan then escorted the soldiers over it in a journey of less than two months.

The gold boom that began in 1862 suddenly turned sleepy Fort Benton into a busy river port and a rough-and-tumble town populated by renegade characters. As the *Montana Post* put it: "As to Fort Benton and its inmates—the imagination can have full play." By 1864, the tonnages of mining equipment landed at Fort Benton exceeded those of Indian trade stuffs; in 1866, porters off-loaded 4,441 tons of cargo for transport to the mining camps. Except for 1863, when drought and low water stopped the steamboats downstream at Cow Island, the number of boats docking at Fort Benton increased each year, disgorging passengers, mining equipment, and supplies and loading up stocks of gold bullion, hides, and wool. The traffic reached a peak in 1867, when thirty-nine boats tied up at the Benton docks, carrying fifteen hundred passengers.

Booming little Fort Benton, thirty-five hundred miles from the Gulf of Mexico, was America's most remote port. Major freighting outfits, such as the Montana and Idaho Transportation Line, J. J. Roe and Company, J. T. Murphy, and King and Gillette, shuttled back and forth between Benton and the mining camps. In 1866, some twenty-five hundred men and three thousand teams of oxen and mules engaged in the freighting of goods from the port. After 1867, however, dockings at Fort Benton fell off each year until they reached a low of six in 1874. The lack of traffic was due to both the decline of placer mining and the completion of the transcontinental railroad through northern Utah in 1869, which increasingly robbed the port of its traffic.

After 1875, Fort Benton sprang back to life again, this time primarily as a base of supply for the isolated settlements on the Canadian prairies. Fort McLeod, Fort Whoop-Up, and other Canadian outposts could be reached more easily by way of the Missouri River and the "Whoop-Up Trail," which ran north from Benton, than they could by way of Winnipeg. For a time, this trade meant big business as Fort Benton's aggressive "merchant princes"—T. C. Power, I. G. Baker, the Conrad brothers, and

W. S. Wetzel—transshipped goods from the river northward over the long Whoop-Up route. They prospered for a time, hauling merchandise and sometimes illegal whiskey for the Indians northward and returning with loads of hides, coal, and produce. The sordid trade on the Whoop-Up Trail fell off in the 1880s, however, as the Royal Canadian Mounted Police brought law and order to the scene. By then, the arrival of railroads was bringing Fort Benton's river commerce to an end.

For residents of Minnesota, Wisconsin, and the upper Midwest, the natural route to the gold mines of the far Northwest lay straight across the broad plains of the Dakotas and Montana. Unfortunately, hostile Sioux Indians made travel hazardous across this otherwise easy country. Promoters of a "Northern Overland Route," primarily Minnesotans, pushed for and got from Congress a special appropriation in 1862 to provide military protection for wagon trains through the Dakota country. The Minnesota-Montana Road, as it was often called, closely followed the route of the 1853 Stevens expedition through northern Dakota and Montana and connected to the Mullan Road at Fort Benton. Between 1862 and 1867, eight wagon trains left Minnesota for Idaho and Montana. Four of them were led by the famed wagon master and Montana pioneer James Liberty Fisk, a tough Yankee frontiersman and a capable organizer and propagandist. Significantly, the "Fisk Expeditions" provided the first real transportation link between Montana and the upper Midwest, and they brought an important Yankee-Republican element into early-day Montana.

The Oregon Trail, which passed through southern Wyoming and Idaho, was the main route of immigration into the Far West, and many Montana-bound pioneers detoured northward from the trail to reach their objective. From a strictly geographical viewpoint, John Bozeman and John Jacobs laid out the most sensible cutoff from the Oregon Trail into Montana in 1863. Their route, the Bozeman Road, left the Oregon Trail near present-day Casper, Wyoming, and flanked northward along the east slopes of the massive Big Horn Mountains. The road then headed westward along the Yellowstone River, over Bozeman Pass, and across the Gallatin Valley to the gold-bearing areas.

Wagon trains could cross the Bozeman Road with relative ease, but the trail passed through the best buffalo lands of the powerful Sioux Indians. The Sioux turned back the first train that Bozeman and Jacobs tried to lead over the road in 1863, but Bozeman succeeded in bringing a caravan through in 1864. In that same year, friends of Bozeman laid out the town bearing his name in the shadow of Bozeman Pass, and for a few years wagon trains continued to cross the road. But the Sioux continued to make such travel extremely dangerous, and finally the federal government abandoned its efforts to keep the road open. Meanwhile, the old mountain man and guide Jim Bridger laid out an alternate route. The "Bridger Cut-off" passed to the west of the Big Horns through the Wind River Canyon and down to the Yellowstone. Bridger's route had the advantage of bypassing the Sioux threat, but shortages of forage and steep grades made it unpopular.

Montanans resented the government's failure to keep the Bozeman Road open, but in truth the road had lost much of its usefulness by 1869. Completion of the Union Pacific Railroad through southern Wyoming to northern Utah in that year meant that Montana immigrants could travel by rail to the vicinity of Ogden, Utah, and then head directly north into southwestern Montana. Even before the rails reached Utah, the route later known as the Corinne–Virginia City Road, or the Salt Lake Trail, connected the Mormon settlements to the Montana gold camps. Mormon merchants did a thriving business over this road, and when the Union Pacific reached Corinne, thirty-two miles west of Ogden, that town became the major freighting depot for Montana. Merchants at Walla Walla, Washington, and Portland, Oregon, tried desperately to compete with Utah for the Montana trade by campaigning for improvement of the Mullan Road, but they never had a chance.

Simple geography made the Corinne–Virginia City Road Montana's primary transportation artery, and the road's connection with the Union Pacific allowed Montanans to ship freight and to travel on a regular, predictable basis. The road headed northward through Utah and eastern Idaho over arid plains and plateaus, and it crossed the Continental Divide into Montana over Monida Pass. Along the Red Rock–Beaverhead River, the road forked, with a branch leading to Bannack and on to the Deer Lodge Valley and the main road leading to Virginia City and Helena, where it connected with the Mullan Road. An alternate fork led from Alder Gulch to the Gallatin Valley.

Keeping this and other roads in decent shape was nearly impossible. Because the territory had few tax dollars to spend, the legislature granted franchises for toll roads, bridges, and ferries. Predictably, this system led to few improvements, poor services, and the gouging of travelers. Freighters, in turn, blamed their extremely high rates on high tolls and the poor condition of roads. Finally, Congress received so many complaints about local roads that it expressly amended the Montana Organic Act so that the legislature could no longer grant such special charters.

At its peak, Montana wagon freighting was big-time business, employing hundreds of men and thousands of draft animals. The Diamond R Freighting Company, founded at Virginia City in 1864 and later based at Helena, came to dominate the local carrying trade. Managed efficiently

Charles Broadwater's Diamond R freight wagons, shown here in Prickly Pear Canyon north of Helena, transported goods from Fort Benton on the Missouri River to gold camps in southwestern Montana.

by the influential C. A. Broadwater and his partners, Matthew Carroll, E. G. Maclay, and George Steel, the Diamond R outfit owned 300 wagons, 350 mules, and 500 yoke of oxen and extended its service throughout the territory. The freighting business involved high overhead, with heavy investments in stock, stables, wagons, and warehouses, but it also returned handsome profits, making fortunes for some of Montana's leading capitalists, such as Broadwater, T. C. Power, and I. G. Baker. By wintering thousands of mules and oxen on the open range, these freighters helped establish Montana's grasslands as land well-suited for livestock production.

Freighting on the Corinne–Virginia City Road or on the Whoop-Up Trail followed general western patterns. In April and May, as the weather moderated and the fields began to green, long lines of mule trains and bull trains began to roll out. Mule skinners usually rode the left-wheel mule and controlled the lead animal with a jerkline. Bullwhackers walked alongside the slower, plodding teams of oxen and expertly cracked their whips over the animals while shouting directions of "Gee" and "Haw." Respected for their skills, the mule skinners and bullwhackers were legendary as hard drinkers and masters of profanity.

Most often in Montana, a hitch of eight mules or oxen drew three coupled wagons holding a cargo of about twelve thousand pounds; really big loads employed as many as twelve teams of oxen. Travel on local roads peaked in mid-summer, when low water ended steamboating on the Missouri and released equipment from Fort Benton for the southern run. It took teams about three weeks to deliver goods from Corinne to Helena; and with time out for resting the draft animals, each unit could make three round trips per season. Freighters who gambled on four trips ran the risks of getting mired down in spring mud or being trapped by late spring or early winter snowstorms. The freighters hauled surprisingly large quantities and varieties of goods. During the early 1870s, shipments from Corinne averaged between six and seven million pounds annually and included everything from tools, machinery, dry goods, and coal oil to whiskey, fresh fruit, and carefully packed eggs.

Freight rates varied widely, depending on such factors as the season, local demand, and the availability of men, animals, and equipment. In June 1873, for instance, the Diamond R charged $3.75 for hauling 100 pounds from Corinne to Missoula, $4.12 to Deer Lodge, and $5.00 to Bozeman. Sometimes the freighters hauled cargoes of wool, hides, furs, or ore to Utah on their return trips. But often they returned with empty wagons, which simply meant higher charges on goods taken north to Montana.

Soon after gold was discovered at Alder Gulch, stage lines began to serve the larger towns, offering regular service to Corinne and Salt Lake City. As early as autumn 1863, the A. J. Oliver and the Peabody and Caldwell outfits operated lines between Virginia City and Bannack. During the winter of 1863-64, Oliver opened regular service between Virginia City and Salt Lake. Ben Holladay, the transportation baron of the West, drove out the competition by gaining a government subsidy to carry the mail to Montana; he, in turn, sold out to Wells, Fargo and Company in 1866. Traveling day and night, the Wells Fargo stages took four and a half or more days to cover the 550 miles between Helena and Corinne. The company charged $145 for the trip, and, even at that, it needed the mail contract to make a profit. Not surprisingly, the stage operators often seemed more interested in the mail than they were in the passengers.

In Montana, as elsewhere in the West, handsome Concord coaches served as the standard carriers. Stage companies maintained "swing stations" every ten to thirteen miles for changing horses and "home stations" every forty to fifty miles where drivers began and ended their runs. Passengers suffered the rigors of cramped quarters, jolting rides, extreme heat and cold, asphyxiating dust, and swarms of insects. But, because the coaches offered the only commercial method of travel, people learned to endure the hardships. Daily stagecoaches from Helena to Fort Benton and Salt Lake did a good business, and the regular mail service that the coaches made possible turned local post offices into community social centers. The arrival of the telegraph in 1866 allowed even closer contact between Montana and "The States."

Yet, even with these improvements in transportation, Montanans were terribly isolated. Elaborate as it was, wagon freighting was often unreliable. Heavy snows during the winter of 1863-64 caused a flour famine in Virginia City that ended in a "Bread Riot." Even in the summer of 1871, the scarcity of flour at Deer Lodge drove the price up to fifteen dollars per sack. So long as the territory relied on roads and waterways for transportation, the local economy would stagnate and the local population would suffer inconveniences. Montanans of the 1860s and 1870s understood this fact, and they waited eagerly for the rail connections that would join them to the outside world.

THE VIGILANTES

Frontier miners, usually moving ahead of federal authority, had to improvise when it came to law and law enforcement. Because most of them were transients, the miners had little civic pride or interest, with the predictable result of inefficient, often corrupt government. Once a gold camp had sprouted up, a miners' meeting usually convened to organize a "mining district" and provide basic laws. Montana's gold towns naturally relied on the precedents of earlier mining frontiers, especially California, when they established their governments and laws. The elected officers of most mining districts included a president, who presided over miners' meetings; a judge, who met with the democratic miners' court; a sheriff; and a "recorder," who kept the records of mining claims. Local laws dealt heavily with mining claims—their size, the number that an individual could acquire, the volume of water each could use, and the amount of work necessary to secure claim titles.

Very often—particularly in Montana—this casual, democratic form of government was woefully inadequate. Mining camps, after all, attracted large numbers of cutthroats, thieves, and fast-buck artists. Sometimes, as in the rush to British Columbia, well-organized government kept lawlessness to a minimum; but more often, as in California, Colorado, and Montana, crime became rampant. When neither federal nor local law provided order, residents accepted a dangerous substitute: vigilantism and lynch law.

The 1862-63 gold rushes to Bannack and Virginia City brought a large, turbulent population to a remote area where the federal government exercised almost no authority. From mid-1862 until the end of 1863, anyone who traveled this area literally risked life and limb. Most of the disorder arose from a violent gang of road agents who followed the gold rush over the Bitterroots from the mining camps around Lewiston, Idaho. Their leader was Henry Plummer, one of the most amazing of western outlaws. Still a young man in 1862, the handsome Plummer combined in one unstable personality qualities of charm and intelligence and also psychotic viciousness. His career of murder and lawlessness took him from California and Nevada to Idaho and eventually to Montana. Amazingly enough, the engaging Plummer was elected sheriff of Bannack, and in 1863 his authority extended to newborn Virginia City. His henchmen, who identified one another by a special knot of the tie and cut of the beard and by the password "I am innocent," received intelligence from Sheriff Plummer and preyed on gold shipments, stagecoaches, and individual travelers. In its brief career, the Plummer Gang may have murdered over a hundred people.

One brutal killing followed another, but the Bannack–Virginia City populace was slow to react. People neither knew nor trusted one another, and the miners were only interested in working their claims, accumulating some cash, and leaving. Even murder committed out in the open went unpunished. In January 1863, for example, two "roughs" named Charles Reeves and William Moore shot up an Indian camp, killing several natives and a white man. A jury voted to banish the murderers for their crime, but a subsequent miners' meeting rescinded even that light sentence.

During the hectic summer of 1863, three of Plummer's cronies—Buck Stinson, Haze Lyons, and Charley Forbes—killed Chief Deputy Sheriff D. R. Dillingham because he had informed on them as outlaws. A Virginia City miners' court acquitted Forbes but convicted Stinson and Lyons and sentenced them to death by hanging. The crowd that made up the miners' court, however, weakened under the influence of weeping women and the outlaws' pleading lawyer. After many of the miners had gone back to work, those remaining voted to reverse the verdict, and both Stinson and Lyons fled.

The beginning of the end for the Plummer Gang came late in 1863 after Plummer's cohort George Ives brutally murdered young Nicholas Thiebalt. When friends of the boy identified the body, they quickly organized a posse to track down his killer and suggested that a vigilance committee be organized. Livery owner James Williams led the group that brought Ives to justice. When Ives came to trial before the miners' court on December 19, a courageous young attorney named Wilbur Fisk Sanders served as prosecutor. After persuading the jury to return a verdict of guilty, Sanders moved that the hanging sentence be carried out at once, before the crowd could be swayed toward leniency. Armed guards surrounded Ives and faced off the crowd, which included many of the condemned man's friends. Ives was hanged within the hour.

Ives's execution led directly to the formal organization of a vigilance committee. Many of the law-abiding majority of citizens knew each other by then, and the agitation of the trial prompted them to act. Among the organizers were both Masons and Catholics, but the Masons seem to have played the key role. On December 23, 1863, men from Bannack, Virginia City, and Nevada City met secretly and organized a vigilance committee based on the California model. They drew up an oath, regulations, and bylaws and appointed a seventeen-man executive committee and captains to head up local committees. The local committees enlisted nearly two thousand men as vigilantes, which suggests that the movement was broadly popular and not the work of a small clique. The key officers included Paris S. Pfouts, president; James Williams, executive officer; Wilbur Sanders, official prosecutor; and John S. Lott, treasurer. As a warning signal and symbol of recognition, they used the numbers "3-7-77" (sometimes "3-11-77"), the meaning of which is still a subject of debate.

Ably led by tough and fearless James Williams, the Montana vigilantes destroyed the Plummer Gang in a surprisingly short time. Their first two victims were G. W. Brown, secretary of the gang, and Erastus "Red" Yeager, who revealed the identities of gang leaders and then resigned himself to his own hanging. Yeager's confession allowed a rapid crackdown on the criminals. Between January 4 and February 3, 1864, the vigilantes tracked down and hanged twenty-four men. Vigilantes from Bannack and Virginia City arrested Plummer and his lieutenants Buck Stinson and Ned Ray on January 10. Stinson and Ray swore and resisted, and Plummer wept and pleaded for his life, but all three were strung up at once. The hanging party departed, "leaving the corpses," as one contemporary wrote, "stiffening in the icy blast."

On January 14, five key members of the gang were seized and summarily hanged in Virginia City. Among them was Boone Helm, reputedly the most violent man in the area. Standing with the noose about his neck, Helm looked casually at the still lurching corpse of one of his pals and remarked: "Kick away, old fellow; I'll be in Hell with you in a minute." Then, just before the rope broke his neck, Helm shouted: "Every man for his principles—hurrah for Jeff Davis! Let her rip!" Some of the road agents fled the territory; others went to outlying areas like Hell Gate (Missoula) and the Deer Lodge and Gallatin valleys. The vigilantes tracked many of them down and hanged them on the spot. In only a month and a half, the vigilantes had ended the road agent menace.

Ever since the 1860s, Montanans have dwelt on these dramatic happenings and honored the vigilantes as men larger than life. State highway patrolmen wear the emblem "3-7-77" on their shoulder patches, and Helena named one of its athletic fields "Vigilante Stadium." But we really know precious little about the secret operations of the vigilantes. Two prominent Montanans, both of them participants in these events, wrote highly influential accounts of what happened, but both men wrote to justify the vigilantes. Thomas J. Dimsdale's *The Vigilantes of Montana*—published serially in the Virginia City *Montana Post* in 1865 and then as Montana's first book in 1866—argued that "swift and terrible retribution is the only preventative of crime, while society is organizing in the far West" and that the "positively awful expense and delay" of established law and order could not be tolerated. Nathaniel P. Langford's *Vigilante Days and Ways*, published in 1890, had a similar interpretation. More recently, scholars have questioned the actions of the vigilantes and have raised doubts about the reliability of Dimsdale's and Langford's accounts, suggesting they might have been covering up widespread local criticism of vigilante deeds. Merrill Burlingame's research, however, emphasizes the large numbers of men involved and their varied backgrounds, indicating that the vigilantes might have been popularly supported.

Certainly, the incredible lawlessness at Bannack–Virginia City called for action, and most of the convictions from January 4 to February 3, 1864, seem to have been necessary and appropriate. But the dangers inherent in secret trials and mob action sometimes led to excesses. For instance, Joe Pizanthia, locally known as "The Greaser," arrived in Montana with a bad reputation, but the vigilantes had no proof that he was a local road agent. In January 1864, when a vigilante group approached his cabin, Pizanthia shot two of them as they entered his door. The enraged crowd outside blasted the cabin with a howitzer, dragged out the badly wounded Pizanthia, hanged him, riddled his corpse with gunfire, and then burned it on a funeral pyre made from his cabin. In a case that caught Mark Twain's fancy, the vigilantes apprehended a local hell-raiser named "Captain" J. A. Slade. Even though Slade had no apparent connection with the road agents, they hanged him dramatically and quickly, before his wife could arrive on the scene and change people's minds.

Perhaps the greatest problem with vigilantism was that of ending it once the courts began to function. When he opened Montana Territory's first official court, at Virginia City in December 1864, Judge Hezekiah L. Hosmer acknowledged the necessity of past vigilante actions but added a note of caution:

> Let us give to every man, how aggravated soever his crime, the full benefit of the freeman's right—an impartial trial by jury. Vigilantes and courts—and all good men can cooperate in fulfilling the grand purpose of the criminal law; that of bringing offenders to justice, without violating any of its provisions; but the very first element in such a warfare against crime, must be the general recognition of courts of law, as the great conservator of peace and safety.

Not everyone heeded the good judge's advice. Alder Gulch vigilantes hanged James Brady in June 1864, then learned afterward that his murder "victim" was recovering nicely from his wounds. In Helena, where the "Hanging Tree" became a local landmark, a number of controversial hangings, like those of James Daniels and John Keene, aroused considerable controversy. On one occasion, a respected and law-abiding young man, on his way from Bannack to Salt Lake City, overtook and rode along with a stranger who, unbeknownst to him, was a horse thief. Vigilantes, who were trailing the thief, caught up with them and promptly hanged both men. Such incidents led to mounting public anger at unauthorized vigilante groups. In March 1867, miners from the Highland District of Alder Gulch posted a notice in the local paper that they would retaliate on a five-to-one basis against any further vigilante executions. Vigilantism had become a menace, and it soon faded into memory and folklore.

THE URBAN FRONTIER

The mining frontier of the Far West differed sharply from the normal pattern of America's westward movement. Ordinarily, as in the westward advances of trappers, stockmen, and farmers, towns and cities arose only

Many gold camps in Montana, such as Virginia City seen here in 1867, quickly took on as much of the shape and style of urban places as conditions allowed.

after the hinterland had been occupied and only in order to serve a rural population. But this process reversed itself on the mining frontier. Instant "cities" sprang up along forlorn gulches, often in remote locations, and then farmers and ranchers settled nearby to feed the towns. Montana's mining region was an "urban frontier." As historian William J. Trimble aptly put it, these ugly and isolated towns seemed to be "ganglia of civilization, comparable to Roman Colonies."

To the boom-and-bust mining towns came not only miners, but also merchants, freighters, saloon-keepers, gamblers, and prostitutes. At first, most of these people came from other mining regions—principally California, Colorado, and Idaho—but before long, Montana's mining camps drew from nearly all regions and nations. This was not a frontier that attracted many families, older people, or single, "respectable" women. In Helena's 1870 census, men outnumbered women three to one, and two-thirds of them were between twenty-one and forty-two years of age. For women, even those with families, mining camps provided opportunity. Many worked in the growing service economy as prostitutes, servants, laundresses, and roominghouse managers.

The mining towns were cosmopolitan places. During Helena's mining boom, for example, conversation in more than twenty languages could be heard on the city's streets. Miners were a relatively tolerant lot, but they noticed distinctive ethnic people, especially if they played an important role in the community. Jewish immigrants from Prussia, Bavaria, and Poland, who had moved to Montana from California mining camps, dominated dry-goods merchandising. French-Canadians and Scandinavians worked in sawmills and construction, and Germans opened breweries and farmed near the camps. And some ethnic groups—notably Indians, blacks, and Chinese—had to endure enmity and persecution.

In contrast to the camps in Colorado, Arizona, or the Black Hills, Montana's gold camps were distant from Native American lands, and their emergence did not lead directly to Indian-white conflicts. Some Indian bands, in fact, frequently camped near the mining camps and traded with whites. But there were still conflicts over the whites' disregard for Indian lands, particularly along trails and roads to the goldfields that often cut directly through Indian hunting territories.

The Montana goldfields attracted a sizable number of African Americans, especially after the Civil War. African Americans in Helena made up slightly more than 2 percent of the population in 1870. Some came as servants of white families, many more to work in the service economy or as day laborers, and a fraction of them as miners and entrepreneurs. In Virginia City, African Americans established a "Pioneer Social Club" in 1867, and in Butte and Helena during the early 1870s, black families established Methodist Episcopal Zion churches that became centers of a robust and multifaceted community life. Although lynchings and physical abuse against African Americans was infrequent in Montana, towns like Helena and White Sulphur Springs passed laws that discriminated against them; and in 1872, the territorial legislature enacted a statute that required school districts to establish segregated schools for African American children.

Montanans directed their most virulent racism against the largest and most distinctive ethnic group in their midst, the Chinese. In 1870, nearly two thousand Chinese resided in the territory, constituting fully 10 percent of the population. At one point, they made up one-third of the total population of both Alder Gulch and Butte. The Chinese came to Montana with the gold rush, but as miners they approached their work differently, preferring to work in small groups at abandoned placers or seemingly worn-out drift mines, where they often extracted surprisingly large quantities of gold. Nearly half of the Chinese, however, lived in mining towns, making their living as servants and operating laundries and restaurants. Many whites saw the Chinese as a despised class, calling them "idolatrous" because of their religious beliefs, "uncivilized and filthy" because of their unfamiliar ways, and "parasites" because of their use of opium. In Virginia City, whites forced the Chinese to live in special districts, charging them with "extreme carelessness as to fires."

Whites tolerated the Chinese only so long as they did menial work and did not pose an economic threat. At one point, the territorial legislature prohibited Chinese ownership of mining claims, an action that federal mining official Rossiter Raymond labeled as foolish, considering that Chinese miners added considerably to the territory's wealth. Had the whites looked at the situation objectively, they would have seen in the Chinese a community of taxpayers who controlled opium use better than they themselves did alcohol and who were more diligent in their religious beliefs. In part because of discrimination, few of the Chinese remained long in Montana. By 1900, most of them had returned to China or had moved to the Pacific Coast.

Life in the mining camps was hard and unromantic. Men worked from sunrise to sunset six days a week during the warm season and usually faced unemployment and boredom when the long winters made placering impossible. During the busy half of the year, the miners left their claims only on Sundays. Most of them enjoyed the Sabbath not as a day of rest but as an opportunity to transact business, attend court, and socialize in town. In the mining camps, Sunday was always the busiest day of the week.

A surprisingly small percentage of Montana miners owned their own claims. Most of them worked for wages, and wages in the remote gold camps were excellent. Men skilled as blacksmiths, carpenters, and butchers often gave up their hopes of quick riches at placering and returned to their original crafts for wages that were as high as fourteen dollars a day. Unfortunately, the high cost of living outpaced the high pay. One woman in Bannack wrote in 1863: "many persons will come here and make more than they could do in years at home. And they ought to; a person ought to make money pretty fast here to pay them for living in such a place." When improved transportation brought costs down, pay scales fell to the more normal level of three to seven dollars per day.

Often, the road to riches was to "mine the miners." Merchants appeared on the mining frontier immediately after the initial strikes were made. "Many men," one Virginia City miner wrote home in 1863, "are to be seen selling merchandise in tents, under brush arbors and in wagons." The genuine fortunes, however, lay not in trading but in investment. Shrewd and enterprising young capitalists like William A. Clark and Samuel T. Hauser were quick to grasp the wisdom of the old frontier adage: "It is good to be shifty in a new country." Some did well speculating in townsites and real estate, but the instability of gold camps made this a risky business. The buying and selling of claims was more lucrative, more hectic, and often less honest. Because claim-holders often "salted" their property with false indications of gold, buyers had to beware. Any prospector could salt his claim by loading shotgun shells with gold particles and firing them into a stream bank, producing the appearance of rich, gold-bearing sands. Another slick scheme was the "freeze-out." Local operators would convince outside investors to buy into a mine, then take out only worthless ore until the outsiders sold out at a loss to their "partners" on the scene. The freeze-out became such a common practice at Alder Gulch that eastern capital began to avoid the area.

The miners suffered many hardships. Few of them, for instance, enjoyed an adequate year-around diet. The mining camps usually had ample supplies of beef and wild game, salt pork and beans. Within a year or two, the bigger towns attracted enough farmers to supply them with potatoes and vegetables, but only at high prices and unpredictable intervals. Fruit and eggs, often imported from great distances, were rare, highly treasured, and costly. So were breadstuffs. When flour supplies ran out or became scarce, prices soared so high that whole towns went on straight meat diets for long periods of time.

Isolated, eating poorly, and dwelling in unsanitary conditions, the urban pioneers lived in constant dread of accident, illness, and disease. Epidemics of typhoid, diphtheria, smallpox, and scarlet fever claimed many victims, especially children; and for much of the population, dysentery became an unpleasant fact of life. Doctors, especially competent ones, were few and far between, and dentists often simply traveled from town to town. Under such conditions, many young men returned to the States broken in body and spirit. The tough realities of mining camp life contributed to the mobility of the population; as any place new seemed better to the miners than where they were.

Some of the restless miners left their claims during the long and idle months of winter, but most stayed and kept an eye on their property. For those who remained, escape from boredom presented a real challenge. As on all frontiers, some turned to drinking and dissipation. The ever-present saloons offered escape and male companionship, and sometimes games and gambling. Nearly as ubiquitous were "hurdy-gurdy" houses, which flourished as places where men could buy both a drink and a dance with a woman. A thin line separated these businesses from houses of ill repute, and some operated as both. These enterprises were often owned by entrepreneurial women, who invested their profits in real estate and engaged freely in the world of legitimate business. As property owners, these women had taken keen advantage of their earnings and frontier opportunities to become capitalists. As mining camps matured, ministers, women reformers, and business leaders campaigned to close down the red-light districts by passing restrictive statutes, taxing them, and harassing prostitutes and patrons. These efforts seldom succeeded, at least for long. The reformers had much better luck eradicating the "opium dens" that whites and Chinese frequented.

Contrary to Hollywood mythology, few mining towns witnessed more drinking, gambling, whoring, and violence than most other places in the nation. The majority of residents, eager to improve their positions in life, behaved with propriety. But the mining frontier could still be hard on family life and marriages. Between 1865 and 1870, there was one divorce for every three marriages in Helena. In most cases, men deserted women and families, leaving them to fend for themselves.

Children lived in a special world in the mining towns, working for pay at a young age yet also occupying a realm of their own. Some industriously swept spilled gold dust or hired on to haul water for miners. Mary Ronan gathered flowers in Virginia City to sell, and Cornelius Hedges's son helped run Helena's library. The coarse-grained society of the camps matured children quickly and caused their parents to worry. Because the youngsters spent so much time near gambling dens and saloons, they learned profanity early. Parents should break them of this habit, a Virginia City editor pronounced, "or else break their necks."

Like all frontier communities, residents came together in entertainment and celebrations. Homespun music and dancing, especially to a

The Alice Mine and Mill in Walkerville, about two years after the Walker Brothers of Salt Lake City purchased it and sent Marcus Daly to manage it.

fiddle, seemed to be the miners' favorite diversion. Picnics and weddings drew large crowds, and everyone celebrated the major holidays, the most festive ones being the Fourth of July, Christmas and New Year's, and St. Patrick's Day. Aside from hunting and fishing, the most popular sports included sledding, skiing, and ice skating, as well as foot and horse races, rock-drilling contests, and baseball. Boxing matches drew big crowds and large wagers. In January 1865, a tremendous Virginia City crowd watched one of the longest fights in history when Con Orem and Hugh O'Neil struggled to a 185-round draw.

Considering the handicaps of their situation, mining towns displayed a hearty appetite for cultural refinement and the theater often provided evening entertainment. Shortly after the first strikes at Alder Gulch, Jimmy Martin staged melodramas and comedies in Virginia City. In 1867, Martin persuaded Denver's Jack Langrishe to come to Montana. During the next three fall and winter seasons, Langrishe and his troupe performed regularly at Virginia City's People's Theater and at Helena's Wood Street Theater. The audiences enjoyed ornate melodramas and farces, but they liked Shakespeare best of all.

The majority of mining-town residents spent far more time with books, magazines, and newspapers than they did in saloons and hurdy-gurdy houses. Books and magazines passed from hand to hand until they literally fell apart; and when newspapers arrived, weeks late from the States, homesick miners read them over and over again. The Stonewall Building in Virginia City symbolized public tastes in the mining West. Although the Gem Saloon occupied the lower floor, the second story housed a reading room where subscribing members enjoyed all forms of reading matter as well as chess, checkers, and dominos. Similarly, the Helena Library Association, organized in 1868, enjoyed wide support.

The forces of stability and civilization came early to the mining frontier. Fraternal groups, most notably the Masons, not only provided benevolences for their members but also worked for law and order, community improvement, and cultural and charitable activities. As always, main street merchants campaigned tirelessly to improve their towns, and newspaper editors, eager to increase circulation by boosting the community, beat the drum incessantly for civic improvement. Virginia City's *Montana Post*, Montana's first newspaper, was edited by schoolteacher Thomas J. Dimsdale and spoke out constantly for the "law and order" virtues of vigilantism and the Republican party.

As on most frontiers, the church and the school were the two primary forces of civilization. Roman Catholic priests, already active among western Montana Indians, moved into nearby mining camps. Father Joseph Giorda arrived at Virginia City in the fall of 1863 and had a chapel ready in time to celebrate Christmas. Among Protestants, the Methodists and Episcopalians arrived first. The Methodists, always in the vanguard on the frontier, were conducting services at Bannack by early 1864; and the Episcopal church of Montana took root in 1867, when Bishop Daniel Tuttle and Reverend E. N. Goddard came to Virginia City. The Baptists and Presbyterians, two other Protestant denominations usually active on the frontier, got off to a slow start in Montana, largely because their churches were so bitterly divided by the Civil War. Churches failed to thrive in most gold camps until women and civic leaders arrived in large enough numbers to lend them strength.

Considering how few children there were in the mining camps, schools appeared at remarkably early dates. Subscription schools, where parents had to pay directly for their children's education, appeared first; Kate Dunlap ran one of these schools at Nevada City, and Lucia Darling operated another at Bannack. Soon after Montana Territory was created in 1864, the first legislature provided for public education by authorizing the county commissioners to levy property taxes for schools. In 1866, Virginia City was the first community to set up a public school district, with the schoolhouse opening its doors that summer. Governor Sidney Edgerton appointed English-born schoolteacher and author-editor Thomas J. Dimsdale as Montana's first superintendent of public instruction, but Dimsdale died of illness in 1866. The legislature soon made this office elective. After gaining election to the post in 1868, Superintendent Thomas Campbell filed his first report, which told of 704 children enrolled in 25 schools throughout the territory. By 1880, Montana was spending considerably more on education per pupil than Oregon, for example, and the territory paid its teachers more than twice as much as Nebraska, New Mexico, or Pennsylvania.

In contrast to their success at founding schools and libraries, the mining towns faced social challenges that were more difficult to master. To begin with, the towns developed at the placer strikes, often along a sizable stream. The inhabitants gave little or no thought to residential and business construction and took any convenient spot. The result was a ramshackle settlement of tents, log cabins, and houses scarcely better than lean-tos. Some miners built cabins in hillsides at the openings of their mine tunnels. Streets were laid out to fit the terrain and connect the goldfields with main roads. Gumbo mud and blowing dust often made traffic impossible even on main streets. Because water was the critical resource, ditches and flumes often laced the camps, forcing unusual residential patterns. Haste in building made the camps firetraps, where small blazes could suddenly roar through town, as happened several times in Virginia City and Helena. These conflagrations encouraged the construction of stone and brick buildings by the early 1870s. In boomtowns of uncertain longevity, the citizens seldom chose to tax themselves in order to build decent water and sanitation facilities. Because they relied on unpredictable property taxes for revenue, local governments were usually anemic and were unable to take much positive action.

To put it simply, the transient population of early Montana took little pride in their towns and little interest in developing the territory. Most of them had no intention of staying, but only desired to "make a pile" and head back to the States. The mining towns, they well knew, would soon disappear, so why worry about improving them? The miners, at least most of them, moved on—to the Black Hills gold rush, to a life of farming in the West, or, in most cases, back home to the East. And their towns became ghosts. Only Butte and Helena lived on to become major Montana communities.

CHAPTER 5

Montana Territory

EACH of the United States of America, except for the original thirteen, Texas, and California, was first organized as a territory before achieving admittance to the Union as a state. Originating with the Ordinances of 1785 and 1787, the territorial system provided the expanding United States with a method of governing frontier areas until they gained sufficient population and economic maturity to qualify for equality with the states. Territories represented a sort of compromise between colonies and states. They had limited powers of legislative self-government, but their executive and judicial officers were appointed by the federal government. Not surprisingly, residents of frontier territories usually demanded quick admission to statehood so that they could gain full control of their local governments. Until they had such control, federal supervision over their local affairs was the source of constant frustration. Montana's time of frustration lasted for twenty-five years, from the creation of Montana Territory in 1864 until the territory was admitted to statehood in 1889.

THE BIRTH OF MONTANA

The mining boom of the 1860s brought the first sizable influx of whites to Montana and, thus, the first demands for government. Until that time, the large eastern and small western sectors of what would be Montana had simply been attached to huge frontier territories whose centers of population lay hundreds, even thousands, of miles away. The eastern two-thirds of Montana, which occupies the far northwestern corner of the Mississippi-Missouri Basin, had formed the far extremity of Indian Territory until 1805, was part of Louisiana Territory until 1812, Missouri Territory until 1821, a general Great Plains "Indian Country" until 1854, and

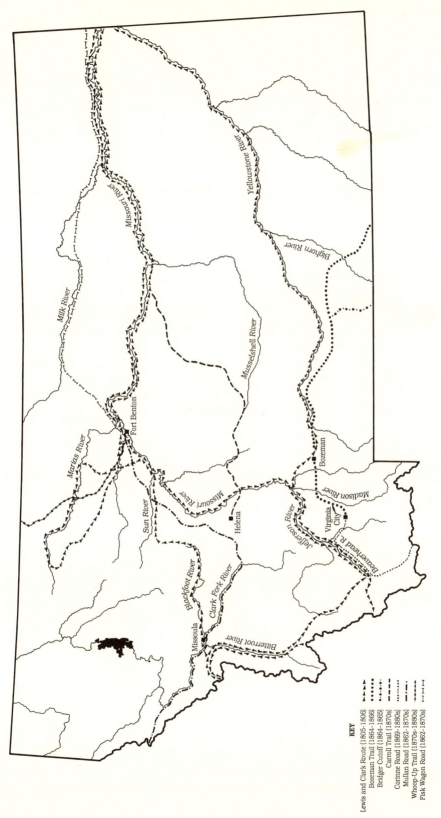

Map 2. Early transportation routes (map by Barbara Lien)

Nebraska Territory until 1861, when it became the western sector of newly created Dakota Territory.

The northwest corner of Montana lies on the periphery of a different geographic province, the Columbia River Basin. The United States and Great Britain held this area, known as "Oregon Country," under a joint occupancy agreement until 1846, when they agreed to extend the 49th parallel boundary to the Pacific as the dividing line between the United States and Canada. The western portion of future Montana then became the easternmost portion of Oregon Territory from 1848 until 1853 and of Washington Territory from 1853 until 1863.

Quite by accident, it was the advance of the mining frontier that caused the eastern and western regions of Montana to be joined together in one political unit. In 1861-62, as miners began the rush into the newly opened goldfields of present-day north-central Idaho, settlers demanded a new territory in the Northern Rockies. Congress responded in March of 1863 by creating Idaho Territory. Carved out of Washington, Dakota, and Nebraska territories, Idaho embraced an enormous area, including all of present-day Idaho and Montana and most of Wyoming. Its capital lay on the far western border at Lewiston. Significantly, the creation of Idaho brought eastern and western Montana within a common boundary for the first time.

Idaho Territory was a geographic impossibility. The massive ranges of the Rocky Mountains divided the territory in half, and a thousand miles separated Lewiston in the west from the far eastern extremities. Even in 1863, Idaho's population was shifting rapidly eastward, across the Continental Divide to the mining camps on the upper Missouri. With good reason, the Bannack-Virginia City miners believed that Lewiston—hundreds of miles away over endless, snow-clogged mountain passes—could never govern them properly. The outrages of the Plummer Gang tended to prove their point. Miners began agitating for the creation of a new territory, to be split from Idaho along the crests of the Rockies.

Fortunately for their cause, Judge Sidney Edgerton, the newly appointed chief justice of Idaho, arrived at Bannack in September 1863. Edgerton, a former Ohio congressman, was unable to proceed to Lewiston because of the approach of winter. He soon learned that the governor of Idaho had snubbed him by assigning him to the faraway judicial district lying east of the Divide. Both Edgerton and his nephew, vigilante leader Wilbur Fisk Sanders, took up the settlers' crusade to divide Idaho Territory. Edgerton personally knew the president and many congressmen, so the miners chose to send him to Washington, D.C., to press their case. Carrying two thousand dollars in gold, Edgerton headed east in January 1864. Meanwhile, the Idaho legislature at Lewiston obligingly petitioned

Congress to carve a new territory named Jefferson out of Idaho, with the dividing line along the Continental Divide and the 113th meridian, locating Idaho's new eastern boundary just west of the Deer Lodge Valley.

Arriving in Washington, Edgerton consulted with President Lincoln and found him agreeable to the idea of a new territory in the Rockies. More important, Edgerton discovered that his friend and fellow Ohioan, Congressman James M. Ashley, had already begun work on a bill to form the new territory. Ashley, who chaired the House Committee on Territories, had the power to make his wishes felt. His political muscle and reports of the area's wealth of gold, which Edgerton reported as influential "in such a mercenary age as ours," pushed the bill speedily through Congress.

While the bill lay in committee, Edgerton and his allies broke with the Idaho legislature by maneuvering the new territory's northwestern boundary three degrees to the west. This meant that the Idaho-Montana territorial line would generally follow the Bitterroot summits northward to the United States–Canada boundary and that Montana would take a 130-mile-wide bite out of northern Idaho. In this manner, Idaho lost the Flathead, upper Clark Fork, and middle Kootenai valleys to its new neighbor. The arrangement reduced the width of northern Idaho by three-fourths, leaving it an awkward "panhandle," cut off from the southern portion of the territory by the rugged Salmon River Mountains. Idaho petitioned Congress to restore these "stolen" lands, but with no success. The Lewiston area even advocated establishing another territory named Columbia, which would join today's western Montana, northern Idaho, and eastern Washington, but the plan got nowhere. So, by circumstance and scheming, the new territory emerged with its jagged western border.

Congress, preoccupied with the Civil War, devoted little time to the matter of founding another western commonwealth. The one serious threat to passage of the bill arose when the Senate voted to force the new territory to give the vote to African Americans. Even though there were few blacks in the Northern Rockies, this explosive issue caused a deadlock with the House of Representatives. The two houses of Congress finally compromised by restricting the vote to citizens of the United States, thus leaving the newly freed African Americans without a guarantee of the ballot on the distant mining frontier.

The House and Senate also debated the name that Congressman Ashley had placed on his creation. "Montana," from the Latin or Spanish adjective meaning "mountainous," first appeared as a place name in 1858, when Josiah Hinman gave the name to a small mining town near Pike's Peak. Governor James William Denver of Kansas Territory remembered the name and suggested it to Senator Stephen A. Douglas as a name for a future territory in the Rockies. Ashley picked the name up from Douglas or somewhere else and liked it enormously. After trying unsuccessfully to give the name to what became Idaho in 1863, Ashley determined to apply it to Idaho's new neighbor.

When Ashley's Montana bill reached the floor of the House, the Democrats began harassing the Republican about the name. The Democrats suggested dropping it and substituting the title "Jefferson" to honor the founder of the Democratic party or even "Douglas" to commemorate the prominent Democratic senator from Illinois. Ashley and the Republicans would have none of it. Congressman Jacob Cox of Ohio suggested "Shoshone," but the name was scuttled when the Colorado delegate pointed out that Shoshone meant "Snake," a word that had unfortunate implications during the Civil War, when pro-Confederates from the North were called "Copperheads." The debate reached the point of true absurdity when Representative Elihu B. Washburn of Wisconsin suggested the name "Abyssinia," taunting the Republicans about their fondness for African Americans.

Although Ashley won his battle in the House, two weeks later the Senate again challenged the name "Montana." Again, several members believed the classical name was inappropriate and argued that an Indian word would be better. But no one could suggest a name with any relevance to the place, so they too settled on Ashley's title, but only after this illuminating exchange:

> MR. HOWARD: I was equally puzzled when I saw the name in the bill. . . . I was obliged to turn to my old Latin dictionary. . . . It is a very classical word, pure Latin. It means a mountainous region, a mountainous country.
> MR. WADE: Then the name is well adapted to the Territory.
> MR. HOWARD: You will find that it is used by Livy and some of the other Latin historians, which is no small praise.
> MR. WADE: I do not care anything about the name. If there was none in Latin or in Indian I suppose we have a right to make a name; certainly just as good a right to make it as anybody else. It is a good enough name.

Montana it became, and Montana it has remained. Following approval by Congress, President Lincoln signed into law the bill creating Montana Territory on May 26, 1864.

THE POLITICAL SITUATION

The infant territory of Montana faced severe political and governmental problems during its first half-dozen years. Some difficulties stemmed from the territorial system itself. Others arose because the territory was born during the Civil War. In drafting the 1864 Organic Act that established Montana Territory, Congress followed a system of government that had become the standard for most western territories. Law-making power was placed in the hands of the territory's citizens through the popular election of a bicameral legislature. The upper house of the legislature was a seven-member "council," and the lower house a thirteen-member "assembly." The Organic Act also authorized the citizenry to elect one non-voting "delegate" to the U.S. House of Representatives, who would speak for their interests.

The Organic Act limited these powers of self-government, however, by mandating that the executive and judicial officers of the territory be appointed by the president of the United States. The principal executive offices of the territory consisted of the powerful governor, who also served as Indian superintendent and commander of the militia, and the secretary, who kept official records and assumed command in the governor's absence. Significantly, the secretary had the exclusive power to authorize the expenditure of federal funds in the territory. The judicial officers were the chief justice and the two associate justices, who combined to make up the territorial supreme court. This system fulfilled its basic purpose: it allowed a measure of self-government while keeping the area under tight federal control. But the system also led to wide-open struggles between the locally elected legislature and the federally appointed judges and executive officials.

Emigrants to Montana came from every section of the country. The first census taken in the territory, which was registered in 1870, reported a non-Indian population of 20,595. Of those people, the largest bloc—7,371—came originally from the northern states. Another 2,272 were western born, and 7,979 hailed from other countries. A total of 891 came from the states of the Confederacy, and 2,060 were from Missouri and other border states. Because these population numbers were posted when the mining boom was in its decline, they do not necessarily indicate the makeup of the mining rush at its mid-1860s peak.

In their political affiliations, a solid majority of Montanans adhered to the Democratic party, and a strong minority were Republicans. Each party, in turn, consisted of moderate and more extreme factions. The more moderate wing of the Republican party—the party of Lincoln and the Union—included those who believed in preserving the Union but did not wish to crush the South irreparably. They often called themselves "Unionists" and welcomed the support of northern Democrats. The more extreme Republicans, sometimes referred to as "Radical" or "Black" Republicans, demanded that the South be crushed and that African Americans be given political rights. In Montana, the Radical Republicans wielded considerable power. They were led by Wilbur Fisk Sanders and

Sidney Edgerton, whom Lincoln had named first territorial governor.

The more powerful Democratic party showed a similar division between moderates and extremists. On the one hand, there were many Union Democrats, who came mainly from the North and supported the Union, even while opposing the Republicans. On the other hand, Montana attracted some Democrats from the South and many others from states like Missouri that bordered the South. These Democrats, along with "Copperhead" Democrats—that is, northerners who sympathized with the South—made up a strong and vocal minority in Montana. They hated the Radical Republicans and especially hated the idea of African Americans gaining equality with whites. The Confederate sympathizers never came near gaining a majority of the Montana vote, but they sometimes raised enough hell to give observers that impression.

During Montana's first years as a territory, which coincided with the close of the Civil War, the more extreme wings of each party thundered at one another and echoed the issues of the war. Radical Republicans, such as editor Thomas Dimsdale of the Virginia City *Montana Post* and the Fisk brothers of the *Helena Herald*, blasted Democrats as disloyal rebels. The venomous Dimsdale referred to "the arch traitor Jeff Davis" and concluded that Democrats "would vote for the Devil himself if his name were on the Democratic ticket." To Dimsdale, the issues seemed simple: "There are but two parties now in this republic—patriots and traitors." N. P. Langford, another zealous Republican, wrote inaccurately to Washington, D.C., that he "was in a Territory more disloyal as a whole, than Tennessee or Kentucky ever were. Four fifths of our citizens were openly declared Secessionists."

Pro-Southern Democrats replied in kind, branding their opponents as "Black Republicans" and "nigger lovers." Their leading newspaper, the *Rocky Mountain Gazette* in Helena, spoke often and heatedly of the race issue and used it as a club against the Republicans: "All the Irish have left them. The Germans (naturally Democratic and lovers of liberty) are leaving them. They now place their last hope on the irrepressible nigger." Racists from both North and South were strong enough in early Montana to prohibit African Americans from testifying against whites in court and, in a statute passed by the first legislature, to ban them from voting in school elections: "Every white male inhabitant over the age of twenty-one years, who shall have paid or be liable to pay any district tax, shall be a legal voter at any school meeting, and no other person shall be allowed to vote." Although some historians have exaggerated the role of Confederate sympathizers in early Montana, the fact remains that they were numerous and powerful enough to challenge the Unionists. As Elizabeth Fisk, wife of radical Republican editor Robert Fisk, remarked in 1868: "Radicalism

in Montana is not the wisest course. . . . with regard to Negro Suffrage—
the time for its successful promulgation has not yet arrived."

CIVIL WAR POLITICS

It was this volatile political situation that faced Montana's first governor,
Sidney Edgerton, when he returned to the territory in mid-1864.
Edgerton chose Bannack to be the temporary capital and ordered a hur-
ried census in order to hold elections that autumn. Because the entire executive and judicial branches of their government were federally appointed, the Montana electorate would vote only for members of the two-
house legislature and for their delegate to Congress.

Montana's first political campaign centered on the race for delegate to
Congress. The Republicans ran their most prestigious party member,
strong-willed Wilbur Fisk Sanders. Sanders enjoyed the advantages of his
fame as a vigilante and the support of his uncle, Governor Edgerton. His
Democratic adversary was Samuel McLean of Pennsylvania, a large,
portly man who drank whiskey by the barrel. Backed by the only newspaper in the territory, the *Montana Post*, Sanders and Edgerton ran a
tough, free-swinging campaign. They attacked all Democrats as Copperheads and traitors and held themselves up as the only real guardians of
the Union. There were only two political parties, Edgerton declared,
"one for the Union and one against it." He put the issue squarely and passionately, but the strategy failed badly. In the election of October 24,
1864, Sanders lost to McLean, who carried the big Democratic counties
of Madison and Jefferson. Otherwise, the Republicans held their own.
The election produced a political balance in the legislature: the Council
went Unionist (Republican) by one vote, and the House went Democratic, also by one vote.

Clearly, if he wished to succeed, Governor Edgerton had to find a way
to work with the Democratic majority in Montana. But that rigid Ohio abolitionist, who had already antagonized the Democrats in the recent election, found compromise impossible. When he addressed the opening session of the legislature, Edgerton referred to former Democratic President
James Buchanan as an "imbecile" and insisted that all legislators swear to
the "Iron Clad Oath," which Congress had drawn up for use in the defeated Confederate states. The oath—which required the signer to swear
that he had never borne arms against the United States government—
needlessly offended the Democrats and forced one lawmaker, Confederate veteran J. H. Rogers, to resign his seat rather than perjure himself.
The governor's actions guaranteed a continuation of political warfare.
Nevertheless, the Democrats seemed willing enough to work with him in

considering badly needed legislation, and the first legislature passed a large number of hastily written laws dealing with such urgent matters as roads, public schools, irrigation, and mining.

Edgerton faced many frustrating problems in his new position, many of them the result of federal negligence. Amid the chaos of the closing months of the Civil War and the aftermath of Lincoln's assassination, Montana was largely forgotten in Washington and key federal positions remained unfilled. During its first sixteen months, Montana had no territorial secretary. Because only the secretary could sign federal warrants, this meant that no federal funds could be spent. Edgerton simply covered many territorial expenses with his own funds, assuming that he would soon be reimbursed.

When the new secretary, Thomas Francis Meagher, finally arrived in late September 1865, Edgerton hurriedly left for the East, turning over his duties to Meagher as acting governor. Edgerton left in order to look after both his own personal affairs in Ohio and Montana's concerns in Washington, D.C., but he had neglected to obtain a leave of absence. When he later sought to obtain a leave, federal authorities refused it and forced Edgerton to resign as governor of Montana Territory in early 1866. The governor apparently lost his job for two reasons: unexcused absences by territorial officials had become an open farce, and President Andrew Johnson hated Radical Republicans like Sidney Edgerton. Thus, after a brief and hectic term, Montana's first chief executive left the scene, never to return.

Edgerton's absence led to one of the most chaotic periods in Montana's political history. At the center of the chaos and controversy stood Thomas Francis Meagher, the territorial secretary and acting governor. This colorful character was a brash adventurer who arrived in Montana with an international reputation and an appetite for glory. Descended from a wealthy Irish family, young Meagher had been a leading figure in the Irish independence movement, a noted orator, and an ally of Irish nationalist Daniel O'Connell. Meagher had narrowly escaped execution by the British because of his revolutionary activities and was banished to the penal colony of Tasmania. After escaping from Tasmania, Meagher had traveled to New York, where he rose to prominence as a leader among the thousands of Irish immigrants in that city. During the Civil War, he had gained fame as the organizer and commanding general of the Irish Brigade, the hard-charging outfit that had seen fierce action at such battles as Malvern Hill and Antietam. The brigade had been practically annihilated in the suicidal charge at Fredericksburg and was later disbanded. It was Meagher's fame and military record that had led President Johnson to appoint him secretary of Montana Territory in 1865.

As acting governor, Meagher faced an angry situation in Montana. At first, both political parties saw him as a friend. He was a Union Democrat, and local Democrats welcomed him as one of their own. But he was also a Union general who had fought the rebels, and he had received his job from a Unionist administration. Meagher sided at first with the Republicans and informed his immediate superior, the United States secretary of state, that the Montana Democrats consisted largely of "turbulent men," pro-Confederates who could not be trusted. A few weeks later, however, Meagher suddenly turned about and allied himself with the Democrats. He notified Washington that he had been mistaken and "that these very Southerners and Southern sympathizers are now as heartily to be relied upon by the Administration . . . as any other men in the Territory."

It is likely that Meagher shifted his loyalty because the Democrats were the majority and were heavily Irish, and he believed he could build a political future as their leader. But he also had a falling out with the local Republican hierarchy, which included such Radicals as Wilbur Sanders and Judge L. E. Munson. Meagher told his superiors in Washington of "the bitter personal animosity of the ultra Republicans who calculated on my being a miserable and mischievous tool in their hands." As for the Republicans, they never forgave Meagher for deserting them. They sent wild complaints to Washington, charging that the acting governor had "been in fact drunk nearly every day since he has been in the territory" and "that the executive office is a place of rendezvous for the vilest prostitutes and *they* state the fact publicly [*sic*] and boast of their profitable *intercourse* with him."

At this time, 1865-66, two crucial issues arose that sharply divided the Democrats from the Republicans, and on each of them Meagher shifted from the Republican to the Democratic position. The most pressing problem involved the legislature. The first territorial legislature had adjourned without passing a redistricting bill that would establish districts for the next legislative election. Knowing that the Democrats held a voting majority, the Republicans opposed holding another legislative session. They argued that, since the legislature had not redistricted the territory, the acting governor lacked the authority to order a special session or to call for another election. But the Democrats insisted that the territory badly needed new laws and that Meagher did have the authority to convene the legislature. After first accepting the Republicans' argument, Meagher suddenly changed his mind and agreed with the Democrats that a new legislature was both necessary and proper. A partisan W. F. Sanders later remarked that "the erratic Meagher" had been "baited with the promise of a senatorship" by the Democrats. Meagher called the lawmakers to assemble in Virginia City on March 5, 1866.

The other important issue confronting Meagher concerned statehood. Knowing they could gain control of a state government, the majority Democrats desired Montana's quick admission as a state. For exactly that reason, the Republicans opposed it. Montana lacked sufficient population to justify statehood, but Congress had bent the rules to make thinly populated Nevada a state only two years earlier. Again, Meagher reversed himself and shifted from the Republican to the Democratic viewpoint. Because territories were required to apply for statehood by submitting a state constitution for congressional approval, Meagher summoned a constitutional convention to meet in Helena on March 26, 1866.

Both of these acts led to pandemonium. During March and April of 1866, the second territorial legislature met and conducted a great deal of business. Following a September 1866 election, the legislators met in a third session during the winter of 1866-67. The Republicans were furious, charging that both sessions had been illegally called by the "Acting One." When a majority of the Territorial Supreme Court, including Republican justices Lyman E. Munson and H. C. Hosmer, declared all acts of the second legislature null and void, both Meagher and the legislators simply ignored the ruling. The legislature even struck back at Munson by creating a "sagebrush" judicial district in eastern Montana and assigning Munson there, with the provision that he must live there.

In sheer rage and frustration, the Montana Republicans responded by sending Wilbur Fisk Sanders to Washington to convince the leaders of Congress that Meagher's legislative sessions should be declared illegal. In a highly unusual move in late February 1867, the Radical Republican leadership in Congress pushed through a measure declaring the second and third Montana legislatures "null and void." This harsh and unfair move by Congress caused howls of protest from Montana and prompted Territorial Delegate Samuel McLean to threaten Montana's secession from the Union and its joining with Canada if the legislature's acts were not restored. Laws essential to the operation of government had been summarily wiped from the books.

Meanwhile, the constitutional convention, which Meagher had originally summoned for March, met in Helena on April 9, 1866. But attendance by the delegates was spotty, and the entire convention lasted only six days. The delegates kept no formal records, but they did produce a state constitution, reportedly drawn largely from those of New York and California. Incredibly, the constitution of 1866 was promptly lost. One story claims that delegate Thomas Tutt lost the document while en route to a printer in St. Louis. More likely, the 1866 constitution burned in a fire that years later destroyed the records of the convention's secretary, H. N. Maguire. It made no difference, in any case, because Montana had no real hope for statehood in 1866. The territory lacked the requisite population, and the Republican Congress had no desire to create yet another Democratic state.

In early October 1866, a new governor finally arrived to succeed Sidney Edgerton. Green Clay Smith impressed Montanans by his adept handling of the third legislative assembly that autumn. At the request of the legislature, Smith soon asked for and received permission to return to the nation's capital in order to pursue Montana's neglected interests there. Once again, Secretary Thomas F. Meagher became acting governor and, once again, the result was chaos.

During the spring of 1867, attacks by Sioux Indians along the Bozeman Road touched off a classic frontier panic in Montana, especially in the Gallatin Valley. The fear spread that the Sioux would sweep westward along Bozeman's route and terrorize the Montana settlements. Although groundless, public fear heightened when John Bozeman himself was killed, reportedly by Indians, along the Yellowstone River in April. Besieged by pleas for military protection, Acting Governor Meagher asked for and finally received federal authority to raise a militia force to guard the Gallatin and surrounding areas.

Affairs quickly got out of hand. Meagher raised an army of over six hundred volunteers, heavily staffed with high-ranking officers. The army encamped in the Gallatin Valley and along the upper Yellowstone, but encountered very few Indians. By the time the "army" was finally disbanded—to the great anger of some of the troops, who wished to remain on the federal payroll—it had run up bills totaling $1.1 million. Realizing that local merchants had egregiously overcharged the militia, the federal government refused to pay the full amount of the bills and eventually settled with local creditors for $513,000. Meagher had waged a senseless and very expensive "war."

Amid this confusion, Meagher's career came to its sudden, and still unexplained, end. On July 1, 1867, while in Fort Benton awaiting the arrival of his wife and an arms shipment by steamboat, Meagher mysteriously disappeared from the docked boat on which he was staying. He apparently fell from the vessel during the night and drowned, but his body was never recovered. Whether accident, suicide, or murder was involved, no one knows. General Meagher remains a hero to the Irish of his homeland, and the thousands of Irish who came to Montana's mining towns celebrated his memory with the impressive equestrian statue that stands before the state capitol. But Meagher's role in Montana's history was less than constructive. In truth, he was overwhelmed and destroyed by the bitter partisanship of Montana territorial politics.

In June 1867, just prior to Meagher's death, Governor Smith returned

The political battle over the location of the territorial capital, which was rife with election chicanery in 1874, spawned this sarcastic caricature in defense of Helena's victory.

to Montana. A Union Democrat from Kentucky and a man of marked ability, Smith had served with distinction in both the Mexican and Civil wars. He had resigned from the army in 1863 with the rank of brigadier general. He took a seat in Congress and rose rapidly in national politics.

Governor Smith was a sensible political moderate who was able to work with both political parties and restore calm in the territory. He wrapped up the bogus Indian campaign Meagher had begun and convened the legislature in special session to pick up the pieces left by the nullification of the two previous sessions. Addressing the legislators, Smith pointed out the desperate need for education and land laws and the urgent problem of reducing the territorial debt, which stood at $55,000. Chouteau, Meagher, and Beaverhead counties had paid no property taxes at all, and the debt would continue to soar until tax collection was enforced.

The legislature responded to the governor's program, and at long last it seemed that the territory might look forward to responsible government. But Meagher's death had again left Montana without a secretary, and the long delay in appointing another left the territory without access to federal monies. To straighten things out, Smith left for Washington, D.C., in the summer of 1868. Apparently deciding to give up politics altogether, he resigned his position and never returned to Montana. The abrupt departure of the capable Green Clay Smith seemed a cruel blow to the territory, which once again faced governmental uncertainty.

For nearly a year, Montana had no federally appointed governor. James Tufts, who was finally designated secretary, served quietly during this period as acting governor. At last, in April 1869, President Grant appointed as governor none other than James M. Ashley, who had just been defeated for re-election to Congress. Because Ashley had engineered the creation of the territory, he might have seemed the ideal person to serve as governor. Actually, he proved to be very nearly the worst possible choice. Ashley was a leading Radical Republican, an outspoken critic of slavery and the South, and was famed as the congressman who had filed the impeachment resolution against President Andrew Johnson. He was rigid and moralistic, a tough, partisan campaigner. During one of his Ohio campaigns, he knocked out a heckler, and once an angry member of the audience had thrown a live goose at him.

To the Democratic majority in Montana, Ashley's appointment seemed a direct provocation. Democratic newspaper editors wailed in dismay at the news. "Angels and Ministers of grace defend us," groaned the *Montana Democrat*. Helena's *Weekly Independent* complained: "The broken down political hack, James M. Ashley, has been appointed Governor of Montana. How long are the people to be scorned and insulted by being told . . . that there is not one among the thirty thousand freemen of

Montana who is capable of discharging the functions of the Executive office?"

Ashley arrived with high hopes during the summer of 1869. He held a fatherly attitude toward Montana and seemed intent on converting his territory to the ways of the Republican party. When the legislature convened late in the year, however, the governor faced overwhelming Democratic majorities in both houses. Ashley demonstrated no skill whatsoever in dealing with the Democrats. He immediately locked horns with them by insisting that key territorial offices—treasurer, auditor, and superintendent of public instruction—must be appointed by the governor, not elected, as the legislature had provided by law. Ashley appointed Republicans to these positions, but the elected Democrats refused to vacate them.

Things got worse when Ashley refused to give the Democrats even one of the appointive offices of the territorial government. In retaliation, the Democrats in the legislature repealed the salary supplement they had provided the governor when Smith held the office; and, more important, they refused to approve any of the governor's appointments to territorial offices. "To the end of December, 1869," historian Clark Spence observed, "the council had rejected eleven nominations for the office of superintendent of public instruction, fifteen for auditor, and sixteen for treasurer."

This was government by deadlock, and it was a sorry situation indeed. It ended suddenly, late in 1869, when President Grant summarily fired Ashley. Evidently, Grant dismissed the governor because of a speech he had made just before going to Montana, in which Ashley had described the Republican party as being "dumb in the presence of a dummy." His dismissal, Ashley said, was "the hardest blow I ever received." Ashley's removal solved the territory's immediate problem, but it left Montana's affairs once again adrift and confused.

POLITICAL MATURITY: THE POTTS ERA

After six years, three governors, and two acting governors, Montana Territory seemed doomed to perennial misgovernment. Much of the trouble had arisen from local politics, but the major problem stemmed from federal mismanagement. Republican administrations in Washington had paid little heed to local complaints and problems, and they had insisted on sending unemployed Republican politicians to govern a strongly Democratic territory. There seemed little hope for improvement when, on July 13, 1870, President Grant appointed Benjamin F. Potts to be the new territorial governor. Like Edgerton and Ashley, Potts was an Ohio

Republican; and like Smith and Meagher, he had served as a brigadier general in the Union Army. He had served with Grant at Vicksburg and with Sherman, who called him a "Sample Vandal."

But Potts gave Montanans a pleasant surprise. Unlike Edgerton or Ashley, he was a moderate Republican, capable of compromising with the Democrats. He would record one of the longest and most successful careers in the history of American territorial government, presiding over Montana from 1870 until President Chester Arthur removed him from office in 1883. A large, powerfully built man of forceful personality, Potts adjusted so well to the Montana scene that after his removal as governor he remained on his ranch near Helena until his death in 1887. Beyond dispute, much of his success stemmed from the fact that by 1870 the violent political hatreds of the Civil War were beginning to abate. The more important factor, however, was Potts's reasonable spirit of conciliation.

Potts worked easily with the Democrats, so easily that the Radical Republicans turned against him. The new governor understood clearly that factionalism worked directly against the good of the territory, which everyone agreed was economic development. He undertook, instead, a pragmatic course, essentially pursuing what historian Kenneth Owens has called a "no-party pattern of territorial politics." As a result of the 1871 election, the Democrats recognized the power of the Irish element and moved toward party unity, which in part resulted in the election and re-election of Martin Maginnis as territorial delegate from 1872 until 1884. The Republicans, however, remained divided. In fact, the Radicals became so angry with Potts that Sanders and the Fisk brothers went to Washington, D.C., in 1877 to lobby for his removal from office.

Radical Republicans had reason to be upset with Potts. Orchestrating a smooth working relationship of moderate Democrats and moderate Republicans, Potts scrambled party lines. At the heart of this system was his business and political alliance with Samuel T. Hauser, the shrewd Helena banker who was the most powerful capitalist and Democrat in Montana. Potts thus presided over a cross-party alliance of businessmen and investors whose chief aim was increasing development. There was little room in this arrangement for the rancorous debates that extremists in both parties seemed to enjoy.

Potts's first concerns as governor were to stabilize the small bureaucracy and to bring the soaring territorial and county debts under control. It took him several years to settle the squabble over filling the executive offices that had begun under Ashley. When an 1870 investigation uncovered wrongdoing by Territorial Secretary Wiley Scribner, Potts forced him from office. The governor worried most about the alarmingly high territorial debt, which had surpassed a hundred thousand dollars, and the

By 1890, when this photograph was taken, Helena's Main Street was lined by impressive commercial buildings, illuminated by electric lights, and traversed by electric streetcars, which belied the city's remote location on the mining frontier.

staggering county debts, which had been amassed by sometimes irresponsible county commissioners. Surely Potts's greatest achievement was
his reform of territorial finances. Under his constant prodding, Montana
Territory and most of its counties began a general refunding of their debts
at 10 percent interest in 1876. By the time Potts left office in 1883, the
territory stood on a sound fiscal basis, and the millage tax had been reduced from 4.5 to 2 mills.

As Montana Territory achieved stability under Benjamin Potts, it began to deal more realistically with its problems. The big political and economic questions in Montana were generally the same as those prevailing
elsewhere in the West. Montanans argued about how best to reduce the
size of the huge Indian reservations and open the lands for white "development," about attracting outside investors during the depression that
began in 1873, and about how to gain more independence from the federal government while acquiring more federal military posts and other investments. Like all western territories, Montana longed for the railroads,
which would surely bring growth and prosperity. And, like other westerners, Montanans sharply debated the question of whether or not the
territory should encourage the railroads by offering them subsidies or tax
exemptions. Potts himself first opposed railroad subsidies, but he later
moved cautiously to support them. Montana finally chose not to run up
large debts in order to finance railroads. They came in good time, and
Montana escaped the terrible indebtedness that rail subsidies forced on
some of its neighbors.

Another hotly contested issue in Montana, as in other territories, was
the location of the territorial capital. Many towns hungered for the honor,
for it would bring jobs and prosperity, prestige and permanence. Bannack
had served as the first capital, simply because Governor Edgerton had ordered the legislature to assemble there. In 1865, the legislators had
moved the seat of government to Virginia City, the center of population.
Even by that time, however, Virginia City was losing population to Helena, and a long struggle over location of the capital began between the
two cities. Virginia City won the prize in an election on the issue held in
1867. As Helena continued to prosper and Virginia City to decline, another election was held in 1869, this time amid widespread accusations of
fraud. Incredibly, after the ballots had been taken to the territorial secretary's office at Virginia City, an "accidental" fire destroyed them. Suspicions abounded.

Helena, by now the center of activity in the territory, continued to
press its case. The legislature ordered a third election on the issue for August 1874, this time giving the voters the choice: "For or Against Helena." Again, widespread irregularities occurred. The Gallatin County

vote was thrown out, the returns from Meagher County were certified as fraudulent, and the matter finally ended in a great legal hassle. After the United States Supreme Court refused to consider the case on appeal, the Montana Supreme Court resolved the irregularities in Helena's favor. Finally, in 1875, Helena—centrally located, flanked by rich quartz mines, and lying on a projected rail route—became the capital city of Montana Territory.

Aside from such colorful squabbles, the quality of government and the tone of politics improved steadily in Montana during the 1870s and 1880s. Competent men began to assume elective and appointive offices—men like Cornelius Hedges, the long-time superintendent of public instruction who played a key role in developing the territorial public school system. The trend toward better government was best reflected in the territorial supreme court. Montana gained recognition as having one of the most efficient court systems among western territories. This reputation was primarily the result of a few dedicated men: Hiram Knowles, the first Montana resident to receive a federal appointment in the territory; Decius Wade, who served as chief justice from 1881 until 1887, and Henry N. Blake, who was appointed to the bench in 1874. Wade, the "Father of Montana Jurisprudence," dominated the territorial court and later played a major role in codifying the laws of early Montana. Wade once estimated that he and Knowles had traveled over twenty-five thousand miles by coach during their years on the bench.

Montanans generally showed good judgment in their choices of delegates to Congress. Of the six men who served as Montana's congressional delegate, four were Democrats, who usually faced the frustrations of dealing with a Republican-controlled Congress. Like all territorial delegates, the men also carried the handicap of having no vote. Nevertheless, they voiced their constituents' concerns and looked after their interests in Washington, and they joined with other territorial delegates to speak for the West as a region.

The most able of the Montana delegates were William Clagett and Martin Maginnis. Clagett served only briefly in 1871-72, but he was a Republican dealing with a Republican government and his talents allowed him to accomplish a great deal for the territory. Democrat Martin Maginnis, who defeated Clagett in 1872 and served ten years as delegate, was surely the most effective and powerful of Montana's men in Washington. He worked smoothly with Potts and the Republicans, and he constantly looked after the interests of Samuel Hauser, C. A. Broadwater, and other local investors. Maginnis proved especially adept at removing lands from Indian reservations and at securing federal forts, agencies, and monies for the folks back home.

Under Governor Potts, responsible government—along with the arrival of railroads and a new prosperity, placed Montana well on the road to statehood. Yet, Congress forced Montana to wait six long years after Potts's 1883 retirement before granting it admittance to the Union. During those years, Montana received five governors in quick succession. One of these, B. Platt Carpenter, reportedly lost his job because of absenteeism. Interestingly, two of the governors were local residents: powerful Democrat Samuel T. Hauser, who resigned, apparently over a dispute with the United States land commissioner, and Benjamin White, a Republican businessman and founder of the city of Dillon.

During the 1880s, Montana's political landscape changed perceptibly. The Republicans increased their numbers, practically reaching parity with the Democrats. Although party platforms often only differed on selected issues, to a large degree the parties represented cultural differences that subtly affected politics. Generally speaking, the Republicans drew their strength from Yankee political and social traditions, and border and middle Atlantic states' influences shaped a large portion of the Democratic party. As the territory's political community matured during the 1880s, the "no-party" system of the Potts era gave way to a closely balanced contention between the two major parties, with both agreeing that increased population and economic activity would benefit everyone.

Not surprisingly, as Montana matured, the more its citizens resented the "colonial" rule that accompanied territorial status and the more they demanded self-government and statehood. With the usual exaggeration, Delegate Martin Maginnis voiced a common complaint in 1884: "The present Territorial system . . . is the most infamous system of colonial government that was ever seen on the face of the globe." In that same year, the editor of *The Missoulian* wrote plaintively: "The President has nominated another carpetbagger for Associate Justice of the Supreme Court of Montana. Seventy-five thousand people in the Territory to make laws for themselves, and a Hoosier sent out from Indiana to tell us what we have done. How long, oh Lord; how long!"

In truth, the territorial system in Montana produced the same mixed record of success and failure that it did elsewhere. It succeeded in providing a measure of local self-government, balanced by federal supervision. Despite Maginnis's complaints, it made of early Montana neither a colony nor a martyr. The territorial system, most significantly, brought order and some form of government to the distant mining camps of the Northern Rockies, and it set those communities on a course that would take them toward political equality with the established states of the Union.

To those who lived in Montana, however, the disadvantages of territorial status far outweighed the benefits. Statehood, it was hoped, would

Created by the Northern Pacific Railroad, Billings grew rapidly during the 1880s and became an important commercial center by 1900.

bring an end to the federal meddling and bungling that had been upsetting the territory since 1864. Perhaps most important, statehood meant the recognition of Montana's coming of age as a community. By the mid-1880s, such recognition was clearly due. No longer did Montana simply echo the issues and concerns of the nation. By then, the territory had revealed a political culture of its own, arising out of the needs and demands of its major economic groupings—industrial miners, stockmen, merchants, lumbermen, farmers, and labor leaders. Statehood was no longer a mere pipedream; it was a justified expectation.

CHAPTER 6

Indian Removal, 1851-1890

EXCEPT perhaps for black slavery, the whites' purposeful destruction of Native American societies is the most sordid chapter of American history. Historians have long focused too much attention on the violent clashes that left the Indians a dispirited and relatively defenseless people. Recently, however, historians have begun to examine the broader aspects of the encounters between Native Americans and white invaders, viewing them as a major turning point in the history of North America. Whites seized control of vast territories while, as ethnologist John C. Ewers put it, Indians were forced into "trading land for a living." It was a genuinely tragic story for the Indians, punctuated by war, disease, and fraud. But for the slowly growing community of whites in western Montana, the Indians' loss meant the opening of their territory to settlement and "development."

THE FIRST TREATIES

Montana Indians had been in contact with whites for nearly three decades before the United States government began to deal with them as independent and sovereign groups. In 1825, the Crows negotiated a treaty that promised United States military protection from their enemies in exchange for the Crows' acceptance of the supremacy of the federal government. This was the first of many treaties that the government negotiated with the Crows and other Montana tribes, but the treaty method of resolving disputes seldom worked well. It assumed that Indian tribes, like sovereign nations, were united under one supreme leader, or one group of leaders, who could speak for all the people. That was seldom the case. More often, one or several compliant chiefs, often persuaded by liquor or

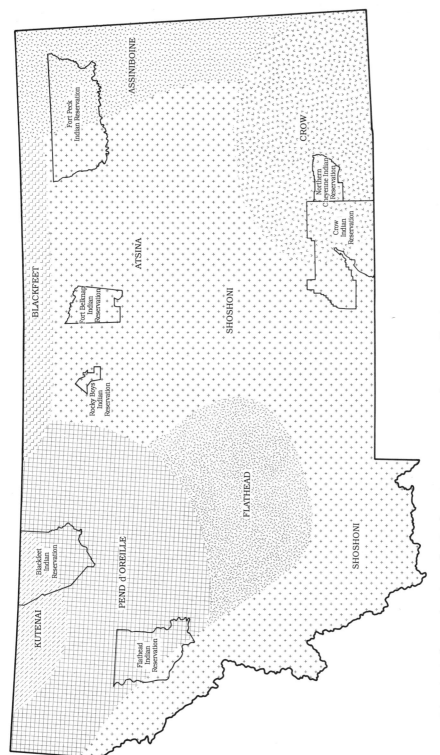

Map 3. Indian tribes (map by Barbara Lien; source: Harley Sorrells after Carling Malouf)

bribes, signed away lands over which they lacked sole authority. In many cases, a carnival atmosphere surrounded the treaty negotiations, and sometimes government agents practiced outright deception and fraud. Almost always, the Indians came out second best.

The first such agreement to affect the Montana area was the Fort Laramie Treaty of 1851. Government officials summoned Great Plains tribal leaders to Fort Laramie, located on the Oregon Trail in present-day southeastern Wyoming. The purpose of the meeting was to negotiate a treaty of peace between warring Indians and between the Indians and the advancing white Americans. In return for the customary "annuities"— annual gifts of food, utensils, and other items—the chiefs signed a number of important agreements. The government promised to respect and protect the Indians' tribal lands, and the Indians agreed to allow the construction of roads and forts on their territory. More important, the Fort Laramie Treaty mapped out each tribe's domain and obligated its members to respect the lands of its neighbors.

The Blackfeet, who had no representatives at Fort Laramie, and the Gros Ventres became the recognized proprietors of the north-central area of present-day Montana east of the Continental Divide. Most of the upper and middle Yellowstone Valley was assigned to the Crows, and the Assiniboines received a sizable tract of land in northeastern Montana. The Fort Laramie Treaty had little immediate impact on the native Montanans. It "kept the peace" for a dozen years, but only until white prospectors found a use for the lands involved. Understandably, the chiefs failed to foresee the treaty's major long-term significance. By assigning specific lands to particular tribes, the treaty opened the way for future agreements in which each tribe could be cajoled or forced into giving up its own lands.

The Fort Laramie Treaty did not cover the mountain tribes who lived west of the plains. Four years later, Washington Territorial Governor Isaac I. Stevens held a series of conferences with the Plateau tribes of the Northwest. Stevens sought to place the tribes on large reservations and thereby open choice areas for white settlement and transportation routes. In July 1855, Stevens convened a major council near present-day Missoula with the Flathead, Pend d'Oreille, and Kutenai tribes, led by their respective head chiefs Victor, Alexander, and Michel.

These tribes, traditionally friendly toward whites, agreed to accept a common reservation; in return for lands thus ceded, the government promised to spend $120,000 over the next twenty years for improvements on the reservation. The problem in Stevens's negotiations arose over the site of the reservation. The Pend d'Oreilles and Kutenais wanted the Flathead Valley near St. Ignatius Mission, but Victor and the Flatheads wanted to remain in their beloved Bitterroot Valley. Finally, all sides agreed to the creation of the enormous Jocko Indian Reservation, embracing over 1,280,000 acres to the south of Flathead Lake. In order to gain the Flatheads' acceptance of the treaty, the negotiators inserted Article 11, which allowed Victor's people to remain temporarily in the Bitterroot above the mouth of Lolo Creek. The president would order a survey of the Bitterroot Valley, the negotiators said, and would ultimately decide whether the Flatheads should be given a reserve there or whether they should remove to the Jocko. This clause would lead to confusion and sorrow, but for the time being the "Salish Council" opened much of western Montana to peaceful white intrusion.

Following the conference, Stevens and his party moved eastward, and in mid-October 1855 they opened a similar council with the Blackfeet near the mouth of the Judith River. Stevens wanted to confine the Blackfeet within a limited area and to persuade them to make peace with both Indians and whites. Again, he proved his ability as a diplomat. In return for annuities, the Blackfeet accepted a general reservation with boundaries reaching from the crest of the Continental Divide to the mouth of the Milk River, and from the United States–Canada boundary southward to the upper Musselshell River. The Blackfeet promised to recognize the general area of southwestern Montana as a common hunting ground, where they would respect the rights of other tribes. They even agreed to limited white usage of their reservation lands. Stevens's Blackfeet Treaty of 1855 appeared to be a major triumph, a guarantee of peace for years to come.

THE WHITE INVASION

The gold rushes of 1862-63 disrupted these fragile treaty arrangements. The Blackfeet felt the full impact of the mining invasion, for the prime goldfields lay along and below the southern limits of their reservation lands. When whites began entering the valuable hunting grounds of southwestern Montana, a number of "incidents," usually isolated killings or thefts of stock, naturally resulted.

The inhabitants of newly created Montana Territory demanded federal military protection. Like most frontiersmen, they panicked easily and exaggerated the Indian threat. They knew that military forts meant not only protection from the Indians, but also juicy government contracts for local businessmen. Following the end of the Civil War in 1865, the federal government began the task of garrisoning the Montana frontier. The army located its first posts in Montana in 1866, when it established Fort C. F. Smith ninety miles up the Big Horn River and Camp Cooke near the con-

In 1880, the army built Fort Maginnis in central Montana after stockmen pressured Congress for protection from feared Indian raids. The raids were few and troops at Fort Maginnis had little contact with Indians.

fluence of the Judith and Missouri rivers. Neither of the isolated forts lasted long. In 1869, the small force from Camp Cooke moved to old Fort Benton, where the troops spent most of their time policing whiskey peddlers and guarding government supplies.

In 1867, the army established its two major bases on the Montana mining frontier, Fort Shaw and Fort Ellis. Fort Shaw, regimental headquarters for the newly formed Military District of Montana, was located near the strategic Sun River Crossing, where the Mullan Road forded that stream and near the location of the first Blackfeet Indian Agency, which Stevens had established in 1854. The fort protected the Mullan Road and guarded the northern fringes of the mining settlements from Blackfeet and other intruders. Built mainly of adobe, Fort Shaw housed four companies of infantry. Fort Ellis, situated at the western portal of Bozeman Pass near the new town of Bozeman, was built in the aftermath of Governor Meagher's "Indian War" of 1867. It protected the southwestern Montana gold camps and the southeastern flank of the Montana settlements against Sioux and other raiders from the Yellowstone Valley. From three to five companies, including cavalry, were usually located at Fort Ellis. In 1870, the military also based one company of infantry at Camp Baker (later named Fort Logan) in the Big Belt Mountains east of Helena.

Trouble between the Blackfeet and the whites was probably inevitable, but federal mismanagement made the situation worse than it need have been. In 1865, Agent Gad Upson, assisted by Acting Governor Meagher and others, had negotiated a Blackfeet treaty at Fort Benton that might have avoided many problems. In return for the usual annuities, this treaty removed from the reservation all lands south of the Teton and Missouri rivers, moving the Blackfeet to the north and away from the white settlements. But the treaty never became law. Believing that neither the whites nor the Indians would observe it, the secretary of the Interior did not even bother to submit the treaty to the Senate.

So events took their natural course. Blackfeet and a few Sioux raiding parties ranged throughout the Montana settlements, stealing horses and livestock and occasionally killing whites. Fort Benton lay in the heart of the troubled area. In mid-1869, following an Indian attack that killed two whites nearby, two innocent young Blackfeet were wantonly gunned down on the street in Benton. One of the slain was the brother of the Piegan leader Mountain Chief, and the Indians retaliated over the next six months with raids that may have claimed well over two dozen lives. When the Piegans killed the well-known trader Malcolm Clarke, who had a Blackfeet wife, whites in the Helena and Fort Benton areas reacted with near hysteria and shouted for military reprisal. Federal authorities demanded that the guilty Blackfeet be surrendered for punishment, but the Indians allowed them to flee into Canada.

Amid a mounting chorus of demands for military action, General Philip H. Sheridan, in charge of the army's Division of the Missouri, decided to act. The hard-boiled Sheridan, who believed in "total war" against Indians, ordered Major Eugene M. Baker at Fort Ellis to retaliate against Mountain Chief and his band. "Tell Baker," he telegraphed, "to strike them hard." He did. In bitter, sub-zero cold, Baker led four companies of the Second Cavalry north from Fort Ellis in January 1870, picking up two infantry troops at Fort Shaw on the way. Baker's scouts found an unsuspecting Blackfeet village on the Marias River, and at dawn on the terribly cold morning of January 23, a reportedly drunk Baker attacked. In the ensuing massacre, 173 Indians, including 53 women and children, were murdered.

Baker had attacked the wrong village. It was not Mountain Chief's camp, but that of several other chiefs, including the friendly Heavy Runner. Heavy Runner rushed out, waving papers certifying his good character, only to be shot down. The carnage ended quickly. When Baker learned that some of the captive women and children had smallpox, he turned them loose in the snow and cold. Because of this vicious slaughter, Baker faced considerable criticism from around the nation, and an angry Congress killed a proposal to return control of the Indian Bureau from the Department of the Interior to the War Department. But many Montanans and military men commended Baker's action. The major's superior, General Winfield Scott Hancock, concluded in his annual report that Baker and his command were "entitled to the special commendation of the military authorities and the hearty thanks of the nation."

The Baker Massacre largely ended Blackfeet resistance to the white invasion. During the next few years, the Indians of northern Montana began the hard adjustment to a new way of life. Beginning in 1868-69, the Department of the Interior established separate agencies and subagencies for the tribes. The Blackfeet agency was moved north from the Sun River to the Teton River and later to the upper Marias. The Gros Ventres, Assiniboines, and River Crows received a subagency at Fort Browning on the upper Milk River; in 1871, the subagency was transferred up the Milk to Fort Belknap. In 1873, other Assiniboines, along with Sioux bands who were pressing in from the east, were assigned to an agency at Fort Peck, near the confluence of the Milk and Missouri rivers.

In 1873, President Grant signed an executive order that restructured the northern Montana reservation. In 1871, the federal government had discarded the old treaty system in 1871 and had begun dealing with the Indians by executive agreements. This meant, in effect, that tribes could be dealt with more summarily and without long negotiations. The order of 1873 set aside—for the Blackfeet, Gros Ventre, Assiniboine, and Sioux tribes—all of northern Montana, from the Continental Divide to the Dakota line, with the southern boundary of the huge reserve running along the Missouri and Sun rivers. A year later, in 1874, the government moved the southern boundary of the Blackfeet territory northward from the Sun to the Marias River, depriving the Blackfeet of some of their best hunting lands.

By the mid-1870s, the Blackfeet and Gros Ventres—and also the more distant Assiniboines and Sioux—had been pushed north of the Missouri River. This arrangement pleased Montana whites, for it opened the lush grasslands of the Judith Basin to penetration by stockmen. For the Indians, however, it meant the narrowing of horizons and a deepening dependence on the federal government. An indifferent Congress and an Indian Bureau riddled with corruption often failed to provide the food and annuities promised by law. The Indians faced a hard and depressing future.

Because neither the Flathead nor the Bitterroot valleys contained major gold deposits, the Indians of western Montana experienced less direct conflict than did the Blackfeet. But the Salish and Kutenai Indians on the Jocko Indian Reservation well understood the meaning of neglect, as their buildings, herds, and crops suffered from negligence and scant funding. South of the reservation, the Flatheads still remained in the Bitterroot Valley. Despite the stipulations of Article 11 of the 1855 Stevens treaty, the president had never ordered a survey of the valley nor had he decided on a permanent home for the Flatheads. Victor, head chief of the Flatheads, died and was succeeded by his son, Charlot. Charlot and his people reasoned that, since their land had not been surveyed and assessed, the government had chosen to leave them there permanently. Once again, federal neglect led to problems.

The agricultural possibilities of the Bitterroot Valley began to attract more and more white farmers. These settlers raised the familiar cry that the Indians be removed, and the Montana legislature memorialized the federal government to this effect. Congressional Delegate William Clagett pressed the case for relocating the Flatheads. In late 1871, President Grant issued an executive order declaring that, a survey of the valley having been completed, he had decided that the Flatheads must move north to the Jocko. But the Flatheads sat tight and refused to move. In 1872, Congress entered the fray by ordering the Indians' removal and opening the Bitterroot lands for sale to white settlers.

In June 1872, the secretary of the Interior sent Congressman James A. Garfield, a former Union general and future president, to negotiate the withdrawal of the Flatheads. Garfield found a tense situation in Montana. The Bitterroot settlers were organizing themselves into militia, demanding arms and ammunition from the governor, and pleading that a fort be built to protect them. Accompanied by a party that included Governor Potts and Delegate Clagett, Garfield traveled to the Bitterroot to confer with Charlot and subchiefs Arlee and Adolph.

In return for government promises of buildings, annuities, and the provision that any Flathead could remain in the Bitterroot by becoming a land-holding United States citizen, Arlee and Adolph agreed to move to the Jocko Indian Reservation. But Charlot refused to join them. While Arlee led some of the Flatheads to the reservation, the majority remained with their head chief in the Bitterroot. Charlot became deeply embittered. The government had not honored the spirit of the 1855 treaty, and he deeply resented Garfield's negotiating with Arlee as if he were the head chief. But most of all, Charlot reacted angrily when published accounts indicated that he had signed the agreement to move to the Jocko. As Garfield himself later admitted, Charlot never signed the 1872 removal pact, but the government nonetheless allowed such reports to appear in print.

Charlot and his small band remained in the Bitterroot Valley for years, living in miserable poverty. The Flatheads remained peaceful, however, and even refused to help their old Nez Perce allies during their 1877 retreat from Idaho. Meanwhile, Peter Ronan, the capable Jocko Indian agent, tried to get Charlot's people to move. Finally, after Arlee had died and after Charlot had learned that Garfield had not forged his name on the 1872 agreement, the chief relented. In 1891, Charlot and his people left the Bitterroot Valley and moved to the Jocko Indian Reservation. The removal of the western Montana tribes was complete.

Even though their domain lay east of the major mining areas, the Crows also felt the impact of the white intrusion. Like the Flatheads, they got along reasonably well with the whites, and also like the Flatheads, they lost most of their lands anyway. The 1851 Fort Laramie Treaty recognized the major portion of the Yellowstone Valley as Crow territory. But a dozen years later, the Montana mining rushes began to cause complications. The Bozeman Road passed through the heart of Crow lands en route to mining camps on the upper Missouri. As more and more prospecting parties entered the upper Yellowstone Valley, clashes mounted between Indians and whites. The result was a prolonged conflict between the United States military and Sioux and Cheyenne warriors, which ended with an ignominious military retreat and a new treaty.

Eager to move the Crows away from their advancing Sioux enemies on the east, the United States government negotiated a new treaty with the Mountain Crows in 1868, which the majority River Crows refused to sign. Promising the usual improvements and annuities, the treaty lopped off the eastern extremities of the Crows' domain. The new reservation was bounded on the north and west by the Yellowstone River, on the south by the Montana-Wyoming line, and on the east by the divide between the Big Horn and Rosebud rivers. The Indian Bureau established an agency for the Crows at the western end of the reservation near present-day Livingston.

Congress had no more than ratified the 1868 treaty than discoveries of gold on the upper Yellowstone led to irresistible pressure for opening the western end of the Crow reserve. Sympathetic to the whites' demands, the government worked out a new agreement in 1873, whereby the Crows would give up their reservation entirely and take instead a much smaller one in the Judith Basin, north of the Yellowstone River. But the plan created too many problems. Although the River Crows had long hunted in central Montana and liked the new location, the Mountain Crows balked at leaving their homeland. Chief Old Crow told the negotiators: "It is too small a country in the Judith Basin. We want from the Yellowstone to the Missouri." More to the point, cattlemen reacted angrily to the prospect of locking up the inviting Judith Basin in a reservation. In 1875, President Grant rescinded his previous order and ended the plan to move the Crows.

Eventually, the cattlemen won the Judith and the miners got what they were after, the upper Yellowstone. In 1880, six Crow chiefs were taken to Washington, D.C., for negotiations; but disagreements in Congress delayed ratification of the agreement they had made until 1882. The final action decreased the Crow Indian Reservation by 1.5 million acres and a 400-foot right-of-way for the advancing Northern Pacific Railroad. These ceded lands included the mining camps along the upper Yellowstone and the site of Crow Agency, so in 1875 the agency was relocated well to the east, on the Rosebud fork of the Stillwater River. Thus, the Crows, crowded from the east by the Sioux and Cheyennes, from the north by cattlemen, and from the west by miners, were pressed into an ever-shrinking remnant of their once great domain south of the Yellowstone River.

THE "SIOUX PROBLEM"

The Montana mining rushes provoked surprisingly little violence from the Indians who actually lived in the areas immediately affected. But some of the immigrants to early Montana traveled routes like the Bozeman and Minnesota-Montana roads, which followed shortcuts across the northern Great Plains. This wide plains province, reaching from western Minnesota and Iowa into eastern Montana and Wyoming, was Sioux territory. Along with their Northern Cheyenne allies, the Sioux Nation had the strength, numbers, and determination to challenge the white thrust into their prized hunting lands.

Several factors drove the western Sioux and the Northern Cheyenne to war. Following a major conflict in Minnesota in 1862, the eastern Sioux retreated onto the Dakota plains, spreading excitement among western Sioux tribes and attracting military pursuit by armies under General Henry Sibley and General Alfred Sully. These engagements involved the powerful, western Teton Sioux, who were driven into eastern Montana and Wyoming. The terrible slaughter of the Southern Cheyennes at Sand Creek, Colorado, in 1864, also spread waves of unrest among the tribes to the north. The Civil War added complications by reducing military forces and creating uncertainty on the western frontiers. But most of all, the Sioux and Northern Cheyennes resented whites entering and disrupting their buffalo grounds.

From its opening in 1863-64, the Bozeman Road enraged the Sioux and Northern Cheyenne because it crossed the Powder, Tongue, and Big Horn rivers, lands that they and their Crow enemies claimed as prime hunting grounds. Teton Sioux, Cheyenne, and Northern Arapaho warriors allied to defend this territory, first in an attack at Platte Bridge Station in July 1865 and then against the troops that General Patrick Connor brought against them. The conflict intensified the following year when the government fortified the road to protect travelers en route to the Montana goldfields. In the summer of 1866, even as peace commissioners at Fort Laramie were trying to bargain the Bozeman Road area away from the Sioux, Colonel Henry B. Carrington and his infantry forces headed northward for the Powder River. Led by Red Cloud, the most powerful of the Sioux chiefs, the majority of the Indian leaders angrily broke off the talks at Fort Laramie and left to protect their lands. Meanwhile, Carrington began building three small posts along the Bozeman Road: Fort Reno at the forks of the Powder and Fort Phil Kearny in the Big Horn foothills, both in present-day Wyoming, and Fort C. F. Smith on the Big Horn River in southern Montana.

Carrington's troops quickly found themselves in an impossible situation. There were simply too few of them and too many Indians. Morale suffered, especially after the cold weather chilled the garrisons. The men were poorly equipped, and most of them had only outmoded Springfield muzzle-loading rifles. Red Cloud's warriors had the advantage; they closed in and placed the forts in a state of siege. Fort Phil Kearny, Carrington's headquarters, faced the worst of it. In December 1866, a young, headstrong, and reckless captain named William J. Fetterman took eighty-one men out of the fort to protect a wagon train and impetuously followed warriors directed by a young Sioux war chief named Crazy Horse

Colonel Myles Keogh, Colonel George Armstrong Custer, and more than 120 other members of the 7th Cavalry died at the Battle of the Little Big Horn in June 1876, an event that has become mythic and symbolic of the Indian-military conflict on the Northern Plains. (Photo by S. J. Morrow)

straight into an ambush. Within forty minutes, Fetterman and his men lay dead and mutilated.

The Fetterman Massacre shocked the nation. By the following summer, the army had nine hundred men, better armed and supplied, on the Bozeman Road, and a new post, Fort Fetterman, was taking shape at its southern end. Still, the Sioux kept the soldiers on the defensive and allowed only a trickle of migration over the road. In late summer 1867, the Indians—some of them carrying repeating rifles obtained from white traders—mounted heavy attacks. Near Fort C. F. Smith, a large force under Red Cloud hit a haying party in what would become known as the "Hayfield Fight," but the Indians were beaten back by soldiers using newly arrived Springfield breach-loading rifles. In the "Wagon Box Fight" near Fort Phil Kearny, the Indians attacked a woodcutting party; again the soldiers drove them off with their more sophisticated rifles.

The violent summer of 1867 cost the Indians dearly in lives, but it clearly underscored the government's dilemma: either Washington must vastly increase troop strength on the Bozeman Road or it must abandon it. The government chose the second alternative, partly because completion of the Union Pacific Railroad across southern Wyoming would now allow Montana-bound immigrants to bypass the Bozeman Road and use instead the Corinne-Virginia City Road north from Utah. Once again, federal peace commissioners journeyed to the council site at Fort Laramie and began bargaining with the warring chiefs.

In the Fort Laramie Treaty of 1868, the Sioux got basically what they wanted. Red Cloud refused to discuss terms until the soldiers left the hated forts. To the angry dismay of white Montanans, the treaty negotiators agreed and closed the Bozeman Road, promising that the areas it had crossed would remain unfortified. The day after the soldiers left Fort C. F. Smith, the Indians put it to the torch. But the chiefs also made concessions. In line with the new federal policy of "concentration," which aimed to place most of the Plains tribes on two large reserves, the commissioners persuaded the chiefs to accept a reservation centering on the Black Hills and consisting mainly of today's South Dakota west of the Missouri River. It was significant that the Powder—Tongue—Big Horn areas, where Red Cloud had just won his war, were not part of the reservation. The treaty denoted this vast expanse as unceded Indian lands, closed to general white entry, making it available for seasonal hunting, but not permanent occupation, by the Indians.

The Fort Laramie Treaty of 1868 seemed a model compromise: the Indians got the hated road closed, and the United States succeeded in concentrating them in a more restricted area. But this treaty, like so many others, turned out to be only a temporary truce, not a lasting peace. Red

Cloud and most of the older and calmer chiefs went on the reservation, but many of the younger Sioux leaders, like the fiery Hunkpapa chief Sitting Bull and the Oglala Crazy Horse, refused to accept the decision of their elders. These nontreaty Indians kept their bands in the unceded lands crossed by the old Bozeman Road. The treaty commissioners fully expected the buffalo hunting to decline and predicted that the nontreaty Indians would end up living on the reservation. But the nontreaty bands adamantly refused reservation life and frequently ventured northward to hunt in and beyond the Yellowstone Valley, giving many white Montanans a bad case of the jitters.

For a few years, the situation remained static. Few whites entered the areas south of the Yellowstone, and many Sioux and Cheyennes simply "commuted" between the neglected agencies in Dakota and the hunting lands to the west. But it was only a matter of time before trouble erupted. This time, the problem involved the Northern Pacific Railroad, which by 1871 was heading across northern Dakota Territory toward the Yellowstone River Valley. By a loose reading of the 1868 treaty, the Sioux and Cheyennes believed that the Yellowstone belonged in their unceded zone; many of the Indians, in fact, denied the legitimacy of the treaty altogether. As railroad surveying parties probed up the Yellowstone with army protection, the Indians moved against them.

In August 1872, a large Sioux party struck an army escort under Major Eugene Baker (whose troops had murdered the Blackfeet on the Marias in 1870) near the mouth of Pryor Creek on the Yellowstone. Baker was too drunk at the time to lead his men, but they managed, in spite of heavy losses, to drive off the raiders. A larger military escort force, which came up the Yellowstone in 1873, also ran into Indians. Then the Panic of 1873 closed down work on the Northern Pacific, leaving the railhead at Bismarck in north-central Dakota. The tensions in the Yellowstone eased for a time, but another one quickly arose in the Black Hills.

The Black Hills lay well within the 1868 reservation, yet rumors of gold drew in armies of white prospectors anyway. In 1874, Colonel George A. Custer led a large and leisurely surveying expedition through the Black Hills and reported the area rich not only in gold, but also in prime agricultural land. Predictably, Custer's and other reports set a rush of white intruders onto the reservation. Although the Indians killed some of the goldseekers and the army halfheartedly threw out others, they continued to come by the thousands. By 1875, Montana boosters were beginning to worry that the Black Hills gold rush would empty their territory.

The Black Hills gold boom made a travesty of the Fort Laramie Treaty of 1868, and again brought the situation with the Sioux to a boil. As whites streamed onto the reservation, more and more Indians left the corruption-ridden agencies and headed west to join the nontreaty bands in the Big Horn-Powder River country. Further complicating the issue was President Grant's "Peace Policy" toward recalcitrant Indian tribes, which emphasized reform of the Indian agent system, the elimination of treaties, and the preference for negotiated executive agreements. Under this new policy, peace commissioners tried to persuade Sioux chiefs Red Cloud and Spotted Tail to sign away the Black Hills, but the Indians balked. Finally, at the close of 1875 and with the "Peace Policy" honored more often than not in the breach, the Grant administration made its fateful decision. While passively allowing whites to enter the Black Hills, it would use military force to drive the Sioux and Cheyennes out of the unceded lands below the Yellowstone and back onto the ruptured reservation. Once again, the United States violated its treaty agreement, and this time the last of the great Indian wars in America was the result.

In early December 1875, the Indian Bureau sent messengers to the bands in southeastern Montana and northeastern Wyoming, ordering them to return to the reservation by the end of January 1876. The ultimatum did not allow the tribes enough time to comply, but the Indians had decided to stand and fight in any case. They became what the United States Army called "hostiles."

THE DEFEAT OF THE SIOUX, 1876-1877

The army eagerly made its first move against the so-called hostiles in March 1876, when General George Crook, who had proven his ability against the Apaches in Arizona, led nine hundred men north from Fort Fetterman, Wyoming. Suffering terribly in subzero weather, Crook's command advanced to the Powder River, where some of his troops under Colonel J. J. Reynolds attacked and captured a large Sioux-Cheyenne village. But Reynolds failed to either hold or destroy the camp, and the "Battle of Powder River" accomplished almost nothing. Largely because of the severe cold, Crook gave up the effort and returned to Fort Fetterman.

Meanwhile, from his Chicago headquarters, General Phil Sheridan, commander of the Military Division of the Missouri, planned a major spring-summer campaign to corral the Sioux and Cheyennes. Sheridan decided to send three large armies into the Powder–Tongue–Big Horn area, hoping that one or more of them would engage the hostiles and either defeat them or cause their surrender. The general's three-pronged offensive began soon after Crook's sad return from the Powder River. During April 1876, the "Montana Column," consisting of 450 infantry and cavalrymen from Fort Shaw and Fort Ellis, began moving down the Yellowstone River under Colonel John Gibbon. Gibbon's assignment, essentially defensive, was to block any Indian movement north or west of the Yellowstone. The "Dakota Column," under the command of General Alfred Terry, left Fort Abraham Lincoln near Bismarck in mid-May. Moving across the Dakota plains and up the Yellowstone Valley, Terry led a large force consisting of the 700-man Seventh Cavalry under Colonel George A. Custer, 225 infantrymen, and a large contingent of scouts and teamsters.

Custer, a national hero because of his colorful career as a Civil War general and a dashing Indian fighter, had originally been assigned command of the entire Dakota Column. But he had angered President Grant by testifying before a congressional committee about corruption in the Indian Services implicating Grant's brother. The president retaliated by removing Custer from the command, and only at the last moment did he consent to allow the prideful young officer to go along as commander of the Seventh Cavalry. Some historians have speculated that Custer—a vain and egotistical, yet capable, man—may have acted as he later did on the Montana plains because of his determination to recover the glorious reputation that Grant had seemingly tarnished.

As the Montana and Dakota columns moved toward a rendezvous on the lower Yellowstone, General George Crook once again led a large army northward from Fort Fetterman. His command included over a thousand cavalry and infantry, an enormous wagon and mule caravan, and over two hundred fifty Crow and Shoshoni warriors, eager to settle some old grudges with their Indian enemies. Crook, Terry, and Gibbon had only a general idea of where the Indians were and how many there might be. Throughout the spring of 1876, bands of Sioux and Northern Cheyennes had fled the reservation and joined the hostile camps near the Rosebud and Little Big Horn rivers in southeastern Montana. By June, their villages may have housed as many as fifteen thousand people, including possibly three to four thousand warriors.

The three advancing columns had to act somewhat independently, since communications were slow and unreliable. The army's greatest fear was that the Indians—who the army estimated had more than a thousand lodges in their camp—would scatter before one of the columns could hit them. With a thousand troops under his command, Crook encountered the hostiles first. On June 17, as his men paused on their way down upper Rosebud Creek, a large Sioux-Cheyenne force under Crazy Horse—probably seven hundred fifty men or more—attacked them. It was fortunate for Crook that he had paused before reaching the canyon, because Crazy Horse had hoped to trap him inside. Instead, the battle turned into a fierce, helter-skelter series of attacks and counterattacks as the Indians fought successfully in well-disciplined units. After six hours of fighting, the Indians withdrew, with as many as thirteen killed, but the capable Crook had in truth been beaten. The Battle of the Rosebud probably cost the general about seventy killed and wounded. Cautiously, Crook moved back to Goose Creek on the upper Tongue River to wait for reinforcements. Meanwhile, Crazy Horse moved his people northwest to join their allies.

The Rosebud battle, in effect, removed Crook's column from the campaign. In the meantime, Terry's and Gibbon's columns converged on the Yellowstone between the mouths of Rosebud Creek and the Tongue River. By scouting to the south, Terry figured that the Indians were located either on Rosebud Creek or, more likely, to the west on the Little Big Horn, a favorite camping spot. Terry and Gibbon knew nothing of Crook's whereabouts and feared that the Indians might get away from them. Sensibly enough, they chose a strategy of attempting to entrap the Indians from both the north and south. They would send Custer's swift Seventh Cavalry on a sweep southward up the Rosebud and then across to and down the north-flowing Little Big Horn. Meanwhile, Terry and Gibbon would march the slower moving infantry-cavalry force southward up the Big Horn and then up its Little Big Horn tributary. Both armies, it was hoped, would reach the Indian village on June 26, 1876. Coordination would be difficult, and the Indians would probably flee if they were forewarned. So Terry gave Custer considerable discretion: he might change the strategy if the Indians seemed likely to escape.

Leading nearly seven hundred men of the Seventh Cavalry, along with some Crow and Arikara scouts, Custer rode up the Rosebud on June 22. On June 24, he made the first of his controversial decisions: instead of following Terry's order and advancing to the head of the Rosebud before crossing over to the Little Big Horn, he pursued an Indian trail westward before reaching the upper Rosebud. Driving his men to exhaustion on a night march, Custer reached the divide between the two streams, and at dawn on June 25 his scouts saw the smoke of an enormous encampment. For whatever reason, whether to have all the glory for himself or to hit the Indians before they could scatter—or, possibly, both—Custer decided not to wait until Terry's June 26 target date. He failed to realize the immensity of the Indian gathering, even though his terrified scouts warned him of it. The Seventh, in his opinion, could whip any number.

By mid-day, Custer's troops were advancing down Reno Creek, southeast and out of sight from the Indian camp on the Little Big Horn, the stream the Indians called the "Greasy Grass." Planning to hit the encampment from two directions in order to stampede it, Custer divided his command into three units. He sent three troops under Captain Frederick

Benteen to scout the hills west of the village, hoping that Benteen could contain any Indian retreat. Major Marcus Reno, Custer's second in command, was ordered to cross the Little Big Horn with three more troops and strike the camp at its southern end. With five troops, Custer would skirt the bluffs to the right of the village and attack at its center.

But there were too many Indians, and they refused to panic. When Reno hit the near end of the enormous village, which stretched for miles along the river and included at least two thousand warriors, the Indians rallied quickly under Chief Gall and rushed their attackers. Reno tried and failed to form a defensive skirmish line. He led his men in a disorganized and bloody retreat back across the river and dug in on the bluffs there. Benteen's returning force soon joined what was left of Reno's. With Benteen in effect taking over from the distraught Reno, their combined command held off the attacking Indians.

Unaware of these developments, Custer emerged from the bluffs to the east of the village and attempted to cross the river and attack it. But Gall's warriors, having left Reno's force behind, moved across the stream and attacked Custer instead. The colonel began his retreat up the ridges to the north, but it was too late. More warriors joined Gall, and Crazy Horse led another attack flanking from the north. The Indians overwhelmed Custer's skirmish lines, and within a half-hour had wiped out his command. While they celebrated their victory, the Indians kept Reno and Benteen under siege until the evening of the next day. Then, aware that more soldiers were approaching, the Indians suddenly dispersed. On June 27, Terry and Gibbon arrived at the battlefield. They buried the more than two hundred and sixty dead and prepared Reno's and Benteen's wounded for removal to the steamboat *Far West*, which waited at the mouth of the Big Horn ready to steam down the Yellowstone to Dakota.

When news of the "Last Stand" on the Little Big Horn reached the American public in early July 1876, it had a shocking effect. Accounts of the "massacre," often highly inaccurate, disrupted the patriotic celebration of the nation's centennial anniversary and sent Americans poring over maps of faraway Montana Territory. Custer became an even larger hero in death than he had been in life; generations of schoolchildren learned of his derring-do, but never of his impetuous recklessness. And every western saloon, it seemed, came to display a romantic Anheuser-Busch painting of the battle. But despite all the attention it has received, the Battle of the Little Big Horn was in no way decisive. The Indians had won a significant victory, but the victory only postponed their inevitable defeat.

Stung by public criticism, both Congress and the army moved to force

L. A. Huffman took this historic photograph at Fort Buford in 1881, where Sitting Bull and other Sioux Indians who had returned to the United States after four years of self-imposed exile awaited steamboat transportation to the Standing Rock Reservation in Dakota Territory.

an unconditional surrender. Congress increased the maximum size of the army and allowed General Sheridan the two forts on the Yellowstone he had long been demanding. Together, Fort Keogh, at the Tongue River's juncture with the Yellowstone and Fort Custer at the confluence of the Big Horn and Little Big Horn rivers, would house over a thousand men when completed in 1877.

During the weeks following the Custer battle, Terry and Crook received reinforcements and led their large, cumbersome armies in a slow and unrewarding pursuit of the hostiles. As summer turned to autumn, Terry broke up his command and sent most of it home, leaving only some infantry behind to guard the Yellowstone. Crook continued his pursuit of the bands scattered between the Yellowstone and the Black Hills. After destroying a Sioux village at Slim Buttes in Dakota, he too disbanded his forces, who returned to their bases.

To the great anger of Montanans, the departure of Terry and Crook left only Colonel Nelson A. Miles, with his Fifth Infantry and eight companies from two other regiments, to police eastern Montana during the coming winter. This small army was based at the mouth of the Tongue River, the site of future Fort Keogh, and the town of Miles City arose to serve it. Miles was a shrewd, tough, and capable man who would gain fame as one of the greatest of all frontier commanders. He was also vain and ruthless, and he had the advantage of being married to the niece of General of the Army William Tecumseh Sherman. Miles drilled his men unceasingly and disciplined them for long winter marches. Although infantry troops were usually believed to be inferior to mounted troops in fighting Indians, Miles's tough foot soldiers proved themselves superior to cavalry, which required feed for horses and large supply trains.

Miles took the five hundred men of the Fifth Infantry into the field in October 1876. After Sioux forces under Sitting Bull had disrupted wagon traffic between Glendive Creek and the Tongue River, Miles confronted the headstrong chief at Cedar Creek north of the Yellowstone. Sitting Bull forthrightly rejected Miles's suggestion that he take his people to the reservation. When the discussion between Miles and Sitting Bull ended, the soldiers turned their artillery on the Indian camp and scattered the bands in two days of fighting. The attack cost the Sioux dearly in irreplaceable food, supplies, and horses, and some gave up and went back to the reservation. But Sitting Bull led others in continued resistance.

The fight at Cedar Creek was only the beginning. Miles obtained winter clothing for his men, and they cut up wool blankets for long underwear. Shrewdly, the colonel acquired Indian spies and an efficient corps of scouts, the most valuable of whom was Luther "Yellowstone" Kelly. In the severe cold of November and December 1876, "Bear Coat," as the Indians called Miles, led his infantrymen north into the Missouri and Musselshell country. One of his battalions under Lieutenant Frank Baldwin hit Sitting Bull's camp on the Redwater River, and the losses suffered soon convinced the chief that he should head for Canada. There, diminishing food supplies and continued pressure from American military south of the international boundary combined to persuade Sitting Bull to return and surrender. In July 1881, after more than four years in Canada, Sitting Bull and about fifty families arrived at Fort Buford, Montana, where he gave up his rifle, symbolically ending his resistance.

General Crook, meanwhile, was rebuilding his forces in Wyoming, and he brought a large army up the old Bozeman Road in November. Discovering the big Cheyenne village of Dull Knife and Little Wolf on the Red Fork of the Powder River, Crook sent out a powerful column under Colonel Ranald Mackenzie to attack and decimate it. The Cheyennes fled with terrible suffering. Miles also closed on the Indians south of the Yellowstone. Leading 350 of his men, who called themselves "walk-a-heaps," he moved up the Tongue River in the last days of 1876. Early in January 1877, Miles and his men expertly fought a stand-off battle with Crazy Horse at Wolf Mountain; both sides had to withdraw from the battleground, owing to weather and supply problems.

While Miles and Crook kept the pressure on the hostile bands, they also sent out emissaries to convince the chiefs that they should give up and return to the agencies. Hungry and demoralized, the Sioux and Northern Cheyenne bands straggled in and surrendered during the spring of 1877. Even the great Crazy Horse gave up in early May. But Lame Deer's Sioux band still held out, and Miles struck his camp on Muddy Creek in May. In the ensuing violence, Lame Deer was killed and Miles narrowly escaped death. The army spent the summer of 1877 rounding up the remnants of Lame Deer's band, and by the following autumn the conquest of the Sioux and Northern Cheyennes was complete. Fort Keogh and Fort Custer stood guard over the Yellowstone country, and white Montanans rejoiced at the removal of the Indian "menace."

THE NEZ PERCE RETREAT

The Nez Perces of north-central Idaho and northeastern Oregon lived on the Columbia Plateau, where their economy included hunting and gathering, fishing, and seasonal bison hunts on the Montana plains. They first encountered whites when Lewis and Clark crossed their lands in 1804. Regarded by other tribes as exceptional horse breeders and practiced traders, the Nez Perces confidently welcomed whites and extended their hands in friendship. In 1855, after missionaries had labored among them for nearly twenty years, some tribal leaders agreed to the cession of some of their homeland in return for annuities. But the Salmon River gold rush of the 1860s brought thousands of miners to the Nez Perce reservation and disrupted their relations with the whites. In 1863, the government forced a much harsher treaty on the Nez Perces, taking away some of their best lands. That action divided the tribe into "treaty" and "nontreaty" factions, the latter refusing to give up their lands and to move to the reservation along the Clearwater River in Idaho.

For a dozen years the nontreaty bands, including that of Chief Joseph in Oregon's Wallowa Valley, continued to live in the traditional way, off the reservation. But by the mid-1870s, increasing white settlement in these areas led to heightened demands for removal of the nontreaty Indians to the reservation. The whites' demands finally came to a head in early 1877. In May, one-armed General Oliver O. Howard, Civil War hero and commander of the army's Department of the Columbia, conferred at Lapwai with Joseph and the other nontreaty chiefs. Howard ordered the chiefs to move onto the reservation within the impossible deadline of thirty days. In mid-June, as the nontreaty Nez Perces gathered east of the Snake River, several bitter young men of White Bird's band struck out angrily and killed a handful of white settlers.

Fearing reprisals before they could explain what had happened, the nontreaty chiefs fell back to Tepahlewam on Camas Prairie near the Salmon River. There, more whites were killed, and General Howard sent out a column to punish the Indians. Although the Indians did not desire a full-scale war, a force of eighty nontreaty Nez Perces determined to fight back and soundly defeated Howard's more than two hundred soldiers, which included infantry, cavalry, and artillery.

In early July, the military widened the conflict by attacking Looking Glass's camp on the reservation, pushing his treaty band into an alliance with the nontreaty groups. By mid-July, Howard's actions had laid the road to war; the Battle of the Clearwater made war a reality. At the Clearwater, barely a hundred Nez Perce warriors fought off more than five hundred troopers. The Indians then paused to determine their options. Some counseled war; others urged that they leave the reservation and find a sanctuary rather than conduct a self-destructive war on their own land. While Howard's forces licked their wounds, Nez Perce warriors and their families—over eight hundred men, women, and children, accompanied by more than two thousand head of stock—moved east over the Lolo Trail into Montana, hoping to find protection and aid from the Crows along the Yellowstone. The Nez Perces literally fled their homeland to preserve their culture.

In Montana, the Nez Perce intrusion set off a near-panic. From his headquarters at Fort Shaw, Colonel John Gibbon hastily put together a force to intercept them. Meanwhile, local volunteers and troops from newly built Fort Missoula under Captain C. C. Rawn tried to block the Indians' passage down Lolo Creek by throwing up a log barricade, later dubbed "Fort Fizzle." But the Indians simply flanked the barrier and headed south up the Bitterroot Valley. Leaving the local settlers alone, except to conduct trade, the Nez Perces crossed over the Continental Divide into the Big Hole Basin. Knowing that General Howard was far behind, they made camp and rested.

What they could not know was that Colonel Gibbon was following them up the Bitterroot with a makeshift army of over two hundred soldiers and volunteers. At sunup on August 9, Gibbon and his men attacked the sleeping camp, peppering the lodges with rifle fire and slaughtering dozens of women and children. The soldiers first gained the advantage but then lost it when the Indians regrouped, captured the army's howitzer, and proceeded to outfight Gibbon's force. Nez Perce sharpshooters picked off Gibbon's men, especially the officers, with deadly accuracy and drove them back into a coulee. The Indians held them under siege there until late the next day and then fled. The Nez Perces beat Gibbon decisively, killing thirty of his command. But they suffered terribly, leaving eighty-nine dead, many of them women and children, at the site of the Big Hole Battle.

As Howard's army gained on them, the crippled Nez Perces, now without the tipis and household goods they had abandoned at the Big Hole, looped back into Idaho. When the slow-moving general drew near them at Camas Meadows, Nez Perce raiders ran off one hundred fifty of his pack mules. Montanans stepped up their criticism of Howard and began to appreciate the Indians' nickname for him, "General Day After Tomorrow." In late August, the Nez Perces entered Yellowstone National Park, captured and temporarily held several tourists, terrorized others, and then headed east into the Absaroka Mountain wilderness. After more than a week of making their way through the dense lodgepole forests and driving their horses up narrow canyons, the Indians crossed the mountains and descended southeast down the Clark's Fork of the Yellowstone, only to find that the Crows wanted nothing to do with them and the trouble they bore.

Now the Nez Perces' goal must be Canada, where they might find sanctuary and aid with Sitting Bull and the Sioux. But when the Indians reached the Clark's Fork, they encountered units of the Seventh Cavalry under Colonel Samuel Sturgis. By feinting southward, they removed Sturgis from their path and then headed north across the Yellowstone River. En route, they shot up the settlements near present-day Billings.

*Soldiers captured followers of Sword Bearer, a Crow prophet who in 1887
led an inspired but unsuccessful resistance to reservation life and imposi-
tion of white culture on the Crow Indian Reservation.*

Sturgis caught up with the Indians at Canyon Creek, north of the Yellowstone, but the warriors smoothly held off his troops while their families escaped.

By mid-September 1877, the Nez Perces were moving northward through central Montana, heading for Canada, with General Howard safely behind them. They might have made it, but Howard now called for help from Colonel Nelson A. Miles at Fort Keogh. Wasting no time, Miles led an infantry-cavalry column on a diagonal march northward to intercept the Indians. The Nez Perces crossed the Missouri River at Cow Island, where they found some troopers from Fort Benton guarding supplies recently unloaded from a steamboat. The Indians ran the troopers off, helped themselves to what they needed, and moved on. Knowing that Howard was far behind, the exhausted refugees halted in late September on the northern slopes of the Bears Paw Mountains, only forty miles from Canada. They had no way of knowing that Miles, who had by chance come upon a steamboat that ferried his command across the Missouri, was fast closing in on them.

Miles's cavalry, with Sioux and Cheyenne auxiliaries riding with them, hit the Nez Perce camp on September 30. They captured most of the Indians' horses, but the Nez Perce marksmen made them pay dearly. The soldiers suffered sixty casualties in the charge and lost many officers. Wisely, Miles laid siege to the camp and used his artillery to pound it. In the meantime, he negotiated for their surrender. At one point, Miles deceitfully seized Joseph under a flag of truce, but the Nez Perces simply captured one of his officers and then exchanged him for their chief. As the Battle of the Bears Paw wore on and Howard finally arrived with his army, the chiefs argued over whether or not to surrender. Joseph favored surrender, and with Toohoolhoolzote and Looking Glass dead, he had his way. On October 5, Joseph surrendered his rifle to Miles and Howard. More than four hundred of his people surrendered with him, while others fled with White Bird across the border to Canada. Although it seems doubtful that Joseph really spoke the famous words, "From where the sun now stands, I will fight no more forever," it was a dramatic and poignant moment.

So ended one of the most incredible Indian wars in history, a war in which the Indians far outperformed their white enemies. With the close of the fighting, a new hero passed into the realm of American legend. Chief Joseph emerged from the newspapers of 1877 and lived on in later books and articles as a "Red Napoleon," a military genius who beat the best the United States Army had to offer. Actually, although Joseph was an exceptional man and a great leader, he shared command with other Nez Perce chiefs and did not play a military role in the battles. The Nez

Perces justly deserved their reputation as superb fighters, but in truth much of their success resulted from the bungling of the armies that pursued them.

After their surrender in the Bears Paws, the Nez Perces faced a miserable future. Although Miles and Howard had assured Joseph that his people might return to the Lapwai Reservation in Idaho, the government sent them to Kansas, and later to the Indian Territory of Oklahoma. There, hundreds died of malnutrition and sickness until Joseph, with the help of Miles and others, gained permission to return to the Pacific Northwest. In 1885, Joseph and his band were allowed to live in exile on the Colville Indian Reservation in Washington; Looking Glass's and White Bird's bands returned to Lapwai. Although he tried repeatedly to return to the Wallowas, Joseph was forced to live out his days at Fort Colville, where he died in 1904.

In 1878, the year following Joseph's surrender, Montana saw its last real Indian "resistance." As a result of wretched conditions on their southeastern Idaho reservation, a number of Indians, most of them Bannocks, fled the reserve and fought a series of skirmishes with pursuing armies. Twice the band of well-known Bannock Chief Tendoy entered Montana during 1878, looking desperately for buffalo. Tendoy agreeably allowed military escorts to police his travels and caused no real problems. Later in 1878, however, larger and more aggressive Bannock parties crossed their old hunting trail through Yellowstone Park and emerged on the Clark's Fork of the Yellowstone. By an amazing coincidence, Colonel Nelson Miles was heading toward the park with some of his men for a vacation. With little difficulty, Miles cut off the Bannocks and ended their flight.

THE END OF THE BUFFALO DAYS

Although the Nez Perce and Bannock campaigns signaled the close of organized Indian resistance, friction persisted between Indians and whites. Stockmen and miners, among others, still trespassed on Indian lands, leading to occasional violence and the inevitable demands for punishment. Sitting Bull and his band remained in Canada, and Montanans feared their return. The heart of the problem, however, was conditions on the reservations. The nomadic tribes had not adjusted to reservation life, and the agencies seldom had enough foodstuffs, seed grains, or livestock to care for them. So the Indians continued to hunt buffalo, as they had for generations.

Tragically, the seemingly limitless herds of buffalo vanished in an astonishingly short time, a result of the great hunts of the 1870s and early 1880s (see discussion in chapter 7). Despite warnings from the agencies,

The government opened an Indian school at Fort Shaw in 1893 to educate
Indian children in the ways of white society and to sever their connections
with traditional Indian culture. The school operated until 1910.

the federal government failed to provide for the day when the Indians could no longer depend on the buffalo for food. The consequences were ghastly. Beginning in the winters of 1880-81 and 1881-82, the tribes began to feel the full impact of the buffalo's disappearance, as their hunters returned almost empty-handed. The Indians gathered desperately around the meager croplands and cattle herds at the agencies. But the agencies, starved by Congress and sometimes drained by corruption, lacked the means to sustain the people. In an atmosphere of nightmarish suffering, large numbers of Indians wasted away from malnutrition and starvation. According to John C. Ewers, "Between one-fourth and one-sixth of the Piegans in Montana must have perished from starvation in the years 1883–84." The Blackfeet recall a man named Almost-a-Dog, who cut a notch in a stick for each Indian who died: the notches eventually totaled 555. Mournfully, the Piegans buried their dead on a hill near Badger Creek, which is still known as "Ghost Ridge."

Ironically, as the Indians lost their capacity to make war, the rapidly increasing white community in Montana demanded even greater military protection from imagined attacks. They especially feared the Sioux under Sitting Bull, who remained in Canada with over four thousand in his camp, some of them fugitive Nez Perces and other Indians. Sitting Bull's people generally behaved peacefully, but they perplexed both the Canadians and the Americans. As the buffalo herds began to thin out in Canada, Sioux bands traveled south to hunt on the reservation lands in northern Montana. Inevitably, the disappearance of the buffalo forced these Indians, like the others, to give up the old ways. During 1879 and 1880, most of the chiefs moved back to the United States and went on the reservations. In July 1881, Sitting Bull surrendered; years later, he would die violently on the reservation.

Amid the tension caused by Louis Riel's first rebellion in Canada, the conflicts between Metis Indians and settlers, and the presence of Sitting Bull in the nearby Cypress Hills, the army built Fort Assinniboine in 1879 on the northwestern slopes of the Bears Paw Mountains. This million-dollar installation grew to become one of the major military bases in the West. As earlier posts like Fort Shaw and Fort Ellis were closed down, Fort Assinniboine's impressive brick buildings became the army's nucleus for all regional operations and headquarters for the District of Montana. In 1880, in part as a response to increasing conflict between Indians and stockmen, the army built Fort Maginnis in the Judith Basin, far from the major settlements. Fort Assinniboine, along with Fort Keogh and Fort Custer, and Fort Harrison, built near Helena in 1892, guarded the Montana frontier during its twilight years.

As the Indian wars faded into memory, the same problems that had

This 1890 photograph of the interior of a ceremonial lodge near Crow Agency shows Tobacco Dance musicians, including Long Bear (fifth from left) and Plenty Hawk (fourth from left).

caused them continued to plague the beleaguered Native Americans. The huge, seemingly near-vacant reservations, especially the one located north of the Missouri River, attracted stockmen, farmers, miners, and rail promoters, all of whom demanded that the reserves be scaled down and the lands opened to whites. Governor Benjamin Potts warned federal authorities that cattlemen might "take matters into their own hands" and force a confrontation with the Indians. Between 1880 and 1882, the Crows submitted to the pressure and ceded a right-of-way to the Northern Pacific Railroad, along with 1.5 million acres that miners had long coveted on the western end of the reservation. By 1884, Crow Agency had been moved from the Stillwater River to a location farther east in the Little Big Horn Valley. In 1887-88, the government used its heavy hand to cut an enormous swath of 17.5 million acres from the Blackfeet Indian Reservation north of the Missouri, primarily to provide a corridor for the westward-building Great Northern Railway. Historian Frederick Hoxie has termed the Great Northern the most heavily Indian-subsidized road in America. In return for long-term annuities, the Blackfeet accepted a smaller reserve in the upper Marias drainage. Similarly, the Gros Ventres and Assiniboines were assigned a reservation on the Milk River, and the Fort Belknap Agency was relocated there in 1889. The Montana Sioux joined Assiniboines on the Fort Peck Indian Reservation in the state's northeastern corner.

In addition to these four reserves and the large Salish-Kutenai reservation in the Flathead Valley, the government created a reserve for the Northern Cheyennes on the Tongue and Rosebud rivers in 1884. Following their defeats in 1876-77, the Northern Cheyennes had been sent to live with their Southern Cheyenne kinsmen in Indian Territory, which later became part of Oklahoma. The Indians suffered in that land from inadequate rations and severe sicknesses, and many died. In 1878, declaring that "we are sickly and dying here and no one will speak our names when we are dead," Chief Little Wolf and Chief Dull Knife bolted from their incarceration in Indian Territory and led their people on a dramatic race back to Montana. Many lost their lives during this epic flight, which has become known as "Cheyenne Autumn," but those who survived eventually joined the Two Moons Cheyennes on the Tongue River Reservation.

Reservation life was difficult and degrading for all Indians. Their nomadic, hunting civilization was destroyed, and, like so many other peoples who have seen their cultural heritage shattered, they had great difficulty reorienting themselves. Increasingly during the 1880s, concerned Americans began to conclude that the reservations offered no real solution to the Indians' plight. Idealistic reformers came up with what seemed a better answer: the "allotment" of reservation lands to individual Indians, so that they could learn to become efficient farmers, like other Americans. Reformers hoped the Indians would adjust to white civilization and accept absorption into white society. Some Montanans cheered the prospect. "Give them their lands in severalty," Granville Stuart said in 1885. "This breaks up their tribal organizations and sandwiches them in among the whites where they must learn by force of example." But this so-called solution to the "Indian problem" was a frontal attack on Indian tribal government and culture, for it increased the pressure on them to give up their traditional ways.

This was the philosophy that produced the far-reaching Dawes Act of 1887. The Dawes Act granted plots of land to each member of a tribe—usually 160 acres or more to heads of families, with lesser amounts to dependents and unmarried persons. In order to protect them from swindlers, the law denied the Indians the right to dispose of their land within twenty-five years. The act sought directly to break up the tribal units and declared that, when the Indians became legal landowners, they would also become United States citizens with all due rights. With the dawn of the twentieth century, the allotment process began to take effect on the Indian lands of Montana. The reservations were surveyed and the lands allotted to individuals. In some cases, as on the Flathead Reserve, the lands remaining after allotment were opened to white settlement. In other cases, as at Fort Belknap, they were not.

In the long run, the Dawes Act was a failure. Under its provisions, in Montana and elsewhere, the Indians lost some of their best lands and got little in return. Most Indians did not make the transition from hunters to agriculturalists. They seldom received sufficient resources on the reservations, and most wanted only to return to their old way of life. As the twentieth century began, the Indians passed into the ranks of forgotten Americans. To most white Americans, Indians were the spirited warriors of the 1870s, not the impoverished people isolated on faraway reservations. It would be many years before the United States would again pay attention to what had happened to its Indian population.

CHAPTER 7

Stockmen and the Open Range

JUST as precious metals first attracted a sizable population to western Montana in the 1860s, the more abundant resource of free grass first lured a permanent white population to the eastern plains during the 1870s. Although gold was Montana's initial attraction, as early as January 1863 pioneer James Fergus predicted that much of Montana "must eventually become the great grazing country of the United States." The natural vegetation of east-central Montana—blue gramma, needle-and-thread, buffalo grass, and western wheatgrass—had, after all, supported millions of buffalo for hundreds of years. Because the range lay open, largely unsurveyed, and seemingly free for the taking, stockmen wasted little time in putting it to use.

During the 1870s and 1880s, while the farmers' frontier passed well to the east of the semi-arid Great Plains, the cattlemen's frontier entered east-central Montana from two different directions. An indigenous livestock industry, which had grown up in southwestern Montana during the mining rushes of the 1860s, began probing beyond the Rockies into the north-central part of the territory in the mid-1870s. By 1880, another invasion of stockmen, many of them driving longhorns north from Texas, entered the Yellowstone drainage from the southeast. Like ocean cross-currents, these two advancing waves of the stockmen's frontier met and commingled in central Montana during the 1880s. All across the eastern two-thirds of Montana, cattle and sheep outfits—some of them large, corporate ranches—sprouted like mushrooms, thriving on the free grass of the public domain. The rapid expansion of livestock on the Montana range was made possible by both the destruction of the buffalo and the confinement of Indians on ever-shrinking reservations.

The open-range ranchers prospered for a short while but soon began to fail, as the terrible effects of the "Hard Winter" of 1886-87 and wasteful overcrowding combined to speed the downfall of the open-range economy. Eventually, as the unfenced open-range system proved to be impractical, the pioneer stockmen abandoned it and turned to the closed-range system of bought or leased land that still thrives throughout Montana.

THE FIRST STOCKMEN

Cattlemen actually entered the Montana area before the 1860s gold rushes. Jesuit missionaries and early traders, such as John Owen in the Bitterroot, kept some domestic stock, but the first real trade in cattle resulted from commerce on the Oregon Trail. By the time travelers on the trail reached present-day southwestern Wyoming or southeastern Idaho, their livestock were usually famished. In 1850, recognizing an opportunity, former fur-trader Richard Grant and his sons, Johnny and James, began acquiring cattle through trade, driving them northward into the Beaverhead Basin of southwestern Montana for grazing. The Grants then herded the fattened cattle back to the Oregon Trail the following spring, trading one fresh animal for two that were trail weary. They soon had a sizable herd, and more pioneer stockmen began to join them in the high mountain valleys of southwestern Montana. In 1853, for instance, Neil McArthur and Louis Maillet brought cattle from the Oregon Country, grazed them for a season in the Bitterroot-Missoula area, and then returned them to the Columbia River Valley for sale.

The first miners to enter southwestern Montana found cattlemen already on the scene. On his second trip to Montana, in the fall of 1863, James Liberty Fisk reported cattle grazing on the Morgan ranch in the Prickly Pear Valley and noted that the Grants had several thousand head in the Deer Lodge country. The mining rushes, along with new military forts and Indian agencies, offered the stockmen lucrative markets. Not surprisingly, men like Conrad Kohrs and Philip Lovell gave up the uncertainties of prospecting and turned instead to buying, butchering, and selling beef.

Some of the prospectors-turned-cattlemen did very well. Conrad Kohrs moved from selling meat to producing it. He bought the Johnny Grant ranch in the Deer Lodge Valley in 1865 and soon ranked among Montana's leading stockmen. Eyeing the isolated and hungry mining-town markets, cattlemen began immigrating to Montana in significant numbers from all points of the compass. In the fall of 1864, for example, William C. Orr of the California-based Poindexter and Orr partnership drove a herd into the Beaverhead Valley for wintering. Within a few

Ranch house interior, Powder River. Pioneer ranchers in eastern Montana used cottonwood to build their ranch houses and furnished them with utilitarian equipment and furniture. (Photo by L. A. Huffman)

years, Poindexter and Orr ran one of the territory's largest cattle and sheep operations. Dan Floweree brought a cattle herd from Missouri in 1865; and in 1866, Nelson Story drove the first Texas longhorns into Montana, locating in the Gallatin Valley.

These early outfits relied almost exclusively on the open, unfenced range. Stockmen allowed their animals to fend for themselves and used natural barriers like forests and rivers to limit their movement. Most ranchers cut only small amounts of hay, which they fed mainly to bulls and saddle horses. They usually drove their stock into the high country for summer grazing and saved the valley floors and foothills for winter pasture. Although a few drovers, like Nelson Story and Dan Floweree, brought in Texas longhorns, few of the lanky creatures arrived in Montana before 1880. The vast majority of early Montana cattle were shorthorns, mainly from the Pacific Coast states and Utah. From the beginning, the Montana livestock industry depended on the territorial government for regulation and law enforcement. As early as 1865, the legislature enacted the first law requiring stockmen to adopt and record distinctive brands as signs of ownership. Poindexter and Orr posted the first brand in Montana. In subsequent sessions, the legislators regulated the use of summer and winter pasture, roundups, and the handling of strays.

By the early 1870s rising meat production and the decline of gold mining had produced a glut on the local market and lower meat prices. In May 1874, the *New Northwest* of Deer Lodge estimated that there were seventeen thousand more cattle in Montana than the populace could use; most of the animals were four and five years old. Under the circumstances, Montana cattlemen had to reach out to new markets by driving their stock to faraway railheads. The first long drives took place in 1868, when Montana drovers sold their animals to Union Pacific construction crews in southern Wyoming. Completion of the Union Pacific in 1869 brought railroads within closer driving distance. By 1873-74, Montana herds began to appear regularly at Granger, Pine Bluffs, and Cheyenne, Wyoming. Some Montana cattlemen, like Con Kohrs, joined the Wyoming Stock Growers' Association in order to secure brand inspection from that powerful organization.

Montana cattle drivers also headed northward into Canada. Robert Ford and other Montana herders drove stock up the Whoop-Up Trail and sold it for slaughter to the Royal Canadian Mounted Police and to Indian agencies. Merchant I. G. Baker, among others, secured handsome beef contracts to feed the crews who were building the Canadian Pacific Railroad. And as early as 1872, stockmen like John McDougall moved animals onto the Canadian plains to form the nuclei of permanent herds there. Some ranchers drove their stock to Dakota Territory during the late

Homesteaders and pioneer ranchers on the eastern Montana plains often lived in remote locations, with miles of unimproved gumbo roads between them and the nearest towns. (Photo by L. A. Huffman)

1870s, either to feed the men in the mining camps in the Black Hills or to reach the Northern Pacific railhead at Bismarck. When the Northern Pacific resumed construction westward in 1879, cattlemen increasingly drove their cattle toward the advancing railhead.

The long drives to and from Montana fit the pattern that prevailed throughout much of the West from 1860 to 1890, the halcyon years of the cattle kingdom. In order to move a large herd of, say, twenty-five hundred cattle, an outfit needed as many as twenty men, several wagons, forty or more horses, and a lot of equipment and provisions. Traveling at about ten miles per day, trail outfits often spent two months covering four hundred to six hundred miles. The drovers broke camp at daybreak, grazed their herds on the move throughout the day, with only a brief break at noon, and then stopped early for the evening. Through the night, pairs of mounted cowboys took turns circling the herd, often singing to pacify the animals. "It must never be thought that the cow has a good ear for music," cowboy John Barrows observed. "If this were true, the herd would have been stampeded by his songs."

By the early 1870s, overcrowded and overgrazed ranges and the rising competition for the land by farmers and dairymen began pressuring Montana stockmen eastward and northward, beyond the mountains into central Montana. The well-grassed Sun River Valley served as the main portal for this northeastward movement of the Montana cattle industry. Possibly as early as the fall of 1869, Con Kohrs brought a thousand head onto the south bank of the Sun River. In 1871, rancher Robert Ford established his famous outfit at the Sun River Crossing near Fort Shaw. Eastward momentum carried the pioneer ranchers beyond the Missouri into the sheltered confines of the Smith and upper Musselshell rivers.

William Gordon and others had cattle in both these areas by 1872; and by 1875-76, the Moore brothers, Perry, Sanford, and John, had a sizable herd on the upper Musselshell. Over the next few years, the cattlemen braved Indian raids and pushed inexorably down the Musselshell Valley. Robert Coburn located his famous Circle C Ranch on Flatwillow Creek in 1877. Conrad Kohrs, in partnership with John Bielenberg, also ran cattle in this area. But most inviting of all to the stockmen was the luxuriant Judith Basin, north of the upper Musselshell. Once the Judith was freed of Indian claim, cattlemen rapidly moved in their stock. T. C. Power, the Fort Benton magnate, established his Judith Cattle Company there in the late 1870s. In 1880, Granville Stuart located the famous DHS Ranch—a partnership between himself, Samuel Hauser, and A. J. Davis—on the southeast flank of the Judith Mountains near Fort Maginnis. Well-known pioneer James Fergus located nearby on Armell's Creek.

By the early 1880s the entire central section of the territory—from the

Sun River eastward to Fort Benton, the Judith Basin, and the lower Musselshell—supported large herds feeding on the public domain. For the most part, these ranchers north of the Yellowstone country were men like Granville Stuart, Con Kohrs, and James Fergus—older, well-established Montana operators. Often in partnership with local bankers and merchants, these men raised mostly shorthorn cattle and worked together easily in local stockgrowers' associations.

Interestingly, sheepmen and horse ranchers shared the range with cattlemen. In contrast to some other places, like Wyoming, the breeders of sheep and horses got along reasonably well with cattlemen in Montana, and many operators raised horses, sheep, and cattle together. By the 1880s, Montana had become famous for its fine horse herds. Among the territory's major horsemen were W. E. Larabie of Deer Lodge, J. S. Pemberston and C. E. Williams of Helena, and Nelson Story of Bozeman, who grazed a large herd on the upper Yellowstone.

Violent clashes between cattlemen and sheepmen, the stuff of western lore, did not characterize frontier Montana. Although cowboys customarily expressed contempt for sheepherders and cattlemen sometimes worried about the effects of sheep on the range, documented instances of violence are rare. One such incident was described by Lyman Brewster, who told of cowboys clubbing to death three thousand sheep near Birney in December 1900. Generally, however, there was no trouble because the same capitalists invested in both sheep and cattle. Also, the sheer enormity of the open range made accommodation of the two enterprises possible until the early years of the twentieth century, when settlers began to constrict the range.

Sheep appeared in Montana about the same time as cattle. Jesuit priests raised sheep at St. Ignatius Mission in the 1850s, and flocks of sheep accompanied herds of cattle onto the ranges of southwestern Montana during the 1860s. In 1869, John F. Bishop and Richard Reynolds began the territory's first major sheep operation when they brought fifteen hundred head from Oregon to the Beaverhead Valley. After wintering the animals there, they sold their fleeces to C. A. Broadwater, who sent them by wagon to Utah for rail transport to the East in what may have been the first commercial wool shipment from Montana.

Until the mid-1870s the sheep industry amounted to little in Montana. The 1870 census recorded only 2,024 sheep in the territory, and most of them were in the Beaverhead Valley. During the decade that followed, sheepmen increased rapidly in numbers and holdings, and they followed the same path of geographic expansion into central Montana as the cattlemen did. In 1874, the A. W. Kingsley outfit moved into the area south of the Great Falls of the Missouri, and Charles W. Cook took sheep into the

Sheep raising in Montana expanded dramatically during the 1890s, making the state one the nation's leading wool producers. Tending the millions of sheep on the range required sheepherders, often immigrants who came as experienced herders. (Photo by L. A. Huffman)

Smith River Valley. William and John Smith led flocks into the upper Musselshell country in 1877. By early 1879, according to the *Rocky Mountain Husbandman*, fifteen thousand sheep were grazing on the Smith River and sixty thousand were on the Musselshell.

During these pioneer years, the sheep industry tended to attract more small investors than cattle ranching did. Like cattlemen, woolgrowers relied on the open range for forage, and raising sheep had the advantages of requiring only small original investments and of providing wool clips—the sheared fleece—for extra profit. Well-established Montana investors began to take notice of the potential of the sheep industry, especially when John Healy, a representative of a major wool-purchasing concern, opened a depot at Helena in 1878. Montana investors stocked the ranges by sending buyers generally to California and Oregon, where they bought up to twenty-five thousand sheep at a time. Drovers trailed the sheep to Montana in bands of three thousand to six thousand, at some points stretching out more than fifty miles. Successful miners such as Thomas Cruse, whose Montana Sheep Company located the N Bar Ranch on Flatwillow Creek, and bankers such as John T. Murphy of Helena, whose 79 Ranch ran both cattle and sheep, exemplified this trend. Eager to broaden their range of investments, these local capitalists usually hired experienced stockmen to manage their flocks and paid them with half the annual number of newborn lambs. During the good years, stockraisers profited handsomely.

THE OPEN-RANGE BOOM OF THE 1880S

The great open-range boom of the 1880s was the result of several factors. The rising urban population of the United States and Europe increased the demand for beef, and newly developed railroad refrigerator cars made safe, long distance delivery possible. The resumption of rail-building throughout the West in the late 1870s gave previously isolated stockmen direct access to world markets. And most dramatically of all, the destruction of the immense herds of buffalo and the confinement of the Indians on smaller reservations opened up huge, new expanses of free, publicly owned land for pasturage.

The destruction of the buffalo offers perhaps the most incredible example in all frontier history of environmental devastation. For years before 1871, Indians killed limited numbers of the buffalo, and white hunters took some in order to supply the small market for robes. In 1871, however, tanners discovered a method of treating buffalo hides for use as marketable leather. Seizing the opportunity, hide-hunters, often encouraged by the railroads to clear away the great herds and joined by thrill-seeking "sportsmen," began the great buffalo hunt that contributed to the animals' obliteration. Small hunting parties, often consisting of a hunter, two skinners, and a cook, took to the field for months at a time. Unlike the sportsmen who hunted from horseback, the professional hunters usually set up a stand downwind from a herd, then used heavy-caliber Sharps rifles rested on stick-mounts to slaughter as many as two hundred buffalo at a single stand. The hunting parties used some of the animals' humps for food and shipped the tongues east, where pickled buffalo tongue was regarded as a delicacy. They left the rest of the meat to rot on the prairie. On a spring trip in 1880, Granville Stuart found the plains littered with rotting carcasses all the way from present-day Forsyth to Miles City.

Perhaps thirteen million buffalo grazed the western prairies and hills before the great hunt commenced. But by 1884, the buffalo stood on the brink of extinction. Those who have written about the sudden demise of the buffalo on the plains have always attributed it to the great hunt, a brief and dramatic episode. Hunting increased in intensity throughout the 1870s and climaxed on the northern range during 1881-82. By 1883, it was over. A survey that year counted fewer than two hundred of the shaggy animals in the entire West. In 1884, when the last trainload of hides pulled out of Dickinson, Dakota Territory, the center of shipment for the northern trade, it carried only enough hides to fill part of one car.

But hunting pressure was not the only or even the most significant cause of the destruction of the great herds. Recent estimates of the effect of the hunt indicate that hunting may not even have destroyed numbers equal to the annual increase. A more efficient killer arrived as domestic cattle encroached on the bison's range, exposing the buffalo to cattle-borne contagious diseases that reached epidemic proportions in 1881-82. It was probably this cause, rather than white and Indian hunters, that accounts for the buffalo's sudden and calamitous decline. And there was the added deadly effect that the cattle-borne diseases may have had on the Indians themselves.

Not even the bones would be left on the plains as evidence of the buffalo's once overwhelming presence. For years after 1883, enterprising individuals scoured the prairies to gather up buffalo bones, often firing the grass to uncover their location. The bones had become valuable because they could be used in a sugar refining process and to make fertilizer. In the meantime, the Indians suffered miserably. Little by little, they saw their once-rich hunting lands lopped off the reservations, to the applause of white Montanans and the stockmen.

In 1880, on the eve of the great invasion of cattle that would boom Montana's livestock industry, Granville Stuart toured eastern Montana and found mostly empty countryside. The census of that year recorded only 428,279 cattle and 279,277 sheep in the territory. Most of the stock grazed the ranges of southwestern and west-central Montana. In the far northern, eastern, and southeastern expanses of the territory, Indian removal was just beginning to open vast new areas to herds brought in by stockmen from outside the territory.

The stockgrowers' invasion into eastern Montana after 1880 was part of a general movement of eastern and foreign capital into the lucrative livestock industry. From Texas to Canada, large, corporate ranches spread over the vast western plains. Local promoters, eager to lure outside capital, painted a rosy picture of the profits to be made in ranching. In 1881, two books appeared that brought attention to eastern Montana rangelands: James Brisbin's *The Beef Bonanza; or How to Get Rich on the Plains* and Robert Strahorn's *Montana and Yellowstone National Park*. Quoting experienced ranchers and selecting their evidence carefully, Brisbin and Strahorn assured their readers that small investments in Montana livestock would bring reliable profits of at least 15 percent per year. Outside "experts" sang much the same song. The *Breeders' Gazette* explained how a five-dollar steer could be run for a season or two and then sold for forty-five to sixty dollars. In 1882, the Cincinnati *Gazette* stated categorically: "In the region traversed by the Northern Pacific lie boundless, gateless and fenceless pastures of public domain, where cattle can be grown and fattened with little operating expense save that of a few cowboys, some corrals and a branding iron. There a poor man can grow rich while a rich man can double or even treble his capital."

The big outside investors came from all parts of the country and even from foreign countries. In the summer of 1882, the Nebraska-based Carpenter and Robertson outfit located three thousand head on the Rosebud, and the Niobrara Cattle Company, also from Nebraska, drove ten thousand cattle into the Powder River Valley. The Concord Cattle Company of New Hampshire established itself on the Tongue River. From Nevada came the Scott and Hanks outfit, which drove herds into the valley of the Little Powder. Texas, of course, provided many of the cattle and some of the largest concerns. The Hash Knife spread, possibly the first Texas enterprise north of the Black Hills, based itself at the head of the Little Missouri River. By late 1883 the Hash Knife had moved northward to the Montana-Dakota state line, where it was joined by other Texas outfits like the 777 and the Mill Iron. Soon, more large Texas investors, such as the XIT and the Matador Land and Cattle Company, also moved into Montana.

The established Montana ranchers—many of whom had never seen a longhorn—reacted to the "Texas invasion" with little enthusiasm. John Barrows remembered that when he and other DHS cowboys came to Miles City in the early 1880s and happened upon some of the wiry Texas longhorns, they considered them an interesting curiosity. Probably reflecting a common Montana opinion, Robert Coburn reported the long-horns as being "all horn and bushy tails" and as inferior to the shorthorn stock that he and other "old-time" Montanans were running on the western and central ranges of the territory. With some justification, men like Coburn, who used graded bulls and took pride in the quality of their stock, feared that the imported, low-quality longhorns would overcrowd the range and endanger their quality-bred herds.

These fears point to an interesting result of the open-range boom in Montana: the division between older ranchers, who generally grazed quality shorthorns to the north and west of the Yellowstone River, and the newcomers, many of them Texans, who entered the territory from the southeast and expanded into the far eastern and northern areas. The established cattlemen were usually "she stockmen," who used the ranges for breeding purposes; the newcomers tended to be "steer men," who brought cattle from Texas for maturing on the northern grasslands. Outfits like the XIT, the Mill Iron, and the Matador Land and Cattle Company drove yearlings and two-year-olds north, double-wintered them in Montana and Wyoming, and then marketed them as four- and five-year-olds. These steer operators were generally more speculative than the older Montana ranchers. They ran bigger herds, overcrowded the range, and aimed for a quick profit.

The two groups differed in other, more subtle ways, too. Teddy Blue Abbott, who worked for Granville Stuart and married one of his daughters, noted how Montana-based owners showed more concern for their men and provided them with better food and shelter. The cowhands also differed sharply. As Walt Coburn observed, the Texans, in comparison with Montana cowboys, "were a different breed of cowhand for the most part." They roped differently, handled their horses differently, even dressed differently. The Texans wore drab clothes and chaps, and the Montana hands often adorned themselves in fluffy angora chaps of bright colors.

Tension between the older "Montanans" and the newly arrived "Texans" flared most openly over the question of a "national cattle trail." The Texans and other operators who drove southern-bred stock north for maturing desperately petitioned the federal government to lay aside a broad corridor of land for their use in moving cattle from Texas to the far northern ranges. Established Montanans opposed the idea vigorously. Because they raised their own calves, they had no need of a national cattle trail, and they argued that it would overcrowd the range and introduce longhorn-carried diseases like the dreaded Texas Fever. The Texans never got their national cattle trail, but long drives continued to move cattle into southeastern Montana until well into the 1890s.

Enthusiasm for the livestock business on the frontier also spread overseas. Some of the foreigners who turned up on the Montana range were known by the locals as "remittance men"—rich and adventuresome youngsters who lived mainly off the funds sent to them by their families. But others were serious cattlemen, like French stockman Pierre Wibaux, who built up a large and prosperous operation in the Beaver Valley along the Montana-Dakota line. Englishmen and Scotsmen predominated among foreign investors. By the later 1870s, so much American meat was being imported into the British Isles that a delegation from the Royal Agricultural Commission conducted a full investigation of the western cattle industry. Its report, brimming with enthusiasm over the profit potential of the Plains grasslands, persuaded many British capitalists to invest in livestock. Englishmen controlled many prominent firms, such as the N-F Ranch on the lower Musselshell, the Montana Sheep and Cattle Company, Ltd., and the Chalk Buttes Ranche and Cattle Company, Ltd. Although the enormous Matador outfit was Texas-based, Scottish investors actually owned it.

Foreign capital continued to pour into western ranching until Congress passed a law in 1887 prohibiting aliens from owning any property in the territories. By that time, the inflow of such heavy investments had drastically altered the organization of the cattle business. Before the boom of the 1880s, most Montana cattle operations were partnerships or family affairs, but many of the new outfits were full-fledged corporations with access to plenty of capital and plenty of livestock. Dozens of corporate ranches held Montana charters by 1886; and many others, such as the Texas-based XIT, 777, and Continental Land and Cattle spreads, were incorporated in other states or territories. By 1886, at the peak of the open-range boom, roughly 664,000 cattle and 986,000 sheep grazed Montana rangelands. A large percentage of the animals belonged to the new corporate ranches, whose managers packed them onto limited ranges with no provisions of winter hay, in the hope of quick profits from minimal investments.

Flocks of sheep intermingled with herds of cattle on the booming open range, and throughout the 1880s the sheep population steadily outpaced cattle in growth. By 1890, Montana ranked as the nation's sixth largest sheep producer. Prior to the 1890s, most of the sheep brought to Montana were Merinos from the Pacific Coast, Idaho, Utah, and Nevada. After the decline of wool prices during the Panic of 1893, however, Montana sheepmen would turn increasingly to mutton breeds such as Cotswolds and Rambouillets crossed with Lincolns and Cotswolds to produce better feeder lambs.

By the late 1870s and early 1880s, sheepmen, like cattlemen, were pressing into the far northern, eastern, and southeastern reaches of the territory. The leading pioneer sheepman of northern Montana was Paris Gibson, who founded the city of Great Falls. In 1874, Gibson and his son Theodore moved sheep into the country near present-day Belt, and soon a partnership that included Governor Benjamin Potts located a band of sheep on the Dearborn River. More and more sheepmen pressed into the northern Judith and eastern Musselshell country and, with the removal of the Indians, into the Yellowstone Valley. Even in the frenzied spring of 1876, John Burgess brought eighteen hundred head of California sheep down the Yellowstone to the site of Miles City—and with no trouble from Indians. Many others followed Burgess's example, and the lower Yellowstone became the center of the great 1880s boom for both sheepmen and cattlemen. A. M. and A. D. Howard pioneered the Rosebud country by driving in eleven thousand sheep in 1884; and several large operators, among them W. E. Harris and the Myers brothers, led flocks into the Tongue and Powder valleys south of Miles City. By the mid-1880s, sheep ranches dotted southeastern Montana; an 1884 map of Custer County revealed that one operation in every five raised sheep.

Some sheepmen trailed their flocks through Montana on their way to markets in the Midwest. J. B. Long of Great Falls, for example, bought wethers in Oregon and trailed them through the mountains to north-central Montana. Each spring, he moved his sheep eastward—sometimes trailing as many as 160,000 head—with shearing stops at Malta and Glasgow. In the autumn, he shipped the fattened animals by rail out of Culbertson. Most operations, however, were smaller, less migratory, and more centrally based at one ranch headquarters. Ordinarily, woolgrowers invested prudently in lambing pens, winter shelter, and at least some hay for use in the most severe cold. Herders tended the animals in bands of about two thousand and corralled or posted them at night to protect them against predators. And each June, the managers hired itinerant shearers to handle the wool clip. The shearers were, by and large, a rough lot. According to Walt Coburn, some of the shearers who worked for his father drank a quart of whiskey a day, and many mixed marijuana with their cigarette tobacco.

THE WAYS OF THE OPEN RANGE

Most open-range cattlemen, and some sheepmen, relied entirely on unfenced pasturage for their animals. There were exceptions, of course, especially among the experienced ranchers of the western valleys and the north-central region. Even in eastern Montana, intelligent newcomers like Pierre Wibaux raised enough alfalfa to provide feed for their animals in severe winter weather. But for the most part, the newer outfits, especially the big corporate ranches, made few investments and took few precautions. Each ranch in a given grazing area laid claim to an "accustomed range," which neighbors ordinarily recognized as private property, even though the land was public domain. The accustomed range, however, meant nothing to wandering animals, so local ranchers had to cooperate in segregating animals and determining ownership. This need gave birth to the central institution of the open range—the roundup.

Cattlemen staged two roundups a year, one in late spring and early summer and one in the fall. By the early 1880s, territorial and county laws laid out roundup rules. Cattlemen divided the territory into districts. In 1886, central and southeastern Montana had seventeen districts, each bounded by the natural configurations of the land. The Musselshell Valley, for instance, encompassed two districts, one for the upper drainage and one for the Flatwillow country. And in each district, ranches joined forces for the roundup. The larger roundups were colorful affairs, employing as many as sixty or seventy men and hundreds of horses, with each outfit contributing according to the size of its herd. A roundup captain oversaw the entire operation and held unlimited authority to hire, fire, and command any cowboy from any ranch.

The purpose of the all-important spring roundup was to gather up the cattle that had scattered during the winter, segregate them by brands, and return them to their home ranges. While segregating the stock, the cowboys branded the new calves and tallied the increases of their herds. Often riding as many as seventy or eighty miles a day, the cowboys gathered the cattle in about three weeks. The work of branding and driving the herds to home ranges sometimes carried well into July. As the roundup proceeded, the owners sent representatives—or "reps," as the cowboys called them—to neighboring district roundups to watch for brands from their ranges. Because the "reps" operated under their own supervision and held responsibility for many different brands, they were considered a notch above most hired hands.

The principal task of the fall roundups, which were much smaller in scale than those of the spring, was to select the mature cattle that were ready for market and then trail them to a railhead. In the process, the cowhands branded the calves that had been missed in the spring. After the fall roundup, the owners laid off many of the hired hands, retaining a select few for winter work. Those who found winter employment on a ranch broke horses, patrolled range lines, and worked at general maintenance. Those who were unemployed frequently "rode the grub line"; that is, they bummed food and shelter from one ranch to another.

Because the stockmen and their roundup associations did not own their rangeland, they faced many perplexing problems. Running bulls on the open range caused constant headaches. If any individual rancher ran inferior bulls, or if he ran them at the wrong time of year, all of his neighbors suffered. The handling of mavericks—that is, calves that could not be identified with their mothers—also led to frustration and trouble. In some districts, local custom dictated that a maverick belonged to the owner of the range on which it turned up; but, predictably, this arrangement led to the dishonest practice of "mavericking," or indiscriminately branding any stray calf that turned up. Many open-range ranchers increased their herds by using such methods. In an effort to control the situation, the district associations prohibited the use of branding irons at any time except during the common roundup. Finally, the stockmen found a solution to the problem by declaring mavericks to be the common property of the district associations and selling them to raise money for association expenses.

The roundup associations faced other, larger problems that could not be handled on the local level. To deal with these difficulties, they organized on a territory-wide basis and turned to the government for help. One such problem arose from Indian hunting parties that stole livestock in the absence of buffalo on the plains. Largely to deal with Indian thievery, northern Montana stockmen formed what may have been the territory's first effective regional cattlemen's organization, the Shonkin Association, in July 1881. The Shonkin Association, which covered the Shonkin, Highwood, Belt, and Arrow Creek districts, joined with other groups during 1882-83 to break up Indian camps south of the Missouri and drive their inhabitants back to the north. In October 1883, the newly arrived ranchers in the east formed a large organization of their own, the Eastern Montana Livestock Association, at Miles City. This group also fretted about Indian raids and petitioned the government to provision the reservations more adequately so that their residents would not have to steal.

Since the early 1870s Montana ranchers had been trying, without success, to create a large, territory-wide organization to pursue their interests. With powerful James Fergus providing the leadership, ranchers held a series of meetings at Helena early in 1879 and put together the Montana Stock Growers Association. But that organization, confined mainly to western Montana, faltered until 1884, when it reorganized and began to seek cooperation with the Eastern Montana Livestock Association. Finally, in April 1885, the older stockmen of the Helena group joined the Eastern Montana Livestock Association at Miles City to create a territory-wide Montana Stockgrowers Association. At last, Montana cattlemen had joined permanently in one, big organization. The Montana Stockgrowers Association wielded great economic and political power, but it never quite matched the strength of its Wyoming counterpart,

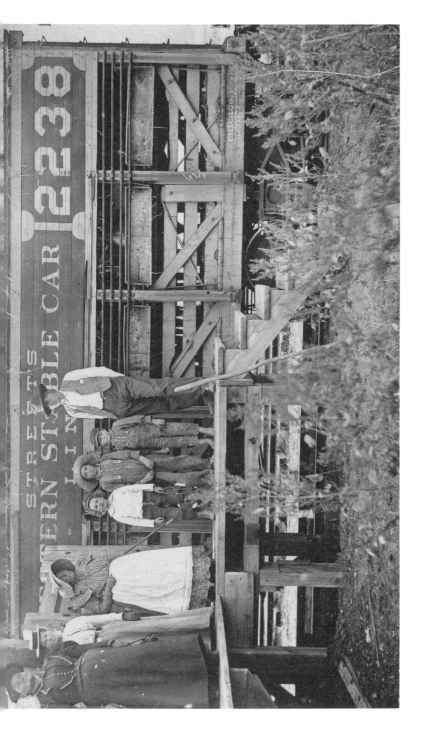

Evelyn Cameron took this photograph of a railroad car full of cattle at Fallon, near Miles City. The construction of transcontinental railroad through Montana in the 1880s helped stimulate the state's cattle boom.

mainly because Wyoming ranchers had no competition from large mining interests.

Montana sheepmen, who faced problems similar to those of the cattlemen, also organized. Although little is known about its antecedents, the Montana Wool Growers Association took shape at Fort Benton in January 1883, with Paris Gibson as its president. The sheepmen had trouble keeping their association going and had to reorganize it in 1895, this time with T. C. Power as president, and again in 1906. These reshufflings lasted until 1921, but the Montana Wool Growers Association still spoke out constantly in the interests of its members, demanding, among other programs, a protective tariff on wool and the establishment of a board of sheep commissioners to help protect the animals against disease and theft.

The open-range cattlemen reached the peak of their power in 1885, the year in which they organized the Montana Stockgrowers Association. That was also the year of the "Cowboy Legislature," when livestock interests had things their own way in Helena. The legislators granted many favors to stockmen that year, such as the law prohibiting branding except during the roundup season. Of special significance, the 1885 legislature created two new functions of government: a territorial veterinary surgeon, who had the power to quarantine cattle, and the all-important Board of Stock Commissioners, which would conduct brand inspection at marketing points and supervise the range industry in general.

But even with support from the territorial government, open-range stockmen faced difficulties that could never be fully mastered, such as the natural and man-caused prairie fires that could destroy their herds at any time. Predators, such as wolves and coyotes, took a heavy toll, and both the territorial government and the associations placed bounties on wolves while ranchers used poison against the animals. Thievery presented the knottiest problem of all, for rustlers could steal stock easily on the unfenced range. By the 1880s, rustling had reached epidemic proportions in southeastern Montana and western Dakota, and it was worse in the Judith-Musselshell areas. Finding refuge in the Missouri Breaks, a motley assortment of unemployed whiskey traders, wolf hunters, woodchoppers, and trappers brazenly stole livestock in Montana and Canada and then took the animals across the border for sale.

In the 1883 legislature, Territorial Council President Granville Stuart and other stockmen had tried to address the problem of theft with HB 49, which would have created a Board of Stock Commissioners with the power to appoint subordinates to make arrests. The bill passed the House by a vote of fourteen to nine and passed the Council by eleven to one, only to be vetoed by Governor John Schuyler Crosby. Crosby did not believe it proper to impose a general property tax to support the single-interest Stock Commissioners. More important, he objected to what he called the "considerable delegation" of executive and legislative powers to the commissioners. The further delegation of power to their subordinates, who Crosby feared "may commit ignorant, corrupt or malicious wrong," created a danger of returning "to the dangerous days of the star-chamber and the Stuarts." The irony of referring to the "Stuarts" was probably unintended.

Like the miners of the 1860s, the cattlemen of the 1880s turned to vigilantism. The problem with theft was a major topic of discussion at the April 1884 meeting of the Eastern Montana Stock Growers Association in Miles City. Hotheads like young Theodore Roosevelt and the Marquis de Mores wanted to raise a cowboy army and rid the region of thieves. Publicly, Granville Stuart stifled such proposals, thereby creating the impression that eastern Montana stockmen would take no action. What he actually wanted, however, was to maintain absolute secrecy and to avoid the publicity that the planned action might attract.

There followed a series of raids in central Montana, in the Powder River country, and along the Little Missouri and Lower Yellowstone rivers. Following the 1884 spring roundup, a group of stockmen in central Montana banded together under Stuart's leadership. Their organization, which came to be known as "Stuart's Stranglers," killed at least fifteen men. In July, they staged a major shoot-out at Bates Point on the Missouri with eleven reprobates who were led by John Stringer (alias "Stringer Jack"). A number of outlaws died that day, and others were later seized from a deputy marshal and hanged. Stuart also joined another group of vigilantes on the lower Yellowstone. That band, whose activities have been lastingly veiled in secrecy, ran a special train down the Northern Pacific tracks, stopping periodically to deal with rustlers. They continued their manhunt in Dakota, and some old-timers figure they killed more than sixty men. James Fergus justified the vigilante killings by reasoning that "we must either gather up what stock we have left and leave the country or gather up these desperadoes and put them where they will kill and steal no more; there is no alternative, and we choose the latter. It is now simply a state of war." The vigilante killings were highly effective as a deterrent to rustling, but, as in the case of the Johnson County War in Wyoming, the stockmen were severely criticized for their arbitrary killings.

In the final analysis, the open-range stockmen faced one insurmountable difficulty: they could not control rangeland they did not own. Few of the big outfits of the 1880s owned much of their "accustomed range." Usually, the owners homesteaded or purchased land along rivers or streams and claimed contiguous rangeland by prior appropriation. Sometimes ranchers had their cowhands file homestead claims on the range and then bought up the claims to form workable landholdings. Walt Coburn remembered that his father located "all the Circle C cowpunchers on the choice bottomlands along the creeks with various springs and water resources within a twenty-five mile radius on all sides of the home ranch."

Montana ranchers found another way to pick up title to rangeland by manipulating the Desert Land Act of 1877. This misguided law, which allowed "farmers" to buy 640 acres for only $1.25 per acre, provided that they irrigated a portion of it, was meant to encourage reclamation and improvement of the arid lands of the West. In practice, however, farmers could seldom irrigate such large plots without government support. Instead, cattlemen often claimed a section of range under the act, made some token effort to irrigate the land, and used it for pasturage until the end of the three-year "prove-up" period. Then they simply forfeited the land to the government, having used it for three years at almost no expense. In another maneuver, stockmen bought or leased sections of land and fenced them in such a way as to enclose public lands as well as their own.

So long as the federal government refused to lease public lands for grazing purposes, a system the Canadian government had found to be practical, open-range cattlemen could not gain firm control of their range unless they bought it or leased it from private landlords. So they "squatted" on their "accustomed range" and protected it as best they could. If an interloper tried to crowd his stock onto someone else's range, local ranchers could refuse to allow him the privilege of belonging to the area roundup district. In 1885, for instance, John H. Conrad, a rancher near Fort Benton, moved six thousand cattle onto rangeland east of the Musselshell River that was claimed by the Niobrara Cattle Company. A fall meeting of Miles City stockmen condemned Conrad for this violation of range law and warned him that they would not handle his stock or cooperate with him in any way. He got the message and withdrew his herd. Such methods were not always so successful, however, simply because the unfenced ranches, especially the large corporate spreads, crowded in and overstocked the grasslands.

As Granville Stuart wrote, "Cattle men found ways to control the other difficulties but the ranges were free to all and no man could say, with authority, when a range was overstocked." So the great open-range boom mounted steadily through the mid-1880s, and the ranges became more and more dangerously overcrowded. At its 1886 meeting in Miles City, the Montana Stockgrowers Association discussed the problem of overstocking with intense anxiety, and during the fall of that year the Little Missouri Stock Growers' Association announced that its members would not cooperate with any more new outfits. Stuart observed: "The range business was no longer a reasonably safe business; it was from this time on a 'gamble' with the trump cards in the hands of the elements."

THE HARD WINTER OF 1886-1887 AND ITS AFTERMATH

Montana cattlemen had seen hard winters before 1886-87. They came through those winters, including the winter of 1880-81, in reasonably good shape, mainly because the ranges were not overgrazed, feed was abundant, and most of the cattle were well acclimated to northern climates. And in those days, before the great open-range boom, a fair percentage of ranchers put up winter hay. But 1886 was different: the plains cattle ranges were recklessly overstocked and prone to disaster. The winter of 1885-86 had been warm and "open," with little snow. A hot, dry summer followed, and by autumn the grass was in poor condition. "Our ranges are already bare," Governor Samuel T. Hauser wrote to the Secretary of the Interior, "or so nearly so that our stock is in poor condition for the winter, and should it prove long and severe great loss must inevitably follow." Still, the range continued to fill. A market glut and falling beef prices in 1885-86 produced a carryover of many steers, which otherwise would have been marketed in the fall. And cattle and sheep poured into the territory in larger and larger numbers. Many of the trail cattle, especially those from the south, arrived late in the autumn, in poor condition to face the winter.

The snow and cold set in during November. Following a brief chinook in January, a long and terribly severe cold spell caked the scant forage with ice. Cold, wind, and snow continued through February, frightfully punishing humans and beasts. Some ranches recorded temperatures of sixty-three degrees below zero. As Joseph Kinsey Howard described it, "Starving cattle staggered through village streets, collapsed and died in dooryards. Five thousand head invaded the outskirts of the newborn city of Great Falls, bawling for food. They snatched up the saplings the proud city had just planted, gorged themselves upon garbage." When chinook winds finally lifted the cold in March, plains cattlemen looked in horror on the results of their ill-planned misuse of the environment. The bloated carcasses of their once-great herds lay scattered across the landscape. For most ranchers it was a wrenching emotional experience. "A business that had been fascinating to me before," wrote Granville Stuart, "suddenly became distasteful. I wanted no more of it. I never wanted to own again an animal that I could not feed and shelter."

The losses were hideous, perhaps 362,000 head of cattle, 60 percent of the territory's beef population. Pioneer sheepman W. O. Pound recalled that in some areas the rotting carcasses were so numerous that it was difficult to find water fit to drink. The losses are impossible to determine accurately, partly because many managers used the winter kill to cover up careless bookkeeping. One ingenious manager was bold enough to blame the hard winter for a loss of 125 percent—50 percent steers and 75 percent cows. West-central Montana ranchers fared much better than the reckless newcomers to the east. From loss rates of less than 40 percent in the valleys of the Sun, Teton, and Marias rivers, the curve reached upward to 90 percent kills on some lower Yellowstone ranches. The winter wiped out many of the speculative, corporate ranches. As creditors demanded liquidation of their assets, these outfits rounded up their remaining steers and shipped them east, furthering the decline in beef prices. A typical casualty was the Niobrara Cattle Company. In the fall of 1886, it listed assets of over a million dollars. By the following spring it had only nine thousand head of cattle left and claimed assets of less than $250,000.

Recovery from the disaster came surprisingly soon. Accustomed to putting up hay, small operators sustained fewer losses than the big, speculative investors. Those who had not experienced large losses were able to buy cattle at low prices in the spring of 1887, as the big outfits threw their remaining cattle on the market in an effort to survive. The winter of 1887-88 was mild, and the following spring brought a good calf crop. A combination of ample rainfall and understocking brought the range back quickly, and the losses of 1887 cut the supply of beef, thus raising prices. Those with financial reserves, intelligence, and stamina stayed on the range, and many prospered. Pierre Wibaux, for example, returned to France, secured further credit, and steadily expanded his eastern Montana herds until he ranked as one of the largest individual cattle owners in the United States. Far more typical, however, was the increase of small operators. Between 1887 and 1889, the number of Montana ranches increased significantly; and by 1890, Montana ranges carried more cattle than before the winter of 1886-87. The acreages devoted to hay crops nearly trebled during the 1890s.

The hard winter broke the back of the open-range empire, but large, unfenced outfits persisted in some areas for years afterward. Cattle drives from the south and west continued to enter Montana throughout the late 1880s and early 1890s. At the same time, further reductions in the huge Indian reservations opened vast new grazing areas to stockmen, especially above the Missouri River. During its twilight years, the open range became increasingly concentrated in northern Montana, especially in that large triangle of land lying between the Missouri River on the north, the

Yellowstone on the south, and the Musselshell on the west—the area that Miles City photographer L. A. Huffman called the "Big Open."

Open-range outfits thrived in the Milk River Valley and other choice northern Montana areas, especially after the Great Northern Railway began serving the region. The North Montana Roundup Association, organized after the open range had declined elsewhere, remained a potent force until well into the twentieth century. The biggest outside corporate operations, such as the Matador and the XIT, continued their open-range grazing. In place of the trail drives from the south, however, they shipped cattle by rail to Miles City or Billings and turned them out on the empty range until the new frontiersmen in bib overalls crowded them out after the turn of the century. Even then, a few persisted. The Matador continued to run open-range cattle on the Fort Belknap Indian Reservation until 1928. But in general the open-range system declined rapidly after the winter of 1886-87. The boom atmosphere evaporated, and the trend toward reckless investment in livestock reversed itself. The hard winter taught everyone the value of winter feed, and hay acreages increased rapidly, from about fifty-six thousand acres in 1880 to more than seven hundred thousand in 1900. Even the larger outfits began to provide feed and shelter for their calves and weak cows.

Another response to the lessons of 1886-87 was the sharp increase in sheep ranching, for sheep had weathered the crisis much better than cattle. Stockmen who had formerly specialized in cattle, like Robert Coburn, invested heavily in sheep. In northern Montana, men like B. D. Phillips and Angus Dunbar ran their flocks over enormous acreages, freed by the recent contraction of the reservations. In 1887, two exceptionally large Montana sheep operations were established. With the backing of New York capital, Lee Simonsen began a large enterprise in the Castle Mountains and the Stillwater country, and Charles M. Bair began building an immense sheep empire based at Lavina, Hardin, and Martinsdale. The sheep population expanded throughout the 1890s until by 1900 it stood at roughly six million head, making Montana the nation's number one wool-growing state. But homesteaders would soon deprive both sheepmen and cattlemen of their choicest grasslands and put an end to the open range.

Like the miners who had come earlier, the open-range stockmen laid one of the cornerstones of the Montana economy. The open range also gave Montana—and the rest of the world—one of our favorite heroes, the cowboy. Ever since he first appeared in late nineteenth century pulp fiction and in Owen Wister's popular novel *The Virginian* (1902), the cowboy has captured the American imagination as the embodiment of free and unfettered manhood. The realities of the cowhand's way of life, however, were hard and monotonous and scarcely warranted such sentiments.

Most cowboys were young, probably in their early twenties, and energetic. Although our folklore fails to say so, they were often either African American or Mexican. Especially when on the trail or during roundups, cowboys worked long days with little sleep. They labored under trying conditions, facing searing heat and bitter cold, drenching rains or snows and choking dust, kicking horses and nervous cattle. For this, they received wages lower than what most workers received in settled areas, thirty to forty-five dollars per month, plus keep. The keep left something to be desired, for the camp cook fed them a steady diet of beef, bacon, beans, bread, and sometimes canned fruit. Canned tomatoes were a luxury and canned milk a miracle.

Cowboys relieved the monotony of their lives with practical jokes and wry humor. They cut loose on infrequent trips to such cow towns as Miles City, Chinook, or Lewistown, where they could find liquor and beer and such exotic foods as eggs, celery, and oysters. Saloons, the cowhands' social centers, offered not only drink but also entertainment and the companionship of prostitutes. In Miles City, the epitome of cow towns, the Cosmopolitan Theater or the Gray Mule Saloon provided popular shows of all kinds. While squandering their pay and raising hell, the cowboys frequently got out of hand and perturbed local residents. According to Nannie Alderson, an astute observer, the residents of Miles City considered cowboys a wild and undesirable lot. "Nice people in Miles City," she recalled, "would as soon have thought of inviting a rattlesnake into their homes as a cowboy." Perhaps reflecting such attitudes, cowboy Teddy Blue Abbott commented that cowhands feared only two things: a decent woman and being set afoot. To be sure, many cowboys had their better side. Most were honest, loyal, and courageous, and most seemed less interested in profit than in seeking adventure.

Despite this hardscrabble existence, the cowboy looms large in America's popular culture. The cowboys would have wondered at their prominence; along with most of their contemporaries, the cowboys saw the bankers and cattlemen as the truly heroic frontier figures. As George T. Armitage, a cowboy for the 79 outfit, put it: "the puncher certainly never thought of himself as romantic. But the new settlers definitely did. They avidly watched our activity." Armitage's observation provides an important clue as to why the cowboy has played such an important role in our folklore. Unlike the colorless and overburdened farmers, cowboys seemed to be the last of the free frontiersmen—mounted, unrestrained, and adventuresome. As America became an increasingly urban and industrialized society, the cowboy became a lasting, romanticized reminder of the way of life being left behind.

Significantly, the cowboy's heyday coincided with Frederick Jackson Turner's pronouncement of the end of the frontier. The conquest of the land that had begun with the founding of Jamestown in 1607 appeared to be at an end. Recognizing this fact, eastern establishment figures such as Owen Wister, Frederic Remington, and Theodore Roosevelt seized on the cowboy as a worthy figure for their writings and their art, and they surrounded the cowboy with an aura of romance. Montanans made their own contribution to this process of romanticization. Writing under the pen name of B. M. Bower, Bertha Muzzey wrote more than five dozen novels of the West between 1904 and 1952, the most famous being *Chip of the Flying U* (1904). The book was illustrated by cowboy artist Charlie Russell, who also contributed heavily to the legend of the cowboy.

Historian Lewis Atherton has reminded us that our preoccupation with the cowboy has led us to neglect the role of the ranch owners themselves, who, after all, made the system work, and the important role that women played on the stockgrowers' frontier. Theodore Roosevelt, a one-time Dakota rancher, put it aptly: "There is an old and true saying that 'the frontier is hard on women and horses.'" Isolated and lonely, ranch women lived in a male-dominated world, dwelling in crude shacks or cabins with leaky dirt roofs and pests such as bedbugs, flies, mosquitoes, and snakes. They often had to haul water a considerable distance and sometimes had to boil it before drinking. Doctors were scarce, and women worried constantly about injury and disease. Those who settled near reservations lived in fear of theft or violence.

Women made the best of a tough situation. Ranchers tried to provide their wives and daughters with such amenities as books and musical instruments, and many of the successful stockgrowers located their families in town. The mail-order catalogues kept women in touch with the larger world, and picnics, parties, and dances broke up the monotony. Hoping for a better future, ranch women tolerated their unenviable situation on the assumption that "civilization" would soon come to them. Perhaps Nannie Alderson best summed up their stoical outlook: "When you live so close to the bare bones of reality, there is little room for sentiment." In contrast to Hollywood myth, life on the open range was hard and demanding.

Yet, the extent to which the demands of ranch life were debilitating varied with each woman's personality. To a Nannie Alderson ranch life was a shattering experience, but others took both the routines and the extraordinary occurrences of ranch life in stride. Recalling the many writings about how pioneer men had made the West safe for women and children, cowboy Floyd Hardin wrote: "In my opinion, the women took quite a hand in making the west safe for themselves and their children." He remembered his mother working as homemaker, nurse, cowhand, and

Madge McLean, Mrs. Kenneth McLean, James Hamilton, and Dot McLean (l. to r.) work at domestic tasks at a sheep camp in eastern Montana. This Evelyn Cameron photograph documents one of the important contributions women made to Montana's agricultural economy.

hunter. It "was all in a day's work for her and her kind, a part of the pioneer women of the West. There are no statues erected for, nor halls of fame dedicated to them, but they had a very big part in the taming of the West and making it a more safe place for the less experienced who were to follow them. We often hear of 'the forgotten man.' In my book, these pioneer women are 'the forgotten women.'"

CHAPTER 8

Railroads, Silver, and Statehood

DURING the decades after the Civil War, railroad-builders turned their attention to the Far West, where stockmen, miners, and town boosters begged for rail connections to eastern markets. To the remote territories of the Far West, the railroads meant everything. Boosters of every region and town prayed and plotted for a railroad that would build to their doorstep and bring them instant prosperity and the guarantee of permanent growth. Ranchers and farmers needed railroad access to reach national and international markets, and mining developers had to have rails to import heavy machinery and to export their precious metals. Once the rails arrived in the territory, a boom in silver mining began that lasted into the 1890s and made Montana one of the leading industrial mining areas of the world. The coming of the railroads, along with the resulting growth of corporate mining and livestock production, led to the flush times of the 1880s and paved the way for Montana statehood in 1889.

NORTHERN PACIFIC AND UNION PACIFIC

The dream of a transcontinental railroad, spanning the continent and linking the Mississippi Valley to the Pacific Coast, had captured men's minds long before the Civil War. But until the southern states left the Union in 1861, jealousies between North and South over the route to be selected made congressional action impossible. Once the South had seceded from the Union, Congress moved quickly to authorize and encourage the building of rails to the Pacific. The first transcontinental was the Union Pacific-Central Pacific line, which reached from Omaha to Sacramento over the old Oregon-California Trail route and was completed in 1869. Both the Union Pacific and the Central Pacific received generous federal aid in the forms of large government loans and huge land grants, which could be sold to defray the costs of construction.

The announcement of the first transcontinental railroad convinced the states and territories far removed from its tracks that they, too, should have lines to serve them. Obligingly, in July 1864, Congress issued a charter for construction of a Northern Pacific Railroad, which would link Lake Superior to the north Pacific Coast. While refusing the railroad the loans that had been granted the Union Pacific–Central Pacific, lawmakers compensated by giving the Northern Pacific the largest land grant in the history of American railroads. In its final form, the Northern Pacific land grant provided twenty sections of land per mile of track built in the states of Oregon and Minnesota and forty sections per mile in the territories lying between those two states. This enormous swath of land, which was granted in alternate, checkerboard sections along each side of the right-of-way, eventually amounted to forty-four million acres. Of this, seventeen million acres were in Montana Territory. Thus the Northern Pacific became, with the exception of the federal government itself, the largest landowner in Montana.

Raising money for construction was difficult in the years following the Civil War. Because the Northern Pacific route crossed a generally uninhabited region, the railroad had little hope of immediate profits. But the land grant offered a powerful lure. In 1870, the great Philadelphia banking house of Jay Cooke and Company, which had handled government loans during the Civil War, agreed to finance construction of the Northern Pacific and floated a one hundred million dollar bond issue to raise the funds. Cooke sold the bonds to over eight thousand investors, and he promoted the Northern Pacific route with such gusto that it soon became known as "Jay Cooke's banana belt." Starting from Pacific Junction, Minnesota, in 1870, crews pressed the rails westward until they reached the Missouri River at Bismarck, Dakota Territory, in 1873.

The enormous expenses involved in such rapid construction proved to be too heavy a burden, even for so great a banker as Jay Cooke. He overextended himself so severely that his bank failed. Its collapse, in turn, touched off a major nationwide depression, the Panic of 1873, which had a deadening impact on all western rail-building. The Northern Pacific fell into bankruptcy. The failure of Cooke and the Northern Pacific deeply distressed the small communities of Montana, who were hard hit by the Panic of 1873 and desperately sought rail connections. "The only hope this Country has," Governor Potts had written in 1870, "is in the Northern Pacific R.R." Suddenly, that hope had faded. Without the railroad, as the *Bozeman Times* put it in 1876, Montana seemed doomed to remain "a dull monotonous Territory, cut off from the world and civilization."

*The construction crews who built the Northern Pacific through Montana,
such as the one shown here just east of Helena, did much of the work by
hand and were composed of many nationalities, including Chinese, Irish,
Norwegians, and Italians.*

Meanwhile, other rail promoters turned their attention toward Montana. For most of a decade, Mormon merchants in Utah had held sway over the markets of southwestern Montana by way of the Corinne-Virginia City Road. After the Union Pacific crossed Utah north of the Great Salt Lake, they could hold their share of the Montana trade by forging a rail spur north from the Union Pacific over the Corinne route, beating the Northern Pacific into the Montana mining region. In the summer of 1871, Mormon investors led by John W. Young, the son of Brigham Young, joined a group of eastern capitalists led by Joseph Richardson to create the Utah Northern Railroad Company, which would construct a narrow-gauge line north through Idaho into Montana.

The Utah Northern also felt the financial squeeze of the 1873 Panic, and to the anguish of Virginia City and other southwestern Montana towns, it crept northward at a snail's pace. By 1874, its tracks reached only seventy-seven miles beyond Ogden to Franklin, Idaho. Recognizing Montana's frustration, Union Pacific executives asked the territorial legislature for construction aid in the forms of tax exemption and territorial bonds, in effect asking Montana to pledge credit to the railroad. Many local businessmen, led by Sam Hauser of Helena, strongly supported subsidies to hurry the arrival of the Utah Northern, and the legislature nearly agreed to grant them. But the subsidies never materialized, partly because the wrangling over north-south versus east-west rail connections set community against community. Local politics, as one observer noted, had turned "red hot." The subsidy bills fell victims to internecine politics, standing, as the *Helena Herald* commented, "as tomb-stones over buried hopes." Critics of subsidy in any form argued that competition between the railroads would bring them into the territory without any financial aid at all. Events proved them right.

Fearful of the resumption of Northern Pacific construction westward, the Utah Northern executives could no longer wait for aid from the legislature. In 1878, Jay Gould and Sidney Dillon of the Union Pacific secured full control of the Utah Northern and reorganized it as the Utah & Northern Railroad. They intended to make the road an adjunct line of the Union Pacific, a feeder that would draw Montana traffic away from the Northern Pacific. Building advanced rapidly, and in 1880 the Utah & Northern reached the Montana line. They built 110 miles into southwestern Montana in 1880, passing through the townsite of Dillon, which was named for the railroad's president, Sidney Dillon. On the evening of December 26, 1881, a night too cold for outdoor festivities, the first Utah & Northern train entered Butte, the railroad's destination. The Utah & Northern-Union Pacific, winning its race with the Northern Pacific, had become the first railroad to enter Montana, and it had captured the fabulously rich Butte mining trade.

The Northern Pacific's Marent Gulch trestle, shown in this F. Jay Haynes photograph of 1883, was one of the road's great engineering achievements.

The Northern Pacific, recovered from the woes of the Panic of 1873, entered eastern Montana soon after the Utah & Northern came in from the southwest. The key figure in reorganizing the Northern Pacific was Frederick Billings, who was determined to forge the road rapidly to the port of Tacoma on Puget Sound. Under the guidance of Chief Engineer W. Milnor Roberts, the road advanced out of Bismarck in 1879. By 1881, construction crews labored along both the Yellowstone River in eastern Montana and the Clark Fork in the west. While work continued, however, a power struggle arose over control of the Northern Pacific.

A group of investors who were interested in Portland, Oregon, and in rail-steamship lines extending eastward from there along the Columbia River feared the plans of Billings and his associates to make Tacoma and Puget Sound their main seaport. The leader of the Portland group was Henry Villard, president of the powerful Oregon Railway and Navigation Company. As a friend of former President Lincoln and the son-in-law of abolitionist William Lloyd Garrison, Villard had excellent political and financial connections. After failing to persuade the Northern Pacific directors to make Portland their major port facility, Villard decided to attempt a direct takeover of the railroad. In 1881, in one of the most spectacular moves in Wall Street history, Villard organized his "Blind Pool," through which he secretly raised eight million dollars to purchase controlling stock in the Northern Pacific.

Villard's maneuver allowed him to take over the Northern Pacific and replace Billings as its president. More of a speculator than a railroad man, Villard set out to invest heavily, build the road quickly, and thus gain the land grant and develop Portland as the terminus of the Northern Pacific. Through 1882 and into 1883, large construction crews extended the line from both east and west. Moving eastward from Washington and Idaho, crews laid rails along the Clark Fork River in western Montana. At the same time, rail gangs moved up the Yellowstone, across the new townsites of Billings and Livingston, through the Bozeman Pass tunnel, down the Missouri system to Helena, and westward over the Continental Divide. The climactic driving of the last spike to complete the Northern Pacific took place in a gala celebration at Gold Creek, Montana, on September 8, 1883. Five excursion trains brought out the celebrities, including former President Grant, who joined in the festivities. The telegrapher's key matched the blows of Villard's sledge as it drove home the final spike.

Montana had ample reason to celebrate in the fall of 1883. By then, two major railroads had linked the territory to the outside world, and a golden age of economic growth seemed near at hand. But the popularity of railroads soon began to fade. Mainly because of Villard's frenzied campaign, the Northern Pacific faced huge debts and severe financial problems. Villard resigned from the presidency of the Northern Pacific in 1884, and a more conservative management began cautiously building branch lines to open up the empty country that the railroad crossed. For Montana boosters, the branch lines inched toward their communities at a disappointingly slow pace.

Local critics also angrily observed how the two railroads in the territory carefully avoided the direct competition that might lead to lower prices. In 1882-83, the directors of the Northern Pacific and of the Utah & Northern-Union Pacific negotiated an agreement specifying that the Northern Pacific would stay out of the rich mining center of Butte if the Utah & Northern would not build northward from Butte to Helena. In order to exchange passengers and freight, the two railroads jointly constructed the Montana Union line from Butte to Garrison. As Montanans well knew and resented, the pooling arrangement meant that rail rates would remain high. But the agreement could only last as long as there was no other competition on the scene.

JIM HILL AND THE GREAT NORTHERN

The vast, windswept High Line of northern Montana, although enclosed in Indian reservations, lay open and inviting to developers. The man who, more than any other, seized this opportunity was James J. Hill. Hill, whom Stewart Holbrook once characterized as "the barbed-wire, shaggy-headed, one-eyed old sonofabitch of Western railroading," was a stockily built man of great forcefulness and ability. A Canadian by birth, Hill came to St. Paul, Minnesota, in 1856. He learned the transportation business from the ground up, first on Mississippi steamboats and later as a freight agent. In close collaboration with Canadian investors, Hill began developing a lucrative steamboat freight route down the rich Red River Valley, which tilts northward along the Minnesota-Dakota line, draining across the Canadian border into Lake Winnipeg.

Hill's prospering freight activities naturally led him into the rail business, and he played an important role in the early building stages of the Canadian Pacific Railroad. His first important entry into the rail business came in 1878, when he joined with a group of Canadian partners to buy control of the St. Paul & Pacific Railroad, an ailing line that reached from Minneapolis to the Red River and aimed northward toward Canada. The main value of the St. Paul & Pacific lay in its land grant, which promised future profits. In 1879, Hill and his partners incorporated the St. Paul & Pacific into the St. Paul, Minneapolis & Manitoba Railroad Company, known popularly as the "Manitoba." The Manitoba quickly laid its rails down the Red River Valley and into Canada. With its generous land grant, its control of a productive agricultural area, and its capable management, the railroad prospered.

Jim Hill's vision extended well beyond the Dakota-Minnesota line. Hill held great hopes for the arid high plains country that seemed to reach endlessly across Dakota toward the Rocky Mountain foothills in central Montana. With the proper promotion, he believed that the prairies could become a rich grain-producing empire, dotted by thousands of family farms. So he pressed the Manitoba's tracks steadily westward across northern Dakota Territory until, by 1886, the railhead stood at Minot, 115 miles east of the Montana line.

In Montana, Hill's nose for investment pulled him toward Butte and the transportation of Anaconda copper. For his part, mining entrepreneur Marcus Daly wished Hill success, especially when Hill promised him rail service at "such rates as will enable you to largely increase your business." Hill had already committed himself to a Montana investment in 1881, when he agreed to aid former St. Paul businessman and Montana sheep rancher Paris Gibson in promoting a new townsite at the Great Falls of the Missouri. And that was only the beginning. With entrepreneur Charles A. Broadwater as his corporate point man in Montana, Hill created the Montana Central, an industrial railroad that would link the westward-building Manitoba road to Butte.

Broadwater headed up the Montana Central; and Hill, taking his advice, pursued opportunities in gold mines near Helena, coal seams east of Great Falls, and investments in Broadwater's Helena bank. Meanwhile, the Hill-Broadwater combine also contorted Helena and Montana politics by splitting up the Democratic alliance of Broadwater, Daly, Sam Hauser, and Martin Maginnis. Hauser operated as the Northern Pacific's man on the scene in Montana, and in that capacity he did the railroad's bidding by trying to block the Montana Central and Hill's other enterprises. He created trouble by challenging Hill's new line in court, by spreading rumors, and perhaps even by sabotaging the rival railroad's operations. Late in the contest, as Montana Central crews approached Helena, desperation got the best of Northern Pacific men, who laid track across the Montana Central right-of-way and parked a locomotive in a futile attempt to block the track-layers.

As Broadwater's crews laid out grades between Great Falls and Helena and located the best route over the Divide to Butte, Hill faced the much tougher problem of persuading Congress to open a corridor through the Indian lands north of the Missouri River. For assistance, Hill turned to another Montana Democrat and erstwhile Hauser ally, former Territorial Delegate Martin Maginnis, who lobbied Congress to open the reservations and who received a handsome retainer for his efforts. President

Cleveland vetoed the first bill, pointedly arguing that "it ignores the right of the Indians to be consulted," but Hill discounted that reason and immediately suspected that Jay Gould of the Union Pacific had played a role in the veto. Hill warned Gould to back off or he would "nail every one of your crooks to the doors of the Capitol by their _____ ears." That warning may have helped, but it was Hill's lobbying efforts that won the day for him in early 1887, when Congress granted the Manitoba its easement through northern Montana's Indian lands. Through all the maneuvering and negotiations, the Indians had no voice at all, as rail ambitions rode roughshod over Native American rights.

What followed ranks as one of the epic chapters in the history of railroading. Beginning in April 1887, huge construction gangs began building the Manitoba Railroad westward from Minot. Hill and his chief contractor, D. C. Shepard, hired veteran contractors who were fresh from building the difficult Canadian Pacific. Eight thousand men worked on the grading crews, and six hundred and fifty more built bridges and laid track. From early May until mid-October 1887, they averaged three and a quarter miles of track a day, reaching from Minot to the Manitoba's rail center of Havre, and from Havre southwest to Great Falls, a total of 550 miles. A month after the Manitoba reached Great Falls, the Montana Central was completed northward from Helena to join it. It had been, as Hill put it, "a long and hard summer's work." The rail connections had an immediate and dynamic effect on Montana. New rail cities like Great Falls and Havre were established nearly overnight. By 1889, when the Montana Central was completed to Butte, Hill could ship the ores of Montana mines directly to the Great Lakes. As a result, the pooling agreement between the Union Pacific and the Northern Pacific broke apart, and Montana freight rates fell sharply. The Northern Pacific cut its Helena–St. Paul rates by a third in reaction to competition by the Manitoba.

With his rails poised along the Continental Divide, Jim Hill still faced the difficult question of whether and how to complete his line to the Pacific. The Northern Pacific completed its Cascade Branch to Tacoma in 1887, gaining a better route to the sea and forcing Hill to make a coastal connection of his own. The main problem was that, with the Northern Pacific's crossing of the Rockies to the south and the Canadian Pacific's route to the north, there was no feasible pass through the mountains, at least none that was generally known.

Hill desperately needed to find a passage through the mountains lying due west from Havre in northern Montana. Legend told of a "lost Marias pass," which had been discovered years before but then forgotten. In 1889, Hill's highly capable location engineer, John F. Stevens, set out to find the elusive passageway. In a terrible December blizzard, so intense that his Indian guide refused to accompany him, Stevens walked into the Marias Pass, at the southern edge of what is now Glacier National Park. Stevens's dramatic rediscovery opened the way to the Pacific, over the easiest crossing of the Northern Rockies. Hill's successor, Ralph Budd, later noted the significance of the discovery:

> The actual location of it [Marias Pass] was at an altitude of five thousand two hundred feet on a 1 per cent grade Westbound and 1.8 per cent Eastbound, and without a summit tunnel. It fully confirmed Stevens' report. At one stroke the discovery of Marias Pass shortened the proposed line to the Coast by over one hundred miles, afforded better alignment, much easier grades, and much less rise and fall.

The path lay open to the sea. Shortly before Stevens's discovery, on September 16, 1889, Hill and his associates had consolidated their holdings into the Great Northern Railway Company. In 1890, the Great Northern formally took over the Manitoba, and with it the Montana Central, becoming the proprietor of 2,770 miles of track. The board of directors of the Great Northern voted at once to "extend its lines westwardly from some suitable point in Montana to Puget Sound." The Great Northern built hurriedly westward from Havre over Marias Pass, down the Middle Fork of the Flathead River to the new towns of Columbia Falls and Kalispell, and then turned northwest to follow the Kootenai River into the Idaho panhandle. Hill's railroad passed through Spokane and crossed the Cascade Mountains to reach Everett, Washington, on Puget Sound in 1893. Great Northern trains soon steamed into the port city of Seattle, Jim Hill's real destination. With justification, Hill could boast to his stockholders that, without a transcontinental land grant, the Great Northern had built a solid line to the Pacific, "shorter than any existing transcontinental railway, and with lower grades and less curvature."

LATER DEVELOPMENTS: THE BURLINGTON AND THE MILWAUKEE

The year of the Great Northern's completion also saw the beginning of a severe nationwide depression, the Panic of 1893. This drastic downturn of the economy spelled disaster for many of the heavily indebted railroads, among them the Northern Pacific, which had never really recovered from the Villard building campaign. For James J. Hill, whose well-managed Great Northern barely came through the panic without going under, the Northern Pacific's bankruptcy presented a glowing opportunity. During 1895-96, Hill and a number of his Great Northern associates, including the powerful banker J. P. Morgan, bought controlling shares of the Northern Pacific and reorganized it under their own management. From that time on, the Northern Pacific and the Great Northern became popularly known as the "Hill Lines," with Hill, the "Empire Builder," as master of the northern transcontinentals.

Meanwhile, yet another major railroad extended its tracks into Montana. The Chicago, Burlington & Quincy Railroad was an older, established midwestern carrier with excellent connections to Chicago, Omaha, and Denver. The efficiently managed Burlington occupied a prosperous area in the Midwest. Pressed by tough competition from transcontinental railroads, however, it needed to lay track to the Pacific in order to maintain itself. Beginning in late 1889, the Burlington extended its main line from Alliance, in western Nebraska, through the Black Hills of South Dakota and into northeastern Wyoming. Its rails reached Sheridan, just south of the Wyoming-Montana line, in late 1892.

For some time, the Burlington directors had considered building their own independent line to the West Coast. A less expensive alternative was simply to extend its tracks northward to connect with the Northern Pacific, if the NP would allow use of its tracks to the west. The two railroads came to terms after the Burlington threatened to build its own line into the lucrative mining areas of Montana if the Northern Pacific did not cooperate. According to their agreement, each railroad would allow traffic from the other over its tracks and into its territories. The Burlington thus gained access to the Northwest Coast, and the Northern Pacific gained an opening into the Midwest. The Panic of 1893 stalled the Burlington for a time, but it reached the Northern Pacific tracks at Huntley, east of Billings, in late 1894. By opening its "Billings Gateway" to the West, the Burlington spared itself the expense of building to the sea. The new line also boosted the economy of the Billings area, especially after the railroad later extended its tracks from Billings-Laurel southward to reach Denver.

For some time, Jim Hill had held an interest in the Chicago, Burlington & Quincy. Unlike the Great Northern–Northern Pacific, the Burlington had a direct connection into Chicago, the rail center of America. It also held the promise of extending Hill's rail empire into the center of the nation. So the Hill-Morgan team set out to buy control of the Burlington. They met stiff competition from Hill's great rival, E. H. Harriman of the Union Pacific; but in 1901 the Great Northern–Northern Pacific jointly purchased control of the Burlington.

Hill had emerged victorious—as the Emperor of the Northwest—but he still faced problems. Failing to gain the Burlington, Harriman retaliated by attempting to buy command of the Northern Pacific. Hill and Morgan were able to stop him, but only at great expense. The solution to such reckless competition seemed to lie in the formation of a holding company, which would weld the northwestern roads together permanently under safe ownership and management. So Hill and Morgan, with Harriman's cooperation, formed the Northern Securities Company, a giant, monopolistic holding company that would formally merge the three Hill carriers. The Northern Securities Company, capitalized at four hundred million dollars, promised Hill and Morgan secure control of northwestern transportation. As J. P. Morgan concluded, it placed these railroads in a firm "with a capital large enough so that nobody could ever buy it."

In Montana and other northwestern states, the creation of the Northern Securities Company brought howls of protest that the rail merger meant monopoly and permanently high prices. Responding to these justifiable charges, the administration of President Theodore Roosevelt charged the Northern Securities Company with violating the Sherman Antitrust Act. In 1904, to the delight of Northwest shippers, the U.S. Supreme Court declared the new corporation an illegal monopoly and ordered it disbanded. In truth, the breakup of Northern Securities made little real difference, for the Hill-Morgan team still maintained control of each railroad concerned. As Hill put it: "Two certificates of stock are now issued instead of one. They are printed in different colors. That is the main difference." A formal merger was postponed for sixty-five years. In 1969, in view of mounting competition from trucks, airplanes, and pipelines, the federal government permitted owners to create the Burlington Northern Railroad, placing the three roads again under one corporate head.

Even after the dissolution of Northern Securities, the Hill-Morgan roads dominated regional transportation. But competition soon arrived in Montana in the form of the Chicago, Milwaukee & St. Paul Railway Company. Like the Burlington, the "Milwaukee Road" was an established midwestern carrier. Fearing that it could not compete with the powerful Hill and Harriman lines unless it built to the Pacific, the Milwaukee management decided in 1905 to build westward to Puget Sound. Rechristened the Chicago, Milwaukee, St. Paul & Pacific, the railroad set to work in 1906 on a 1,385-mile westward extension of its tracks from Glenham, South Dakota. Large construction crews laid tracks rapidly into eastern Montana, entering the Yellowstone Valley near Fallon. Their path then led westward toward one of the Milwaukee's prime objectives, the Musselshell Valley of central Montana, which lay between the domains of the Northern Pacific and the Great Northern.

Part of this promising agricultural area was crossed by the Jawbone Railroad, so named because its owner, Richard Harlow, relied more on fast talk than wage payments to keep his men working. Harlow, who gave his name to the town of Harlowton, had mortgaged his road to Jim Hill, causing problems for the Milwaukee, which desperately needed control of Harlow's line. Despite the threat that Hill might gain control of the Jawbone, the Milwaukee leased Harlow's line and was later able to purchase it outright. The Milwaukee built southwesterly from Harlowton to Butte, north through the Deer Lodge Valley, and west along the Clark Fork and into the Coeur d'Alene mining area of Idaho. By the time the last spike was driven in May 1909 at Gold Creek, Montana, the Milwaukee had reached through Spokane to touch the sea at Seattle.

The Milwaukee ran up huge debts in this great construction program, and it faced hard competition from the Hill carriers flanking it. At the instigation of John D. Ryan of the Anaconda Copper Mining Company, who was also a member of the Milwaukee Road's board of directors, the railroad decided to electrify its tracks from Harlowton across the Rockies to Avery, Idaho. The railroad contracted with various small electric companies, which Ryan was organizing into the Montana Power Company, and by 1916 the Milwaukee had 438 miles of mountain rails electrified with inexpensive power. It was the first long-distance, electrified rail span in America, and it paid off well, both for the Milwaukee and for Ryan's Montana Power Company. But the Milwaukee, locked in hard competition with the Hill railroads and staggering under the massive debt of its western construction, failed to prosper. In 1925, it fell into receivership.

The driving of the Milwaukee's final spike in 1909 signaled the end of main line rail construction in Montana. In the course of thirty years, the railroads had literally transformed the state. They gave birth to important new cities like Great Falls, Billings, and Havre, and they breathed new life into towns already established, such as Butte, Miles City, Bozeman, and Missoula. The railroads spurred the development of Montana's major industries—mining, stockgrowing, and lumbering—and in 1909 they were just beginning to promote Montana to farmers of the United States and Europe. As the nineteenth gave way to the twentieth century, Montanans, like other Americans, became more and more critical of the railroads, and they eventually came to rely more on other forms of transportation. The fact would remain, however, that from 1879 to 1909, the railroads, to a large extent, had built the economy of Montana.

THE SILVER YEARS

Among the Montanans who longed for railroads, no one waited more eagerly than mining promoters. By the depressed 1870s, the easily mined deposits of placer gold had almost played out. Only with rail transportation could the much richer bodies of rock-imbedded quartz gold and silver be developed. These deposits required heavy stamping mills, smelters, and other machinery, as well as ore shipment capacity, which only railroads could adequately supply. These mining operations also required large investments, skilled workers, and intricate new methods of extracting and treating complex ores. Montana miners learned first how to handle quartz gold. Then, mainly after the railroads arrived, they tackled the more abundant but harder to mine veins of silver, whose riches contributed so much to the boom of the 1880s.

The large veins of quartz gold, which through erosion had supplied the glittering placer deposits, usually lay in the same vicinities as the here-today, gone-tomorrow gold camps. Prospectors set to work seeking out the rich quartz deposits, digging them up, and extracting the gold. The first mining of quartz gold in Montana reportedly took place at the Dakota Lode near Bannack. During the winter of 1862-63, William Arnold and J. F. Allen built a crude stamp mill from old freight-wagon parts and began working the Dakota ores. Over a dozen gold mills operated in the Bannack area by mid-1864, possibly two dozen by 1867. The cumbersome machinery for the mills came either by Missouri steamboats or by wagons across the plains.

During the placer rushes of the 1860s, several locations produced significant quantities of quartz gold. One was the Summit District of Alder Gulch, the site of F. R. Steel's Mountain Sheep Vein, and the Oro Cache, Lucas, and other lodes. To the north, Silver Star on the Jefferson River became a center of quartz gold output, as did Radersburg. Helena became the early center of quartz gold milling, and it drew most of the gold from its southern hinterland. Even as placer output near Helena began to decline, quartz lodes like the rich Whitlatch Vein and the deposits in Oro Fino and Grizzly gulches poured their riches into the future capital city and gave it a new lease on life.

Most of Montana's early mills handled "free milling gold." This was rich, oxidized ore that lay near the surface and could easily be recovered by milling and amalgamation, without roasting or chemical treatment. Even so, development was painfully slow. The United States Mint reported in 1867 that the output of quartz compared with placer gold in Montana was so small that it could not be estimated. In 1870, the census listed 172 underground miners in Montana, all of them working in four mines near Helena and eight others in Madison County.

Until the early 1870s, Montana miners paid little attention to the silver ores that were frequently intermingled with the gold. Silver, after all, was harder to treat and of less value than gold. Montana's first recorded silver discovery occurred in 1864 at Argenta, near Bannack. Silver mining progressed slowly, partly because silver ore bodies were amalgams of lead and zinc, base metals that were difficult to separate from silver. It meant the construction of costly mills and smelters, and few were willing to take such risks. As late as 1874, United States Commissioner of Mining Statistics Rossiter Raymond observed that Montana had "not been fruitful of inventions and improvements in mining. Its isolated and remote position has caused it rather to lag behind other mining regions of the country, even in the adoption of improvements already known."

Local silver promoters faced many other problems besides metallurgy. The most serious was transportation. Montana's isolation meant that machinery and construction materials had to be freighted in, with great difficulty and at high cost. The Missouri River provided the best freight route; but steamboats could reach Fort Benton only a few months out of the year, and the freight had to be transshipped more than a hundred miles from the port to the mining areas. There was also a lack of skilled labor. Placer miners formed a highly unreliable labor force; they were unskilled at deep mining and usually unwilling to work for any but the highest wages during the warm season. But above all, the promoters of industrial mining needed capital—capital to invest in the mines, in stamping mills, in smelters and concentrators. Because investment capital was scarce on the frontier, mining promoters usually had to lure outside investors and convince them that the high risks of investing in unproven mines would pay off.

Among the first and most influential of Montana's silver promoters was Samuel T. Hauser of Helena, the territory's most powerful capitalist. Drawing on his family and business connections in Missouri, Hauser helped organize the St. Louis and Montana Mining Company in 1866. The firm invested thirty-six thousand dollars in machinery and equipment and constructed Montana's first silver smelter at Argenta in December 1866. To manage operations, the firm employed August Steitz and Philip Deidesheimer, the inventor of the square-set timbering that was first used in Nevada's Comstock Lode. The St. Louis and Montana Company soon gave up its Argenta operation to concentrate on its investment at Flint Creek, west of Deer Lodge.

At Hauser's direction, Deidesheimer inspected the Flint Creek area and recommended investments there. The company bought up several claims, including the Hope Lode. In 1867, Deidesheimer completed construction of the James Stuart Mill, named for its superintendent, the brother of Granville Stuart. The Stuart Mill employed the pan amalgamation process and was the first mill of its type in Montana. To serve the local mill and mines, the town of Philipsburg, named after Deidesheimer, grew up at Flint Creek and by 1867 had six hundred inhabitants. But the local veins proved disappointing, and the Stuart Mill shut down in 1868. The St. Louis and Montana Company, which reorganized in 1872 as the Hope Mining Company, laid off all its employees except for the few it kept on at the Hope Mine. Philipsburg nearly became a ghost town during the 1870s, but with an increased demand for silver it boomed back to life in the 1880s.

The Panic of 1873 sharply curtailed the mining of quartz silver and gold in Montana. Outside sources of investment dried up, and the vital railroads lay stalled faraway. But even during hard times, some Montana promoters persisted, and limited amounts of high-grade ore found their way to Fort Benton and Corinne during the mid-1870s. From these points, the Montana ores went clear to California, Germany, and Swansea, Wales, for smelting. In the meantime, Montana miners stockpiled lower-grade ore until either railroads or local smelters could make its treatment possible.

By 1875-76, the worst effects of the depression were wearing off, and the mining horizon began to brighten. Concentrators at Argenta converted low-grade ore into first-class shipping product, and the growth of a silver industry in Utah brought final treatment facilities closer to the territory. Montana's silver output for 1875 nearly doubled that of 1874. More and more experienced silver miners, many of them foreign born, began immigrating to Montana from that center of American silver mining, the Comstock Lode. As the great Comstock declined, highly skilled workmen, especially the Cornishmen ("Cousin Jacks"), headed for the land of new opportunity and brought their desperately needed talents with them.

It was at this same time, the mid-1870s, that the inconspicuous little town of Butte began its rise, eventually to become Montana's greatest silver and copper producer. Butte began as a placer gold camp in 1864, but its shallow diggings and remoteness from a water supply supported only limited growth. The Butte–Silver Bow camps reached their peaks in 1867 and then faded rapidly. Prospectors near Butte found promising quartz lodes from the start, but the gold was difficult to mill and remained largely neglected.

William L. Farlin was the first to recognize that silver, not gold, held the key to Butte's future. Farlin, a typically restless placer miner, first drifted into the camp in 1864. Over the next decade he moved about constantly, but he never forgot the silver leads that he had seen at Butte. He returned late in 1874, and in early 1875 he located a lead that he called the Travona. Recognizing that his ore would have to be treated on the spot in order to pay returns, Farlin began building the Dexter Mill. At about the same time, Helena merchant John How started work on his Centennial Mill. Both the Dexter and the Centennial began operations in 1876. When Farlin failed to make payments on his loans, Deer Lodge banker William A. Clark took over operations of his Travona-Dexter properties and built them into big-time producers.

By the centennial year of 1876, Butte's fame was spreading. Visiting the camp in July, R. N. Sutherlin of the *Rocky Mountain Husbandman* found this "quartz eldorado of the great North-West" to be a beehive of activity, as new silver mines like the Lexington and the Nettie were beginning to produce. In August, an event of major importance occurred: the highly respected miner Marcus Daly arrived in town. Daly, a veteran of the Comstock, went to Butte to assess local silver properties for the Walker Brothers of Salt Lake City, prominent bankers and mining investors. Taking their agent's advice, the Walkers purchased the Alice Mine, and they hired Daly to manage it. These events held much significance. They heralded the arrival of big-time investors from the outside and brought one of the world's greatest miners to Montana.

The arrival of the railroad in western Montana during 1880-83 boomed the already rising silver industry. Improved transportation brought many new ore deposits within range of smelters and reduction works. More important, it allowed the finished metals from the new plants to enter the stream of national commerce on a large scale. In 1880, before the railroad arrived, Montana produced less than three million dollars in silver, roughly 7 percent of United States production. By 1883, the territory ranked as the nation's second largest supplier of silver, a position it maintained until the mid-1890s—except for 1887, when it ranked number one. Montana produced about one-quarter of the nation's silver in 1889, and from 1890 through 1893 its annual silver output averaged about twenty million dollars. With the fantastic increase of deep silver mining came a rebirth of gold mining, for veins of gold, zinc, lead, and other metals intermingled with the silver. By the late 1880s, Montana had shifted between second and fourth ranks among American gold producers.

In addition to Butte, which was very much *the* silver town in Montana, the industry also centered at the booming towns of Philipsburg and Helena. The key figure in the 1880s rebirth of Philipsburg was Charles D. McLure, who became superintendent of the Hope Mine in 1877. McLure played a major role in organizing both of Philipsburg's renowned silver firms, the Granite Mountain Mining Company and the Bi-Metallic Mill. For a time, each outfit was a fantastic producer. At its peak, Granite Mountain may have been the world's greatest silver mine. One large, picturesque town sprawled across the Philipsburg-Granite-Clark area. By the early years of the twentieth century, the mines of the Philipsburg district had yielded an estimated thirty-two million dollars, most of it silver from Granite Mountain.

Helena, already flanked by active gold and silver mines, enjoyed a major quartz boom when the Northern Pacific arrived in 1882-83. Marysville, a few miles north of the city, became a major gold-mining center, and it was there that Thomas Cruse discovered his fabulous Drumlum-

Wickes, one of several camps in the silver mining region south of Helena, is a classic example of how important rail connections were to industrial growth in Montana. The Northern Pacific had reached the town one year before F. Jay Haynes took this photograph in 1886.

mon Mine in 1876, which he named after his native parish in Ireland. The Drumlummon, which eventually yielded nearly sixteen million dollars in gold and silver, was the greatest gold mine in Montana's history. In 1883, Cruse sold the mine to the Montana Company, Ltd., one of over thirty British corporations that invested in Montana mining. As so often happened with great ore bodies, the Drumlummon became the object of a long-term legal argument over ownership. The courtroom fight for the Drumlummon, waged between the Montana Company and the St. Louis Mining and Milling Company, began in 1889 and lasted for more than twenty-four years, costing the Montana Company over four hundred thousand dollars in lawyers' fees.

Many rich silver lodes lay to the south of Helena. Large deposits at isolated and remote Elkhorn, which were developed by Helena tycoon Anton M. Holter and later purchased by British capitalists, created a bustling mining camp that at one time had passenger train service three times a day. During the late 1870s, energetic Sam Hauser shifted his focus from Philipsburg to the mines south of Helena and set to work consolidating claims and organizing eastern investors. In 1876, a syndicate of Montana and New York capitalists headed by William Wickes had formed yet another Montana Company and built an elaborate reduction-smelting works at the town of Wickes. The Wickes complex came under the control of Hauser's Helena Mining and Reduction Company, and it became the center of operations throughout the region. Ores were sent to the Wickes smelters from as far away as the Coeur d'Alene district of Idaho. In addition to its own mines, the Comet and the Alta, the firm relied on dozens of other small mining concerns to keep it supplied with ore from the surrounding area.

Although the heart of Montana's silver industry lay in a triangle joining Butte, Philipsburg, and Helena, silver towns sprouted randomly elsewhere. Two major silver centers, Lion Mountain and Glendale, were developed in the Big Hole country west of present-day Melrose. At Glendale, the prosperous Hecla Consolidated Mining Company paid dividends every year from 1881 until its demise in 1901. The silver boom also reached across the Missouri River into the Little Belt and Castle mountains of central Montana. Several silver towns boomed in the Little Belts, including Barker, Hughesville, and especially Neihart. The remoteness of the area retarded its growth until the smelter at Great Falls was completed in 1888 and the Great Northern's Belt Mountain branch opened it to the outside world. Southward in the Castle Mountains, promising silver-lead deposits began to attract population during the late 1880s. The town of Castle arose to serve the area, and the Cumberland Mine there thrived for a time. But rail service did not reach the area in time to help its development, and the Castle Mountains boom, like that in the Little Belts, collapsed quickly in the mid-1890s.

By focusing exclusively on the great operations, like Granite Mountain, it is easy to lose sight of an important aspect of the silver boom: silver, unlike copper, attracted many small operators. Especially during the later 1870s and early 1880s, dozens of small outfits, some with fewer than ten employees, survived in the business. Although outside capital was involved in Montana quartz mining from the beginning, local residents, most of them men of limited means, clearly controlled the industry. Of the sixty-eight deep mines reported in the 1880 census, not one was foreign owned, and over 84 percent of the capital invested in local mines came from local sources. Even in 1890, at the peak of the silver boom, two-thirds of Montana's seventy-five active mines produced less than a hundred thousand dollars worth of ore annually, and only eight yielded more than five hundred thousand dollars during the year.

Inevitably, as Montana's silver boom reached major proportions, the big investors came to dominate the scene. Some of the big-time silver men were local magnates, like Sam Hauser and the Butte silver-copper baron William A. Clark; but most were outsiders, locally faceless individuals who poured money into silver firms that promised a quick profit. The states providing the largest investments in Montana quartz mines included Minnesota, New York, Missouri, Utah, Colorado, and California. Throughout the 1880s and early 1890s, more and more foreign capital, especially British capital, poured into Montana mining investments. The large outside-owned mining corporations, such as the British-controlled Montana Company, Ltd., or Butte's Colorado Smelting and Mining Company, led in local efforts to professionalize mining. They brought in college-trained foremen and superintendents from such prominent centers of mining and metallurgy education as Freiburg, Germany, and New York's Columbia School of Mines. The English often refused to invest in American mines unless an experienced Cornish expert was placed in charge.

Silver mining was always a fragile and risky business. Because so much silver was sold for use as currency around the world, prices rose and fell sharply according to the monetary policies of various nations. The great western silver boom coincided with a worldwide increase in silver production and a subsequent steep decline in price. Silver that had sold for $1.30 per ounce during the early 1870s dropped to $.935 by 1889. Nonetheless, Montana's mines continued to increase production, even though the demand for silver coins steadily decreased. Watching boom turn to bust, western producers wailed at Congress for relief and succeeded in cajoling it to pass the Sherman Silver Purchase Act of 1890, which essentially pledged the government to purchase all of the domestic output. Silver prices climbed immediately to $1.21 per ounce in September 1890. But investors had begun to discount silver and to horde gold as a hedge in a faltering economy, and the artificial prop could not long stand. When gold reserves fell too low in the federal treasury early in 1893 and when Great Britain closed its silver mints in India in mid-year, the price fell through the floor to $.62 per ounce, triggering a national panic.

The Panic of 1893 devastated the silver industry of western America. President Grover Cleveland had become convinced, rightly or wrongly, that the silver purchase program was the prime cause of the depression. The president called a special session of Congress in mid-1893 and prevailed on the lawmakers to repeal the Sherman Silver Purchase Act and end the mandatory government purchases of silver. As silver prices plummeted, the effect on such mining states as Montana, Colorado, Idaho, and Nevada was quick and disastrous. One mine after another shut down, some never to reopen. The Wickes plant closed in 1893, and the company dismantled it. In August 1893, the great mining-smelting operation at Granite ceased operations. The management tied down the plant's steam whistle as a shrill, frightening announcement that employment was ended. According to some contemporaries, as many as three thousand people left the Granite-Philipsburg area within twenty-four hours.

The silver bust did not knock down all of Montana's mines. Silver deposits typically lay near the surface, so major producers during the 1880s had already begun mining marginal veins when the depression hit. But mines such as those in the Lump Gulch District near Clancy, the Nettie in Butte, and the Hope in Philipsburg had richer ore bodies, and they continued producing throughout the 1890s. At the Drumlummon and other larger mines, where silver commingled with gold, silver production also continued. But most of the silver mines failed, some permanently and some later to reopen when prices climbed again to profitable levels. For instance, a reorganized combination of the Granite Mountain and Bi-Metallic companies resumed mining in 1898, only to close down again in 1905 due to renewed price failures. At various times during the twentieth century, such as during the mid-1930s, rising silver prices have breathed new life into Montana's sagging silver industry. But in the broad perspective of the state's history, the age of silver ended abruptly during the mid-1890s. Once-great silver camps, such as Castle, Granite, and Elkhorn, became fascinating ghost towns, whose collapsing stamps and smelters remind us of past glories. After 1893, silver came to be for the most part a mere byproduct of large-scale copper mining at Butte.

The 1884 Constitutional Convention, which convened in Helena and included entrepreneurs William A. Clark, Marcus Daly, Matthew Carroll, and T. C. Power as delegates, wrote a document that ultimately served as a model for the successful constitution five years later.

THE WINNING OF STATEHOOD

To frontier westerners, who felt neglected and left out of national political life, statehood signified a "place in the sun," a recognition of their coming of age as a community. Statehood meant more concrete benefits as well. Once a territory became a state, it gained full representation in Congress, full power to tax local corporations, large grants of land to support education, and other functions of state government. Most important, statehood meant that local citizens could elect their own executive and judicial officers, thus ending the long procession of federally appointed "carpetbaggers" whom Washington had sent to govern them.

Montana's first try for statehood, under Acting Governor Meagher in 1866, had been premature and impossible from the start. The territory had simply lacked the necessary population and political maturity. During the 1870s, economic depression and sagging population temporarily cooled the fires of statehood sentiment. But by the early 1880s, the arrival of the railroad and the booming quartz mining and livestock industries combined to send Montana's population soaring and breathed new fervor into hopes for statehood. From a mere 38,159 in 1880, the territory's population climbed to a respectable 132,159 in 1890. By the close of the boom decade of the 1880s, Montana's treasury held an impressive surplus of over $130,000.

With good reason, Montanans believed by 1883 that they had a solid case for admittance to the Union as a state. Completion of the Northern Pacific Railroad that year strengthened their argument. It also whetted their appetite for statehood, for only states had the legal authority to tax that great landholding railroad. Surely, if Montana drafted a proper state constitution and presented it to Congress, the lawmakers must respond favorably. This logic moved the 1883 legislature to call a special election for delegates to a constitutional convention. Following a November 1883 election, forty-one delegates assembled at Helena on January 14, 1884, to convene Montana's second constitutional convention.

The men of the 1884 constitutional convention had been elected on a nonpartisan basis, and they now organized themselves in the same manner. Naturally, mineowners and stockmen had strong representation, and Butte mining king William A. Clark was elected president of the gathering. The convention met for twenty-eight days and produced a charter that drew heavily from precedents found in existing state constitutions. In the general election of November 1884, the voters ratified the document by an easy margin, 15,506 to 4,266, a degree of approval that demonstrated the voters cared less about the constitution than about its function as the key that would open the door of statehood.

Montanans suffered a cruel disappointment, however, when Congress failed to approve their request. The problem in Washington arose not from any fault in Montana or its constitution, but from political considerations. As a result of the 1884 election, the two national political parties faced each other in delicately balanced competition. While the Democrats controlled the House of Representatives and the White House under Grover Cleveland, the Republicans held a majority in the Senate. Several western territories were clamoring for statehood, and neither political party would allow a new state into the Union that had voted regularly for the opposition. Among the territories in question, the Republican majority in the Senate wanted to confer statehood on Republican Washington Territory and also to admit Republican Dakota Territory as not one, but two states (to allow four Republican senators from the two Dakotas). The Democratic House of Representatives opposed the plan and favored statehood instead for the Democratic territories of New Mexico and Montana.

Political considerations, as usual, prevailed. Various efforts at compromise failed, and from 1885 through 1888 the Republican Senate regularly blocked the pleas of any Democratic territories seeking statehood while the Democratic House held back the Republican territories. The logjam finally broke when, in the election of 1888, the Republicans scored a clean sweep. They won control of both houses of Congress and elected Benjamin Harrison to the presidency. Realizing that the Republicans had only to await the seating of the new Congress to have their way, the outgoing, lame-duck Democratic majority in the House gave up the fight. They agreed to allow statehood to Republican Washington and to a North and South Dakota, while denying it to Democratic New Mexico.

As for Democratic Montana, the Republicans were willing to allow it admission, too. They knew that the railroads were bringing in more and more Republican immigrants from northern states and that Montana might soon show a Republican majority. Congress acted speedily, and on February 22, 1889, outgoing President Cleveland signed into law the so-called Omnibus Bill. The bill was an "enabling act" that, in effect, notified North Dakota, South Dakota, Washington, and Montana that, if they drew up proper constitutions, they would be granted immediate statehood.

The Northwest was jubilant, for the citizens knew that statehood lay within their immediate reach. The federal Alien Land Law, passed in 1887, added to their desire for haste. The law restricted foreign investment in the territories but not in the states, and it threatened to cut off needed overseas investors from entering the Montana mining industry. Following a special election in May, Montana's third constitutional convention opened its deliberations on July 4, 1889. This time, in contrast to

Joseph K. Toole,
Montana's first state governor

Wilbur Fisk Sanders,
a Republican stalwart and one of
Montana's first U.S. senators

Martin Maginnis,
Helena Democrat

Paris Gibson,
Great Falls Democrat

1884, the delegates were elected and organized on a partisan basis. The close political balance, thirty-nine Democrats and thirty-six Republicans, indicated the rising power of the Republicans. As in 1884, mineowners and stockmen were well represented, and, as before, W. A. Clark won election as presiding officer.

The constitutional convention of 1889 did its work in an orderly manner, with a minimum of discord. No one wanted a fight over the constitution that might cause its defeat and thus delay statehood. Using the 1884 constitution as a starting point, the delegates in committee put together a document typical of its time. Fearful of arbitrary government, they sharply limited the authority of the governor and the executive branch. On only one major issue, apportionment in the state senate, did the delegates divide bitterly. The less populous counties, which were for the most part those in eastern Montana, demanded that each county be allowed one, and only one, state senator.

Although such an arrangement was obviously anti-democratic, the small county delegates argued that only this protection would allow them any voice in government. Otherwise, the large mining counties could always outvote them in both houses of the legislature. The big counties fought back, but they realized that their smaller neighbors might reject the whole constitution over this issue. So they gave in, and the rural counties won over-representation in the Montana legislature. Otherwise, the delegates held down controversial issues. They voted against woman's suffrage, mostly out of fear that they might offend male voters and thus jeopardize the constitution and delay statehood. Fearing also the emotional issue of the permanent location of the state capital, they decided to leave that issue to the voters in a future election.

The mining interests had things pretty much their way in the convention. With little debate or acrimony, they managed to imbed in the constitution the same sort of "net proceeds" tax they had inserted in the 1884 document. The measure exempted unmined ore from taxation, which meant that mineowners would pay taxes only on ore extracted and on surface land, buildings, and machinery. Surprisingly, the non-mining delegates offered little protest to this tax advantage. They apparently agreed that mining must be encouraged, at all costs, in order to build up the state economy. One wonders whether anyone winced when W. A. Clark, a mining millionaire himself, offered the delegates this tongue-in-cheek justification of mining-caused air pollution:

> I must say that the ladies are very fond of this smoky city, as it [Butte] is sometimes called, because there is just enough arsenic there to give them a beautiful complexion, and that is the reason the ladies of Butte are renowned whereever [sic] they go for their beautiful complexions. . . . I say it would be a

great deal better for other cities in the territory if they had more smoke and less diphtheria and other diseases. It has been believed by all the physicians of Butte that the smoke that sometimes prevails there is a disinfectant, and destroys the microbes that constitute the germs of disease . . . it would be a great advantage for other cities, to have a little more smoke and business activity and less disease. . . .

After six weeks of work, the delegates produced a state constitution. On October 1, 1889, Montanans approved it overwhelmingly, by a vote of 24,676 in favor to a mere 2,274 opposed. The populace cared little about the substance of the new constitution, viewing it primarily as a means to achieve immediate statehood. Federal approval of the Montana constitution followed quickly, and on November 8, 1889, President Harrison formally proclaimed Montana the forty-first state of the Union. After twenty-five years of frustration as a territory, Montanans celebrated their coming of age as a state.

Unfortunately, the happy consensus Montanans displayed on the statehood question did not extend to other issues. In the same October 1, 1889, election that so resoundingly approved the constitution, the voters divided evenly and heatedly along party lines. Democrat Joseph K. Toole beat Republican Thomas C. Power by fewer than a thousand votes to become Montana's first state governor. And by a less than two thousand-vote margin, Republican Thomas Carter downed Martin Maginnis to become the lone congressman.

Incredible as it seems, fierce partisanship literally destroyed Montana's first state legislature. As a result of the extremely close 1889 election, the state senate divided evenly, with eight Democrats facing eight Republicans and the Republican lieutenant governor holding the tie-breaking vote. In the house of representatives, twenty-five Republicans faced twenty-five Democrats. But a crucial five seats were disputed because of irregularities in Silver Bow County Precinct 34, where each party accused the other of manipulating the election returns. Due to legal confusion over how such disputes should be settled, both parties laid claim to the five seats. Whoever gained them would control the house. More to the point, whichever party gained them would control the joint balloting of the legislature in choosing Montana's first two United States senators. The stakes were high.

In the end, Montana legislators allowed partisanship to overcome good sense and disgraced themselves. Because neither the Republicans nor the Democrats would give up the five contested house seats, each party met in separate chambers in order to protect its five elected members in Precinct 34. In effect, the state had two houses of representatives, and they continued to meet separately throughout the ninety-day session, from

November 23, 1889, to February 20, 1890. Meanwhile, the state senate also deadlocked. Attempting to stop the Republicans from organizing the senate and then joining their colleagues from the house to elect the two United States senators, the senate Democrats refused at first to take their seats. Then, under legal compulsion, they attended but refused to vote for organizing the senate. When the Republicans counted them as present but not voting in order to organize the upper chamber, the Democrats refused once again to attend. Incredibly, the senate president finally ordered arrest warrants for the missing Democrats, who promptly fled to avoid capture. Before he could escape, Senator W. S. Becker was caught at Glendive, taken to Helena, and released on the promise that he would remain. Becker then departed for Idaho, where Montana officers could not touch him.

As a result of this foolishness, the first Montana legislature accomplished almost nothing. Each of the two houses of representatives passed bills, but the deadlocked senate failed to enact them. The main bone of contention all along, of course, was choosing the United States senators. Acting on advice from their friends in the U.S. Senate, both the Democratic and the Republican factions met separately, and each elected two United States senators. The Republicans chose Wilbur Fisk Sanders and T. C. Power, and the Democrats elected W. A. Clark and Martin Maginnis. Then Montana calmly sent the four senators to Washington, leaving the final decision to the Senate itself. Since the Republicans controlled that body, they seated Sanders and Power and sent the two Democrats home.

These ludicrous events severely embarrassed the new state of Montana, and they made for a rough start on the road of self-government. The legislators raised real doubts about their own integrity, and badly needed laws had to await the convening of the second legislative session. When the second session met at Helena in January 1891, the stigma of the previous session's nonsense remained, as the deadlock over the Silver Bow members continued. As Helena politico Richard Lockey lampooned the situation: "We are convinced that our insane department is improperly managed, as seventy-five lunatics are abroad who labor under the hallucination that they were elected to the state legislature." The stickiest issues before the legislature, once it organized in February 1891, were the division of the spoils of statehood and the location of state institutions, particularly the state capital. The state capital fight would play an important role in the political war between copper barons William A. Clark and Marcus Daly, but the squabbling over other state institutions was nearly as intense.

Each region and each major town in the new state vied for the state university, the agricultural college, the normal school, the mental hospital, the school for the deaf, and other institutions. As representatives of each locality hurled threats and allusions to conspiracies and suspicions of bribery, political rhetoric again descended from decency. And once again, the legislators failed to make any decisions. During the 1893 session, the legislature courted disaster again and nearly tore itself asunder trying to select a replacement for the United States senator who had drawn the short term in 1890. Republicans and Democrats split on vote after vote, with the mutually antagonistic forces loyal to Clark and Daly providing most of the fireworks. The Republicans finally prevailed and selected a compromise candidate, Lee Mantle of Butte. Mantle had won out over the lackluster Wilbur Sanders, but he might as well have stayed home. The Democrat-controlled U.S. Senate refused to seat him, leaving Montana under-represented in Washington.

The deplorable politics of Montana's first years of statehood were not all disastrous. Because of the indefatigable labors of Will Kennedy, a political reformer from Boulder, Montana became the first state to adopt and use the Australian or secret ballot. And the 1893 legislature finally succeeded in siting all state institutions except the capitol—locating the state university in Missoula, the agricultural college in Bozeman, and the normal school in Dillon. Nonetheless, the early 1890s did not see fair winds blowing across the "Treasure State." And even darker storm clouds loomed on the horizon.

CHAPTER 9

Copper and Politics, 1880-1910

THE small community of "Montanians" who lived in Montana in the 1870s, gripped as they were by the hard times following the Panic of 1873, had one overriding obsession: to lure big outside investors whose capital meant prosperity. By the late 1870s, the investors had begun to arrive and were pouring their money into livestock production and quartz silver mining. But events during the 1880s and 1890s proved that copper, not silver, was the real key to Montana's mining future. The massive copper deposits of Butte brought some of the world's greatest capitalists onto the Montana scene, and they, in turn, brought development and a measure of prosperity. Then "big money came to Butte," as K. Ross Toole wrote, and the state enjoyed its benefits. Unfortunately, the Treasure State also had to pay a high price, for copper came to dominate its economy and to rule the roost politically, sometimes with grim results. Today, the copper dome atop the capitol in Helena symbolizes the legacy of the days when copper was king.

THE RISE OF KING COPPER

Butte began as a middling gold camp in the 1860s, nearly faded into oblivion, and then came to life again with silver mining in the mid-1870s. Even as silver rose to dominate Montana mining, the ever-deepening mines of Butte proved to be richer in copper than in any of the other commingled metals. As new technologies such as the electric light and the telephone drove up the value of copper, Butte developers began to mine and market the red metal. They hauled their ore to Utah and shipped it from there to such distant points as Newark, Baltimore, and even Wales and Germany for processing. But high freight rates ate up the profits. So Butte mineowners stockpiled the ore and waited eagerly for the rails and machinery to reach them.

The man who waited most anxiously, and who read the future of Butte most clearly, was William Andrews Clark, who lived the classic rags-to-riches success story on the Montana frontier. Born in Pennsylvania, Clark moved as a youngster to Iowa and later followed the mining frontier to Colorado. From there he traveled with several companions to the boom-town of Bannack, arriving in 1863 when he was only twenty-four years old. Clark was a small man, with pinched and delicate features and cold, penetrating eyes. But beneath his unimposing exterior worked a remarkably keen mind; he was a financial genius and had a hard and ruthless ambition. "Inordinately vain," wrote C. P. Connolly, "he loved the flattery and adulation of women. He was a Beau Brummel in the midst of the awkward inelegance of the West."

With an unfailing instinct for profit, Clark moved quickly from prospecting into a variety of business investments—hauling produce from Utah, carrying the mail from Walla Walla, merchandising in Helena. By 1872 he had moved to Deer Lodge where, with two partners, he opened a profitable bank. Butte, with its depressed but valuable mines only forty miles from Deer Lodge, attracted Clark irresistibly. He invested heavily in silver-copper properties, picking them up at ridiculously low prices, and he persuaded a group of Coloradoans to join him in a large-scale smelting enterprise. Remarkably, even while pulling together these multifarious holdings, he managed to work in mining and mineralogy studies at New York's Columbia School of Mines. Clark's mines, smelter, banks, and other investments made him, at a very young age, one of the leading capitalists in the Mountain West, and surely one of the most egotistical and ambitious. He longed, according to those who knew him, to be Montana's richest man and its most prestigious statesman.

Clark's great rival-to-be, Marcus Daly, came to Butte in 1876 at the age of thirty-five. A stocky, likable, and gregarious Irishman, Daly had immigrated to America in the 1850s and had followed the mining frontier to California. Working in the bowels of Nevada's great Comstock Lode, he learned the ins and outs of hardrock mining. Daly came to be known as a "miner's miner," an expert whose "nose for ore" and practical knowledge of geology and mining methods won him considerable prestige. The wealthy Walker brothers of Utah hired Daly and sent him to Butte in 1876 to assess the potential of the Alice Mine. Knowing that Daly represented outside capital, Butte's newspaper, *The Miner*, welcomed him as "the best miner who has ever been in Montana."

Daly remained in Butte to manage the Alice property for the Walkers, and he was soon convinced of the hill's richness. Eager to strike out on his

Marcus Daly   *William Andrews Clark*

In 1884, the construction of the huge Washoe Smelter on Warm Springs Creek in Anaconda brought large-scale industry and the attention of eastern and foreign investors to Montana. (Photo by N. A. Forsyth)

own, he sold the interest he had acquired in the Alice and invested it in the Anaconda Mine, a silver operation on the southeastern side of the Butte Hill. The Anaconda had been developed by Michael Hickey, who had named it after General Winfield Scott's famous strategy of wrapping the Confederate army in a snakelike grip. Daly poured thirty thousand dollars into the mine, but he needed large-scale support to convert the Anaconda into a major producer. Breaking with the Walkers, Daly turned to some powerful friends, the "Hearst-Haggin-Tevis syndicate" of San Francisco. These men—George Hearst, the father of William Randolph Hearst, James Ben Ali Haggin, and Lloyd Tevis, who eventually became chief of banking at Wells, Fargo—ranked among the West's most powerful capitalists. They knew and respected Daly, and they readily joined him in the Anaconda enterprise. The Hearst-Haggin-Tevis syndicate, joined by Daly as an occasional fourth associate, would eventually extend its control over one hundred different mines, including America's greatest copper producer (the Anaconda), greatest gold property (the Homestake in South Dakota), and greatest silver mine (the Ontario in Utah).

With almost limitless backing, Marcus Daly rapidly developed the Anaconda. The mine proved, like others in Butte, to be much richer in copper than in silver. In late 1882, at the three-hundred-foot level, Daly's men struck a copper glance of remarkable richness and purity. As they soon learned, the Anaconda contained the richest bodies of copper sulphide the world had ever seen. Daly had the foresight to anticipate the expanding market for copper; and his partners, especially Haggin, had enough confidence in him to pour millions into a copper venture that was entirely new to them. By early 1883 they had driven the Anaconda shaft to the six-hundred-foot level, where the copper vein widened to one hundred feet and 55 percent in purity. When Daly sent some of the ore for treatment to Swansea, the experienced Welsh copper men wrote back expressing their amazement at its richness.

Daly feverishly bought up the properties adjoining the Anaconda. According to Butte legend, he first assured their owners that the Anaconda was not proving out and then acquired the adjacent mines cheaply. Fully supported by his partners, Daly poured over fifteen million dollars into new mines and the highly expensive facilities to treat their ores. A twenty-stamp reduction mill was built at Butte to handle the silver, but the heart of the syndicate's copper investment took shape on Warm Springs Creek, twenty-six miles west of Butte. There, where there was plenty of water, the partners built in 1883-84 their massive copper reduction works and the Washoe Smelter, the greatest of its kind in the world. There, too, arose the small city that Daly would have given the tongue-twisting name "Copperopolis" had not another Montana burg pre-empted that title.

Daly called the town Anaconda, and it became one of the classic "company towns" of the American West. Anaconda was Marcus Daly's bailiwick, his pride and joy. He chose the townsite personally and dominated its management. He built the Montana Hotel there (later renamed the Marcus Daly), famed for its beautiful Victorian bar and its enormous dining room, where Daly often dined alone in regal splendor. Except for escapes to his magnificent ranch in the Bitterroot Valley, where he raised some of America's greatest race horses, Daly spent most of his time at Anaconda. By 1894 the little Butte, Anaconda & Pacific Railroad—which never quite made it to the sea—shuttled back and forth, carrying the Butte ores to Anaconda for treatment.

Year by year, Daly steadily expanded his operations. He invested heavily in Montana and Idaho timberlands to provide fuel and lumber for his mines and smelters. He bought up coal fields in Montana and Wyoming. Like Clark and the other mining barons, he imported thousands of laborers, engineers, and hardrock miners. Many of them, especially Daly's men, were Irish, either straight from the Emerald Isle or by way of Nevada, Colorado, Utah, or California. Increasingly in the mid-1880s, as the great silver mines of Nevada faded out, large numbers of Cornishmen began to arrive in Butte. The "Cousin Jacks" were the aristocrats of metal mining, and they often clashed with the "Micks." There were others, too: English, Germans, Finns, Chinese, and, by the 1890s, Italians and Eastern European Slavs. Butte-Anaconda, East Helena, and Great Falls became "melting pots," where diverse nationality groups mingled, played, and fought with one another. But the Irish, with their strongly held Catholic and Democratic beliefs, usually prevailed, sometimes resenting and making life uncomfortable for those who came later, as in this bit of Butte verse:

> O Paddy dear and did you hear the news that's goin' round?
> They're firin' all the Irish that are workin' underground.
> Oh I've rustled at the Belmont, and I've rustled at the Con.
> And everywhere I've rustled they're puttin' Bohunks on.

Immigrant workers left a lasting imprint on western Montana, especially in Butte and Anaconda. Butte rose to fame as one of the toughest, most picturesque towns in America. It had Finntown and Chinatown, Slavic and English districts, and the suburbs of Meaderville, Dublin Gulch, and the remote neighborhood of "Seldom Seen." Beneath the somber gallows frames that towered over the mineshafts, Butte had some of the most famous saloons, gambling dens, and whorehouses in the

The electrification of Butte's mines increased production and introduced a new generation of machines that made miners more efficient but also put them at greater risk of accidents.

United States. Not surprisingly, Butte came to dominate the new state of Montana, and it held that dominance until the middle of the twentieth century. Writing in the 1940s, Joseph Kinsey Howard could still refer to Butte as the "black heart of Montana."

The hardrock miners, especially the veterans from Nevada and California, brought labor union loyalties with them, and they soon made Butte a "Gibraltar of Unionism," one of the strongest labor bastions in America. Labor first raised its head in Montana during 1878, after the Walker brothers and other employers had selectively cut wages from $3.50 to $3.00 per day. Led by Aaron C. Witter of Indiana, the real "father" of Montana unionism, local miners organized the Butte Workingmen's Union, with Witter as president and a constitution based on Nevada precedents. The organization became the Miners' Union of Butte City in 1881 and welcomed all laborers into its ranks.

Unionism registered few gains in Butte until the mid-1880s, when the booming copper industry formed a large and highly skilled proletariat. By 1885 Butte had become the greatest mining camp in the West, with the largest army of organized miners—eighteen hundred strong. In that year, the union reorganized once again, this time as the Butte Miners Union, which was strictly a miners' organization. Other workers formed their own unions and joined the BMU in creating the Silver Bow Trades and Labor Assembly in 1886.

Led by Cornish miners like William Penrose and Irishmen like Peter Breen and Patrick Boland, the Butte Miners Union sometimes rocked with tension between the English and the Irish. But it made solid gains, winning the closed shop in the Butte mines by 1887. Much of the BMU's strength and success arose from its friendly relationship with management. Marcus Daly easily identified with his men, and they with him. Arguing that contented employees meant safer profits and bigger gains than could be had by exploiting labor, Daly stoutly resisted any efforts to cut wages or discourage unionism. Other local employers, like W. A. Clark, generally shared Daly's paternal attitude toward labor. Until the turn of the twentieth century, Montana workers benefited from working mostly for locally managed operations. They earned comparatively high wages; and, in contrast to miners in Idaho or Colorado, they usually refrained from strikes and violence.

The Butte Miners Union steadily expanded its authority into other Montana camps, such as Granite and Neihart, and it became the pacesetter of mining unionism for the entire Mountain West. Montana revealed the full measure of its union strength in May 1893, when delegates from throughout the West met in Butte and founded the Western Federation of Miners. The Western Federation was launched, with the BMU as Lo-

The city that Butte's copper deposits created, as seen here in 1890, became one of the most famous mining camps in the world, noted for its multicultural population, labor solidarity, and wide-open lifestyle. (Photo by F. Jay Haynes)

cal Number One, in an effort to bring all western metal miners into one big organization. Although it gained a reputation for toughness and violence in states like Idaho, Colorado, and Utah, the Western Federation of Miners enjoyed peace and political harmony with the mineowners in its Montana birthplace. Unionism thus came early and peacefully to Montana, and peace would prevail as long as Marcus Daly was in charge of Anaconda.

When the Anaconda Reduction Works began full production in late 1884, Montana moved rapidly into the forefront among copper-producing states. At first, though, it seemed that the Anaconda partners stood little chance of breaking the powerful Michigan producers' hold on the American copper market. Backed by Boston investors and led by the great Calumet and Hecla Company, the Lake Superior operators enjoyed heavy advantages over their western competitors. The Michigan copper was high-grade ore compared to the generally mid-grade Montana deposits. Furthermore, the Lake Superior mines enjoyed the advantages of being well established and lying in closer water and rail proximity to the major eastern markets.

But the Anaconda partners had less obvious factors working in their favor, too. They had a modern and highly efficient plant, capable of mass producing the red metal at a low cost. They enjoyed ready and inexpensive access to such vital raw materials as coal and wood, and they had almost unlimited capital reserves to fund their copper operations. Calumet and Hecla thus ran into trouble when, beginning in 1883, it attempted to close down the Anaconda upstarts by driving down the price of copper. Prices fell from eighteen cents a pound in 1883 to ten cents in 1886; but to the amazement of many observers, Anaconda continued to expand production. Daly's highly efficient reduction, concentration, and smelting plants allowed him to maintain operations, and the price war forced only a momentary shutdown in Montana. The price war became even more complicated when a group of French speculators attempted to corner the world market. They failed, and so did Calumet and Hecla's effort to drive Anaconda from the field. In 1889, the war ended with a negotiated agreement to peg the price of copper at twelve cents a pound. By then Montana was producing 43.3 percent of the nation's copper, compared to Michigan's 38.7 percent. The Treasure State ruled supreme, and it would continue to do for the next two decades, until the booming open-pit mines of Arizona and Utah would catapult those two states into the lead.

Although the Anaconda Company was establishing itself as the nation's leading copper producer, other large investors were also moving into Butte copper mining. Their operations, combined with Anaconda's, made Butte-Anaconda the greatest metal-mining center in the United States by the 1890s. The powerful Lewisohn brothers of New York, for instance, joined Boston copper men to found the Boston and Montana and the Butte and Boston Consolidated Mining Companies. The Boston companies poured large investments into both Butte and Great Falls and gained control of some of Butte's greatest mines, such as the Leonard, Mountain View, East Colusa, Gambetta, and Michael Davitt properties. Also prominent among Butte mineowners were the colorful millionaire James Murray, the Heinze brothers of New York, and William A. Clark. The tightfisted Clark owned a sizable share of Butte's silver and copper wealth, as well as the Centennial and Dexter mills, the Butte Reduction Works, a hardware firm, electric and water utilities, and a great deal of real estate. In addition, the Midas of the West was building a new financial empire around his phenomenally rich United Verde Mine in Arizona.

Towering over all of these stood the giant Anaconda, the undisputed master of Montana mining. The Panic of 1893, which toppled so many silver producers, did much less damage to the copper market. In fact, the panic strengthened the local position of the copper industry by destroying the silver operators and leaving silver as primarily a derivative of copper mines in the Treasure State. The Anaconda underwent a highly significant series of reorganizations during the 1890s. In 1891, the year George Hearst died, the Anaconda's owners incorporated for the first time, taking the name Anaconda Mining Company and issuing capital stock to the sum of twenty-five million dollars. Assessing the corporation, renowned mining authority Hamilton Smith called it "the most extensive mining property in the world." The firm reorganized in mid-1895, this time as The Anaconda Copper Mining Company, with James Ben Ali Haggin as president and Marcus Daly as superintendent. "The Company," as Montanans called their home-state colossus, would retain this title until 1955, when it renamed itself simply The Anaconda Company.

Few Montanans understood the importance of this incorporation, for management remained in the hands of Haggin and Daly. But the incorporation and issuance of stocks meant that "outsiders" would now share in, and might possibly gain control of, the firm. During the last years of the nineteenth century, control of American industry was becoming increasingly concentrated in fewer and fewer hands. It is hardly surprising that the lucrative Anaconda got caught up in this monopolistic trend. In 1899, executives and directors of the powerful and much feared Standard Oil Company—led by Henry H. Rogers, William Rockefeller, and A. C. Burrage—purchased control of the Anaconda Copper Mining Company. These men already dominated the petroleum industry through Standard Oil, and now they aimed to extend the same kind of control over the rapidly expanding copper market.

Determined to corner Montana copper, and ultimately world copper production, Rogers and his associates had first bought heavily into the stock of the Anaconda and the Boston and Montana and Butte and Boston companies. Then they merged the last two firms. When they purchased the Anaconda outright in 1899, the Rogers group created the Amalgamated Copper Company as a "holding company" to control the Anaconda and the other firms they planned to add to it. They floated seventy-five million dollars in Amalgamated stock to fund the venture. In one of the most notorious chapters of Wall Street history, they soon manipulated down the price of Amalgamated stock to squeeze out and fleece stockholders. Then they bought it back cheaply.

What did all of this mean to the Treasure State? As Montanans soon learned to their sorrow, it meant plenty. It meant that the industry that dominated their economy had passed out of the comparatively benevolent control of Marcus Daly and J. B. Haggin and into the hands of a group of corporate executives who were notorious for their ruthless dealings. Haggin sold out his Anaconda interest for fifteen million dollars. Daly became vice-president of the new Amalgamated holding company. But it meant little, for he was a dying man. The real power lay in the hands of the president of Amalgamated, Henry Rogers, and its secretary-treasurer, William Rockefeller, the brother of John D. Rockefeller. The significance of the Standard Oil group's takeover of Anaconda would soon become appallingly clear. To understand that significance, we must first examine the political results of the rise of King Copper.

POLITICS: COPPER KINGS AND POPULISTS

The 1890s was perhaps the most turbulent period in Montana's political history. During those years, two major political developments combined to scramble party lines and disrupt affairs of state: the famous "Clark-Daly Feud," and the less famous rise and fall of the Populist party. The legendary struggle between mining barons W. A. Clark and Marcus Daly apparently began at an early date. One story has it that their mutual hatred began as early as 1876, when Clark's bank refused to accept a draft from Daly in his purchase of the Alice Mine. Another identifies their first disagreement with Clark's fleecing of Daly when he purchased water rights on Warm Springs Creek. Other accounts recall such petty issues as Clark's supposed reference to J. B. Haggin as a "nigger" or Clark's childish envy of Daly's mining reputation.

Whatever the original provocation, rivalry between two such powerful men may have been inevitable. For a time, Clark and Daly cooperated in their common financial interest—for example, at the 1884 constitutional convention. They became known, along with Helena capitalists Samuel Hauser and C. A. Broadwater, as the "Big Four" of the ruling Democratic party. The factor that turned the Clark-Daly feud into an explosive issue was Clark's unquenchable thirst for the glories of public office. Although Daly found ample satisfaction in business achievement and in such gentlemanly pursuits as horse breeding and racing, Clark desired a seat in the United States Senate as the crowning achievement of his career. His desperate efforts to gain that position would polarize and disgrace Montana politics.

Clark first tasted public acclaim as Montana's centennial orator at the Philadelphia Exhibition in 1876, and he clearly relished the praise he received as a constitution-maker in the 1880s. In the election of 1888, Montana's last as a territory, Clark went after federal office for the first time and secured the Democratic nomination as delegate to Congress. The nomination, in a territory famed for its Democratic leanings, should have assured his election. When the votes were tallied, however, Clark learned that he had lost by over five thousand votes to a less than renowned Republican named Thomas H. Carter. Clark had suffered a humiliating defeat, and he never forgot it. Clearly, Marcus Daly had played a hand in upsetting him, although other factors, such as Clark's antagonizing the Irish, were also involved. Those counties that the Anaconda Company "controlled"—Silver Bow, Deer Lodge, and Missoula—went Republican, even though all were confirmed Democratic areas.

Daly may have acted out of spite in opposing Clark, but he also acted in self-interest. Along with the Northern Pacific Railroad and a group of Missoula capitalists, in 1882 Daly had created the Montana Improvement Company, a lumber firm that became a vital supplier of timber and fuel to the Anaconda Company. This outfit, like others in the West, ran afoul of federal laws that prohibited lumbering on public lands, laws often violated in the absence of accurate surveys. Federal lawsuits against the Montana Improvement Company resulting from these violations posed the direct threat of cutting off the Anaconda's access to cheap timber. Reading national political trends accurately, Daly and his associates foresaw that Republican Benjamin Harrison would probably win the presidency in 1888. If he did, Democrat Clark would stand little chance of getting the lawsuits withdrawn, but Republican Carter might prove to be effective. Thus, Daly's backing of Carter made political sense. Although the Montana Improvement Company and its successors continued to face federal litigation for many years, Congressman—later Senator—Thomas Carter proved to be an unfailing friend to Marcus Daly.

Daly acquired a friend in Carter, and he also acquired a bitter enemy in W. A. Clark. With a fair measure of truth, Clark's newspaper, the *Butte*

Miner, accused Daly and his friends of "influencing" their employees to vote Republican. In response to Clark's attacks, Daly employed an experienced and capable New York newspaperman, John H. Durston, to establish a paper that would present his viewpoint. Durston's paper, the *Anaconda Standard*, gained wide recognition as a well-edited sheet. But the *Standard*, like the *Miner*, often seemed less concerned with reporting the news than with advancing the interests of its owner. Unfortunately for Montana, the press was becoming a weapon of the warring copper kings.

W. A. Clark unflinchingly continued his quest for high political office. Statehood made two seats available in the United States Senate, which was sometimes referred to as the "Millionaires' Club." In 1890, Clark was one of two Democrats sent to the Senate by Montana's fractured first legislature. Once again he tasted defeat as the Republican majority in the Senate accepted the two Republican senators and sent the Democrats home. The persistent Butte mining king got his next chance during the legislative session of 1893. Throughout the sixty-day session, rumors abounded of vote-buying by the Clark and Daly forces. On the last day of the legislature, Clark sat in the front row of the assembly, ready to deliver a speech of acceptance. Amid great excitement, however, he fell three votes short of victory. The legislature adjourned without choosing a United States senator, and Montana had only one man in the Senate until the lawmakers met again in 1895. In addition to corrupting politics, the mining barons had also cost the state its proper representation.

These burning defeats proved nearly unbearable to the vainglorious Clark, but he finally gained his chance for revenge during the election campaign of 1894. The 1889 constitution had left the permanent location of the state capital up to a vote of the people. The 1892 election had failed to produce a majority vote for any one city, so a runoff election in November 1894 would determine the issue. The contenders were Helena, the "temporary capital," and Anaconda, which Daly mightily wished to make the center of state affairs. Clark stepped forth as the champion of Helena, not just to spite his foe, but also because he had investments there, the loyalty of Helena's people, and strong financial and political allies among them.

The contest turned into a wide-open frontier Donnybrook. Pointing to the obvious danger of placing the seat of government in a company town, the Clark-Helena forces dwelt on the feudal hold that the Anaconda Company supposedly had on its workers. The proponents of Anaconda answered, less persuasively, by ridiculing Helena's social airs, its cultural pretensions, and its black and Chinese elements. Helena, they intimated, was a sissy and un-American town! Playing on the prevalent animosity toward the Chinese, the *Anaconda Standard* boasted that "the people of

Anaconda have succeeded in reducing the total number of pigtails in this city to less than a dozen all told." For their part, Helena boosters tried enticing African American voters throughout the state, especially in Butte, by financing the *Colored Citizen*, a statewide weekly for African Americans, edited by J. P. Ball Jr. Ball asked his readers why any black would support Anaconda, "the iron claw of corporate infernalism which has always crushed out the black man from every factory and workshop."

Both sides generated more heat than light. There were gala parades with imported bands, barrels of free booze, and even free money on occasion. The Clark people cleverly struck off small copper collars, with the obvious message of what an Anaconda victory would mean. A well-informed observer guessed that Daly spent over two and a half million dollars and Clark at least four hundred thousand dollars on the campaign. Since the state cast just over fifty-two thousand votes in the election, that meant roughly fifty-six dollars invested for each vote.

In the end, the "company town" issue, along with others, sealed Anaconda's fate, and Helena won by just under two thousand votes. Marcus Daly was brokenhearted and never really got over his defeat. For once in his life, W. A. Clark was a hero, an object of real public affection. In celebration on the night of November 12, as light flickered down on the city from a giant bonfire atop Mount Helena, more than two hundred grateful citizens joyously met Clark's victory train at the Great Northern depot, unhitched his carriage, and pulled it through the streets, leading a parade of nearly fifteen thousand. After Clark's victory speech, the saloons of the capital city roared with free drinks on his tab, no doubt the grandest party in the city's history. Clark had won the heart of Helena forever. Behind the celebrating, though, lurked a dark truth: like a spreading cancer, mining money was eroding and consuming the state's frail political integrity.

While the Clark-Daly feud kept the political pot boiling, another important development also unfolded—the rise of the Populist party. The Populist, or People's party, was one of the most significant "third parties" in American history. Arising mainly in the Midwest and South during the 1890s, the party consisted primarily of hard-pressed farmers. Its famous Omaha Platform of 1892 reflected the radicalism that economic hardship had spawned throughout the agricultural regions of the country. Among other things, the platform demanded a graduated income tax, government ownership of railroads, telephone and telegraph service, postal savings banks, and more direct democracy to counter the power of great wealth. Most important, silver provided the key to the Populist program, which called for the "free and unlimited coinage of silver," at a ratio of sixteen to one with gold. This provision would cause inflation, and thus raise farm prices and reduce the burden of their indebtedness.

Even though few farmers had settled in Montana, the Populist party took immediate and deep root in the state. The Populists gave voice to a growing anti-corporate dissent that developed in step with perceived abuses by railroads. But also, as Thomas A. Clinch pointed out, the silver issue galvanized the opposition to politics-as-usual. Although many small farmers in Montana lined up under the Populist banner, the majority came from mining communities, especially after the silver collapse in 1893. The Populists' demand for "free silver" promised miners and mining investors renewed government purchases of silver, full employment, and restored profits. Montana Populists also complained about railroad rates, commercial monopolies, importation of immigrant labor, and the use of strikebreakers.

The Populist movement surfaced in Montana during early 1892, when a gathering of reformers—including laborites who had failed to organize a workers' party in 1890, ex-Greenbackers, proponents of Henry George's "Single Tax" plan, and prohibitionists—met with silver miners and angry agriculturalists. They held their first nominating convention at Butte in June. Their platform echoed most of the concerns the party voiced nationwide, but the Montanans also had concerns of their own, arguing, for instance, that the Northern Pacific should be forced to forfeit its land grant.

The Montana Populists produced some able candidates for office, such as *Boulder Age* editor Will Kennedy for governor and Caldwell Edwards of Bozeman for congressman. For attorney general, the party nominated lawyer Ella Knowles of Helena, the second woman in American history to be nominated for that office. She was the first woman admitted to the bar in Montana and then the first woman to run for statewide office. Ironically, although Knowles's nomination was surely an affirmation of the Populists' support for women's rights, Kennedy had earlier opposed the special legislative statute that admitted her to the state bar. Knowles's selection underscores the rising power of feminism in Montana and the close ties between the Populist and feminist movements. On the campaign trail, Knowles drew great attention and was labeled by the press as the "silver tongued orator of Montana" and the "Portia of the People's Party." She generally drew very favorable responses, although Helena's Elizabeth Fisk was horrified at her conduct on the platform: "She swung her arms and opened her mouth and yelled. No other word expresses it." Although the Populists' major candidates lost in 1892, they made a respectable showing. Three members of the party were elected to the legislature, and they ended up holding the balance of power during the contentious 1893 session. Ella Knowles soon took a job on the staff of her successful opponent, Henri Haskell, and subsequently married him.

The Panic of 1893, with its disastrous impact on the silver industry, added many new converts to the Populist ranks. The depression devas-

The Populist political protest in Montana included a group of Coxeyites—followers of Jacob S. Coxey—who demanded debtor relief and monetary reform and "borrowed" a Northern Pacific train in 1894 on their way to join a march on Washington, D.C. L. A. Huffman photographed these Coxeyites at Forsyth, where federal troops captured them.

The industrial apparatus at Butte's mines included boxlike cages that lowered miners thousands of feet below the surface to work in the labyrinthian tunnels, blasting the ore and ferrying it to the surface. (Photo by N. A. Forsyth)

tated Montana, sending banks and railroads into receivership and producing widespread unemployment in Butte, Anaconda, and Great Falls. In the spring of 1894, a group of disgruntled Butte miners "borrowed" a Northern Pacific train and drove it across Montana in the hope of joining the highly publicized march on Washington led by Jacob S. Coxey. Captured near Miles City, Montana's "Coxeyites" were brought to Helena for trial, and the leaders received jail sentences. Two months later, railroad workers in Montana joined the nationwide boycott against the Pullman railroad car manufacturing firm, further increasing tensions in the state and attracting more voters to Populist ranks.

In the 1894 election, Montana voters elected three Populists to the state senate and thirteen to the house of representatives. In the election campaign of 1896, the Populists reached the peak of their influence in the United States. The Populists joined the Democratic party in supporting the presidential candidacy of William Jennings Bryan, a Democrat who was wedded to the idea of free silver. Bryan's popularity in the silver state of Montana allowed him to carry its presidential vote by a four-to-one margin. According to Bryan's biographer, Marcus Daly contributed fifty thousand dollars to the campaign, making him the largest single contributor to the nationwide Democratic-Populist cause.

In Montana, the Populists followed a similar policy of "fusion" and united with the Democrats. The "Popocrats" ran a strong state ticket, led by Populists Robert B. Smith for governor and A. E. Spriggs for lieutenant governor. In the November 1896 election, the "fusion" ticket won sweeping victories, which easily put Smith in the governor's chair and gave the Democrats-Populists overwhelming control of the house of representatives. Charles S. Hartman, a "Silver Republican" whom the fusionists supported, captured the state's lone seat in Congress.

Like most political marriages of convenience, the Democratic-Populist fusion soon came unstuck. In joining with the Democrats, the Populists had destroyed the integrity and organization of their party. They had sacrificed their key ideals for political expediency, although it is true that the Democrats had forced their hand by embracing free silver. By 1898, Democratic king-makers Clark and Daly had drifted away from the fusion idea, and Populists like Governor Smith were returning to the Democratic party. The Montana Populists, like their compatriots throughout the West, saw their power melt away by the early years of the twentieth century. The Clark-Daly feud helped destroy their unity and speed their demise, and many eventually closed ranks behind copper baron F. A. Heinze. By late 1906, according to legend, so few loyal Populists remained in Butte that they held their last county convention in Barney Shanahan's cab.

The Populists left a great deal to Montana. They left the two-party system—which was never particularly strong in Montana—in a shambles. Populism and its legacies are major causes of the lack of party regularity that persists in Montana and in other western states. Although the Populists failed in their campaign for the free coinage of silver, they gave a great boost to many reforms in Montana: the eight-hour workday; mine safety reforms; democratic measures like the initiative and referendum; the direct election of senators; and political equality for women.

Most important, the Populists laid the groundwork for twentieth century progressives and reformers in Montana and in other mining-agricultural states of the West. Their political philosophy—based on grass-roots democracy, distrust of the East, and enmity toward railroads and other large corporations—has passed from one generation of Montana liberals to another, and it still thrives amid such heated debates as development versus environmentalism. The heirs of Populism—like senators Burton K. Wheeler and Lee Metcalf and state legislator Tom Towe—have always been in the forefront of Montana politics.

MR. CLARK GOES TO WASHINGTON

Following the "Capital Fight" of 1894, the Clark-Daly rivalry eased off until the 1899 legislative session, when the legislators once again took up the matter of choosing a United States senator. Sixty years of age, William Andrews Clark was determined to be elected, apparently without regard for the moral or monetary cost. From the day that the legislature convened, January 2, 1889, rumors abounded in Helena. Clark's son, Charles, supposedly promised: "We will send the old man to the Senate or the poorhouse." The Clark and Daly organizations lined up for a fight to the finish.

Reports that Clark's agents were bribing legislators became so widespread that the lawmakers chose to create a joint committee to investigate them. On January 10, when balloting for senator was scheduled to begin, the committee presented sworn testimony to a joint session of the legislature, bringing the whole bribery matter into the cold light of day. The key testimony, read aloud to the legislators, was that of State Senator Fred Whiteside of Flathead County, a prominent contractor who had earlier exposed wrongdoing in the construction of the state capitol. Whiteside testified that Clark's henchmen, led by attorney John B. Wellcome, had given him thirty thousand dollars to purchase his vote and the votes of several other legislators. In an atmosphere of indescribable tension, the clerk presented the money in evidence, and Whiteside stood to speak. He said that his exposure of Clark's bribe had brought threats to his life, but "if this be the last act of my life, it is well worth the price to the people of this state." The fearless Whiteside blistered his colleagues: "Men of apparent respectability and good standing in this community are trafficking in the honor of members of this body as they would buy and sell cattle and sheep. . . . What new code of morals or of ethics has been discovered which makes of bribery a virtue, and condones the crime of a man because he is rich?" The Daly and Clark newspapers responded emotionally, with Daly's *Anaconda Standard* flaying the "Clark bribers" and Clark's *Butte Miner* charging a Daly frame-up. On the first senate vote, Clark received a mere seven votes.

As the senate deliberations continued, a Lewis and Clark County grand jury looked into the evidence of bribery. Over the next eighteen days, frenzied political manipulations continued to pollute Montana politics. The community of Helena, unfailingly loyal to Clark, seemed to accept bribery as a necessity and to shun those who stood against it. Journalist C. P. Connolly called it "a city hysterical with guilt and greed." Connolly wrote that "the morning salutation with everyone was 'What's the price of votes today?'"

Just before the final vote on the United States Senate seat, the Helena grand jury delivered a verdict of inconclusive evidence. Rumor had it that the grand jurors had been bribed to the tune of ten thousand dollars apiece. Incredibly, on the same day that the grand jury announced its decision, the senate voted to unseat Fred Whiteside, following a committee ruling that certain contested votes belonged to his opponent, John Geiger. The brave Whiteside stood before the joint assembly of the legislature and bade them farewell:

> I understand that the fiat has gone forth, that this is the last day I am to be a member of this body, and if I failed to express myself at this time, I feel that I would be false to myself, false to my home, and false to the friends that have stood so manfully by me.
>
> Let us clink glasses and drink to crime. The crime of bribery, as shown by the evidence here introduced, stands out in all its naked hideousness, and there are forty members seated here who, today, are ready to embrace it. And what is the motive? Answer me that question, you who sit with bloodless lips and shifting eyes—answer if you dare.
>
> There are some features of this senatorial contest which would be ridiculous if it were not for its serious import to the people of this State. It has reminded me of a horde of hungry, skinny, long-tailed rats around a big cheese. . . .
>
> I am not surprised that the gentlemen who have changed their votes to Clark recently should make speeches of explanation, but I would suggest that their explanations would be much more clear and to the point if they would just get up and tell us the price and sit down.

But nothing could stop the Clark bandwagon. On January 28, 1899, the Montana legislature elected the mining king to the United States Senate, with eleven Republicans giving Democrat Clark their votes. Clark later admitted to an outlay of over $272,000 in the campaign; he may have spent over $400,000. Usually crediting some "lucky" circumstance, many Montana legislators turned up with large sums of money after the election, and Helena put on another gala celebration for its favorite "statesman." The old man reportedly spent thirty thousand dollars on champagne alone.

But Clark's victory was not quite complete. The Daly-Whiteside forces petitioned the Montana Supreme Court to disbar attorney John Wellcome on charges of bribery. According to published reports, the Clark forces attempted to "influence" two members of the supreme court and the attorney general in a desperate effort to clear Wellcome's—and thus Clark's—reputation. But these public officials proved to be honest, and Wellcome was disbarred. He never implicated Clark in the charges against him.

Wellcome's disbarment marked a defeat for Clark, but the main battle took place in Washington, D.C. Through Senator Thomas Carter, the Daly organization petitioned the Senate to refuse Clark his seat on the grounds that he had obtained it improperly. From January into April of 1900, the Senate Committee on Privileges and Elections conducted an investigation of Clark's election, which included the questioning of some embarrassed Montana legislators. The committee voted unanimously to recommend that the Senate refuse to seat W. A. Clark (the committee also found some questionable dealings by Daly). But on May 15, before the Senate could act, Clark resigned his office. He went out with a fighting speech in which he defended his incredible outpourings of cash as a heroic effort to save his home state from the clutches of Marcus Daly and the Anaconda Company.

Clark had one last card up his sleeve, a maneuver so preposterous that it is still difficult to believe. Clark's resignation from the Senate left Governor Robert B. Smith with the responsibility of appointing a successor to Clark's seat. Smith was an outspoken foe of Clark, but the lieutenant governor, A. E. Spriggs, was a friend. Apparently, Clark's associates lured Smith out of the state on legal business. While he was gone, Spriggs, who had been attending a Populist gathering in South Dakota, returned to become acting governor. Charlie Clark presented his father's letter of resignation to Spriggs who, amazingly, appointed none other than W. A. Clark to the Senate seat that he had just vacated.

Governor Smith angrily returned to Montana and revoked Spriggs's appointment of Clark "as being tainted with collusion and fraud." Eventually, the vacant Senate seat went to the distinguished Paris Gibson of Great Falls, who served from 1901 to 1905. But in the meantime, as in 1893-95, Clark's intrigues lost Montana one of its seats in the United

States Senate. More important, the episode disgraced the state, as observers across the nation watched with amazement and horror. The *St. Paul Dispatch* published a large cartoon showing William Jennings Bryan fainting over the Montana situation and pictured a thousand dollar bill with the note: "The kind of bill most frequently introduced in the Montana legislature." Montana, it seemed, had been thoroughly debauched by mining money. Yet, even after all of his intrigue, William A. Clark's political hopes were still alive.

As Clark's position in the Senate crumbled under his feet during 1899-1900, events in Montana were quietly working in his favor. Standard Oil's takeover of the Anaconda Company through the formation of the Amalgamated Copper Company occurred at the same time, in effect giving Clark a new life. Now he could stand forth as Montana's loyal son, defying the soulless corporate monster to which Daly had handed his company and his employees. Of equal importance to Clark was the rising power of the man who now became his ally against Anaconda-Amalgamated, F. A. Heinze.

Fritz Augustus Heinze occupies a unique and enigmatic place in Montana's history. The son of a wealthy and cultured German immigrant family, he received a fine classical education in both Europe and America and attended the prestigious Columbia School of Mines, where he received his engineering degree in 1889. He arrived in Butte the same year and went to work for the Boston and Montana Company. Heinze possessed a quick intelligence, and he rapidly learned the Butte ore bodies and the secrets of how to work them. He also became a leading social figure in the gaudy nightlife of the city. Handsome, vigorous, yet well-mannered and somewhat shy, Heinze became a leader of men and a favorite of women. His talents included a fine oratorical ability, a shrewd sense of politics, and, so valuable to him in Butte, a glaring lack of moral scruples.

Heinze was only twenty years old when he arrived at Butte, but he was young, brash, and shrewd, and he rose rapidly to prominence. After learning the opportunities at Butte firsthand and then working briefly for the *Engineering and Mining Journal* in New York, he decided to launch his own business. In partnership with his influential New York brothers, Otto and Arthur, in 1892-93 he opened the Montana Ore Purchasing Company and built a large, modern, and efficient smelter. Heinze's smelter handled the ores of independent companies at reduced rates, which naturally made him a favorite of the smaller-scale mineowners of Butte. In 1895, he purchased the rich Rarus Mine, which, along with other, leased properties, fed a steadily mounting flow of raw copper into his reduction works and smelter.

In the early 1890s, Heinze invested in Canadian mining with a smelter at Trail, British Columbia, a venture that turned out to be a dress rehearsal for later and larger events in Montana. He became a vocal champion of the isolated provinces against the Canadian Pacific Railroad and threatened to build a competing line of his own. In the end, he sold out to Canadian Pacific for "a splendid profit." By 1899-1900, the swashbuckling Heinze was the most celebrated and controversial man in Montana mining. He had also begun an incredible legal battle against the Boston and Montana Company that would have repercussions for the entire state.

The election campaign of 1900 ranks as one of the most significant in Montana's history. In this wild and wide-open contest, W. A. Clark allied himself to F. A. Heinze. Both were Democrats, both opposed the newly created Amalgamated Copper Company, and both had something to gain. Clark desired the election of a legislature that would quietly send him back to Washington, this time without any charges of bribery. Heinze wanted control of the government of Butte–Silver Bow County, especially the election of friendly district judges who would aid him in his legal battles.

The two "copper kings," who were so different in personality, made a powerful team—Clark with his millions and his established political organization and Heinze with his ability to woo the voters. Clark's *Butte Miner* and Heinze's free-swinging newspaper, *The Reveille*, began firing broadsides at Standard Oil and pointing with alarm to its lengthening shadow over Montana. In order to win the crucial support of organized labor, Clark and Heinze granted their miners the long-sought-after eight-hour workday, with no cut in pay, and they challenged Amalgamated to do the same. Amalgamated's directors refused. Clark and Heinze also encouraged the Clerks' Union to demand a general six o'clock closing time. Most other firms agreed, but Hennessy's "Company Store" refused. Thus labor broke ranks without Daly at the head of Anaconda and fell in line behind Clark and Heinze. Amid the wildest of cheering, the triumphant copper barons rode together in a carriage to lead Butte's Miners Union Day parade in June 1900. With labor's backing, the Clark men won control of the Democratic party organization away from the Daly, now Amalgamated, forces.

Even with the power of Standard Oil and Anaconda behind it, Amalgamated could not match the Clark-Heinze effort. As orator and campaign organizer, Heinze flailed the Amalgamated "copper trust," its directors, and its political servants. He branded Henry H. Rogers, William Rockefeller, and their associates as the "kerosene crowd" who aimed to use ruthless, Standard Oil methods to crush Montana. As for Daly's friend, Republican Senator "Oily Tom" Carter, Heinze dismissed him as an

Amalgamated stooge and nicknamed him "Polly," in reference to his parroting of the Company line. Heinze's *Reveille*, edited by the acid-penned P. A. O'Farrell, tore the hide off the "trust" with biting editorials and cartoons. A typical *Reveille* cartoon depicted Standard Oil–Amalgamated as a giant gorilla hulking up a mountainside with the unconscious maiden Montana held in its grasp. In reaction to these attacks, the Amalgamated began buying up Montana newspapers in an effort to win the battle of public opinion.

In the ensuing, frenzied campaign, party lines became hopelessly scrambled. One wing of the Democratic party followed Heinze and Clark. So did some of the Republicans and most members of the smaller Populist, Labor, and Social Democratic parties. Most of the Republicans, along with the "Independent" Democrats, followed Senator Carter in backing the Amalgamated. The *Anaconda Standard* described the wide range of forces lined up against Amalgamated as the "Heinzeantitrustbolting-democraticlaborpopulist ticket." The November 1900 vote count registered a major victory for the Clark-Heinze team. While Clark obtained a friendly Democratic legislature, Heinze cemented his control over the government of Silver Bow County.

The 1900 campaign marked a major turning point in the "War of the Copper Kings." It ended the Clark-Daly feud and began a bitter contest between F. A. Heinze and the Amalgamated Copper Company. Only a week after the election, the fifty-nine-year-old Marcus Daly died in his New York hotel room. He died knowing that Clark, his archenemy, would win the Senate seat that Daly had so long denied him. Daly's death meant that the Anaconda Company, now completely under the control of Standard Oil–Amalgamated Copper, would no longer be subject to the policies of a loyal Montanan; it was now a "foreign corporation."

Clark savored his victory. The legislature, without Daly's influence at work, quietly sent Clark to serve his term in the United States Senate (1901-7). Almost immediately after the election, Clark broke his alliance with Heinze and became, in effect, an ally of the Amalgamated. Rumor had it that Henry Rogers had given the old man a simple ultimatum: either break with Heinze or face another challenge to his Senate seat. At any rate, Clark evidently found the Senate to be a less desirable place than he had imagined. Catering to the voters back home went against his grain. He proved to be, not surprisingly, a staunch Senate conservative and a vigorous opponent of Theodore Roosevelt's conservation policies. In a characteristic attack on the creation of federal national forests, he remarked: "Those who succeed us can well take care of themselves." When his term expired, Clark did not seek re-election, but for the rest of his long life he was known as "Senator Clark."

Montana saw less and less of W. A. Clark after 1900. He spent more and more time in Europe, Los Angeles, Washington, and New York, where he built an incredible mansion that cost a reported three million dollars and contained 121 rooms, 31 baths, and 4 galleries for his massive art collection. As always, most of his attention was given to his investments, which included cattle, lumber, sugar beets, real estate, utilities, banks, newspapers, and a Los Angeles–Salt Lake City railroad, along which the city of Las Vegas in Clark County, Nevada, was built. But mines remained the key to the Clark empire. He owned six, each of which produced ores worth several millions of dollars. His great United Verde Mine in Arizona yielded nearly one hundred million dollars in dividends.

When Clark died in 1925 at the age of eighty-six, he left behind one of the great American fortunes, but he left no monuments to his memory at "home." Clark's heirs gave the William Andrews Clark Memorial Library to the University of California at Los Angeles, not the University of Montana, and a million dollars went to a new law school at the University of Virginia. The Clark fortune also endowed the Los Angeles Philharmonic Orchestra. The Columbia Gardens, his pretty trolley park at Butte, was closed in the late 1970s. The Clark name remains an uneasy if imposing memory in Montana. Perhaps his legacy is best symbolized by the notorious statement that he may or may not have made: "I never bought a man who wasn't for sale."

The Triumph of Amalgamated

Although stung by the Clark-Heinze attacks of 1900, the newly formed Amalgamated Copper Company pressed inexorably toward its goal of completely taking over Montana's copper industry. Once W. A. Clark entered the Senate and abandoned the fight, F. A. Heinze and his political allies stood nearly alone in opposing the Standard Oil–Amalgamated "copper trust." But Heinze proved to be a tough opponent.

Heinze entered the legal-political arena even before his fight with the Amalgamated holding company. In 1898, he launched an incredible five-year war against the Anaconda Company, which raged on many fronts at the same time. The hottest disputes centered on the rich Michael Davitt Mine. A property of the consolidated Boston and Montana–Butte and Boston Mining companies, the Davitt bordered Heinze's Rarus Mine. In March 1898, a legal battle erupted in federal district court between the Boston firms and Heinze's Montana Ore Purchasing Company over ownership of the veins that merged along the boundaries of the Davitt and Rarus mines. At issue was the federal Apex Law, a great source of litigation in the mining West. The Apex Law provided that the owner of the claim where a vein of ore "apexed" (that is, touched the surface) could pursue that vein wherever it led, even laterally under the borders of adjoining claims.

Federal District Judge Hiram Knowles directed the jury to decide in favor of the Boston and Montana Company, but such was "Fritz" Heinze's popularity that the jurors defied the judge in their verdict. This forced a retrial, which took place at Helena in 1900. By that time the Amalgamated was in the process of absorbing the Boston and Montana–Butte and Boston firms, and Heinze found himself in a larger battle than the one he had entered. At Heinze's instigation, the Helena newspapers blistered the Amalgamated, and the jury again found against the holding company. Arguing that Heinze's propaganda had influenced the verdict, Amalgamated won a second retrial, this one in a circuit court at San Francisco.

Because a court injunction forbade mining the disputed veins, Heinze was now cut off from ores that he desperately needed to keep his smelters running at capacity. With his back to the wall, he began to fight ruthlessly. He and his brothers transferred the holdings of the Montana Ore Purchasing Company to another of their firms, the Johnstown Mining Company. Then, arguing that the Johnstown Company was not subject to the injunction, they began mining the rich veins that were in dispute. The loyal Heinze miners drove intricate crosscuts into the Davitt from the Rarus Mine and then sealed off the veins with bulkheads to keep out the Amalgamated crews.

The distant roar of underground blasting alerted the Amalgamated to Heinze's scheme. Soon the Company's men were pouring into the disputed Davitt veins from the adjoining Pennsylvania Mine. An "underground war" erupted, as Amalgamated and "Johnstown" miners skirmished with jets of high-pressured water, smudge fires, slaked lime poured through vents, and even dynamite. Two Amalgamated men died in a dynamite blast, and it seemed that widespread violence would engulf the Butte Hill. But the war in the Davitt soon wound down. The court ordered inspectors into the mine, who uncovered the extent of Heinze's looting—an estimated million dollars worth of ore. For this he was fined a ridiculous twenty thousand dollars. The Davitt Case remained in federal courts for years. It eventually reached the U.S. Supreme Court, which ruled entirely in favor of the Amalgamated.

As "underground warfare" flared in the Michael Davitt, Heinze and his army of over three dozen lawyers engaged the Amalgamated on other fronts, too. In creating the Amalgamated holding company, Henry Rogers had aimed to absorb not only the Anaconda Company but also the Boston and Montana–Butte and Boston companies. When Rogers tried to arrange an Amalgamated takeover of the consolidated firms in 1898, he found to his discomfort that two of Heinze's cohorts had each bought one hundred shares of Boston and Montana stock. The Heinze men brought suit in court, arguing that the Boston and Montana could not legally be transferred to Amalgamated without the consent of the minority stockholders. Accepting the argument, the Montana Supreme Court halted Amalgamated's takeover of the Boston firms and disrupted Rogers's strategy until the 1899 legislature dutifully passed House Bill 132, which allowed stock transfers with the approval of only two-thirds of a company's stockholders. In the meantime, the court placed the Boston and Montana Company in receivership, which cost it dearly in legal fees and falling stock values.

In this case, and in others as well, Heinze's trump card was his "friendship" with the judges elected to the district courts in Silver Bow County. William Clancy, a Populist and curbstone lawyer, won election to one of the judgeships in 1896. Judge Clancy soon became famous for his unkempt appearance and his peculiar courtroom behavior, which included dozing during legal arguments and casually spitting tobacco juice at well-placed spittoons. He also gained fame for his unfailing support of Heinze, which was so obvious that rumors of bribery abounded. During his 1900 alliance with Clark, Heinze won another friend when, with Heinze's support, Edward Harney won election to the second district bench in Butte. With his allies sitting on the local courts, Heinze could easily drive the titans of Standard Oil to absurd lengths.

For instance, there was the incredible case of the "Copper Trust Company." While plotting the complex claims of the Butte Hill, Heinze's brother, Arthur, discovered a thin, triangulated sliver of unclaimed land that lay between three of Amalgamated's greatest mines—the Anaconda, the Neversweat, and the St. Lawrence. With a fine sense of humor, Fritz Heinze claimed this forty-square-yard trace of land, named it the "Copper Trust" claim, and went before Clancy's court with the argument that all three of the mines were really his because they "apexed" on his claim. The judge unflinchingly shut all three mines down in early 1900 and, pending a court ruling, put three thousand Amalgamated miners out of work. But this time Heinze had gone too far. When an angry mob of workers threatened to lynch the judge, Clancy hurriedly reversed his decision, and the mines reopened.

Heinze posed a much greater threat in the case of the Minnie Healy Mine. He first leased the Minnie Healy from Miles Finlen, a friend of Marcus Daly's who had had no luck in developing it. With his uncanny "nose for ore," Heinze soon uncovered rich veins in the mine. Because Heinze had acquired the lease by an oral agreement, however, Finlen took him to court in an attempt to regain what had become a very valuable property. But even before the case reached court, Amalgamated, desperately afraid that Heinze would use the mine for more raids on adjoining properties, bought up Finlen's claim.

The Minnie Healy case came before newly elected Judge Edward Harney in 1901, and the judge predictably upheld Heinze's claim. The Amalgamated decided to play dirty. Learning of Harney's fondness for liquor and his relationship with a Butte stenographer named Ada Brackett, Charlie Clark and Amalgamated attorneys A. J. Shores and D'Gay Stivers attempted to blackmail and bribe him. They acquired copies of correspondence between Harney and Brackett—they became known as the "Dearie letters"—which seemed to indicate that Heinze had influenced the judge. The Amalgamated group confronted Harney with the threat of impeachment and offered him $250,000 to sign an affidavit admitting that he had accepted bribes from Heinze. Harney steadfastly refused to make any such admission, and he attempted to have lawyers Stivers and Shores disbarred. The judge was never impeached, and the two lawyers were acquitted.

Because of the evidence arising from the Minnie Healy case, the Montana Supreme Court reversed Judge Harney's decision and remanded the case to the other Butte district judge—none other than William Clancy. While the issue lay in court, underground warfare erupted in the Healy, just as it had in the Davitt. In the rich veins of the "firing line" sector of the Minnie Healy, Heinze's men skirmished with Amalgamated miners who entered from the adjacent Leonard Mine. Each side attempted to flood the other's shafts, and large-scale loss of life seemed imminent until averted by a truce between Heinze and the Amalgamated. The Healy case remained in Clancy's court from 1901 through most of 1903, and the tension in this and other cases mounted toward an explosive climax. On October 22, 1903, Clancy awarded Heinze full title to the multimillion-dollar Minnie Healy. It was a stunning defeat for the Amalgamated, which not only lost the mine but would also face new Apex litigation along the Healy's boundaries. Even more important, on the same day Clancy ruled against Amalgamated in the case of the Parrot Mining Company.

The Parrot Mining Company was an Amalgamated subsidiary. In a familiar move, two of Heinze's lieutenants had bought some Parrot stock and had then gone to court in 1903. They charged, in effect, that the Amalgamated holding company, by managing the Parrot in the interests of its subsidiaries, was infringing on the rights of Parrot stockholders. The case struck at the very heart of the Amalgamated, and, once again, Clancy ruled in Heinze's favor. The judge declared, in essence, that the Amalgamated could not operate legally in Montana. According to Clancy's decision, Amalgamated subsidiaries that were organized before House Bill 132 made such stock transfers legal could issue no dividends to the parent company or its stockholders.

The Parrot decision prompted Amalgamated to square off for a fight to the finish. Even though the Montana Supreme Court would later reverse Clancy's ruling, the trust now had the opportunity to turn the tables, once and for all, against F. A. Heinze. Only hours after Clancy's decisions, the Amalgamated shut down most of its Montana operations. In the mines, smelters, refineries, and lumber camps, the doors swung shut. Fifteen thousand men, the majority of Montana's wage-earners, were suddenly out of work. The question on everyone's mind was whether the Amalgamated, which had large surpluses of copper on hand, would reopen before winter. And if it did, what would be the conditions? The Company laid down its terms. It demanded that Heinze's lieutenants, John Mac-Ginnis and Daniel Lamm, sell their stock in the Parrot. Quickly, the Butte Miners Union, along with Senator Clark and other interested parties, offered to purchase and hold the troublesome stocks. But the Company wanted more: it wanted to smash Heinze's hold on the courts.

Under the pressure of the Amalgamated's lockout, Heinze's popularity among Butte miners began to fade. On the afternoon of October 26, 1903, he appeared before a crowd of ten thousand men who had assembled at the Silver Bow County courthouse. Many of the men were hostile, and some were armed. Heinze offered evasive proposals to turn over the Parrot stock, offers that he knew the Company would never accept. Dramatically, he lashed out at the Standard Oil–Amalgamated octopus and warned the crowd of what might happen to them:

> My friends, the Amalgamated Copper Company, in its influence and functions, and the control it has over the commercial and economic affairs of this state, is the greatest menace that any community could possibly have within its boundaries. . . .
>
> Rockefeller and Rogers have filched the oil wells of America, and in doing so they trampled on every law, human and divine. . . . The same Rockefeller and the same Rogers are seeking to control the executive, the judiciary, and the legislature of Montana. . . .
>
> You are my friends, my associates, and I defy any man among you to point to a single instance where I did one of you wrong. These people are my enemies, fierce, bitter, implacable; but they are your enemies, too. If they crush me today, they will crush you to-morrow. They will cut your wages and raise the tariff in the company stores on every bite you eat, and every rag you wear. They will force you to dwell in Standard Oil houses while you live, and they will bury you in Standard Oil coffins when you die.

It was a brilliant and moving speech, and Heinze once again won Butte's loyalty. The miners and their families knew that much of what he said was true, that with Daly gone they were the pawns of a cold, merciless employer.

The Amalgamated's leadership rejected any compromise with Heinze. Instead, they demanded that Governor Joseph Toole call a special session of the legislature in order to pass an unprecedented law that would allow a litigant to have a judge removed from a case on the rather simple charge of bias. The "Clancy Law" would permit a much easier escape from hostile judges than more complicated change-of-venue statutes. And the law would destroy Heinze's advantages in the Butte courts.

Governor Toole recognized naked coercion when he saw it and resisted. But in the end, with the state facing economic ruin, he had no choice. The legislature convened in special session on November 10, 1903, passed the Fair Trials Bill, and adjourned. Montanans went back to work, but on Amalgamated's terms. The giant trust had literally beaten the state into submission and taught it the price of defiance. Observers around the nation watched in awe as a "sovereign state" was held up by a corporation. As the *Idaho State Tribune* observed: "It took the Amalgamated Copper Company just three weeks to coerce Montana into falling on her knees with promises of anything that big corporation might want."

The battle for Butte, for its mineral riches and its political mastery, was over. F. Augustus Heinze, who had presented the only real obstacle to Amalgamated's drive to "consolidate" control of the Butte Hill, lost the war when he lost control of the courts. In the 1904 election, Montana voters removed Heinze's friends from the district court. Despite his promises that he would never sell out to Amalgamated, Heinze began secret negotiations with John D. Ryan, who in 1904 had become the Company's managing director in Montana. After fifteen months of maneuvering, the Heinzes announced in February 1906 that they had sold their Butte holdings to the Amalgamated. The Company paid a whopping twelve million dollars to remove Heinze from its path. But it bought more than mines and smelters. It also bought the end of about one hundred lawsuits that were tying up fifty million dollars worth of Amalgamated property. To manage the Heinze properties, Amalgamated formed a new subsidiary, the Butte Coalition Mining Company. The question must always remain: did Heinze fight Standard Oil on principle, or did he merely shake them down? The answer, perhaps, is that he did both.

Fritz Heinze took his newly gained fortune and departed for Wall Street. He bought into a major banking chain and began developing a firm he had founded earlier, the United Copper Company, as a Wall Street syndicate through which he would compete directly with the Amalgamated. But the former Butte copper king had started something he could not finish; according to the *Copper Handbook*, United Copper was nothing more than a "piece of stockjobbery." Within months, "myste-rious" purchases and sales of United Copper stock, along with runs on his major New York bank, had driven Heinze and his brothers from Wall Street. Standard Oil and its allies were unmistakably behind the Heinzes' ruin, aided no doubt by Fritz Heinze's own mistakes. The Heinzes' fail-ure on Wall Street, along with other factors, triggered a brief but sharp depression known as the Panic of 1907.

F. A. Heinze never recovered from his Wall Street shellacking. He faced trial on charges of fraud arising out of the whole affair, but he was acquitted. Heinze attempted with some success to rebuild his western mining empire, but in truth he had burned himself out. After a 1910 mar-riage to actress Bernice Henderson, which brought little happiness, Fritz Heinze died in 1914 of cirrhosis of the liver and massive hemorrhaging. Only forty-five years old when he died, Heinze had packed a lot into his brief life, but he had left little but destruction behind.

Heinze's defeat in 1903 and his sellout in 1906 brought "peace" to Butte and allowed the Amalgamated to consolidate its grip on Montana mining. Under the tough-minded John D. Ryan, who succeeded Henry Rogers as president of Amalgamated in 1909, the Company became the proprietor of the Butte Hill. In 1910, Amalgamated bought W. A. Clark's Montana copper mines and smelter and merged all of its subsidiaries into the Anaconda Copper Mining Company. The Amalgamated Copper Company, with only one major operating subsidiary, was fast becoming an anachronism. Also, the federal government was threatening to double-tax holding company profits. In 1915, the Amalgamated was liquidated and was replaced by the Anaconda Copper Mining Company. Since 1915, the Anaconda has had no affiliation with the old Standard Oil group.

The newly independent Anaconda Copper Mining Company bore little resemblance to the firm purchased by the Rogers-Rockefeller group in 1899. With assets of $118 million, and a copper production capacity of 300 million pounds a year, the Company was the giant of the world's copper industry. Its Montana empire included thirty mineshafts on the Butte Hill; reduction works and smelters at Anaconda, Great Falls, and East Helena; a lumber operation based at Bonner; coal fields; a railroad; hard-ware stores and hotels; and a growing chain of newspapers, including most of the state's major dailies.

By 1910-15 the Anaconda clearly dominated Montana's economy and political order. In contrast to the days when Marcus Daly seemed to man-age the Company with the state's interests in mind, Montanans found that they were locked in the grip of an insensitive corporation controlled from Wall Street. Montanans would often forget that it was Clark who had first tampered with the legislature and turned journalism to his own purposes and that it was Heinze who had first corrupted the courts, but they would always remember the shutdown of 1903 and the awesome political power of the Anaconda. To many observers, both inside and outside the state, Montana appeared to be the classic example of a "one-company state," a commonwealth where one corporation ruled.

The Homestead Boom, 1900-1918

 T HE farmers' frontier came late to the plains of east-central Montana. This semi-arid region, the far corner of the great Mississippi-Missouri Basin, seemed hopelessly dry to frontier farmers in the nineteenth century. Many of their maps and schoolbooks designated the rolling prairies, which reached from the 98th meridian to the Rocky Mountains, as the "Great American Desert." Westward-moving farmers passed by this forbidding land and headed to the inviting valleys of the Rockies and the Pacific Coast. It was only after 1900, with the advent of new land policies, new farming machines and methods, and new land promotions that the farmers opened the last frontier on the immense emptiness of the Montana plains. The sodbusters' invasion would set off the greatest land boom in Montana's history and would transform the state's politics. As early as 1909, official promotional literature began using the name "Treasure State," but Montana might have been more appropriately named the "Homestead State." Under various public land laws, more people took up more land in Montana than they did in any other state. In the fifteen years between 1909 and 1923, settlers filed 114,620 homestead claims on almost twenty-five million acres of land.

AGRICULTURAL BEGINNINGS

The first white farmers in what would become Montana were fur traders and missionaries, who surrounded such fur posts as Fort Benton and Fort Connah with vegetable gardens, crop fields, and grazing livestock. In the Bitterroot Valley, Jesuit priests began farming successfully in the 1840s. They imported seeds and domestic stock from the Columbia River Basin and used irrigation to raise impressive crops of potatoes and wheat. They even built a crude flour mill. By the 1860s, other isolated farmers, like the O'Keefe brothers near present-day Missoula, were also tilling the soil. But it was only with the great gold rushes of the mid-1960s, and the far-removed and hungry mining towns they produced, that there were large demands for foodstuffs in the area. Farmers quickly took up residence in Montana in response to the demand.

The placer gold towns of southwestern Montana faced severe food problems. Located four hundred miles to the south, the Mormon settlements in Utah eagerly welcomed the Montana trade. But the prices were high, and sometimes winter and spring snowstorms blocked the roads. During the hard winter of 1864-65, for instance, flour shortages in Virginia City drove the price of a hundred-pound sack up to $150 and riots broke out as a result. The high price of food persuaded many prospectors to give up mining and take up farming instead.

Often to their surprise, the pioneer farmers found that the high mountain valleys surrounding the gold fields were richly fertile and well-watered. By selectively irrigating and by protecting crops against the late spring and early autumn frosts, they produced fine harvests of grain, vegetables, and even fruits. Small farms soon dotted the Jefferson, Ruby, Madison, Bitterroot, Deer Lodge, Prickly Pear, and other valleys along the Continental Divide. The broad and beautiful Gallatin Valley surpassed all others in the territory in productivity and housed three flour mills by 1867. With good reason, Bozeman, the principal community in the Gallatin, boasted that it had a much more secure future than the gold towns lying to the west and north.

Yet, agriculture in early Montana remained limited for many years, restricted economically to local mining markets and confined geographically to the southwestern valleys. By 1870, the placer gold towns were fading rapidly and Montana farmers faced a troubled future. The 1870 census found only 851 farms and 150,000 cultivated acres in the entire territory. During the next three decades, the farmers' frontier crept eastward and northward, but at a snail's pace. The aridity of the land, the lack of rail connections, and the enormous Indian reservations and huge open-range livestock outfits all combined to hold back the farmers' advance. Even the arrival of railroads failed to touch off a rush to Montana's plains. During the 1890s, some farmers irrigated bottomlands along the Yellowstone, Missouri, and Milk rivers, and a few even tried dry farming on the benchlands of northern and central Montana. But they were few and far between.

As the twentieth century dawned, the eastern two-thirds of Montana lay wide open, with a settlement or Indian village here and there, occasional herds of cattle and flocks of sheep, and nearly everywhere vast expanses of vacant public lands. The cutting edge of the farmers' frontier stood far to the east, in central North Dakota and South Dakota. The farmers' advance, which had begun along the Atlantic seaboard early in the seventeenth century, had paused at the 98th meridian, the "rainfall line" that divides the subhumid from the semi-arid Great Plains. Those acquainted with eastern Montana and the western Dakotas understood the central fact of its geography: the lack of adequate rainfall meant that farmers must rely either on large-scale irrigation or moisture-conserving dry-land farming.

In the minds of many Montana and Great Plains boosters of the 1890s and early 1900s, reclamation seemed to be the key to prosperity. They saw big rivers, like the Missouri, the Milk, and the Yellowstone, carrying their heavy spring runoffs to the sea, leaving parched but fertile uplands unwatered. Paying little heed to the enormous amounts of land as compared to the light annual streamflows, the boosters argued passionately that, once the Missouri and its tributaries were dammed and diverted, the deserts could be made to "blossom like the rose." Addressing Montana's constitutional convention in 1889, John Wesley Powell, the director of the United States Geological Survey, made the incredible prediction that one-third of Montana's land mass could be irrigated: "It means that no drop of water falling within the area of the state shall flow beyond the boundaries of the state. It means that all the waters falling within the state will be utilized upon its lands for agriculture." Boosters of Montana reclamation, such as Governor Joseph K. Toole, U.S. Senator Thomas H. Carter, and Billings promoter I. D. O'Donnell, saw their fondest dreams come true when Congress passed the Newlands Reclamation Act in 1902. This important law committed the federal government to a long-range program of building large-scale irrigation projects throughout the arid West. A prosperous era of high dams, gleaming canals, and verdant croplands seemed at hand.

The grand vision of the early-day reclamationists proved to be mostly mirage. Between 1904 and 1906, construction began on several large and important federal reclamation developments: the Huntley Project east of Billings, the Lower Yellowstone Project along the Montana-Dakota state line, the Milk River Project in northern Montana, and the Sun River Project west of Great Falls. These federal irrigation developments meant a lot to Montana. So would others built much later, like the Canyon Ferry and Tiber dams in the 1950s. But the federal reclamation projects still left most of Montana's wide open spaces unwatered. The simple fact is that Montana has relatively little land that is well-suited to irrigation, and reclamation is less central to its farm economy than it is to such states as Arizona, California, or Idaho. Realizing this inescapable fact, agricultural

Fertile valleys, such as the Gallatin, shown in this turn-of-the-century photograph by Albert Schlecten, attracted farmers and would-be farmers to Montana during the homestead era.

promoters abandoned their hopes of turning the semi-arid western plains into an irrigated "garden," and they turned instead to the promise of dry farming.

Behind the Boom

The great Montana land rush began late in the first decade of the twentieth century. Viewed in proper perspective, it marked the culmination, the final thrust, of the three-century advance of the American agricultural frontier. A number of complex developments lay behind this agricultural invasion of the Northern Plains. Perhaps most basic was the industrial revolution, which by 1900 had supplied farmers with steel moldboard plows, grain drills, twine binders, discs, harrows, steam-powered threshers, and other increasingly effective machinery. It had also produced a growing and hungry urban population in the eastern states and in Europe. Three important factors gave rise to the homestead boom in Montana: the dry farming system of agriculture, the availability of large tracts of land either free or at low prices, and the mammoth promotional campaign that cranked up around 1908.

"Dry farming," wrote historian Mary Wilma M. Hargreaves, "may be generally defined as agriculture without irrigation in regions of scanty precipitation." By the early twentieth century, experienced farmers in such semi-arid regions as Utah and eastern Washington had worked out various methods of moisture-conserving tillage. They allowed their lands to lie in summer fallow during alternate years, and they learned to work the ground intensively in order to retain soil moisture. Many enterprising individuals contributed to the development of dry farming, but by 1900, Hardy Webster Campbell was easily the best known. Campbell, a South Dakota farmer, stoutly maintained that, by applying scientific principles to agriculture, the dry Dakota-Montana prairies could produce just as abundantly as the well-watered croplands far to the east. As he phrased it in 1909, "I believe of a truth that this region which is just now coming into its own is destined to be the last and best grain gardendry of the world."

The "Campbell System" of dry farming was aimed almost exclusively at conserving water in the soil. Campbell worried little about expanding acreages or encouraging crop rotation or diversification. Instead, he preached deep plowing and intensive cultivation in order to retain the precious moisture in the earth. Campbell's famous subsurface packer tamped the subsoil while loosening the topsoil. In order to maintain a fine surface mulch that would hold down evaporation, his system then called for constant discing and harrowing, especially after each rain. Campbell's theory was music to the ears of Great Plains promoters. Regional railroads soon had him, and others like him, running experimental farms and lecturing to enthusiastic audiences.

Campbell's influence came late to Montana. Prior to 1905 only a few local promoters, such as Paris Gibson of Great Falls, had advocated dry farming. Noting that not all Montanans could "be cattle kings, sheep barons and bonanza miners," Gibson believed that his own farm operation had proved as early as the late 1880s that dry farming could succeed in Montana. But it was not until the first decade of the twentieth century that the dry-farming movement became popular and expanded across the Northern Plains. The railroads, first in Dakota and then in Montana, pushed Campbell's program with much fanfare. The Montana Agricultural Experiment Station, located at Montana State College in Bozeman, reacted more cautiously. Experiment Station experts like F. B. Linfield and Alfred Atkinson never fully trusted Campbell's optimistic theories. Not only was he too enthusiastic about moisture conservation, they thought, but Campbell also paid little heed to such worthy ideas as developing drought-resistant plants or combining crop farming with livestock production. Despite their reservations, however, the Experiment Station experts generally agreed that dry farming could work and that it was well-suited to much of east-central Montana. With mounting enthusiasm, they lent their full support to the movement.

Although Hardy Campbell hesitated to admit it, dry farming required large tracts of land, units that were big enough to allow for summer fallowing and for smaller crop yields per acre. The potential settler could either buy land from realtors or railroads or get it free from the government. Ever since passage of the Homestead Act in 1862, the federal government had offered free farms to all American citizens. The act gave each interested individual a quarter-section of land—160 acres—at no cost except for an incidental filing fee. Following a five-year "prove-up" period, a homesteader acquired full legal title to the land.

The original Homestead Act meant little to Montana, where farmers came late and where, in most areas, 160 acres was far too little land for a family farm. Slowly realizing that Great Plains agriculture demanded larger acreages, Congress passed several supplementary laws in order to provide more land to the homesteaders. One of these was the Desert Land Act of 1877, which allowed for the sale of a full 640-acre section of land for only $1.25 per acre, if the buyer proved up in three years and irrigated part of the plot. This ludicrous measure, which was pushed through Congress by organized stockmen, offered little hope to real farmers, who could seldom bear the costs of irrigation. The Desert Land Act was used widely in Montana, but mainly by ranchers who violated the spirit of the law in order to gain grazing lands. Over three million acres of public lands in Montana passed into private hands under its auspices.

Settlement of the Montana-Dakota plains obviously demanded a land law that was better suited to local conditions. Finally, in 1909, Congress appeared to meet this need by enacting the Enlarged Homestead Act. This measure, which Montana Senator Joseph M. Dixon played a major hand in formulating, offered a 320-acre half-section of land free to settlers in parts of Arizona, Colorado, Montana, Nevada, Oregon, Utah, Washington, and Wyoming. In 1912, Congress supplemented the law with the Three-Year Homestead Act, which reduced the waiting period for ownership from five to three years and permitted a settler to be absent from his homestead five months of each year. The westward-looking home-seeker, not realizing that even 320 acres was usually far too little land on the arid plains, responded eagerly. Eventually, nearly thirty-two million acres of Montana land would pass from public to private hands under the homestead acts.

Not all of the sodbusters obtained their land free from the government. Many who had some capital bought choice plots from private speculators. Some purchased land directly from the Northern Pacific Railroad, which in 1900 still held 13,450,816 acres of its enormous land grant in Montana. Over the next seventeen years the Northern Pacific sold off most of its grants at rates of up to $8.56 per acre. By 1917, only 2,751,637 acres of the railroad's Montana domain remained intact. Many other homesteaders bought from realty companies, who often purchased railroad or ranch lands in blocs for resale to farmers. Some of these realtors were out-of-state speculators, like W. H. Brown and Company of Chicago; others, such as W. G. Conrad of Great Falls, were local talent. Many stockmen with large holdings eagerly platted their rangelands for sale to the farmers. Joseph Baker summarized the attitude of many ranchers when he said: "Dry farming is the coming salvation of the west. . . . I plan to put the dry farming system into effect on my Highwood land which has heretofore been considered by men as nothing but poor grazing land."

The ready availability of free or inexpensive land and the new methods of dry farming made the Montana homestead boom possible. But what really launched it was the great promotional campaign that began after 1908. Montana's promoters came in many guises. There were chambers of commerce, bankers' groups, and newspaper editors from the towns and cities. There were real estate boomers, state agencies like the Bureau of Agriculture, Labor, and Industry, and experts from the state college. And there were the railroads, which had a vital stake in building up the region they served. They also had advertising resources that no one else could

Homesteaders at Moore in Fergus County were typical of thousands who shipped themselves and their goods by rail to Montana, hoping to find good land and a new start on the nation's last great agricultural frontier.

match. Prior to 1906, the Northern Pacific, the Great Northern, and the Burlington—all dominated by James J. Hill—had advertised the northwestern plains to farmers, but theirs was a modest effort compared to the one launched by the Milwaukee Road. The Milwaukee promoted its prime areas, especially the Musselshell Valley and the Judith Basin, in such glowing terms that an Iowa immigrant ventured the opinion that the Judith was the most heavily advertised area in North America.

The most capable and powerful of all the railroad promoters was Jim Hill—or "Yem" Hill, as his Scandinavian friends called him. Never one to be outdone, Hill had his own promotional campaign in full swing by 1909, the year that Billings hosted a well-attended Dry Farming Congress. At the height of the boom, advocates of the Campbell System held an annual congress in a different city each year, and the Billings meeting was one of the liveliest. Promoters, not farmers, dominated the conventions. At Billings, both Jim Hill and his son Louis, who was president of the Great Northern, went so far as to urge the group to drop the term "dry farming." They believed that the emphasis on "dry" was unflattering to the area and that it was bad publicity. The Hills lost that round, mainly because of opposition from F. B. Linfield of the Montana Agricultural Experiment Station. In solemn terms, Linfield warned the delegates that they were being asked to trifle with the truth.

The railroad advertising campaign reached its climax in 1911. The Milwaukee and the three Hill lines used nearly every conceivable method to publicize the fertility of the northern Great Plains and to lure farmers there. They offered prizes for crops and livestock, sponsored farm exhibits, ran agricultural display trains around the country, and spread advertising leaflets and brochures throughout the United States and Europe. They encouraged Europeans, especially Germans and Scandinavians, to migrate and offered them easy trans-Atlantic rates. Most important, they offered the home-seekers cheap rail fares to their new homes, either in boxcars or in the more comfortable "Zulu" cars that provided sleeping facilities. For as little as $22.50, a homesteader could buy space in a freight car to bring his family, all his belongings, even seed grains and livestock from St. Paul to eastern Montana.

Jim Hill, largely controlling three of the five regional railroads, had an obvious financial interest in promoting immigration. But he pursued motives other than mere economic gain. Hill was very much a Jeffersonian democrat, who believed in rural virtues and saw the family farm as the backbone of American society. He envisioned the fertile plains of Montana and the Dakotas as the granary of the world, neatly partitioned into small family farms and populated by tens of thousands of hearty yeoman farmers and their offspring. With Hill's railroads linking the Great Lakes to Puget Sound, the "Empire Builder" dreamed of opening new markets in China and the Far East for the high protein wheat from the abundant harvests of the Northern Plains.

So the energetic Jim Hill outdid all the other boosters. He took a personal interest in livestock breeding and in importing new drought-resistant grains. His agricultural expert, Thomas Shaw of the Minnesota Agricultural College, surpassed even Hardy Campbell after 1910 as the region's leading advocate of dry farming. Although Shaw was more open-minded than Campbell, more understanding of the need to diversify regional agriculture, he still fully shared Campbell's devotion to deep plowing and intensive cultivation.

Jim Hill gazed on the homesteaders in the Northwest as a father might. "You are now our children," he told the 1909 Billings Dry Farming Congress, "but we are in the same boat with you, and we have got to prosper with you or we have got to be poor with you." In his massive settlement campaign, he saw the fulfillment of a great national purpose. "Population without the prairie," he once observed, "is a mob, and the prairie without population is a desert." Mercifully, Hill would not live to see his dreams blighted by drought, depression, and the exodus from small farms; nor would he read the words of Montana historian Joseph Kinsey Howard, who singled him out, polemically and inaccurately, as nearly the sole architect of later disaster. Hill would never know about the wild denunciation by North Dakota journalist-historian Bruce Nelson, who spoke for a generation that had endured the "bust" by flaying Hill as the "unremitting wrecker of the empire of the northern plains."

THE LAND TAKING

Under the stimulus of a propaganda barrage, the farmers' frontier swept dramatically into east-central Montana after the turn of the twentieth century. Prior to 1900, farmers had already occupied some lands around Great Falls and Billings and in a few other favored locations east of the mountains. During the next half-dozen years, they probed into the "golden triangle" north of Great Falls and into central Montana areas like the Judith Basin. Then, beginning in 1908-9, the railroads started moving a tidal wave of farm families into northern and eastern Montana. The boom swept westward across the High Line area north of the Missouri and engulfed the broad valleys and rolling plains above and below the Yellowstone River. New boomtowns seemed to spring up overnight: Plentywood, Scobey, Rudyard, Ryegate, Baker, and Hardin.

The rush surged dramatically in 1910. The Great Falls land offices, which served north-central Montana, processed between a thousand and fifteen hundred homestead filings a month during that turbulent year. During the first quarter of 1910, the Great Northern moved over a thousand emigrant cars into northern Montana. On one spring evening, that railroad debarked 250 homesteaders at Havre alone. The flood tide of immigration leveled off somewhat during 1911-12 and then rose again during 1913-18. Statistics revealed the mounting effects of the farmers' frontier. Even by 1910 agriculture had surpassed mining to become Montana's major source of income. The state's population climbed from 243,329 in 1900 to 376,053 in 1910. During the same period, the aggregate number of farms and ranches increased from 13,370 to 26,214. An official state promotional publication claimed that Montana's population in 1918 had increased to 769,590. By 1920, even after the boom had collapsed, the census found 548,889 Montanans and 57,677 farms and ranches in the state.

Nature, it seemed, conspired with man to lure the homesteaders to Montana. The boom period of land-taking, from 1909 through 1916, was a time of generally ample rainfall, averaging sixteen inches of precipitation a year. Equally important, the rains came at the right time, during the late spring and early summer months. Newcomers assumed that this was the normal, predictable climate in Montana. Wheat harvests averaged over twenty-five bushels to the acre. In 1909, total wheat production in Montana reached to slightly less than eleven million bushels, and in the "miracle year" of 1915 it totaled over forty-two million bushels. During the wet years of 1915-16, many northern Montana farms harvested thirty-five to fifty bushels per acre. And grain prices were high, especially after 1914, when World War I increased demands for United States wheat. Montana's high quality, high-protein, hard spring and winter wheat held top rank on the booming international markets. It is small wonder that the farmers came and that they foresaw a rosy future.

Who were the homesteaders who changed forever the face and complexion of Montana society? Writing in the 1940s, not long after John Steinbeck's *The Grapes of Wrath* was published, Great Falls journalist Joseph Kinsey Howard described the new pioneer as "the Joad of a quarter century ago, swarming into a hostile land: duped when he started, robbed when he arrived." Howard demonstrated not only a tendency to stereotype and to overdramatize, but also to romanticize history. He saw Montana's history from the cattleman's perspective and tended, like painter Charles M. Russell, to view the dirt farmers as rubes and hayseeds who were despoiling the good earth. Howard resurrected the term "honyocker" to describe the homesteaders. In its earlier usages, "honyocker" was a slur that was a corruption of a German expression meaning "chicken chaser." To some "native" Montanans, all of the newly arrived farmers were "honyockers," and all of them were stupid and undesirable. By continuing to use the degrading cowboy slang, Howard and historians after him have tended to portray the homesteaders as social misfits and incompetents. In much the same spirit, cattlemen used the term "scissor-bill" to refer derisively to homesteaders.

In truth, the homesteaders were a very diverse group. Although many were foreigners—primarily from Germany and Scandinavia—most were native-born Americans. The 1920 census indicated that only 17.1 percent of all Montanans were foreign born. Beyond dispute, many of them lacked farming experience, which undoubtedly caused hundreds to fail. In a sample of fifty-eight farmers in a "typical township" of Montana's north-central "triangle" region, agricultural expert M. L. Wilson found only twenty-three who listed their former occupation as "farmer" in 1922. Among the others, Wilson found two physicians, two schoolteachers, three "Maiden Ladies," six musicians, two wrestlers, and one "World Rover."

Wilson's sample was somewhat misleading because it failed to record how many of the farmers, regardless of their former occupations, were originally from farm families and had some farming experience. Moreover, many of the homesteaders who had no farm backgrounds were literate, and they relied on publications from the U.S. Department of Agriculture and the Agricultural Experiment Station at Montana State College. But Wilson's research clearly indicated the broad variety of people caught up in the net of railroad promotion. "The one trait they had in common," noted Marie Peterson McDonald, "was youth. They were men and women in the prime of life, in their twenties and early thirties." A surprising number were single women who in some areas comprised close to 20 percent of those filing claims. The homesteaders were neither the "Joads of their day"—1930s-style farm refugees—nor were they "dumb honyockers." Some were sophisticated businessmen. Thomas D. Campbell, for instance, acquired the backing of J. P. Morgan to lease 150,000 acres in the Big Horn Basin. At one time, he operated the world's greatest wheat farm, with 500 plows, 600 drills, 72 binders, and 32 combines and threshing machines. Campbell later taught farmers in Russia the dry-farming methods he had worked out in Montana.

Montana's homesteaders were the last wave of the agricultural frontier, and they found in Montana a hard way of life. Most came by rail, but others arrived in Studebaker wagons and lurching Model T Fords. At the depot they often ran into "locators," frontier promoters and salesmen who, for a fee of from twenty-five to fifty dollars, would find them a choice homestead plot or perhaps a lucrative piece of railroad land. Joseph Kinsey Howard described the locators as villains who fleeced the homestead-

One-room, tar-paper-sheathed shacks, and even automobiles among the better heeled, typified Montana's homestead frontier, where thousands located farms in isolated areas, miles from the nearest town and railroad.

ers. And it is true that locators who worked for railroad or land companies on a commission sometimes left pioneer families in desolate settings. But bureaucratic requirements for claiming land were complicated, and homesteaders often needed help. As historian William E. Farr has pointed out, the locator was "an indispensable frontier institution," and an honest one like George Sollid of Dutton was "a permanent, steadying force in the life of his growing town."

Many homesteaders lived in sodhouses constructed from slabs of turf, which were so common on the plains to the east and south. But more often the newcomers to Montana built two-, three-, or four-room shacks out of roughcut lumber. The homestead shanties usually had tarpaper, at best, for an outer covering and often had nothing more than old newspaper sheets for interior "insulation." With only a pot-bellied stove for heat, the crude shacks could be frigid in the winter and terribly hot in the summer. Faced with constant wind and dust and long, bitterly cold winters, with spells of subzero weather when both children and valuable farm animals had to be huddled indoors, farm wives often aged prematurely.

Women's experiences on the homestead frontier were often harsh, but there is little evidence to support the view that women were the reluctant or unwilling victims of their husbands' frontier urge. To be sure, many women experienced loneliness and most had no other women nearby. But there were wide individual differences in the extent to which isolation produced debilitating or even pathological degrees of loneliness. To some women, homesteading meant new and unsettling experiences; others welcomed frontier challenges and preferred farm work to domestic chores.

Wood and water were often scarce necessities. Some families traveled up to twenty-five miles to cut fence posts or to find wood for the woodpile. Where trees were even less accessible, homesteaders sometimes burned lignite or bituminous coal, which abounded in eastern Montana. The availability of easily dug coal was often a factor in determining a homestead location. But water was the most precious commodity. In that arid and rocky land, drilling wells was difficult, expensive, and unpredictable. Some settlers trapped rainwater in cisterns, and others used tank wagons to haul water over long distances. Waterholes often had to be cleared of frogs, snakes, bugs, and dead mice before barrels could be filled, and the mineral content of the water frequently made laundering difficult. More important, water impurity led to the constant threat of disease, especially typhoid, cholera, and the "Colorado quick-step" diarrhea. Childhood diseases terrorized frontier families more than any other threat, and the gravestones of children in the weed-grown cemeteries of homestead ghost towns tell a heart-rending tale of the horrors of scarlet fever, pneumonia, smallpox, and other dreaded killers.

Life on the farm was often hard and monotonous, but it also had many rewards: the closeness of family, neighborly ties, the excitement of week-end visits to town, and long-awaited events like buying the family's first automobile or piano. There was also the unique joy of breaking the soil and the fine sense of accomplishment when the land bore its harvest. In his memoir, *The Generous Years*, Chet Huntley remembered the exhilaration of spring and the feeling of communion with nature that it aroused:

> I sat in the warm sunshine on tops of the hills overlooking the ranch house, the barns, the fields and the lake bed. I lay down and put my head on the grass. I could hear it! I could hear spring! The ground was a moving, writhing, stirring mass of movement and growth. Millions of tiny shoots were probing at the warm earth, drinking its moisture, absorbing its goodness and sending their growth to the sunlight. The earth, the sky, the air, the universe were throbbing with life . . . and it was good!

There were also social rewards. Each year, for example, neighboring farmers and their families joined to help each other with threshing rings. The work was hard, but the men and teenaged boys enjoyed the camaraderie. For most women, though, threshing was a hard and stressful time, with long hours and little sleep. Cooking on wood- and coal-burning stoves, sometimes in mobile kitchens, women had the heavy burden of cooking five meals a day for voraciously hungry threshing crews of as many as twenty-five men.

Where settlement was sufficiently compact, nieghbors maintained an active social life centering on the community hall (often built with the proceeds of box socials), which usually also served as the school. The hall was the scene of Saturday night dances, one of the most common forms of recreation, as well as card parties and the animated literary and debating contests that reflected the broad reading programs of many homestead families. In summer, there were baseball games combined with Saturday afternoon picnics. In some areas, efforts to overcome isolation even included constructing cooperative telephone systems by using barbed wire fences as lines.

The homesteaders had come to Montana by the tens of thousands, and most came to stay. They put down roots and built for the future, for no matter how forbidding the land, it was *their* land. Like American farmers of the previous three centuries, Montana homesteaders valued a farm of their own above all other earthly possessions. Their determination to remain on the land, to turn the land to their own will, made them the last, the most important, and ultimately the most tragically afflicted of all the Montana pioneers.

This homesteader family, photographed while picnicking on Beaver Creek near Havre in 1912, found their relaxation and recreation, as others did, in Montana's abundant natural attractions.

THE AGE OF OPTIMISM

Not surprisingly, this era of land-taking was a time of heady optimism and high hopes. Joseph Kinsey Howard described many homesteaders as land speculators who had no intention of putting down roots. Some certainly fit that description, and they sold out shortly after gaining patents to the land. But a substantial majority, at least initially, looked forward to staying and becoming part of a new community. Both the homesteaders themselves and the residents of the small towns that grew up to serve them shared in the belief that they were building model communities on the high plains and in the mountain valleys. In those days, before the great "bust" of agriculture that followed World War I, time and human affairs seemed to be moving in Montana's direction. The Montana settlers were the true heirs of Thomas Jefferson, and of the many farming generations that had come before them, in their belief that farm families and small towns formed the bulwark of America. As a 1914 state promotional pamphlet put it, land in Montana provided "an assured future," and "there is no place where failure is so remote."

Well aware that they stood on the last frontier of American agriculture, Montana homesteaders saw themselves as taming the last wilderness and advancing the cause of civilization. In their eyes, growth was progress and progress was good. The editor of *The Montana Churchman* expressed this sentiment in 1907:

> That time [the cowboy days] has gone forever. Already in her westward march Civilization has planted her feet firmly on this territory. Ten years from now "the West" will be as the womb of the earth, teeming with people, seething with industry, alive with manifold activities—the center of population and civilization!

The settlers saw in this "inland" or "midland empire" not only the last West but also the best West. By taking advantage of modern technology and the lessons learned on earlier frontiers, they would remove much of the drudgery of farm life, and their upright farms and towns, they believed, would soon overbalance the sinful and debased mining and cattle towns. The open-range grazing era and the wide-open spaces would give way to a more healthy social system. *The Gallatin Farmer and Stockman* predicted: "The rancher of the future will know the color of the smoke from his neighbor's chimney. The covert of the deer will be the retreat of the domestic animal and the lair of the wild beast the play house of the children. There will be no wilderness anymore."

The most enthusiastic of the homestead era boomers were the city fathers and newspaper editors of the farming communities. These towns sprang up literally by the hundreds during the three decades following

1890. Their names still punctuate the Montana map: Shelby and Chester, Geraldine and Joliet, Gildford and Bloomfield. Geographer John C. Hudson has likened homestead towns to "beads on a string," laced about every ten miles along railroad lines by the roads and by local promoters. From either a physical or a cultural viewpoint, the homestead towns bore little resemblance to cowtowns like Lewistown or Miles City, which had served the basic economic and social needs of cowboys and cattlemen. The farmers' towns looked like what they tried to be—transplanted midwestern villages.

These small towns made up the heartland of the Montana prohibition movement, which succeeded, at least in a legal sense, in "drying up" the state in 1916. It was Middle America. Each town, it seemed, looked forward to a rosy future of unlimited growth. Each, as Robert G. Athearn wrote, planned to become a "great railroad center." But none of them ever did, and today's travelers can find dozens of towns that were abandoned or nearly abandoned. Of those that continue to support the population of rural Montana, most are either static or declining in population. Today, these towns, and others like them throughout the nation, are fighting against desperate odds to hold their population and to save a way of life that is being steadily eroded by modern economic trends.

The boom psychology of those years had perhaps its greatest and its most negative effect in the form of the county-splitting movement. Surely it was inevitable that, with the great land rush, the huge counties of eastern Montana would be broken up. The vast distances involved and the needs of citizens to be near their county seats demanded it. As late as 1910, the northern-eastern 60 percent of Montana still remained enclosed in nine huge counties—Teton, Chouteau, Valley, Cascade, Fergus, Dawson, Yellowstone, Rosebud, and Custer. During the fifteen years that followed 1910, twenty-eight new counties were formed, as the larger counties divided and then divided again.

Counties did not usually divide along sensible geographic lines, with the most intensive breakups taking place in the south-central and the northeastern regions. But then, county-splitting was not a rational process. Fast-talking promoters and political con men dominated the movement. The best known of these was Dan McKay, who had a personal hand in breaking up a dozen counties. Usually riding into town atop "the biggest horse in the Milk River Valley," McKay had the political knack of rallying public opinion behind his cause. McKay and other county-splitters simply went from town to town, whipping up enthusiasm about the advantages of smaller counties and the blessings that a county courthouse and its payroll would bring to any village, no matter how remote. Then, for a small fee, the county-splitters would organize the signing of petitions

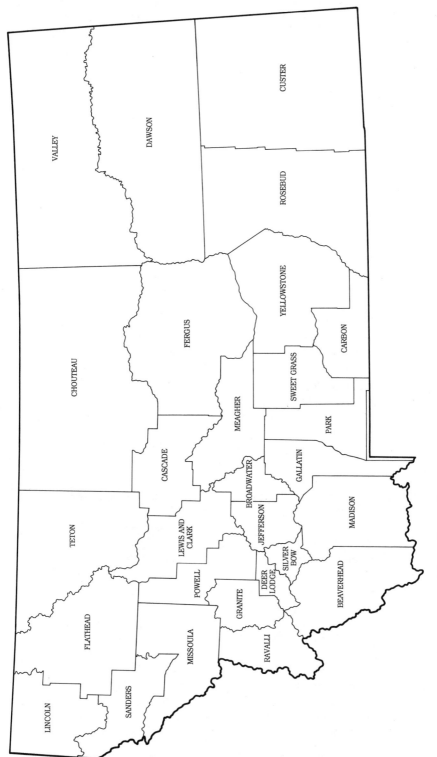

Map 4. Counties, 1909 (map by Barbara Lien)

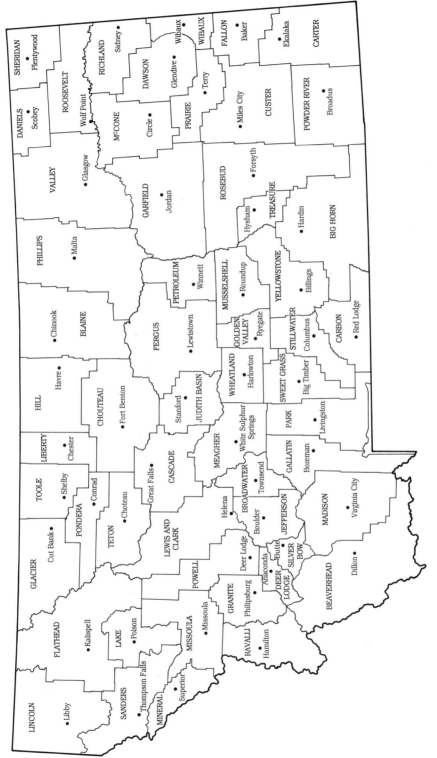

Map 5. Counties, 1990 (map by Barbara Lien)

and arrange the elections necessary to break up the units of government.

The county-splitting frenzy peaked during the boom decade of 1910-20. At the height of the land rush, in 1915, the Montana legislature enacted the Leighton Act. Passed in an irresponsible moment, the Leighton Act gave counties an almost completely free hand to subdivide as they saw fit. They did. And by the time the multiplying process ended, the number of Montana counties had doubled to the present total of fifty-six. The new county governments and their courthouses and employees cost plenty of money, and during the flush times, property taxes increased to pay the bills. But when the boom turned to bust, property owners increasingly failed to meet their taxes. The counties ended up seizing lands for tax delinquencies, devouring their own property owners. Today, the problems arising from reckless county-splitting are still very much with Montanans. Many rural counties have either lost or barely gained population since 1920, and they find themselves hardpressed to support their own local governments.

AGRICULTURE AND THE FIRST WORLD WAR

Few Montanans of those robust, optimistic years foresaw the hardships their future held. The state entered the year 1917 on a tidal wave of prosperity. Over the past eight years, ample rainfall and high food prices had nurtured a persistent farm prosperity; and since 1915, lucrative new markets for American foodstuffs had opened in war-torn Europe. Then, in the spring of 1917, the United States entered World War I. Entry into the Great War had an immediate, decisive effect on agriculture, as the demand for food and the prices of commodities soared. In order to assure maximum farm output, Congress enacted the Lever Food and Fuel Control Act, which empowered the president to peg the price of wheat at not less than two dollars per bushel.

President Woodrow Wilson placed the Lever Act program of conserving food and assuring all-out farm production under a new federal agency, the Food Administration. Under the capable direction of Herbert Hoover, the Food Administration bombarded the nation's farmers with the message that they must produce to the utmost: "Food Will Win the War!" In addition, each state had its own food administrator. Alfred Atkinson of Montana State College held the post in the Treasure State. In countless speeches and newspaper advertisements, he told his fellow citizens: "The government of the United States, as well as its war associates, is in great need of wheat. Every available pound is needed if the German flood is to be stemmed."

Farmers responded to this patriotic appeal, but they responded even more to the rising price of grain. By authority of the Lever Act, the Wilson administration, through the Food Administration, set the price of wheat at roughly $2.20 per bushel for the duration of the conflict. Grain farmers criticized this move, because they believed that wheat prices without controls might have climbed to four dollars a bushel. But the controls still guaranteed them good profits, as they well knew. Uncle Sam encouraged farmers to expand production in other ways as well. The newly created Federal Reserve System extended easy credit to national banks, which then offered loans to farmers on appealing terms. A rising chorus of federal officials, bankers, patriotic orators, and, of course, land speculators urged farmers to expand their operations. With readily available credit, farmers could mortgage their land, buildings, and machinery and buy more land, buildings, and machinery. And with wheat going for more than two dollars a bushel, they could even plow up pastureland and plant it in grain. Surely the war would last at least until 1920, and by then profits would make repayment of the loans easy. "Food Will Win the War!"

By a curious twist of fate, the peak of the Montana homestead rush had coincided with America's entry into the Great War. High wartime prices and the patriotic urge to produce for victory added the final boost to the great Montana boom. The last great plow-up took place in 1917-18. Betting on continuing prosperity, the homesteaders went further into debt and turned their plows toward the uncultivated pasturelands. Why leave the scrublands in their natural grass condition? If they would yield any crop at all, it seemed sensible to plow them up. The land rush reached its climax in the enthusiastic spring and summer seasons of 1917 and 1918. But even at that optimistic moment, the first signs of drought were beginning to appear on the plains of eastern Montana.

CHAPTER 11

The Progressive Era and World War I

AMERICAN historians usually refer to the years between the turn of the century and World War I, from 1900 to 1916, as the "Progressive Era." During that period, many thoughtful Americans, increasingly concerned with mounting social problems, took up the cause of reform. Progressive reformers identified a wide range of social ills, many of them rising out of the industrial revolution, including business abuses, the exploitation of women and children, the traffic in alcohol, and political corruption. The progressives did not, by any means, seek radical answers to these problems, nor did they always agree. Most progressives were moderate, middle-class Americans who believed that the "system" could be made to function properly with only a few alterations. Generally speaking, they believed that what America needed was direct democracy. With great optimism and moralism, they reasoned that things would be set right if the mass of citizens gained political power.

Progressivism had its impact on every level of society and government and on every region of the nation. It took root in both major political parties and produced two presidents, Republican Theodore Roosevelt and Democrat Woodrow Wilson. Although some historians have argued that progressivism had little effect on remote Montana, the facts prove otherwise. Progressivism took deep root in the Treasure State, producing a number of lasting reforms and four political leaders who reached nationwide prominence—Joseph Dixon, Thomas J. Walsh, Jeannette Rankin, and Burton K. Wheeler. In Montana, as in the rest of the nation, those years also produced a powerful radical movement on the far left. Throughout the United States, and especially in Montana, World War I brought the political passions of an entire generation to a boil, deflating the movement for progressive reform and destroying the radicals.

In Montana, as in Oregon and other states of the Northwest, progressive reformers began making their influence felt during the first decade of the twentieth century. The Montana progressives included many different groups with many different concerns, but they all aimed at improving public life, public health, and public morality through direct action. In 1907, Randall J. Condon, secretary of the Helena Civic Club, summarized the goals not only of his organization but of progressives in general: "Better schools; better churches; better public buildings; better playgrounds; better public service; better support of disinterested public officials; unsightly bill-boards abolished; cleaner streets and alleys; a better enforcement of all laws and city ordinances."

Montana progressives shared, for the most part, the same aims as reformers throughout the country. At the local level, cities like Billings, Butte, Helena, Missoula, and Great Falls produced civic clubs and citizens' leagues that concentrated on beautifying their towns and cleaning up government through such innovations as city managers and city commissions. At the state level, Montana progressives aimed to curb the power of large corporations, especially the Amalgamated Copper Company. They pushed an impressive number of reforms through the legislature, including laws that expanded popular participation in government, such as the initiative and referendum, direct primaries, and the direct election of senators; laws that protected workers, such as mine safety measures and workers' compensation; and laws that protected the public, such as railroad regulation, pure food and drug legislation, milk and meat inspection, and the creation of a state board of health.

Political reforms were the key to the progressive program. Once the mass of educated voters gained real political power, progressives believed, they could then put into effect all the other reforms that were necessary. Montana had a heritage of practicing direct democracy, of placing political power directly in the hands of the people. In 1889, Montana had become the first state to use the Australian ballot, thus assuring its citizens the right to cast their votes secretly. The most important political reforms on the progressive agenda were the initiative and the referendum, which allowed voters to legislate directly and bypass state legislatures that frequently seemed under the control of large corporations. The initiative permits the electorate to enact laws by a direct vote, and the referendum allows voters to repeal unpopular laws passed by the legislature.

Political crusaders fought for ten years to win the initiative and referendum in Montana. Beginning in the early 1890s, the Populists pressed hard for these direct legislation measures, and they gained firm support from the Montana Federation of Labor and later from progressive leaders such as Livingston lawyer E. C. Day, Judge Theodore Brantly, and journalists William Greene Eggleston and Will Kennedy. The long struggle finally ended with victory in November 1906, when the voters approved a constitutional amendment that wrote the initiative and the referendum into enduring law.

Another instrument of direct democracy favored by the progressives was the direct primary system of nominating candidates for public office. Like progressives in other states, Montana reformers watched in anger while political "bosses" such as William A. Clark and Marcus Daly gained control of the party nominating conventions. A direct primary law could curb such abuses by allowing the voters to nominate party candidates by secret ballot in special primary elections. Beginning with the Populists in the 1890s, the campaign for the direct primary paralleled the fight for the initiative and referendum. Newspapermen like Miles Romney of the Hamilton *Western News* and W. K. Harber of the Fort Benton *River Press* and lawyers like Thomas J. Walsh of Helena led the attack, and by 1903 public opinion clearly favored such a system. The 1905 legislature enacted a local option system of direct primary nominations, but that experiment proved unworkable and was repealed in 1917. Finally, using the new initiative method, the citizens of Montana approved a statewide direct primary law in the election of 1912.

Yet another element of the formula for putting political power directly in the hands of the people was the direct election of United States senators. The U.S. Constitution had placed responsibility for selecting senators in the state legislatures, but legislators were often "influenced" or bribed outright. The system had become riddled with scandalous behavior and, in the minds of reformers, had filled the United States Senate with millionaires and flunkies for big business. The answer to the problem seemed obvious to those who believed in direct democracy: a constitutional amendment that would allow the people to choose their senators by popular ballot.

Montanans reacted to this issue with special enthusiasm. After all, W. A. Clark's bribery of the 1899 Montana legislature offered an especially sordid example of how badly the current system worked. After 1893, almost every session of the Montana legislature memorialized Congress to pass a constitutional amendment providing for the direct election of senators. By the early 1900s, both political parties in Montana favored the system in their platforms. When Congress failed to act, the 1911 Montana legislature followed the examples of Oregon and other states and passed the Everett Bill. Through a complex system of permitting citizens to vote for U.S. senators and then forcing the legislators to ratify their choice, the Everett Bill, in effect, allowed Montanans to choose their own senators. This complicated system became unnecessary in 1913, when the Seventeenth Amendment to the Constitution went into effect, making direct election of senators the law of the land.

In addition to these basic political reforms, Montana progressives also pushed many humanitarian measures through the legislature. In 1903, Montana lawmakers created the Bureau of Child and Animal Protection. Under the capable direction of Otto Schoenfeld and with the support of the Montana Federation of Labor, the Montana State Federation of Women's Clubs, and the Women's Christian Temperance Union, the bureau mounted a major campaign to outlaw child labor. They won a major victory in the 1904 election, when the voters approved a constitutional amendment setting sixteen as the minimum age for employment in the mines. Other victories followed. The legislature created a compulsory school attendance law, and in 1907 it extended the minimum employment age of sixteen to other industries. Also in 1907 lawmakers created a juvenile court system to assure that a "delinquent child shall be treated, not as a criminal, but as misdirected and misguided, and needing aid, encouragement, help and assistance."

Like their counterparts around the country, progressive-minded Montanans saw the nation's number one problem in the emergence of the new supercorporations, or "trusts." Editor Miles Romney voiced a common progressive sentiment in 1906 when he declared that "the greatest living issue that confronts the nation today" was whether "the corporations shall control the people or the people shall control the corporations." This issue hit close to home in Montana, especially after the Amalgamated Copper Company's 1903 shutdown and shakedown of the state government. Following the November 1903 special legislative session that the Company forced on the state, six hundred angry Montana citizens assembled at Helena to form an Anti-Trust Party. But the organization was dominated by copper king F. A. Heinze, and it accomplished very little. As Governor Toole pointed out in his 1907 state-of-the-state message, there was precious little that the states could do to regulate great corporations like Standard Oil or Amalgamated Copper. Only the federal government, by using the antitrust laws, could tackle them.

One class of corporation that states could regulate was the railroad. Montanans complained that the railroads failed to pay their fair share of taxes, that accidents were far too frequent, that service was poor and rates were too high, and that the railroads "bought" politicians by giving them free passes. The radical Populists favored a government takeover of the railroads; the more cautious progressives wanted them regulated through a state railroad commission. Led by lawyer Thomas Walsh and other experts, the Montana progressives triumphed in 1907, when the legislature created a Montana Railroad Commission. In 1913, the agency became the Montana Public Service Commission, with authority over other public carriers and electrical utilities.

PROGRESSIVISM AT HIGH TIDE, 1912-1916

The reform movement in Montana climaxed immediately after the hard-fought election campaign of 1912. At the national level, a three-way fight for the presidency dominated the 1912 campaign. Woodrow Wilson, a progressive Democrat, faced William Howard Taft, a conservative Republican, while former President Theodore Roosevelt broke with the Republican party and led its more reform-minded wing into the ranks of the newly organized Progressive or "Bull Moose" party. Because the Republicans were bitterly divided, the Democrats won the race, with Wilson taking the White House, Roosevelt finishing second, and Taft an embarrassing third. Events in Montana closely paralleled national trends, with the state's Republican party splitting in two. In the Senate race, the conservative Republicans ran Henry C. Smith; but the real contest was between the state's two leading progressives, Democrat Thomas J. Walsh and the incumbent, Joseph M. Dixon, a Bull Moose Progressive.

Dixon, an intelligent, handsome, and high principled businessman-politician, was the leading figure of the Montana progressive movement. Born and raised in a North Carolina Quaker community, he moved to Missoula in 1891. Dixon took up the practice of law, made several profitable business investments, and moved into Republican party politics. After serving briefly as Missoula county attorney and as a state representative, he won election as Montana's lone congressman and served two terms, 1903-7. Joe Dixon's ability and ambition led him toward the United States Senate. Even though he clashed openly with powerful Senator Thomas Carter, the leader of the conservative Republicans, Dixon managed to gain his party's support for the Senate. In 1907, the legislature sent him to Washington to succeed retiring Senator W. A. Clark.

Once in the Senate, Dixon began to sound more and more like a hard-nosed progressive, attacking the railroads and the Company and speaking out for such reforms as the direct primary. Always an admirer of Theodore Roosevelt, Dixon served as chairman of the Progressive party convention at Chicago in 1912 and agreed to act as Roosevelt's national campaign manager. Back in Montana, Dixon's friends Sam Goza and Frank J. Edwards led in forming a state Bull Moose organization, aimed at putting Roosevelt in the White House and Dixon back in the Senate. The Montana Bull Moosers fought the Company head-on. Their stationery carried the letterhead: "Put the Amalgamated out of Montana Politics."

Dixon's Democratic opponent for the Senate was Thomas J. Walsh of Helena, who was also a progressive but was closer to the middle of the road. Born into an Irish immigrant family, Walsh grew up in Wisconsin, taught in country schools, and then took a degree from the University of Wisconsin Law School. He practiced law briefly in South Dakota, where he also became involved in politics, but greater opportunities led him to Helena in 1890. Dixon built a great legal reputation in Helena, especially through his handling of the cases of injured workmen, and both he and his wife became active in Democratic and progressive circles. Prior to the 1912 Senate race, Walsh made two tries for national public office and failed both times. He lost a 1906 congressional race and was denied a seat in the Senate in 1911, when the Company opposed him in the legislature.

At the height of his powers in 1912, Thomas Walsh stood on the threshold of a magnificent public career. Recognized as a great legal mind, Walsh commanded more respect than affection from the people. He was small of stature and mustachioed, cold and dour in personality. Photographs show him glaring icily at the camera, even while surrounded by cheering crowds and grinning politicians. But no one ever doubted Walsh's ability or his integrity. As a newspaperman wrote, asking Walsh for special favors "would be like asking the statue of Civic Virtue for a chew of tobacco."

Due mainly to the split in the Republican ranks and the Company's determination to defeat Dixon, the Democrats swept the 1912 election and Walsh easily captured the Senate seat. The Democrats also won the governor's chair for Sam V. Stewart, the eastern and western congressional districts, and both houses of the legislature. Soundly beaten, Joseph Dixon retired temporarily from politics and concentrated on his western Montana business investments. Like Roosevelt, Dixon and the Montana Bull Moosers would soon return to the ranks of the Republican party. Thomas Walsh, meanwhile, went triumphantly to Washington, beginning a twenty-year Senate career that would prove to be one of the most distinguished in modern American history. He quickly developed a close relationship with President Woodrow Wilson and earned a reputation for honesty and efficient care of his constituents.

The 1912 campaign bears great significance in Montana's history. It not only launched Walsh's Senate career, but it also revealed the rising power of Treasure State progressives. For the first time since Heinze's fall, Montanans were organizing against the Company. The election also witnessed the first large-scale use of direct legislation in Montana. The voters considered and passed four initiative proposals in 1912, writing into law a direct primary system, a campaign expenditures and corrupt practices act, a presidential preference primary, and a measure clarifying the popular election of senators. In a referendum vote, they also rejected a law passed by the 1911 legislature that had given the governor more liberal powers to call out the state militia. Organized labor, joined by many other progressives, had opposed the law, arguing that the Company had pushed it through so that the militia could be used to crush strikes. In striking down the militia law in the 1912 election, the progressives believed they had handed the Amalgamated a significant defeat.

The sweeping direct legislation victories of 1912 owed much to a progressive organization that had formed the year before, the People's Power League, which grew out of a June 1911 meeting at Deer Lodge. The delegates at the meeting included many of Montana's leading reformers, such as lawyers Walsh and Judge E. K. Cheadle of Lewistown, journalists Miles Romney and W. K. Harber, labor leaders M. M. Donoghue of the Montana Federation of Labor and Henry Drennan of the United Mine Workers. In forming the People's Power League, they elected Romney as their president and Max McCusker of Livingston, a Northern Pacific machinist, as their secretary-treasurer. The sole purpose of the new organization, the progressives announced, was to secure "beneficial legislation through the initiative and referendum."

After its 1912 victories, the People's Power League continued to press for reform. It found support from the Direct Legislation League, another progressive body that took shape in late March 1913. Made up heavily of Bull Moose Republicans, the Direct Legislation League worked hard to raise taxes on mining and other corporations. The two groups shared many of the same aims, of course, and some of the same members. Leaders of the People's Power League, like Romney and Bozeman attorney Walter Hartman, also worked through the Direct Legislation League. Cleverly, the militant progressives pushed two measures that they hoped would serve to form an alliance between farmers and workers against corporate power. They sponsored an initiative providing for a badly needed workers' compensation system to care for the many victims of industrial accidents, and they pushed an initiative that would enable the state to invest money from its common school fund in farm mortgage loans.

The progressives failed in their attempt to create a farmer-labor alliance. In the 1914 election, labor helped rural areas pass an initiative providing for the farm loans. But the Amalgamated and its allies were able to cut down farm votes for workers' compensation by forming the Montana Advancement Association, which sent speakers into the rural areas warning of the dangers of such a system, and the initiative failed to pass. A workmen's compensation law did pass in the 1915 legislature, but it was less sweeping than the one envisaged by the reformers and more in line with corporate wishes.

Jeannette Rankin, the first woman elected to Congress, shown here in her Washington, D.C., office in 1918.

The Argus *in Lewistown, Fergus County, was typical of dozens of newspapers that served agricultural towns in Montana and played critical roles in creating and maintaining community identity.*

Although the progressives lost on some issues, they gained on others. After the 1912 campaign, Montana reformers had two triumphs that they had sought for years—the vote for women and prohibition of alcoholic beverages. In the November 1914 election, Montana voters approved a constitutional amendment granting woman suffrage, capping a thirty-year struggle for women's equality. Montana women had enjoyed a limited suffrage during territorial days, when they could vote on special tax levies as property owners. They also had the right to vote for school district trustees and county school superintendents. Women's political rights first came up for serious discussion at the 1889 constitutional convention when Perry W. McAdow and other delegates tried, without success, to guarantee women the vote in the state constitution.

During the 1890s Montana women made several attempts to secure a constitutional amendment for woman suffrage. Especially encouraged by the Populist party's endorsement of the measure, leaders such as Dr. Mary Moore Atwater of Marysville and Sarepta Sanders and Ella Knowles of Helena constantly hammered away at the legislature. But after a long string of defeats the woman's suffrage movement lost its momentum. A handful of determined suffragettes, such as physician Maria Dean and Mrs. Thomas Walsh of Helena, fought on but made no headway.

By 1905 the woman's suffrage movement in Montana appeared to be dead. But the rising winds of progressivism breathed new life into the cause and gave it a more militant tone. Women had previously demanded the vote on the simple grounds of equality, but now they began to argue that the world needed women's superior social and moral qualities. As one of them said, "Now, it is woman, only woman . . . who can rescue poor, indiscreet and misguided man and lift him to the height above the seething, rotten condition into which he has gotten himself." Aided by progressive organizations and by feminist groups in neighboring states, the women's cause in Montana also benefited from the homestead movement. Most homesteaders, male and female, supported women's equality in the belief that it would serve to cleanse society of its evils.

Leadership of the feminist cause in Montana passed to Jeannette Rankin, an attractive, willful, and capable organizer. Rankin, the daughter of a prominent Missoula family, had gained prominence in national feminist circles and had worked on the 1910 campaign that had won the vote for women in the state of Washington. During the 1911 legislature, the women won a round when Representative D. J. Donohue of Glendive introduced a bill providing for a woman suffrage amendment to the Montana constitution. The house of representatives granted Jeannette Rankin the privilege of appearing to discuss the bill, and Mary Long Alderson, Dr. Maria Dean, and Dr. Mary Moore Atwater were honored with seats

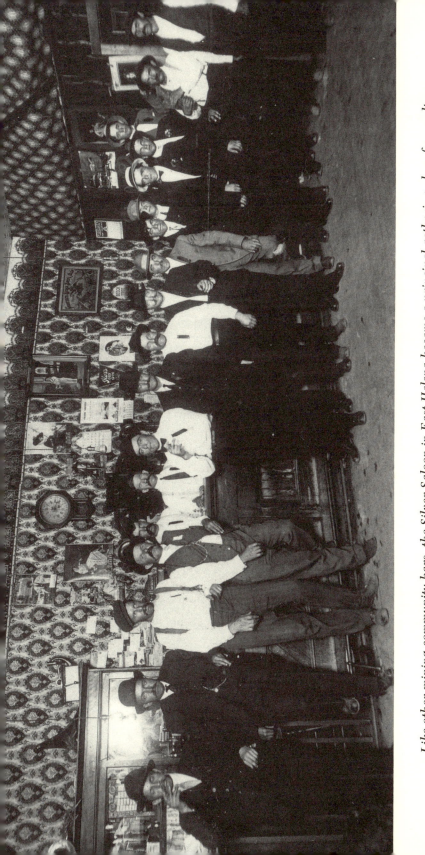

Like other mining community bars, the Silver Saloon in East Helena became a principal gathering place for smelter workers and other union laborers.

on the speaker's platform. Although the suffrage bill failed in 1911, the vote on the measure showed mounting support, especially from the homestead counties.

During the 1912 campaign, Rankin and other suffragists persuaded the major political parties to put woman suffrage planks in their platforms, and they organized the Montana Equal Suffrage Association to lobby politicians. The women's crusade gained momentum rapidly. In its 1913 session, the Montana legislature passed a suffrage amendment bill, which the voters would consider in 1914. Other groups hurriedly joined the Montana Equal Suffrage Association in the campaign to rally public opinion. Wellington D. Rankin, Jeannette's brother and fellow progressive, headed a Montana chapter of the Men's League for Woman's Suffrage, and additional help came from the Montana Federation of Women's Clubs and from the Women's Christian Temperance Union. In their campaign for the vote, the Montana feminists did have their differences. The WCTU, for instance, wanted to link the suffrage movement with prohibition and to rally the support of immigrant groups. Rankin and the Montana Equal Suffrage Association wanted to avoid the prohibition issue and distrusted the foreigners. Rankin even argued that women voters would and should help keep the immigrants from gaining political power.

In the election of November 3, 1914, Montana voters narrowly passed the woman suffrage amendment by a vote of 41,302 to 37,588. The women gained their best support from the new homestead counties and found the toughest going in the older mining and agricultural areas. Savoring their victory, the suffragists met at Helena in January 1915 and organized the Montana Good Government Association, the forerunner of the Montana League of Women Voters. They demonstrated their political clout in the 1916 election when, for the first time, they had the power of the ballot box. Emma Ingalls and Maggie Smith Hathaway won seats in the Montana legislature, and May Trumper was elected superintendent of public instruction. Most significantly, Jeannette Rankin secured a lasting place in American history by gaining election to one of Montana's two congressional seats, becoming the first woman to sit in Congress. When Rankin arrived in Washington to assume her duties early in 1917, the nation watched intently to see whether a woman could handle the responsibilities of high office. Events proved that she could.

Montana feminists had other goals beyond gaining the vote. Like many other progressives, most of them viewed saloons and the traffic in alcohol as great social evils, and they wanted to remove them through prohibition laws. The prohibition movement, like the women's rights movement, had begun far back in the nineteenth century, but it gained strength rapidly during the progressive period. The prohibition campaign received much of its local support from the homestead communities, where strait-laced farm wives were determined to stamp out saloons. Local chapters of the Women's Christian Temperance Union spread rapidly throughout Montana from 1896 to 1910, and so did the highly effective Anti-Saloon League, especially after 1905. When Idaho and Washington passed prohibition laws, Montana prohibitionists gained a powerful arguing point, warning that exiled saloon elements from those states were retreating to Montana.

During the 1915 legislative session, the "dry" forces, led by Joseph Pope, a Billings clergyman and head of the Anti-Saloon League campaign, pressured Montana lawmakers by showering them with petitions demanding a referendum on prohibition. The Catholics joined the offensive, and Bishop John P. Carroll of the Helena diocese and Mathias C. Lenihan of the Great Falls diocese endorsed the referendum. When the people voted on the referendum in November 1916, they approved the prohibition of alcoholic beverages by an overwhelming margin, 102,776 votes to 73,890. Montana officially went "dry" at the end of 1918, and in 1920 prohibition became national law through the Eighteenth Amendment to the United States Constitution.

The prohibitionists breathed a sigh of relief and concluded that their victory had been securely won. But prohibition failed all across the country, and nowhere more spectacularly than in Montana. Soon, numerous illegal "whiskey roads" in Montana reached across the United States–Canada border, and rural residents grew accustomed to the roar of "rum-runners" hauling their cargoes of booze over country roads. By the 1920s, prohibition was an obvious failure in the hard-drinking Treasure State. Liquor flowed openly, especially in working-class towns like Butte and Havre. When the "great experiment" of prohibition ended in 1933, most Montanans seemed relieved.

In supporting reforms like prohibition, the progressives, in Montana and throughout the nation, demonstrated a highly optimistic and moralistic outlook. If only the people had the opportunity to vote and if only the necessary laws could be passed, they believed, then evil would surely be eradicated and progress would be guaranteed. Miles Romney of Hamilton summed up the progressives' attitudes well. Through that "invincible force, enlightened public opinion," he wrote, the "people will control. The railroad corporations, the beef trust, the timber trust and every other predatory adjunct of capitalism that seeks special privileges and to unjustly tax the public will be brought up with a short turn and caused to obey laws." Always optimistic, the progressives were basically enlightened conservatives. With only a few changes, they argued, the system would again work nicely and all would be well. Many of the reformers would later become disillusioned when they found that their reforms did not work as perfectly as they had imagined. Prohibition would fail; direct democracy would not rid the state of political bosses; workers' compensation would lead to scandal; the Public Service Commission would not always regulate industries in the public interest; and the Company would still be there, awesomely powerful, when the progressives were dead and gone. But despite their failures, the progressives had a major impact on the political development of Montana.

THE RADICALS

Progressives did not control Montana politics during the first two decades of the twentieth century. The stage was held instead by other political groups that spoke forcefully on the issues and expressed opinions contrary to the positions taken by the Progressives. During the Progressive Era, thousands of conservative Montanans generally opposed reform and favored the status quo. Represented by men like Republican Senator Thomas Carter and Democratic Governor Sam Stewart, conservatives had no quarrel with the Company and no use for the progressive reformers. Interestingly, Montana in the early twentieth century also produced a powerful radical movement on the far left. To those heirs of the 1890s Populists, piecemeal progressive reform was not enough; the capitalist system itself had to be fundamentally altered or replaced. The radicals reached the peak of their strength in Montana on the eve of World War I.

Of the organizations on the far left, the most famous and the most feared was the Industrial Workers of the World, known as the IWW or the "Wobblies." Founded in 1905, the IWW was a radical labor organization that advocated working-class solidarity, conflict with the capitalist system, and the gathering of all workers, skilled and unskilled, in one large industrial union. The Wobblies opposed capitalism and favored replacing industrial management with "syndicates" made up of workers. Butte labor leaders played a significant role in organizing the national IWW, and the union had a sizable following in Montana's mining towns and lumber camps. Although it never came near to gaining a majority of local workers as members, the IWW aggressively agitated against perceived abuses in the workplace and energetically organized workers. The IWW's tactics and the responses by employers resulted in considerable unrest between management and the working force.

A large and powerful Socialist party also flourished in Montana during the progressive period. Like the Wobblies, the Socialists relied on the laboring class for support and drew most of their strength from the industrial counties of Silver Bow, Deer Lodge, and Cascade. The Socialist party surfaced in Montana in 1902 when one of its members, George Sproule, ran for Congress and received three thousand votes. In 1903, the Socialists surprised everyone by winning municipal elections in Anaconda, only to be defeated the next year. Over the next few years, however, Socialist strength mounted rapidly. By 1908 Socialists held positions in the governments of working-class towns like Red Lodge and Livingston; and in 1911, they joined forces with the IWW to elect a Socialist city government in Butte, with Unitarian minister Lewis Duncan at its head. The Socialists reached the peak of their strength in 1912-14. Lewis Duncan polled over 12,500 votes in his run for governor in 1912 and received only slightly fewer votes in the 1914 congressional race.

As radical discontent spread through the laboring class, it also appeared in the rural areas. The farmer-radicals voiced their anger, as they had during the Populist period, at the unfairly low prices they received for their products while being gouged by railroads and other corporations. In 1914, local branches of the American Society of Equity began to appear in Montana. The society concentrated on forming marketing and purchasing cooperatives, but it also supported equity insurance programs, fought for lower rail rates, and—so significant in Montana—demanded a more equitable system of taxation. The reappearance of rural radicalism sent shudders of fear through the ranks of Montana conservatives, for the homestead invasion was bringing new voting strength to northern and eastern Montana. What might happen if the labor radicals and the farmer radicals joined forces? Despite their differences, such an alliance was a real possibility. As historian Theodore Saloutos put it: "Common hatreds, not a feeling of common interests, threatened to bring the two together; the farmers hated the mining interests because of tax-dodging and their stranglehold on state politics, and labor hated them because of their labor policies."

By late 1916, an organization that was far more powerful and radical than the Society of Equity began to take root in eastern Montana. Founded in North Dakota, the fiery Nonpartisan League advocated a sweeping program of state-owned banks, grain elevators, packing plants, marketing facilities, and insurance systems. The League was outspoken in its opposition to railroads and large corporate interests. More than the Montana Society of Equity, the NPL favored direct political action. Its aim was not to form a Populist-style third party, but to use the direct primary to seize control of either of the established parties. By such guerrilla action, it could nominate its friends in either the Democratic or the Republican columns.

As drought and depression hit the Northern Plains after 1917, support for the Nonpartisan League spread rapidly beyond the boundaries of

North Dakota and thousands of hard-pressed dirt farmers in northern and eastern Montana joined its ranks. In Montana, the League lashed out at the Anaconda Company, arguing that, by avoiding its fair share of the state's tax burden, it was forcing farmers to pay the costs of government. As in North Dakota, the Montana NPL attempted to attract workers as members. William F. Dunne of the Butte Electricians' Union supported the League, spoke before its meetings, and later voiced many of its policies through his radical newspaper, the *Butte Bulletin*. Wherever the Nonpartisan League appeared, it roused feverish debate between friends and foes. Progressive reformers, although suspicious of the League's radicalism, often welcomed its political support. Conservatives hated and feared the "wild men from the prairies" and attacked them as Socialists, anarchists, and Bolsheviks. Like the Wobblies in western Montana, the Nonpartisan Leaguers were on the rise as America entered the Great War.

THE IMPACT OF WORLD WAR I

When war erupted in Europe during the summer of 1914, the United States and its faraway province of Montana quickly felt the impact. At first, the fighting between Germany and Austria-Hungary on the one side and France, England, and Russia on the other merely disrupted the trade of neutral America. But soon the combatants, especially England and the "Allies," turned to the United States for foodstuffs and manufactured items. Throughout 1915-16, trade with the Allies fueled a major boom in the American economy. Skyrocketing farm prices intensified the great plow-up of eastern Montana, and the western mining towns flourished under escalating demands for copper and zinc. Butte reached the peak of its production and population during these years.

After nearly three years of nervous neutrality, the United States finally entered the Great War in the spring of 1917. The decision to go to war, though supported by a majority of American citizens, caused great dissension, and nowhere did the debate flare hotter than in Montana and the Northwest. Most Montanans supported the war enthusiastically, believing with President Woodrow Wilson that the war would lead to lasting peace and would "make the world safe for democracy." Montana demonstrated its support of the war by surpassing all other states in enlistment rates and draft quotas for the armed forces. Twelve thousand five hundred young Montana men volunteered for service; and due apparently to confused population estimates, the Selective Service drafted nearly twenty-eight thousand more. So, nearly forty thousand men—almost 10 percent of the population—went to war, a rate of contribution that exceeded that

The 2nd Montana, 163rd Infantry paraded down Helena's Main Street on October 24, 1917, before shipping out for duty in France during World War I.

of the next highest state by 25 percent. Montanans also suffered a record percentage of casualties—939 Montanans died—many at the French village of Gesnes, whose citizens later erected a monument to them.

Although the majority of Montanans waved the red, white, and blue, many people openly opposed the nation's involvement in the war. In the farming regions, many immigrant homesteaders turned instinctively against the war effort. The large German population naturally disliked making war on Germany, and thousands of the state's Scandinavian farmers had brought neutral, antiwar sentiments with them across the Atlantic. The large Irish population of Butte and western Montana detested America's alliance with Britain, which was once again using military force to beat down an independence movement in Ireland. But the most vehement foes of the war were the radicals on the left, who viewed the conflict as a capitalist conspiracy, "a rich man's war and a poor man's fight." Many spokesmen for the IWW and the Socialist party condemned the war, and so did some of the Nonpartisan Leaguers.

With patriotism and antiwar sentiment rising to fever pitch, suppression and violence were probably inevitable. In Montana, as elsewhere in the United States, German-Americans and suspected opponents of war were hounded and sometimes openly terrorized. German immigrants often had to demonstrate their loyalty to America by kneeling to kiss the flag or by buying Liberty Bonds under threats of punishment. Many towns and cities established a Liberty Committee to police local nonconformists. Billings had a Third Degree Committee to look after "troublemakers," and a local mob in Glendive nearly lynched a German Mennonite minister because of his pacifist views. Bullies frequently took advantage of patriotic feelings to push people around; and extreme conservatives sometimes whipped up public opinion in order to beat down the antiwar radicals. Will Campbell, the wild-eyed editor of the *Helena Independent*, kept up a running attack on the radicals and promoted a constant search for German agents. The October 18, 1917, *Independent* asked: "Are the Germans about to bomb the capital of Montana? Have they spies in the mountain fastnesses equipped with wireless stations and aeroplanes? Do our enemies fly around our high mountains where formerly only the shadow of the eagle swept?"

The often hysterical drive to crush critics of war became entangled in the most violent wave of strikes in Montana history. Many of the strikers were antiwar radicals, and patriotic Montanans argued that the strikes hindered the war effort by interrupting the production of desperately needed goods. Amid the shouting and bitterness, many people failed to recognize that the workers had legitimate grievances. Even though the war brought full employment, runaway inflation was wiping out wage gains, and working conditions were miserable in most of the lumber camps and many of the mines.

The trouble in western Montana began with a wildcat strike at the Eureka Lumber Company in mid-April of 1917. In less than a week, Governor Stewart had sent national guardsmen to Eureka to protect company property. The strike collapsed in a short time, and work had resumed by the end of the month. Unfortunately, the end of the strike at Eureka did not end the horrible conditions in the lumber camps. Working long hours at low pay in remote locations, the lumbermen, many of them illiterate transients, lived in company bunkhouses, ate in company commissaries, and bought at company stores. They slept, often two to a bunk, on straw ticks, and almost all of them suffered from lice and bedbugs. Eating and cooking areas swarmed with insects, and kitchens were often set up next to outhouses, stables, and pigpens.

Just before the Eureka strike, the Industrial Workers of the World had called a general strike to shut down the entire lumber industry in the Northwest. By June 28, Montana's two largest lumber mills were closed. An easy end of the strike seemed impossible, as the radical IWW opposed negotiation and Anaconda and the other employers refused to bargain with any union. In the meantime, most of the state's newspapers favored the operators and pointed with alarm at the IWW's antiwar position. Some editors even charged that German money and saboteurs stood behind the strike.

Finally, the federal government moved in. During late August and early September, government agents unleashed a series of raids on IWW headquarters and meeting halls throughout the West, and over a hundred Wobblies eventually ended up in prison on such charges as sedition and obstructing the draft. As a result of the federal crackdown, the Northwest lumber strike ended in a union defeat on September 7. Despite the IWW's defeat, however, the workers had made a few gains. Eager to avoid further work stoppages, the Montana Lumber Manufacturers Association, led by Kenneth Ross of Anaconda's lumber division, agreed to make some desperately needed improvements in working conditions.

As quiet returned to the lumber camps, bitterness continued to sour relations in Montana's mining industry, especially at Butte. Wartime problems brought to a head the restive labor situation that had been festering since at least 1906. For more than a generation, Butte had been a relatively desirable place to work. The steady expansion of the copper industry had employed a growing work force and made the city's industrial life attractive. Butte's miners were among the nation's highest paid workers, and many families owned their own homes. But things had worsened since the end of the "copper wars," so that by the eve of World War I

Butte seemed to be just one more industrial town with all of the attendant problems.

One key factor in creating working conditions in Butte was the new style of corporate management that had followed Heinze's sellout in 1906. The new style emphasized an increasing opposition to labor unions and an irate enmity toward the radicalism of the Socialists and the IWW. The Amalgamated Copper Company under John D. Ryan and Cornelius Kelley handled its workers with little sensitivity and an increasing regard for labor as a mere commodity. At the same time, the Amalgamated faced stiffer competition from copper interests in South America and the open-pit mines in Utah and Arizona. Amalgamated officials responded with an emphasis on efficiency and set shift bosses in competition with each other to fill production quotas. Management also utilized new technology—steam-powered hoists, electric-powered trams, and machine drills called "buzzies"—to increase cost productivity. But with the changes came new hazards. Working conditions deteriorated as workers became more and more alienated from their employers. The machine drills required strength rather than skill, and the incidence of respiratory diseases increased because of the fine silica dust the drills produced.

Accompanying the technological innovations were changes in Butte's labor force. An all-time high of 14,500 workers labored underground in Butte in 1916. The city's labor force became more and more divided as thousands of Slavic and Italian workers, many of them illiterate, poured into Butte after 1900. Most were single men who lived in boarding houses. The older, established Irish and Cornish families often rejected them. Whereas the older workers were often highly skilled and well-established in the community, the newcomers were usually unskilled and transient, and they sometimes presented hazards on the job to themselves and their coworkers. In addition to these strains, rising rates of inflation during the first two decades of the new century caused problems for all workers.

Combined, these conditions spelled trouble in a city that had become known as the "Gibraltar of Unionism." For more than a dozen years prior to 1917, the long-powerful Butte Miners' Union and its companion organizations had seen their strength deteriorate. Butte's workers, especially the newer and younger ones, increasingly came to believe that the Butte Miners' Union was incapable of dealing with a growing list of labor problems. So Butte, traditionally a uniquely quiet labor community among the strife-ridden mining cities of the West, began to seethe with unrest. Discontented workers seemed to be more and more interested in the extremist goals of the IWW, which stepped up organizational drives in Butte. Frightened by the radicals, the Company hired spies to infiltrate the unions and, according to rumor, "influenced" union leaders to do its will.

Challenged by the IWW on the left and infiltrated by the Company on the right, the Butte Miners' Union began to break under the strain. The union bitterly divided into two factions: a conservative wing that was peaceful toward the Company and the established Western Federation of Miners leadership, and a radical wing that was more friendly toward the IWW. In December 1912, the union revealed just how weak it had become by accepting the new "rustling card" system that Amalgamated-Anaconda had put into effect. Under this heavy-handed procedure, a worker had to obtain a "rustling card" from the Company before he could work on the Hill. By refusing to grant the cards to troublemakers or radicals, the Company could ignore the union and favor whichever workers it chose. Not surprisingly, BMU members increasingly lost faith in their leaders.

The mounting labor frustration exploded violently in 1914. June 13 was Miners' Union Day at Butte, the most festive holiday of the year. But when the traditional parade began that year, the "radical" or reform wing of the BMU boycotted and then, with Wobbly support, attacked the marchers. The rebels roughed up some of the union heads and then sacked the union hall, throwing the organization's records out the window into the street. Rioting persisted throughout the day and into the night, as angry union men searched for their "copper-collared" leaders. For the next several days, the pot continued to boil. The reform wing of the Butte Miners' Union gathered together and formed a new organization, the Butte Mine Workers' Union, under the presidency of miner Muckie McDonald. Although the new union insisted that it had no IWW affiliation, many of its members obviously sympathized with the Wobbly program.

The trouble at Butte climaxed on June 23, 1914. When the Butte Miners' Union held its meeting that night, an unruly crowd gathered outside. Shots were fired, and two men were killed. After the BMU leaders and the Butte police had fled the scene, a group of men—who may or may not have been Wobblies or members of the new union—set off twenty-five dynamite blasts and destroyed the old Miners' Union Hall. For weeks afterward, the great mining city trembled on the brink of anarchy. Finally, on September 1, Governor Stewart declared martial law and sent in the National Guard. Organized labor in Butte had suffered a total defeat. While the troops occupied Butte, Muckie McDonald and other leaders of the new union were tried and imprisoned. Socialist Mayor Lewis Duncan and Sheriff Tim Driscoll, following a summary grand jury investigation, were removed from office. And on September 9, Anaconda announced that it would no longer recognize either union. The once-powerful Butte miners now found themselves impotent under the hated "open shop" system. The Company had had its way, and the mining labor movement in Butte lay broken and helpless.

When America entered the Great War in 1917, the labor situation in Montana was dormant but still tense. Labor conflict erupted again in early summer after a terrible disaster at the Speculator Mine, a property of the North Butte Mining Company. On the night of June 8, a carbide lamp accidentally ignited some frayed electrical insulation in the Granite Mountain shaft of the Speculator. The fire spread rapidly as the updraft fanned the flames. Gases, especially carbon monoxide, quickly permeated the tunnels, and some men died before they knew what was happening. Despite heroic rescue efforts, 164 men lost their lives.

On June 11, a wildcat strike hit the Elm Orlu Mine. Two days later, a spontaneous gathering of laborers created yet another organization, the Metal Mine Workers' Union, with Tom Campbell as president and Joe Shannon, a known Wobbly, as vice-president. The MMWU disclaimed any affiliation with the Industrial Workers of the World, but many of its members either belonged to or sympathized with the IWW. Launching an all-out membership drive, the new union demanded recognition by the mineowners, an end to the despised rustling card system, and better wages and working conditions. Furthermore, they pledged to avoid the kind of violence that had occurred three years before. Nonetheless, Anaconda and the smaller mineowners refused to bargain with the new union. They branded the unionists as being the same troublemakers that had stirred things up in 1914; and by pointing to the antiwar views of some Wobbly leaders, they labeled the MMWU men as unpatriotic. Another major strike was called. As smaller craft unions on the Hill joined in, roughly fifteen thousand men had abandoned their posts by the end of June. The "richest hill on earth," one of the nation's key sources of copper, was shut down. The Company and its allies brought in over two hundred detectives as spies and "goon squads," and once again violence threatened.

Onto this inflammable stage stepped Frank Little, "the toughest, most courageous and impulsive leader the IWW ever had." Little, a mixed-blood Indian, arrived in Butte on July 18 and immediately tried to draw the MMWU directly into the ranks of the IWW. He also delivered biting speeches against United States involvement in the war, which bitterly angered Montana patriots and made Little a subject of intense hatred. On the night of August 1, six masked vigilantes entered the Wobbly's boarding house where Little stayed, beat him up, tied him to the back of their car, dragged him to the outskirts west of town, and hanged him from a railway trestle. The note left on Little's corpse bore the old vigilante insignia, "3-7-77." The murderers of Frank Little are still unknown. They may have been company agents, rival union men, or superpatriotic vigilantes. Except for the *Helena Independent*—which brushed aside the murder by remarking, "Good work: Let them continue to hang every I.W.W. in the state"—most of the press disapproved of Little's murder, if not his departure. Butte's workers gave Frank Little an impressive send-off. Three thousand people marched in his funeral column, while thousands more watched in solemn silence.

The murder of Frank Little raised wartime emotions to a frenzy. Fearful of civil war and a permanent shutdown of the mines, the federal government sent troops into Butte on August 11. The strike had already begun to lose momentum, and with the army occupying their town and public opinion turning against them, the MMWU strikers marched despondently back to work. By early autumn, the Butte mines were working at roughly 90 percent capacity. As in 1914, mining unionism collapsed in Butte, the victim of internal labor divisions, anti-radical public opinion, and company manipulation.

Little's aggressive speeches and his spectacular murder further inflamed the frantic search for traitors and subversives in Montana. The man who found himself in the center of this storm and who eventually became the most powerful politician in the state's history was Burton K. Wheeler, the United States district attorney for Montana. A native of Massachusetts and the son of Quaker parents, "B. K." Wheeler first came to Butte in 1905. A tall, gangling young lawyer with a quick wit and an engaging personality, he moved up quickly and, while serving in the 1911 legislature, struck up a friendship with Thomas Walsh by supporting him for the Senate. After Walsh later won election to the Senate, he rewarded Wheeler by arranging for his appointment as district attorney for Montana, making him the chief guardian of federal laws in the state. The outbreak of war placed Wheeler in the hot seat, as superpatriots and conservatives demanded that he prosecute radical antiwar groups like the IWW and the Nonpartisan League for obstructing the war effort. But Wheeler was tough and would not be stampeded. As an advanced progressive, he sympathized with some of the radicals' beliefs, and he refused to prosecute people on flimsy or false evidence. Soon, Wheeler himself became the target of the superpatriots.

The demand that Wheeler either prosecute the antiwar critics or resign came from many quarters, but especially from the Montana Council of Defense. Governor Stewart created the Montana Council at the request of the Wilson administration, which had asked each state and county to establish such councils, to be coordinated under a Council of National Defense, in order to help further the war effort. Like other state councils, the Montana Council of Defense spread war propaganda and promoted the sale of bonds, and it also got completely carried away in the search for traitors, "slackers," draft dodgers, and other nonconformists.

Aided by most of the Montana newspapers and by several local and statewide groups, the Montana Council of Defense hounded Wheeler and Attorney General Sam Ford, demanding more prosecutions. In the spring of 1918, Ford vainly appealed to the Montana Council of Defense for its aid in restraining county councils from unlawfully imposing restrictions on freedom of assembly and speech. The superpatriots found another archvillain in the person of flamboyant Judge George M. Bourquin of the Butte district court. Like Wheeler and Ford, the strong-willed and domineering Bourquin kept a cool head in wartime and refused to convict people simply because they held unpopular opinions. He once dismissed his critics by saying, "This court may be wrong, but not in doubt." More than any other incident, it was the Ves Hall case that raised the storm of rage against the judge. Hall, a rancher in remote Rosebud County, got into trouble merely by uttering remarks that were critical of America's involvement in the war. When the Hall case came before Bourquin's court early in 1918, the judge found that Hall had broken no law and correctly directed a verdict of innocent. The advocates of total loyalty never forgave him.

Faced by federal prosecutors and judges who would not do their bidding, the Montana Council of Defense and its allies pressured the governor to convene the state legislature in special session. Meeting in February 1918, the legislature set to work beating down the antiwar crowd. It considered, but failed to pass, resolutions demanding that the federal government remove both Wheeler and Bourquin from office. It did manage to impeach and remove from office Judge Charles L. Crum of Montana's Fifteenth Judicial District, simply because Crum had criticized the war and had testified on behalf of Ves Hall. The lawmakers also passed a Criminal Syndicalism Act aimed at outlawing the IWW and expanded the powers of the Montana Council of Defense so that it could act as a fully constituted arm of state government. Incredible as it may seem today, the frightened legislators even passed a gun registration law. Most significantly of all, they enacted the Montana Sedition Law.

In effect, the Montana Sedition Law made it illegal to criticize the federal government, the armed forces, or even the state government in wartime. The law stated:

. . . any person or persons who shall utter, print, write or publish any disloyal, profane, violent, scurrilous, contemptuous, slurring or abusive language about the form of government of the United States, or the constitution of the United States, or the soldiers or sailors of the United States, or the flag of the United States, or the uniform of the army or navy . . . or shall utter, print, write or pub-

Columbia Gardens, a gift to the city by mining baron W. A. Clark, was a popular entertainment park on the eastern edge of Butte, where children and families spent summer days listening to concerts, watching boxing matches, enjoying carnival attractions.

lish any language calculated to incite or inflame resistance to any duly constituted Federal or State authority in connection with the prosecution of the
War . . . shall he guilty of the crime of sedition.

Under terms of the act, forty-seven people ended up in prison, some with
sentences of twenty years or more. Moreover, through the efforts of Senator Walsh and Senator Henry Myers, the act became the model for the
federal Sedition Law of May 1918, which was widely used to stifle criticism of the war and which many authorities consider to be the most
sweeping violation of civil liberties in modern American history.

The campaign against dissenters continued even after the war ended in
November 1918. The Montana Council of Defense even banned the use
of the German language in the state, a ban that hastened the demise of
Montana's German community. In the face of such suppression, the
Staats-Zeitung, Montana's German language newspaper, ceased publication, and the Sons of Hermann lodges and other German-American organizations disbanded. At Lewistown, anti-German hysteria produced a
public burning of German high school textbooks and books by German
authors. To no avail, the Reverend J. E. Schatz of Plevna begged Governor Samuel Stewart for an exception to the ban, because many of his pa-
rishioners knew no English and were not "able to understand a word of
what the Gospel of our Lord brings to them."

The Montana Council of Defense, the Montana Loyalty League, and
other organizations also pressed hard against the Wobblies and the Nonpartisan League. In Montana and elsewhere, the IWW and other radical
labor groups rapidly lost their influence. The federal government aided
the mineowners and labor conservatives in crushing the left-wing laborites: between September 1914 and April 1920, national guardsmen and
federal troops occupied Butte six different times, sometimes with dire results. During the strike of April 1920, Company-paid guards shot into a
group of picketers at the Neversweat Mine, killing one and wounding fifteen others.

By the early 1920s, the Wobblies were beaten and scattered and mining unionism seemed little more than a corpse. The Nonpartisan League
suffered much the same treatment. Its organizers and speakers were frequently harassed and refused the right of free speech. At Miles City,
League organizer Mickey McGlynn was dragged into the Elks Club base-
ment and beaten severely. Attorney General Ford and local authorities
pressed charges against the perpetrators of this crime, but a local justice
of the peace dismissed them. The Nonpartisan League held on for several
more years, but by the early 1920s its influence was fast melting away.

Under storm clouds of wartime hysteria, the radicals and the more outspoken progressives were driven from the field, and the Company and

the far right appeared to control the state. Those who had hoped for a liberal farmer-labor alliance saw their dreams dashed and their two favorite politicians—Burton K. Wheeler and Jeannette Rankin—driven from office in 1918. Wheeler, the darling of the workers and small farmers, held a federally appointive office, but spokesmen for the Company and other conservative elements pressured Senator Walsh, who was up for re-election in 1918, to secure Wheeler's removal. Torn between conscience and his desire for re-election, Walsh buckled and got Wheeler to resign as district attorney. Wheeler thus stuck to his principles and lost his job, while Walsh bent with the wind and kept his. As for Rankin, a lifelong pacifist and progressive, she created a major sensation and lost much support by voting against war in 1917. Openly backed by the Butte workers and the Nonpartisan League, she ran for the Senate as an independent in 1918 and went down to defeat. As World War I came to an end, its main casualties in Montana were the radical and progressive reformers, who appeared to be beaten beyond recovery.

CHAPTER 12

Drought, Depression, and War, 1919-1946

During and immediately after World War I, a severe drought and an international decline of farm prices combined to produce a serious depression in Montana and the Northern Plains. The events of those years mark a significant turning point in Montana's history, the end of the homestead boom and the frontier settlement process and the beginning of a twenty-year period of drought, wind, and poverty. Slowly, almost imperceptibly, the experience of those years changed the course of the state's development. The agricultural frontier boom cycle turned into a bust, the flood of immigration reversed itself and became an exodus to greener pastures elsewhere, and the dreams of the boosters soured into bitter memories. Montanans, once the classic frontier optimists, became more and more the cautious cynics, hardened to adversity and suspicious of change. Montana was entering its modern era.

The Post-War Depression

The agricultural depression began during the war and then intensified at its conclusion. Once again, as in the collapse of the open-range cattle industry, the region's roller coaster, boom-and-bust economic cycle plummeted downward. Again, it seemed as if the forces of nature and of man had conspired against the Treasure State. Nature struck first. Cycles of drought, as the old-timers knew, are a natural part of the Great Plains climate. But most of the homesteaders were ignorant of those cycles. They had immigrated to Montana during a time of unusually ample rainfall, and to them this exception seemed the general rule. The drought cycle began, stealthily, in 1917, the first year of America's participation in the Great War. At first, only certain areas, mainly the High Line counties north of the Missouri River, felt its withering force. Then in 1918 the drought moved southward, encompassing the eastern two-thirds of the state.

In 1919, perhaps the most calamitous year Montana ever saw, the drought became generalized, even spreading into the normally well-watered valleys of the western mountains. The dry cycle brought other problems in its wake. Forest fires swept the western woodlands, and hordes of gophers and swarms of locusts plagued the beleaguered farmers. In their desperation, Montana farmers imported over a hundred thousand turkeys to eat the grasshoppers, but it was no use. The turkeys thrived, but so did the locusts, and roast turkey soon became a cheap staple in dozens of small-town restaurants. High winds set in during 1920, whipping away great clouds of pulverized topsoil into the hideous dust storms that would become so familiar a decade later. Homesteaders paid dearly for their wasteful methods of cultivation. Deep plowing conserved soil moisture, but it also led to wind erosion—and to disaster.

As if the natural calamity were not enough, economic dislocations following World War I brought Montana even more severe complications. The prices of wheat and other commodities had been inflated by high wartime demands and federal price controls. Farm prices remained high after the war ended. But by 1920, as Europe recovered from the war, it began once more to supply most of its own food needs. Farm prices entered a period of international decline; and to make matters worse, the United States government abruptly removed its price controls. Farm prices fell off sharply. Wheat, which had sold for $2.40 per bushel in August 1920, dropped to $1.25 per bushel in October. Farmers also faced light harvests because of the drought. Accustomed to yields of 25 bushels to the acre, Montana farmers averaged a pitiful 2.4 bushels per acre in 1919. In 1920, they were staggered by yet another bad crop year.

Montana's mining and lumber towns also felt the squeeze, as the end of swollen wartime demands for raw materials meant local shutdowns and unemployment. All of this added up to a region-wide disaster. Although the nation as a whole suffered a sharp recession after the war, the national economy had generally recovered by 1922. But in this agriculturally dependent region, the depression hit harder and lasted longer. The worst was over by 1922, but the crisis did not really pass until the return of adequate rainfall in the mid-1920s.

Meanwhile, the people suffered. The summer of 1919 saw the worst of it. In Hill County of northern Montana, three thousand people faced the coming winter without adequate means of support. Wagons and jalopies rolled out of Big Sandy, with mattresses and belongings tied on their sides and occasionally a grimly humorous sign, such as "Goodby Old Dry!" Who could help them? The Red Cross had little to offer and neither did

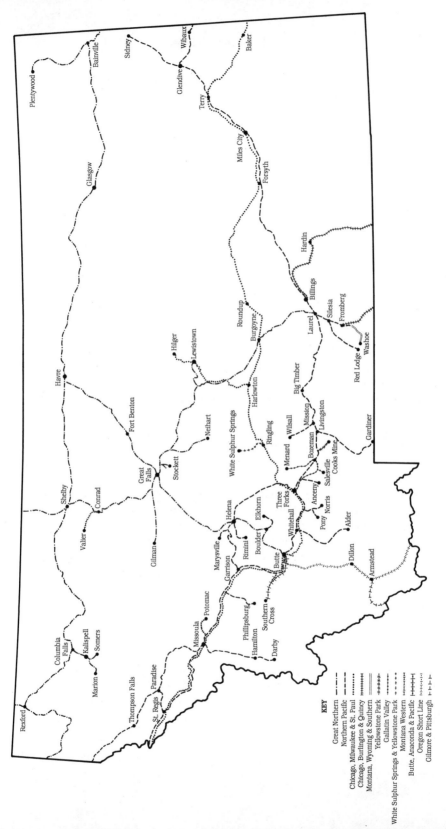

Map 6. Railroads, 1913 (map by Barbara Lien; source: Montana Railroad Commission, 1913, copyright © Rand McNally & Company)

KEY

Great Northern
Northern Pacific
Chicago, Milwaukee & St. Paul
Chicago, Burlington & Quincy
Montana, Wyoming & Southern
Yellowstone Park
Gallatin Valley
White Sulphur Springs & Yellowstone Park
Montana Western
Butte, Anaconda & Pacific
Oregon Short Line
Gilmore & Pittsburgh

the state government. Governor Sam Stewart called a special session of the legislature in midsummer, but the state lacked the tax base to offer much assistance to its distressed citizens. The legislators enacted a law authorizing the county commissioners to issue road construction bonds, hoping that such projects might employ the destitute farmers. But the bonds found few buyers, and the homesteaders found few jobs. Uncle Sam offered little assistance. The Wilson administration extended over two million dollars worth of seed loans to local farmers during 1918-20, but such scant relief barely scratched the surface.

So Montanans faced the depression on their own, and the grim statistics tell their story. During the period 1919-25, roughly two million acres passed out of production and eleven thousand farms, about 20 percent of the state's total, were vacated. Twenty thousand mortgages were foreclosed, and half of Montana farmers lost their land. The average acrevalue of farmlands fell by 50 percent. During the flush times prior to 1918, Montana had become heavily overstocked with banks, and many of them had been reckless in their lending policies. Now the overextended banks fell like dominoes. Between 1920 and 1926, 214 of Montana's commercial banks—over one-half of the state's total—failed, carrying thousands of family savings accounts down with them. Montana had the highest bankruptcy rate in the United States. Whereas in 1914 a state promotional publication had urged prospective settlers to hurry because in a short time the "free homestead will be but a memory," in 1921 a state document tried to turn would-be settlers away by pointing out that no "good homestead opportunities are to be found in the state."

The haunting face of depression appeared everywhere: roads and gullies blown full of dust and sprouting weeds and thistles, homestead shacks abandoned and forlorn, quiet main streets with boarded-up storefronts. Many families were nearly destitute, with little food, inadequate clothing, and insufficient fuel to keep warm. The most ominous sign was the great exodus of the state's rural population. An estimated sixty thousand people left Montana during the 1920s, many of them moving to Washington, Oregon, and especially California. It is likely that more would have left, but they did not have the means. Montana was the only state of the fortyeight to lose population during the "prosperous" 1920s. As rural Montanans moved on, the state began to assume a different population profile. Before the war Montana had been a typical frontier state, with a young and ambitious citizenry. But as many younger families fled, Montana came to be more and more a state of the very young and the very old, with disproportionately few young and middle-aged adults. And it has remained that way.

Who was to blame? Typical of many people of that era, some who lost their farms tended to internalize failure and saw the loss as their own fault. But many others sought out villains. Like other rural Americans who suffered losses during the 1920s and 1930s, Montanans lashed out at the boosters who had misled them, especially the bankers and the railroad promoters. When Joseph Kinsey Howard, the eloquent journalist from Great Falls, singled out Jim Hill as the archvillain in his widely read *Montana: High, Wide, and Handsome*, many agreed with him. And Montana children of the time sang this ditty:

> Twixt Hill and Hell, there's just one letter:
> Were Hill in Hell, we'd feel much better.

Howard also sounded a common sentiment when he accused the federal government of bungling. Montanans remembered that the government had encouraged them, through price supports and patriotic sermons, to plow up their marginal lands during wartime. After the war, the Wilson administration had dropped the supports with what seemed a cruel haste. Montanans also remembered that, on a per capita basis, they had sent more men to fight in the war than any other state and, as a result, had lost a greater proportion of their men. Howard's most angry, and popular, indictment focused on the Federal Reserve Board, particularly on the district bank in Minneapolis. According to Howard's accusations, which were not entirely accurate, the Federal Reserve had restricted credit to Montana banks at exactly the time when it should have extended it, thus making a bad situation much worse.

In the final analysis, there was blame enough to share. The bitterness of those years becomes much easier to understand when we realize how serious the postwar crisis really was. The collapse of the Montana homestead movement after 1918 marked the end of the frontier. The closing of the frontier ended a cycle of spectacular economic growth and began an era of economic stagnation and population loss. As prosperity vanished, so did optimism. Montana lost more in the postwar depression than its marginal farmers. To a considerable extent, it also lost its self-confidence and its faith in the future.

The suffering and privation that came with the depression of the early 1920s convinced some that the homestead movement had been a hideous mistake. Some concluded that old-time cattlemen had been right: the grasslands should never have been plowed. But most homesteaders, including many who went "bust," later looked back on those years of hardship with nostalgia and without bitterness. Defenders of the homestead movement do not ignore the difficulties and disappointments of that period in Montana's history; rather, they maintain that there are important reasons why the homesteaders should be honored as pioneers. The survivors of that movement, after all, helped create one of the world's greatest granaries.

THE DIXON ADMINISTRATION

Interestingly, the hard times produced considerable political discontent and breathed new life into the progressive and radical groups that had been staggered during the war. The Nonpartisan League, which wartime patriots had placed on the defensive, appealed once again to thousands of small farmers who suddenly found the victims of a cruel economic system. Both the progressive and radical forces in Montana regrouped for one last campaign against the Company. The gubernatorial election campaign of 1920, perhaps the most bruising political encounter in the state's history, became a showdown between the reformers and the Anaconda Company.

The hottest issue in the campaign involved the taxation of mines. Almost since the 1889 constitutional convention, liberal forces had tried—and failed—to increase the levy on metal mines. After the war, their arguments took on new urgency, as the depression dried up the income from the property tax. In 1919, the mine tax question suddenly burst into public view when Louis Levine, a young economics professor at Montana State University in Missoula, published a small book entitled *The Taxation of Mines in Montana*. Levine's book was hardly radical. It simply revealed what well-informed Montanans already knew, that mining taxes were inequitably low. Levine gained notoriety, however, partly because he was a Russian Jew at a time when "subversives" and "Bolsheviks" were being hunted down throughout the nation and partly because the Company and its friends pressured the university to dismiss him. In a flagrant and highly publicized abuse of academic freedom, Levine lost his job. Although the university later reinstated him, the tormented professor soon moved on to a distinguished career elsewhere. Levine's little book, followed by his dismissal, drew Montanans' attention to the tax situation.

In August 1920, progressive candidates won the gubernatorial nominations of both political parties. Both nominees were long-time foes of the Company, and both advocated an increase in the mines tax. Joseph M. Dixon, the veteran reformer, won the Republican nomination; and controversial Burton K. Wheeler, backed by the Nonpartisan League, accepted the Democratic nod. The campaign was hard fought and sometimes vicious. The Anaconda Company identified Wheeler as its main enemy and mutely accepted Dixon. An emotional and effective campaigner, Wheeler attacked the Company, its newspapers, and its political empire from one end of the state to the other. The Anaconda papers and other conservative spokesmen returned the attack by roasting Wheeler. Nick-

Burton K. Wheeler, campaigning during the fiercely contested 1920 governor's race

naming him "Bolshevik Burt," they accused him of being a socialist and even reported that Wheeler and the Nonpartisan League advocated free love. Public opinion turned heatedly against the outspoken Democrat. Denouncing the Nonpartisan League's "takeover" of their party, thousands of conservative Democrats deserted Wheeler. He could not even gain access to speaking facilities in Miles City; at another location, opponents chased him off the speaker's platform.

Meanwhile, Joseph Dixon billed himself as a moderate alternative to Wheeler, neither a radical nor a Company man. As a result, Dixon won a great victory and Wheeler went down to one of the worst defeats in Montana's political history. Ironically, Dixon's victory launched him into a sea of troubles, and Wheeler's defeat soon turned to triumph. In 1922, only two years after his landslide burial, Wheeler ran for the United States Senate. This time he struck a more moderate pose, neither attacking the Anaconda nor suffering attack from it, and kept his distance from the sagging Nonpartisan League. As a consequence, he gained the support of a reunited Democratic party and won an easy election to the Senate, where he would hold forth for the next quarter-century.

The newly elected governor, Joseph Dixon, was an earnest, capable, and honest man, who understood the state and its problems. He may have been the best governor Montana ever had, but he faced terrible problems. He had the misfortune to govern during a severe depression, which inevitably meant that he would take the blame for the bad times, the declining tax revenues, and the mounting state debt. Dixon also faced unfriendly legislatures. Although his fellow Republicans controlled both the house and the senate, they were mostly conservatives and generally friendly toward the Company. These conservative Republicans, remembering the Bull Moose rebellion of 1912, had no love for the progressive Republican who sat in the governor's chair.

Undaunted, Dixon pressed forward with a general reform program. True to his campaign promises, the governor aimed at tax reform. He presented the legislatures of 1921 and 1923 with a blueprint for a modern and equitable tax system, including a tax commission and new levies on mines, oil and gasoline, motor vehicles, and inheritances. Under a blitz of Company lobbying, the lawmakers refused to follow the governor's lead. Only the oil and inheritance measures passed, the latter just in time to nail the estate of William A. Clark. Both in 1921 and again in 1923, the key tax commission and mines tax bills went down to defeat. Dixon coldly pointed out the glaring fact that Montana's metal mines produced over twenty million dollars in 1922 but paid only $13,559 in state taxes. Not surprisingly, the Company newspapers chose not to circulate this information; instead, it lambasted the governor for his "reckless" extravagance.

Although one frustration followed another, Dixon still managed some gains. Most significantly, he employed Nils P. Haugen, former director of the Wisconsin Tax Commission, to initiate new methods of assessing railroads and utilities, thus increasing their taxable value. This marked a major progressive victory. So did the enactment of an old-age pension law in 1923, a feat that made Montana, along with Nevada, one of the first states to provide such support for elderly citizens. Courageously, Dixon fired Frank Conley, the iron-handed and controversial warden of the state penitentiary. Responding to this entirely proper act, the *Helena Independent* accused the governor of coddling "slackers, seditionists, highwaymen, rapists, porch climbers, and jail breakers."

The issue of mine taxation, so symbolic of Anaconda's power, remained unresolved as Dixon's term expired. In good progressive fashion, Dixon decided to take his case directly to the people, and he prepared Initiative 28 for submission to the voters in the 1924 election. The initiative called for the levy of a graduated tax of up to one percent of gross production on any mine that produced over one hundred thousand dollars gross per year. This meant war. The Company and its newspapers, which had reluctantly accepted Dixon in 1920, tore into him as he stood for re-election in 1924. Charging the governor with such serious "extravagances" as buying expensive silver dishes for the governor's mansion, the Anaconda press predicted more shutdowns and deeper depression if he were re-elected.

Dixon never had a chance. His Democratic opponent, John E. Erickson, was backed by the Anaconda and beat him soundly by running on a low-keyed platform of thrift and retrenchment. But as the people removed Dixon from office, they also passed his Initiative 28, which would raise the Company's taxes dramatically over the years to follow. Joseph Dixon fell victim to the Company's attack but other factors also contributed to his loss, especially the fact that he was a depression governor who got blamed for the bad times. Dixon never regained political power in Montana. After failing to win a 1928 Senate race against Wheeler, he served as assistant secretary of the Department of the Interior under President Herbert Hoover and died in 1934.

Dixon's 1924 defeat marked the end of a political era in Montana. He was the most powerful of the Montana progressives, and his failure at the hands of the Company signaled the end of the age of reform. In the years since then, many Montanans have seen in Dixon's fall the failure of liberalism in the state. The progressive impulse was spent, while the awesome might of the Company remained. But the forces of liberalism did not die with Joseph Dixon; they merely went into eclipse. In the aftermath of 1924, the conservatives and the Anaconda Company ruled supreme.

PROSPERITY AND POLITICAL CALM

During the years immediately following Dixon's defeat, Montana entered a brief period of renewed prosperity. The rain cycle returned during the middle and late 1920s, and with it came good crops. At the same time, the great nationwide boom of 1922-29 began to improve the state's dormant economy, as local industries responded to rising nationwide demands for metals, lumber, and oil. For a time at least, the bad times seemed to be over. This short interlude of prosperity brought with it a period of political calm that contrasted sharply with the heated atmosphere of the Dixon years. It was during this time, the later 1920s and early 1930s, that a political pattern began to appear that has persisted to the present—a pattern of conservative government at the state level, curiously balanced by liberal representation in Washington, D.C.

Conservatism clearly prevailed in Helena during this period, as it did in most states. From 1925 until 1931, the Republicans controlled the state legislature with lopsided majorities. The Republicans steadily stressed the need for economy, not innovation, in state government and demanded a reduction of the large state debt that had accumulated during the depressed years of the Dixon administration. Governor John E. "Honest John" Erickson was a conservative Democrat who got along well with the Republicans. The tall and strikingly handsome son of Norwegian immigrants, Erickson won three gubernatorial elections and served Montanans from 1925 until 1933. A conservative and party regular, he had no desire to fight the Company. Having beaten Dixon in 1924 on a platform of "economy and efficiency through retrenchment and clean business methods," Erickson ran a low-keyed operation. He was proud of his administration's reductions of the state debt and its efficiency in cutting down and managing the bureaucracy. As long as the prosperity lasted, so did Erickson's popularity. Ironically, however, after having defeated a depression governor, Erickson was about to become a depression governor himself and to suffer the same loss of esteem as Dixon had.

While conservatives ruled at home, Montana gained widespread fame during the 1920s for its liberal representation in the United States Senate. Both of Montana's senators—Thomas J. Walsh, in office from 1913 until 1933, and Burton K. Wheeler, who served from 1923 to 1947—were progressive Democrats, and both became favorites of the national liberal community because of their investigations into the corruption of President Warren G. Harding's administration. The two men, so often compared and considered together, were quite different in personality and in political profile.

Walsh, a seemingly cold and aloof man, was a moderate progressive and an unexciting campaigner. He made his reputation, both in Montana and in the U.S. Senate, as a great legal mind and as an honest and dignified public servant. Walsh gained nationwide fame during 1923-24 when he directed the brilliant investigation that uncovered the Teapot Dome scandal, which involved the improper leasing of naval oil reserves in Wyoming and California. As a result of Walsh's and others' efforts, Secretary of the Interior Albert B. Fall became the first cabinet member in United States history to serve a prison term. After Teapot Dome, Walsh rose to the highest ranks of political prestige and power. He served as chairman of the Democratic national conventions of 1924 and 1932, and in 1928 he made an unsuccessful bid for the Democratic presidential nomination. By 1925, Walsh was unquestionably the most powerful political figure in the state.

While serving his first Senate term, Walsh's young colleague, Burton K. Wheeler, also joined in exposing the wrongdoings of Harding's cabinet. Wheeler led in the Senate investigation that eventually forced Attorney General Harry Daugherty to resign from office. This effort, which prompted eastern newspapers to speak of the "Montana mudgunners" or "Montana scandalmongers," also made Wheeler a leading force among American liberals. In 1924, he ran unsuccessfully for the vice-presidency on the Progressive party ticket, which put forth Robert La Follette for president. Unlike Walsh, Wheeler was an advanced progressive who leaned toward Populist-style radicalism. He loved political infighting and was a natural campaigner. Joseph Kinsey Howard once recalled a typical Wheeler performance:

> He was a solid man on the platform, nearly six feet tall with broad shoulders and a big head; he wore comfortably rumpled suits with ill-fitting coat collars. He would bring his knees together, weave almost to the floor, and thrust his hands out beseechingly—or gesture with fingers spread just above the footlights, as if he were playing on a concealed piano keyboard. He was never a good speaker, but he was entertaining—a good campaigner. His effective use of pauses, seeming to grope for phrases and then repeating them, lent his words an air of sincerity.

Wheeler, much younger than Walsh, looked forward to a long and distinguished career.

This "political schizophrenia," by which Montana presented a liberal face nationally and a conservative face locally, has provoked some interesting explanations over the years. Some conservatives have argued that Montanans are simply realistic: they keep the thrifty conservatives at home while sending the spendthrift liberals off to fetch them federal monies. Liberals have replied that the real explanation lies in the simple fact that local conservative interest groups focus their attention on state, not national, offices. Neither theory seems entirely convincing, since both are simplistic. Whatever the real reasons for this peculiar political posture, one fact appears obvious: there is a delicate balance in Montana of competing liberal and conservative forces.

The conservative community in Montana, which held the upper hand during this period, had powerful forces behind it. The Anaconda Copper Mining Company—with its highly efficient political network, its chain of newspapers, and its corporate partner, the Montana Power Company—was clearly the most powerful conservative force in the state (on the formation of Montana Power, see chapter 13). As seen in the case of Governor Dixon, the Company did not hesitate to lash out at its enemies. Its newspapers were a potent weapon, and its lobbying team in Helena wielded legendary strength. The Company ran twenty-four-hour-a-day "watering holes" for the free use of legislators and maintained a free bill-drafting service and an efficient information bureau to assist the lawmakers. A Company lobbyist once boasted to John Gunther: "Give me a case of Scotch, a case of gin, one blonde, and one brunette, and I can take any liberal." But the Company was not immune to change. And by 1930, younger executives were beginning to soften its political approach and curb its methods.

Many Montanans, and many outside observers as well, believed that the Company ran the state as its own private bailiwick. This was never literally true. Other groups also contributed their support to conservatism. Among corporate interests, five major railroads did business in Montana, including the Northern Pacific with its huge landholdings. Coal, oil, lumber, and smaller metal-mining firms also made their influence felt, as did bankers, merchants, and chambers of commerce. There were also the cattlemen and woolgrowers, who were highly organized through the Montana Stockgrowers Association and the Montana Wool Growers Association. The two associations leaned heavily toward conservatism and toward the Republican party, and their strength in the legislature was often even greater than that of the Company. Naturally, the conservatives also drew considerable support from the broad middle and upper middle classes who worried about big government, excessive spending, and maintaining the status quo.

Who were the liberals, the voters who sent men like Walsh and Wheeler to Washington? Despite its image as a conservative, corporate-dominated state, Montana had some powerful liberal organizations. As in other states of the Northwest, the leading liberal elements in the Treasure State were labor unions and small farmers, both of whom inclined toward the Democratic party. Organized labor had been beaten down during World War I, but its strength would reappear during the turbulent 1930s.

During the 1920s, the depression put smaller farm operators in an angry mood. Some farmers who lived near the northeastern Montana community of Plentywood even organized an active Communist movement and published their own newspaper, the *Producers News*, edited by Charles E. "Red Flag" Taylor. But few moved that far to the left. Instead, as the Nonpartisan League lost influence during the early 1920s, more and more small farmers moved into the ranks of the National Farmers Union. Although the liberal Farmers Union had first organized in Montana in 1912, it took deep root only after the organizational drives of the later 1920s. Montana became, and has remained, one of the six states where the Farmers Union is the leading agricultural organization. The Farmers Union was, and still is, the true heir of Populist-style liberalism, and it has long been a bulwark of liberal causes in Montana.

Montana remains a delicately balanced state, where Democrats and Republicans, liberals and conservatives, usually compete on fairly even terms. This close balance has tended to make the state a political weather vane. In only one presidential election since 1900, the Kennedy-Nixon contest of 1960, did Montana fail to support the winning candidate. The period following Joseph Dixon's defeat was a time of conservative rule, but a new cycle of drought and depression was about to lift liberal Democrats into power.

THE GREAT DEPRESSION

The brief period of prosperity during the late 1920s vanished abruptly during 1929-30, as a new ordeal of drought and depression began in Montana. This time, the droughts would last longer than before, intermittently for nearly a decade. And this time, a terrible nationwide and worldwide depression would vastly complicate Montana's problems. The drought began sporadically in 1929, intensified in 1930, and reached disastrous proportions in 1931. By midsummer of that terrible year, twenty-eight of Montana's fifty-six counties had filed for aid from the Red Cross. Most of those counties lay in the arc of dry-farming and stockgrowing lands that reached from the High Line north of the Missouri River to the southeast along the Dakota state line. Rain fell in many localities in 1932 and 1933, but again in 1934, 1936, and 1937 there were more searing droughts and frightening, dust-laden winds.

Along with the drought came a steep drop in food prices, as the worldwide depression led to declining food purchases and mounting crop surpluses. An amount of wheat worth $100 in 1920 brought only $19.23 in 1932, when the going price stood at 32 cents per bushel. The drought withered forage and hay crops, and meat and wool prices collapsed. Beef cattle sold for $9.10 per hundredweight in 1929; in 1934, the price was only $3.34. Sheep brought $8.14 per hundredweight in 1929 but only $3.12 in 1934.

Once again, hunger, poverty, and desperation stalked the countryside. Daniels County, in the state's northeastern corner, typified the crisis. During the good years of the late 1920s, the county seat, Scobey, had advertised itself as the world's largest wheat shipping point. By the spring of 1933, after four years of sub par rainfall, thirty-five hundred of the county's five thousand people needed relief assistance. After touring the eastern reaches of the state in August 1931, Governor John Erickson could only bury his head in his hands, lamenting, as an associate later recalled, that if only someone could find a solution to the problem, he would gladly embrace it. The people, he wrote, were "in rather a desperate condition. The grain crops and feed crops are practical failures." In some areas the only green vegetation the governor saw sprouted forlornly where the last winter's snowfences had trapped some traces of moisture.

Montana did not lie in the heart of the Dust Bowl of the "dirty thirties," but like other Great Plains states it fully experienced the ravages of drought, dust, and depopulation. Many farmers left the land, as others had ten years before. The number of Montana farms fell from 47,495 in 1930 to 41,823 in 1940. Like the "Okies" described by John Steinbeck or the "Dokies" from the neighboring Dakotas, Montanans joined the general exodus of poor people toward the West Coast. Many of those who stayed in Montana would eventually prosper during the wet and profitable years of World War II. But until then, most of them would feel the squeeze. The aggregate value of Montana farms, including both land and buildings, totaled $527,610,002 in 1930. By 1940, despite the farm relief programs of the New Deal, farm value had fallen to $350,178,461. The average Montana farm, valued at $11,109 in 1930, was worth only $8,373 in 1940. While the post-World War I agricultural depression had knocked down many of the state's shakiest banks, at least twenty went belly-up between 1929 and 1933. Slowly, inexorably, the rural depression squeezed the lifeblood out of the parched Great Plains.

To a much greater extent than in the depression of 1918-22, Montana's industries and cities suffered along with the farmers and ranchers. Like most states of the Mountain West, Montana lacked heavy industry. Its industries were extractive and relied on raw materials, so they were slow to feel the full impact of the "Great Crash" of 1929. By 1931, however, the Treasure State was reeling under the full brunt of the Great Depression. As construction business fell off across the nation, so eventually did the lumber industry of Montana and the Pacific Northwest. As such major copper consumers as the brass companies and the electrical utilities cut back production, so too did western producers.

*Stenographers at the Anaconda Company's main offices, 1927. After
1900, women made up an increasingly larger proportion of Montana's
workforce.*

At this time Montana relied heavily on copper mining; and oil, coal, and lumber industries, which would be so important to the state in the 1970s, were small operations then. Throughout the 1920s, the Anaconda Copper Mining Company expanded into a worldwide enterprise. In the process, it had become heavily indebted. When the Great Depression hit, it flattened the highly competitive copper industry, especially the overextended Anaconda. As markets contracted, copper prices steadily fell, from eighteen cents per pound in 1929, to eight cents per pound in 1931, to five cents per pound in 1933. Anaconda stock, which sold as high as 175 on the New York Exchange in 1929, dropped to an incredible low of three in 1932. At its lowest point, the stock was worth six cents on the dollar of book value. Cheap African and South American copper flooded the market, and the American copper industry cut back production to a quarter of its 1929 peak level.

These trends spelled disaster for Montana's mining towns. The Company steadily cut back its Butte production, from over three hundred thousand wet tons of ore monthly in early 1929 to thirty thousand per month early in 1933. In Butte and in the smelting and refining towns of Anaconda, Great Falls, and East Helena, machinery ground to a halt and thousands of urban workers lost their jobs. At Butte and Anaconda, poverty was grim and undisguised. A 1934 Department of Commerce survey revealed that 64 percent of Butte's homes needed repair, 32 percent had inadequate space for the inhabitants, nearly 20 percent had no indoor toilets, and almost 30 percent had neither baths nor showers. A Consumers' Council survey of the same year concluded that for every well-fed child in Butte, five lacked sufficient nourishment.

Montana had seen hard times before, in the Panic of 1893 and the post-World War I depression, but it had never known anything like this. Tens of thousands of Montanans were in desperate need of relief by the early 1930s, but to whom could they turn? President Herbert Hoover argued that private charities and state and local governments, not the federal government, should meet the emergency. But private charity had little to give. The American Red Cross, as part of its nationwide drought relief program, dispensed food, clothing, medicines, fuel, and feed throughout eastern and northern Montana during 1930-32. But the Red Cross lacked the adequate resources to help much; its average food grant was a pathetic ten cents per person per day.

The state government offered little more. Like the governor, most legislators were conservatives with little inclination to let the state slide into debt in order to support the poor. But they seemed to have little choice. Montana relied on the property tax, but the depression increasingly devalued property and the wellsprings of state revenue dried up. Borrowing offered little hope either. The Montana constitution required a special election in order to exceed an indebtedness of a hundred thousand dollars. Erickson, like most governors of his time, saw inaction as the only alternative. When the state legislature met in early 1931, the governor advised the lawmakers to slash appropriations and avoid new commitments. They were happy to oblige. The lawmakers did pass a state income tax law, but its importance lay in the more distant future. Aside from authorizing a six million dollar debenture to finance road construction work, the legislature steered away from new obligations. As the politicians knew, Montana did not have the financial means to solve its problems.

From 1929 through 1932, the state and the nation sank deeper into depression. As things got worse, the demand for federal assistance to the needy mounted. President Hoover generally resisted the demands, and his resistance, more than any other factor, led to his defeat at the hands of Democrat Franklin D. Roosevelt in 1932. With Roosevelt's inauguration in 1933, the New Deal was underway. It was the greatest reform movement—and the most revolutionary period in federal-state relations—that the United States has ever seen.

THE NEW DEAL

The New Deal reform movement began in March 1933 and continued until it lost momentum in 1938-39. Historians still argue about Roosevelt's motives and about the success or failure of the New Deal in ending the depression. Roosevelt's basic purpose was simple enough: he sought to use the spending and regulatory powers of the federal government to combat the deadening impact of the depression. This meant a sudden funnelling of government funds into every state in the Union. More significantly, the New Deal sparked enormous changes in federal-state relationships. The New Deal began a massive increase in the power of the federal government, and it prompted state governments to expand their operations. By the close of the 1930s, both the federal and state bureaucracies had ballooned in size and assumed large new roles in the lives of the people.

The Roosevelt administration poured a lot of money into Montana during the 1930s. From 1933 through 1939, the federal government spent $381,582,693 in Montana and loaned the state another $141,835,952. On a per capita basis, Montana received $710 per person and another $264 per person in loans, making the state second in the nation in per capita New Deal investments. This high per capita expenditure was largely the result of the few people in Montana and the huge tracts of public lands and miles of federally funded highways.

How were the New Deal dollars spent? Much of the money went directly to farmers. In 1933, the ambitious Agricultural Adjustment Administration began operations, with Montanans prominently involved in its organization. Montana State College professor M. L. Wilson played a key role in planning the AAA, and a local farm editor, Chester Davis, directed the agency for a time. The AAA attempted to raise farm prices through a variety of means aimed at reducing the huge crop surpluses that glutted the market. Most notably, the AAA made direct cash benefit payments to farmers who agreed to restrict crop acreages.

The Agricultural Adjustment Administration program had a revolutionary impact on the wheat-producing state of Montana. For the first time, its farmers received massive federal aid. In turn, they became increasingly reliant on Uncle Sam. Between 1933 and 1937, the AAA made nearly 140,000 contract agreements with Montana farmers and channeled from $4.5 million to nearly $10 million annually into the state's prostrate economy. For many farm families, the new money meant a change of clothes, or a movie for the first time in years, or, for the truly fortunate, a family automobile. To dozens of small farm towns, it meant busy main streets and ringing cash registers for the first time since 1929 or 1930. By 1938, as the rains again began to fall, local farmers enjoyed a 98 percent increase in cash income over what they had received in 1932.

Rural Montana received other New Deal benefits, too. The Farm Credit Administration extended low interest loans to farmers and ranchers, allowing them to refinance on reasonable terms and to avoid the calamity of mortgage foreclosures. FCA loans totaled nearly seventy-eight million dollars in Montana by mid-1938. Ranchers obtained a major windfall with the 1934 Taylor Grazing Act, which allowed organized groups of stockmen to lease federal lands cooperatively for grazing. Through the act, ranchers gained reliable pasturage at low cost without the obligation of purchasing the land. The Rural Electrification Administration was another New Deal agency that meant much to rural Montana. Before 1936, only a handful of farms and ranches had electricity. But beginning in 1935-36, the REA extended loans to farmers' cooperatives and other organizations, enabling them to build rural electrical distribution systems. As a result, the number of electrified farms in Montana jumped from 2,768 in 1935 to 6,000 in 1939, and that was only the beginning. Over the next forty years of development, more than two dozen rural electric cooperatives would make power available to practically every farm and ranch in the state. A new way of life had come to the countryside.

The Civilian Conservation Corps, among the most popular of all New Deal programs, appeared on the scene in 1933. Directed by the Forest Service and the army, the CCC aimed to employ young men and teach

*Civilian Conservation Corps crew, Beaverhead National Forest, 1933.
During the Great Depression, the CCR employed thousands of young men
in Montana to work in national and state forests and parks.*

them job skills by putting them to work in conservation camps on forest and rangelands. Beyond dispute, the CCC did a lot for Montana. Throughout the 1930s, an average of twenty-four camps were established in national and state forests and in federal and state parks in Montana. By 1938, the CCC had employed more than twenty-five thousand young men in the state. The CCC boys, who had to be unemployed and between the ages of seventeen and twenty-three, fought insects and blights such as the terrible Blister Rust fungus; built mountain roads, lookout stations, and reclamation dams; fought forest fires; and planted trees in the woodlands and grasses on the prairies. They left behind many enduring monuments, such as the visitors' facilities at Lewis and Clark Caverns on the Jefferson River and the Squaw Creek Ranger Station in the beautiful West Gallatin Canyon.

Many other New Deal efforts also had their impact on the Treasure State. The Silver Purchase Act of 1934, for example, instituted a government buying program that raised the price of silver and thus stimulated silver mining but also the mining of copper and other ores that commingled with it in Butte's mines. The Home Owners Loan Corporation refinanced home loans and saved families from losing their homes to mortgage foreclosures. During this period, the busy Reconstruction Finance Corporation made over 160 major loans to Montana banks and financial institutions, saving many from failure. Of all the New Deal programs, however, none aroused more praise or protest than the efforts to provide direct relief for the poor.

In 1933, the Roosevelt administration set out to provide work for the unemployed. As a first step, the Federal Emergency Relief Administration offered federal matching funds to the states in order that they might give relief to the needy. By 1935, more than 22 percent of Montana households were on some kind of relief, which meant receiving aid for food, shelter, or clothing either by direct cash payments or work relief. In eastern Montana, more than 35 percent of the families had to rely on relief. The FERA was soon supplemented by the Public Works Administration, a federal agency created to build large-scale projects and to provide jobs for skilled and semi-skilled workers. Neither of these agencies worked out very well: the FERA became snarled in red tape, and the PWA moved too slowly and employed too few men. In 1935, the New Deal came up with its final answer to the relief problem, the Works Progress Administration, a federal agency that offered work to all employable men who could find no jobs.

The New Deal agencies brought vital relief to hard-pressed Montana, with the Works Progress Administration directly benefiting more Montanans than any of its counterparts. As late as mid-1939, the WPA directly employed over fourteen thousand local workers, thus supporting perhaps forty thousand people. Some WPA projects involved "make work" or "boondoggling," but most were of real value. By the spring of 1940, WPA workers in Montana had built 7,239 miles of highway, 1,366 bridges, 301 school buildings, 31 outdoor stadiums, 81 athletic fields, 30 swimming pools, 40 skating rinks, 16 golf courses, 10 ski jumps, and more than 10,000 rural privies.

Although construction projects were the most visible, the Montana WPA also offered special programs such as the National Youth Administration for young people. Women worked in WPA-sponsored gardens throughout the state and in twenty-three sewing rooms, five of them on Indian reservations. The sewing rooms produced over a million garments between 1935 and 1938. Artists produced dozens of major works with WPA sponsorship, including murals in post offices from Sidney to Dillon. A Writers' Program for authors yielded three significant books: *Montana: A State Guide Book, Copper Camp,* and *Land of Nakoda.* Relief programs thereby enabled thousands to hold the threads of their lives together; but for many, such government assistance, even work relief, evoked a demoralizing sense of guilt over what seemed to be individual failure, and the thought of being on relief aroused fears of permanent loss of individual independence.

New Deal programs also brought relief to Indians on Montana's reservations. The decades of neglect that Indians had suffered at the hands of often insensitive federal bureaucracies had taken a heavy toll. On the Blackfeet Indian Reservation in 1934, more than 65 percent of families received some form of relief. The Wheeler-Howard Act in 1934 brought a fresh approach to Indian policy by allowing tribes to write their own constitutions and govern themselves. Aid programs like the WPA brought badly needed relief. Among the most important and productive WPA efforts in Montana was the Blackfeet Craft Guild, which helped women produce beaded and quilled garments and other artwork for sale in their craft shop at St. Mary and to tourists in Glacier National Park. The result was not only badly needed revenues for the tribe, but also a creative explosion in Blackfeet artistry and crafts.

The greatest of all New Deal work projects in Montana—and one of the largest in the nation—was construction of the enormous, earth-filled Fort Peck Dam on the Missouri River. That huge project, which was the result of demands of downstream states for flood control, was placed under the jurisdiction of the Public Works Administration and the Army Engineers. At the peak of construction in 1936, over 10,500 workers labored along the barren banks of the Missouri. They lived in small, makeshift communities like New Deal, Square Deal, Delano Heights, and Wheeler. For

The largest New Deal investment in Montana was the construction of Fort Peck Dam, at the time the largest earth-filled dam in the world. This photograph of the spill gate construction in 1937 shows the enormous dimensions of the project, which employed more than 10,000 workers.

diversion, they hit the "hot spots," such as Ruby Smith's place, where a worker could buy a nickel beer and, for the price of another beer, enjoy the company of a "taxi dancer." The bustling red-light district, "Happy Hollow," also had a large clientele.

At the time of its completion, Fort Peck stood as the greatest earthen dam in the world: 242 feet above the riverbed, over nine thousand feet across, and backing up nearly twenty million acre-feet of water. It is, quite simply, the greatest single alteration that humankind has ever made on the Montana landscape. During the 1930s, before the shantytowns were deserted, Fort Peck was more than just a big dam. It symbolized the New Deal effort: jobs for the unemployed, over $110 million pumped into the local economy, and a harnessing of the forces of nature. To both supporters and detractors, Fort Peck Dam became the epitome of the New Deal in Montana.

By 1940, the year the Fort Peck Dam was completed, the New Deal had ground to a halt as the nation became increasingly preoccupied with the war in Europe. But that greatest of American reform movements would have a lasting impact on the Treasure State. Not only did the New Deal offer temporary relief to thousands of citizens, but it also left behind dams, roads, schoolhouses, city halls, reservoirs, and forest trails. The New Deal began an enduring program of federal support to agriculture, and it sparked a massive resurgence of the labor movement. It offered Social Security to the elderly and insurance to the unemployed. And in Montana, as in all states, the New Deal began a "new federalism" that expanded the role of the federal government so that average Montanans came to look increasingly to Washington, not Helena, for the solution of their problems. By 1940, Uncle Sam wielded as great an influence in Montana as did the Company or the stockmen.

Significantly, the New Deal also stimulated the most dramatic expansion of state governmental activity that Helena has ever seen. At Roosevelt's urging, the Eighteenth Amendment was repealed in 1933, ending the era of prohibition. Like other states of the Northwest, Montana responded to the legalization of alcoholic beverages by placing their sale under a system of state monopoly. The 1933 legislature created a Montana Liquor Control Board, which was empowered to supervise the distribution and sale of liquors and wines through a system of state-owned stores. The state liquor system immediately became a major source of revenue. It also became one of Montana's largest bureaucracies, a fount of political patronage, and an occasional source of scandal.

The unfolding New Deal prompted the Montana legislature to create new boards and agencies that would enable the state to obtain federal matching funds and to coordinate state with federal activities. The new boards included a Water Conservation Board, a Grazing Commission, a State Planning Board, and a Highway Patrol and Patrol Board. Most important of all was the New Deal's Social Security Act of 1935. This highly complex law provided for much more than federal old-age pensions; it also offered federal grants to the states for unemployment insurance and care for the crippled, the blind, and dependent mothers and children. Like most states, Montana moved quickly to secure these federal benefits; and in doing so, it laid the foundation of the state's modern welfare system. The busy 1937 legislature created two important new agencies: a modernized Department of Public Welfare and an Unemployment Compensation Commission. The New Deal had not only expanded federal authority, but it had also triggered a boom in state activities.

THE POLITICS OF THE NEW DEAL ERA

Predictably, the New Deal spending programs, as well as Franklin D. Roosevelt personally, enjoyed enormous popularity in depressed Montana. Roosevelt visited the state in 1932, 1934, and 1937, and each time he received a hearty welcome. The Sioux and Assiniboines even made him a chief in 1934. Borrowing a well-known New Deal symbol, the tribes gave him the name "Fearless Blue Eagle." In each of his four presidential campaigns, Roosevelt carried Montana by wide margins. FDR's popularity and power gave Montana's Democratic party an enormous boost. From 1933 until 1941, the Democrats overwhelmingly dominated state government. Never before or since has one political party so completely held sway over the Treasure State.

Early in the game, Montana political leaders allied themselves to Roosevelt. Senator Burton K. Wheeler was one of the first nationally prominent figures to endorse him for the presidency, and Montanans played major roles in the triumphant Roosevelt cause at the Democratic National Convention of 1932. Senator Thomas J. Walsh, an FDR man, served as permanent chairman of the convention, and the state's national committeeman, J. Bruce Kremer, chaired the all-important rules committee. When Roosevelt swept Montana in the 1932 election, he carried many local Democrats into office on his coattails, including Governor John Erickson for a third term and two new congressmen, Roy Ayers and Joseph Monaghan.

In part to reward Montana for its support, President Roosevelt chose Walsh to be his attorney general. The Walsh appointment drew widespread praise, but tragically the seventy-three-year-old Montanan did not live to assume office. En route to the inauguration in early March 1933, he suffered a massive heart attack and died. With his passing, Montana

New Deal programs in Montana included support for native crafts. This photograph taken in Browning in 1933 shows Blackfeet basketweavers, Wolf Plume and Calf Robe, at work.

In one of his few trips to Montana, President Franklin D. Roosevelt is seen here at Glasgow in 1934, as part of his inspection of the Fort Peck Dam project.

lost perhaps the most distinguished citizen it had ever known. In addition to depriving his adopted state of a powerful voice in Washington, Walsh's death also raised serious political complications. As Governor Erickson set about choosing a Senate successor, he was besieged on all sides by Democrats who wanted the job. The governor finally made a decision that was immediately and inevitably denounced as a "deal." On March 13, 1933, Erickson resigned and was replaced by the Democratic lieutenant governor, Frank H. Cooney, who then appointed Erickson to fill Walsh's seat in the Senate. Erickson's "self-appointment" provoked howls of anger throughout Montana. The Sidney *Herald*, for instance, considered him a poor successor to the distinguished Walsh, "whose shoes he can no more fill in these trying times than could a child." The Erickson-Cooney "deal" turned the expected Montana political pattern upside down by placing a conservative in the Senate and a liberal in the governor's chair.

Like the other governors of his day, Frank Cooney faced enormous problems and hectic conditions. The New Deal dollars pouring into the state, the demands for state matching funds, and the rapidly expanding state bureaucracy all aroused political appetites and tempers, and the governor stood in the eye of the storm. An Irish Catholic Democrat and a successful Butte and Missoula businessman, Cooney leaned toward an independent, progressive position, but he had never held statewide office before 1933 and no one knew what to expect of him. He set out at once to assert himself as a legitimate, not a caretaker, governor; and when he did, powerful interest groups quickly rallied against him.

Cooney struggled mightily, and with some success, to bring the expanding bureaucracy under control and to get maximum New Deal benefits for Montana. He placed the state liquor system on a solid footing and fought successfully to channel federal funds into the water conservation program, which was his pride and joy. He fought with Company employees and friends whom Erickson had appointed to direct the state relief operation, and with federal support he got some of them removed. Not surprisingly, he made some enemies. When Cooney called the legislature into special session to raise matching funds for relief during the winter of 1933-34, his conservative enemies filed impeachment charges against him. The charges were mostly trivial, but the governor only narrowly escaped being removed from office. Until he died of heart failure in late 1935, the scrappy Cooney continued to govern and to demonstrate his independence. After Cooney's death, the president pro tem of the state senate, W. Elmer Holt of Miles City, served as acting governor until an elected governor could be seated in 1937. With Cooney's passing and Holt's appointment, the governorship passed back to conservative hands.

Montana's governor during the later New Deal years was Roy E. Ayers, a Fergus County rancher who had been a Democratic congressman from 1933 until 1937. During his term, 1937-41, Ayers became deeply embroiled in controversies that reflected the expanding state bureaucracy. The key issue arose from the 1937 legislature's passing of House Bill 65, the "Hitler Bill," which gave the governor sweeping powers over the hiring and firing of state employees. Republicans, and many Democrats as well, accused Ayers of using the new powers to build a large political machine within the state bureaucracy. By the end of his administration, Ayers had lost many of his earlier political supporters and faced an uphill battle for re-election.

Although the New Deal created headaches for administrators, it also opened up great opportunities for the Democrats. In the 1934 and 1936 elections, almost all Democratic candidates won easily. They gained control of both houses of the legislature, which they would hold until 1941. Both Montana seats in the United States Senate were put to the vote in 1934. Running as a Roosevelt ally, Senator Burton K. Wheeler faced Republican conservative Judge George M. Bourquin, who denounced the New Deal and attacked the Fort Peck project as a useless "duck pond." Wheeler destroyed Bourquin by a better than two-to-one margin and carried every county in the state.

The short, two-year term left in the Senate seat vacated by Thomas Walsh was also contested in 1934. In the hard-fought Democratic primary, wealthy Butte attorney James E. Murray took the nomination away from John Erickson, whose appointment to the seat the year before had aroused such bitter controversy. Murray easily went on to win the general election, thus beginning a highly successful political career and the longest Senate tenure in Montana's history, from 1935 until 1961. Little-known outside Butte before 1934, the liberal Senator Murray soon became a favorite of both President Roosevelt and the progressive farmer-labor groups in Montana. By the late 1930s, this "Millionaire Moses" had become one of the most powerful New Dealers in the Senate.

The Democrats made even greater gains in the Roosevelt landslide of 1936, when they won a full six-year term for Murray, the governorship for Roy Ayers, control of the legislature, and, incredibly, every elective administrative office. Both congressional seats went to freshman Democrats, Jerry J. O'Connell in the western district and James F. O'Conner in the east. The Republicans, and conservatives in general, seemed to be securely buried. But immediately after the 1936 landslide, the great New Deal–Democratic majority began to break up. In Montana and in the rest of the nation, the Democratic party began to split into liberal and conservative factions, pro- and anti-Roosevelt in their viewpoints. In Montana, the breakup of the party ushered in a period of fierce partisanship and crumbling party lines. By the close of the New Deal era, party loyalty—

never an abundant resource in Montana—had been shattered and the forces of conservatism were again on the rise.

Open warfare erupted within the Democratic party in 1937, when powerful Senator B. K. Wheeler broke with the president over Roosevelt's controversial attempt to "pack" the Supreme Court with friendly judges. Wheeler, who was fast moving away from his earlier progressivism, led the Senate forces that defeated the Court bill and thus began his famous feud with President Roosevelt. When FDR visited Fort Peck in October 1937, he snubbed Wheeler and did not even invite him to attend the occasion. More to the point, the president began to deprive the Montana senator of political patronage and to distribute it instead to other Democratic leaders.

Joined by many Republicans, the more conservative Democrats applauded Wheeler's defiance of the president. But Montana's liberal Democrats, the farmer-labor groups that had always before supported Wheeler, began to turn against him. Senator Murray openly feuded with his colleague, and freshman Representative Jerry O'Connell, an outspoken young radical, reported that the president had encouraged him to "go out there and fight like hell to defeat Senator Wheeler's machine so he wouldn't be back in 1940." The fiery O'Connell announced that he would challenge Wheeler for the Senate nomination in 1940.

In opposition to Wheeler, to Governor Ayers, and to Montana's conservative interests, the left wing of the Democratic party rose up in open rebellion. Representatives of the American Federation of Labor, the Congress of Industrial Organizations, the Farmers Union, and the unemployed joined hands in 1938 to create the Montana Council for Progressive Political Action. The council was outspokenly liberal and opposed to the Company and its allies. A year after its founding, the council supported publication of a reform-minded newspaper, the *People's Voice*, which would carry the liberal banner in Montana for the next three decades. Montana had, in embryonic form, a potentially ultraliberal farmer-labor party similar to parties that had taken power in Minnesota and North Dakota. Once again, as on the eve of World War I, there was thunder on the left in Montana.

Alarmed by these developments, the more conservative Democrats reached out toward an alliance with the Republicans. Wheeler and his political allies helped engineer the defeat of Jerry O'Connell when the young Democratic congressman came up for re-election in 1938. Blacked out by the Company press and undercut by the Wheeler Democrats, the firebrand O'Connell lost to an obscure Republican named Jacob Thorkelson, who soon gained nationwide attention for his anti-Semitic views in and out of Congress.

The chaotic campaign of 1940 demonstrated how liberal-conservative factionalism had broken up the New Deal majority. Angrily, the Montana Council for Progressive Political Action, which consisted mainly of liberal Democrats, set out to defeat the more conservative Democrats, especially Senator B. K. Wheeler and Governor Roy Ayers. They succeeded against Ayers, who lost the election to Republican Sam C. Ford, but they failed to unseat Wheeler in the primary. The tough old warhorse gathered in thousands of Republican votes to win a landslide re-election for a fourth Senate term. In addition to electing Ford to the governor's chair, the Republicans made other substantial gains in 1940. They regained control of the state senate and re-elected the antiwar crusader Jeannette Rankin to the U.S. House of Representatives.

In the 1940 election, the Democratic party lost its near monopoly of Montana politics, and the New Deal era came to a close. Once again, things returned to normal, and Montana's political parties competed on fairly even terms. The burning issues raised by the New Deal, however, centering on the proper role of government and on spending and taxation, carried into the 1940s and beyond. The New Deal had restored the power of the liberal community in Montana, and it closed in 1938-40 with an incredible scrambling of party lines. Liberal and conservative Democrats parted company, and the Republicans were able to regain power by joining hands with the conservative Democrats.

This confused political situation would make the next half-dozen years one of the most peculiar times in Montana's history. But out of the crucible of this confusion emerged a new style of Montana politics that would prove to be more characteristic of western politics in general. Senator Murray's partisan loyalty and his consistent liberal identification with the less fortunate would fade, while Senator Wheeler's willingness to ignore party organization and platforms and to engage in a politics of personality would prove to be increasingly successful. This would become the political trend of the next half-century in Montana.

WORLD WAR II: A TIME OF CHANGE

Between 1941 and 1945, World War II brought significant social and economic changes to every part of the United States. The war caused massive movements of population, unprecedented prosperity for farmers and ranchers, and new industries in most western states. In one way or another, all of these trends had a profound impact on Montana. Montana saw a great agricultural boom during the war years, a result of ample rainfall and high wartime demands and prices. In 1941, the state enjoyed its best crop year since 1927. The yields of 1942 were the best since World War I, and 1943 was the best year Montana farmers had ever seen. Crop values in 1943 surpassed $188 million, and cash income from livestock and livestock products totaled over $134 million. With somewhat lesser yields, the trend continued through 1944-45. Farmers and ranchers prospered, property valuations soared, and operators increased their investments in land and machinery. Between 1940 and 1948, the net cash income of Montana ranchers increased by 188 percent. Montana had fewer farms and ranches, but those that had hung on during the lean years were rapidly growing in size, moving toward mechanization, and increasing in value and income.

The war also had a strong impact on Montana industries. Lumber production increased as small operators moved into western Montana from the Pacific Northwest. Soaring demands for minerals quickly intensified the mining of copper and other metals at Butte, revived the coal-mining industry in Red Lodge, and shot crude oil production up to roughly 8.5 million barrels annually by 1944-45. Compared to many other western states, however, Montana's wartime growth seems less than impressive. The state acquired no significant new manufacturing industries that could compare with the Geneva Steel Works in Utah or the shipyards, airplane factories, or aluminum mills in Washington. Those war-born industries tended to cluster around the few urban centers of the region, leaving the rural states of Montana, the Dakotas, and Wyoming without competitive employment.

Defense spending did directly touch Montana in 1942, when a large Army Air Corps base was located near Great Falls. The complex installation, first called "East Base" and later Malmstrom Air Force Base, was a primary staging point for Lend-Lease airlift flights to Alaska and Russia. Women made up an important segment of the work force at East Base as aircraft mechanics, drivers, and warehouse workers. At Rimini, near Helena, the army established the War Dog Training Center to prepare men and sled dogs to help downed pilots in the Arctic. Training for fighting in Arctic conditions was carried out at Helena's Fort Harrison, where a special, combined U.S.-Canadian First Special Service Force was created. As fierce fighters on the European front, the unit was known as the "Devil's Brigade" by its German adversaries. As in World War I, Montana contributed more than its share of military manpower—roughly forty thousand men by 1942—and the state's death rate in the war was exceeded only by New Mexico's. The 163d Infantry Regiment, originally a Montana unit known as the "Sheepherders," experienced particularly tough fighting and high casualties in New Guinea and the Philippines.

The war caused the most massive, rapid, and hectic population movements in American history, and the migrations touched the Treasure State in contrary ways. Thriving mining and lumbering industries and the

During World War II, the Anaconda Company and other industrial employers emphasized the role their work played in the overall war effort by encouraging employees to buy war bonds and work more efficiently.

high demand for farm labor combined to lure thousands of restless Americans into Montana. At the same time, however, the armed services and high-paying defense industries, especially those on the Pacific Coast, drew tens of thousands of young Montanans away. As John Gunther asked at the time, why should men work for $7.75 a day in the dangerous underground mines of Butte when they could make $14.00 a shift rolling aluminum at Spokane or riveting B-17 bombers at Seattle? The state's population figures showed the results. From a 1940 total of 559,456, Montana's population fell to about 470,000 in 1943, according to estimates based on the issuance of wartime ration cards. This population decline would later reverse itself when the veterans came home and new job opportunities opened up after the war's end. But surely no other period—not even the gold, copper, or homestead boom eras—ever witnessed such dramatic population shifts in Montana as did World War II. Reminders of this fact are still found in the thousands of Montanans who remember their arrival in the state during the war and by the tens of thousands of people who wistfully attend "Montana Day" picnics in Los Angeles, San Francisco, Seattle, and Spokane.

The war years were a curious and confusing time in Montana's political history. As in most other states, the forces of New Deal liberalism lost ground to a reviving conservatism. This trend was complicated in Montana by the incredible scrambling of party lines that resulted from the 1940 election. During the war, state government was dominated by an informal alliance of moderately conservative Republicans led by Governor Sam C. "Model T" Ford and conservative Democrats led by Senator Burton K. Wheeler. Despite their party labels, Wheeler and Ford were old political friends. Both had broken into politics as outspoken liberals, and both had moved to the right as the years passed. In Joseph Kinsey Howard's view, both were "tired radicals" by the 1940s.

The precarious bipartisan alliance among Ford, Senator Wheeler, and their powerful and wealthy Republican ally Wellington Rankin was open and effective. Two well-known Democratic friends of Wheeler's, J. Burke Clements and Barclay Craighead, presided respectively over the Montana Industrial Accident Board and the Montana Unemployment Compensation Commission under Republican Governor Ford. Even though some suspected a Wheeler-Ford-Rankin "axis" or "triumvirate," the arrangement never amounted to a genuine political "machine." It was, rather, an alliance of convenience, and critics from both the right and the left attacked it. Republican National Committeeman Dan Whetstone, a conservative and an intelligent newspaper publisher from Cut Bank, hotly criticized Ford for passing out political jobs to Wheeler Democrats. And from the left, liberal Democrats, led by Senator Murray and the ultraliberal Montana Council for Progressive Political Action, thundered at both Ford and Wheeler.

Throughout the war years, neither conservative Republicans nor liberal Democrats were able to break up the Ford-Wheeler-Rankin alliance. The most formidable challenge came in the gubernatorial election campaign of 1944, when liberal Democrat Leif Erickson ran against Ford in a heated, free-swinging contest. The hottest issue was the proposal for a Missouri Valley Authority, sponsored by Senator Murray and the Roosevelt administration. Patterned after the Tennessee Valley Authority, the Missouri Valley Authority looked toward the massive federal development of the Missouri Basin based on a series of dams built to provide public power, reclamation, and flood control. Erickson and the liberal Democrats pushed the MVA, and Ford and the conservatives opposed it. In the end, Ford won re-election and the controversial MVA bill died in congressional committee.

Like Ford, Wheeler also faced mounting opposition from the left. Following his landslide re-election in 1940, the shrewd senator seemed unbeatable. He rose to new heights of international fame as an isolationist critic of Roosevelt's foreign policy, claiming that the president was steering the country toward involvement in another war. Early in 1941, while speaking against FDR's Lend-Lease Act, Wheeler made his oft-quoted remark denouncing lend-lease as "the New Deal's triple-A foreign policy; it will plow under every fourth American boy." Deeply angered, Roosevelt publicly replied: "That is really the rottenest thing that has been said in public life in my generation."

Until America's entry into the war in late 1941, Wheeler's popularity and political power remained impressive. Representatives O'Connor and Rankin, as well as Governor Ford, were his friends and allies. But the bombs that fell on Pearl Harbor undercut Wheeler's position, as the isolationists found themselves in an untenable situation. The liberal farmer-labor groups, who had always backed Wheeler until his break with Roosevelt, turned against him as he moved to the right. When Wheeler sought renomination to a fifth Senate term in the 1946 primary, he confounded most observers, including himself, by losing to his liberal opponent Leif Erickson, the man who had lost to Ford in 1944. Generally speaking, two factors caused Wheeler's defeat. His outspoken isolationism cost him the votes of many veterans and their families; and his movement to the right turned the liberals, especially the labor unions, against him.

Wheeler's defeat marked the end of a political era in Montana. He was the last of the old-style progressives who had cut their political teeth on battling the Anaconda Company. But by 1946 the young progressive had become an elderly conservative. Wheeler had first entered Montana politics with the nickname "Bolshevik Burt"; a quarter-century later he left under attack as "America's Number One Fascist." Neither label was accurate, but they did signal his passage from the left to the right side of the political spectrum. With his departure, a certain vigor and controversy disappeared from Montana's political life. As his biographer Richard Ruetten observed, no one, before or since, ever wielded such political power in Montana as did Burton K. Wheeler.

CHAPTER 13

The Modern Montana Economy, 1920-1990

S INCE 1920, Montana's fragile economy has become increasingly stable and diversified and, therefore, healthier. When viewed in a national context, however, the state's economic growth is much less impressive. Montana, like other states of the agricultural West, languished in depression throughout most of the 1920s and 1930s. World War II ushered in a period of unprecedented prosperity, which endured into the early 1950s. The economy expanded in uneven cycles of growth and decline during the 1950s and 1960s, boomed in the 1970s, and then fell into sharp depression in the 1980s. Although the hard times of the terrible 1930s have never returned, the economy of Montana, in comparison to that of most other states, has grown at a snail's pace. The basic historical explanation of this sluggish growth rate is simple enough: the two traditional mainstays of the Montana economy, agriculture and metal mining, have sharply declined in employment since the 1920s. Meanwhile, the new growth areas of lumber, petroleum, tourism, and government employment have only filled the gap. Montana still relies heavily on unpredictable extractive industries, and it still lacks traditional major manufacturing and the "high-tech," "high-service" industries that have revitalized so much of America since 1970. As a result, Montana continues to lag behind most other states in employment and prosperity.

TRENDS IN AGRICULTURE

Following the collapse of Northern Plains agriculture during the depression of 1919-22, Montana's farmers and ranchers faced a dismal future. Low farm prices and recurring droughts drove many of them from the land and punished those who stayed throughout the 1920s and the "dirty thirties." The long road to agricultural prosperity would demand major readjustments. Farmers would have to acquire more property, mechanize their operations, experiment with new scientific methods, and inevitably would require aid from the federal government. Most dramatically, the road back to prosperity would force the abandonment of thousands of small homesteads, because homesteading had brought a far more intensive farm population to the region than the environment could sustain. In the future, fewer and fewer operators would work larger and larger farms and ranches.

The hard times of the 1920s and 1930s prompted farmers and stockmen to experiment with and adopt new techniques. Beginning in the 1920s, those local farmers who could afford it began to mechanize their operations in a big way. By 1930, nineteen thousand small, internally geared gasoline tractors were at work on fourteen thousand Montana farms. Trucks came into common use at about the same time, as did mobile, tractor-drawn grain combines. These complex and expensive machines, and others like them, revolutionized farming and vastly increased the acreage that one operator could work efficiently. They also introduced to rural America what the distinguished geographer Isaiah Bowman had aptly termed a "gasoline culture," in which draft animals gave way to motor vehicles and small towns lost their consumers to more distant cities.

Increasingly, Montana farmers diversified their operations, combining wheat production with the raising of other crops like barley or irrigated hay and sugar beets. Many grain growers converted to "combination farms," which joined crop farming with the raising of livestock. Summer fallowing, or alternate-year cropping, was used more and more as a way to build up moisture and fertility in the soil. To combat the wind and soil erosion that resulted from intensive cultivation and summer fallowing, farm experts during the 1920s advocated a clod mulch, developed by such implements as rod weeders and duckfoot cultivators. By the 1930s that system had been supplanted by a "trashy fallow," prepared with the Noble Blade and other implements. From Canadian experiments, local farmers coped with wind erosion by using such effective techniques as strip cropping and contouring. During the "Dust Bowl" years of the 1930s, many farmers planted long rows of trees, or "shelterbelts," to blunt the knifing, highly destructive winds. They found that new drought-resistant varieties of wheat, such as the Ceres, Yogo, Winalta, and Cheyenne, made dry-land farming much safer than it once had been.

Montanans were pioneers in many types of agrarian reform during the 1920s and 1930s. Some of the innovations were sponsored by the Montana Extension Service and the Agricultural Experiment Station at Montana State College in Bozeman. M. L. Wilson of the Extension Service,

M. L. Wilson, agricultural researcher at Montana State College (now Montana State University), instructed farmers, such as this group at Circle in 1912, on the merits of growing flax and other marketable crops.

an intelligent and likable agricultural economist, gathered together a unique and fascinating group of young scientists, economists, and county extension agents. By using such imaginative techniques as "farm success" studies and the "Fairway Farms" project, which set up experimental farms around the state, Wilson and his associates generated ideas that gained nationwide attention. In Teton County, Robert Clarkson, Otto Wagnild, and their neighbors worked out a land classification-tax assessment program that contributed greatly to unified county planning across the state and region. And in Phillips County a group of grass-roots planners developed the "Malta Plan," America's first "resettlement program" of retiring submarginal farmlands and relocating the impoverished families who had been working them.

Throughout the dry and depressed years between the two world wars, Montana ranchers faced the same basic problems as the farmers did. They too staggered under the burden of low commodity prices and found that they must adapt more efficient and scientific methods. During the 1920s, the rising nationwide demand for younger beef led Great Plains ranchers to move increasingly to a "calf crop basis" and to market their animals when they were only two years old. More and more Montana ranchers sold their stock to midwestern feedlots for finishing instead of keeping them on range pastures until maturity. At the same time, the breakup of the great central beef markets in Chicago led to the establishment of local auction markets throughout the Midwest and Far West. Montana's first permanent livestock auction market was held at Billings in 1924. By mid-century, ten such markets operated in the state, and over half of the Montana cattle sold each year passed through the local markets. Since the 1950s, many area ranchers, especially the larger operators, have turned to contract sales, through which they deal directly with meat processors and cattle buyers.

Although Montana ranchers learned early in the game that they had to put up hay for winter feeding, their most persistent problems still centered on their primary resource, the range, and on how to control and manage it. The homestead movement had severely damaged much of the best rangeland, and it had broken up ownership patterns and driven up land prices. Ranchers throughout the West concluded that leasing rangeland, from either public or private owners, usually made more sense than buying it at a high cost. Again, Montanans, compelled by hardship, pioneered new techniques.

In 1928, a group of southeastern Montana ranchers, cooperating with the federal and state governments and the railroads, created America's first "cooperative grazing district." Forming the Mizpah–Pumpkin Creek Grazing Association, the stockmen took a lease on over a hundred thousand acres of public and private rangeland in Rosebud and Custer counties. By carefully controlling the number of animals allowed on the range, the grazers soon restored the land to full productivity. The Mizpah–Pumpkin Creek Project was a stunning success, proving the feasibility of leasing public lands to stockmen who organized grazing districts. In 1933, the Montana legislature provided for the general formation of grazing districts, and in 1934 the United States Congress passed the Taylor Grazing Act. Based in part on the Montana precedent, the act began the modern practice of leasing federally owned rangelands to stockmen.

The Great Depression and the droughts of the 1930s proved that agriculture could never hope to solve the problems of overproduction and low farm prices without federal aid. Beginning in 1933 with President Roosevelt's New Deal program, farmers and ranchers began to receive massive federal assistance for the first time in American history. The Agricultural Adjustment Act of 1933 and later legislation that paid farmers to withdraw land from production were based on the complex "domestic allotment" plan, which M. L. Wilson and other agricultural reformers had promoted for years. Soon, the federal government was pouring millions of dollars into depressed Montana.

Under the New Deal, Montana agriculture also received other forms of federal assistance. Beginning in 1938, the federal government initiated a system of "price support" payments in order to maintain fair ("parity") prices for wheat and other commodities. Various federal agencies refinanced farm loans, subsidized the building of electrical lines into rural areas, eradicated groundhogs and gophers, bought up surplus livestock to provide meat for the unemployed, and helped restore the range. With federal assistance, roughly 1.5 million acres of Montana farmland were reseeded with nutritious crested wheatgrass by 1941. Federal monies also helped the State Water Conservation Board build dozens of dams and storage reservoirs across Montana. After World War II, the Bureau of Reclamation developed the Canyon Ferry and Yellowtail dams, which would provide further aid to agriculture. By 1940, whether they liked it or not, Montana's farmers and ranchers had come to rely heavily on their Uncle Sam.

Although the New Deal programs provided invaluable support, real prosperity returned to Montana farmers only with the high food prices and abundant rainfall that came during World War II. There was a downside for agriculture, as the war pulled away many badly needed farm workers, both to the armed forces and to high-paying wartime jobs elsewhere. And the war hurt the labor-intensive sheep industry badly, as did declining markets for mutton and the invention of synthetic fibers, such as nylon. But the war also brought vastly increased profits to those who

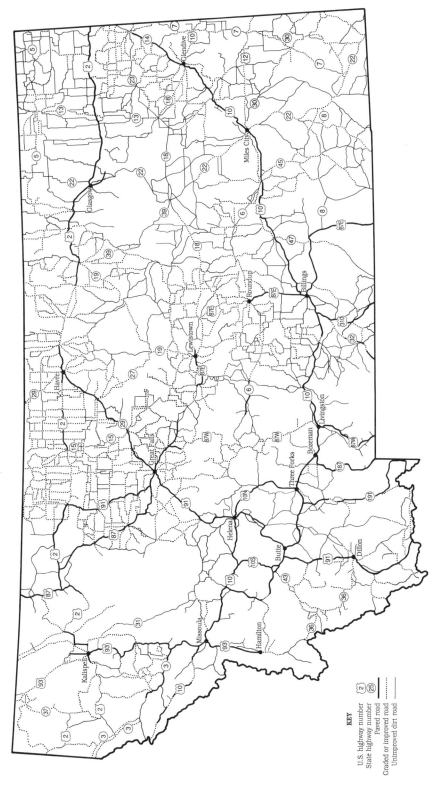

Map 7. Highways, 1934 (map by Barbara Lien; source: Montana State Highway Commission, copyright © H. M. Gousha Co.)

KEY

②	U.S. highway number
㉕	State highway number
	Paved road
	Graded or improved road
	Unimproved dirt road

had held on through the Depression. High food prices and generous federal price supports kept Montana's farms prosperous for several years after the war's end. Booming new food markets on the West Coast, especially in California, gave the agricultural economy of Montana a further boost. By 1946, California led all other states in the consumption of Montana beef. But in the early 1950s, the great wartime and postwar boom began to level off.

Since 1950, rising and falling prices and alternating wet and dry cycles have combined to make Montana agriculture an unpredictable livelihood. Amid the bountiful years of 1950, 1951, 1958, and 1966 were the poor years of 1954, 1959, 1961, 1984-85, and 1988. But never have things fallen apart as they did during the 1930s. Federal aid, in the form of price supports, food purchase programs, and soil conservation payments, have stabilized Montana agriculture, but aid programs such as the Reagan administration's dubious PIK (Payment in Kind) endeavor are controversial and expensive and may be cut back. Another source of stability is the ever-increasing mechanization and scientific management of Treasure State farms and ranches.

Many modern-day visitors are surprised at the extent to which agriculture is diversified in Montana. Some local stockgrowers specialize in sheep or hogs rather than cattle. Dairy farms dot the floors of the high mountain valleys. Cherry orchards beautify the shores of Flathead Lake, and irrigated crops of sugar beets, corn, and hay ripen along the river bottoms. And barley, of both the malting and feed varieties, is a major cash crop, worth over $150 million in cash receipts by the mid-1980s.

But what is most striking about Montana's agricultural economy since World War II is not diversification. It is the concentration on the production of two major commodities, wheat and beef, which together with barley total roughly 86 percent of most years' farm marketings. With few exceptions, Montana operations that do not specialize in either cereal grains or cattle are isolated, small, or in decline. Beaten down by nationwide and worldwide competition, the local production and processing of fruit and vegetables have eroded badly and have nearly vanished altogether from many areas, like the Gallatin Valley, where it used to thrive. The production of sugar beets, although still an important Montana commodity, has given way in many areas to fields of hay or corn. Heavily reliant on import quotas for protection, and with only one refinery left in the state, sugar beet producers face an uncertain future. And the state's once mighty sheep industry—oppressed by declining markets for lamb and wool, by predators, and by rising labor costs—earned less than twenty million dollars annually in 1983. Although some signs of diversification seem promising—such as the production of seed potatoes, honey, and especially hogs—wheat and beef are by far the most important commodities for Montana's agricultural industry.

Montana's expansive wheat and barley farms are "factories in the field" that bear little resemblance to the homesteads of the 1910s and 1920s. Riding in air-conditioned cabs atop huge and highly expensive four-wheel-drive tractors and self-propelled combines, today's farmers can work incredibly large tracts of land with few or no hired hands to help them. Synthetic fertilizers, highly effective pesticides, and new varieties of drought- and rust-resistant grain have all contributed to the quality, quantity, and dependability of agricultural production. As always, Montana's high-protein spring and winter wheat is in demand in national and international markets. In more recent years, the wheat has been sold increasingly to markets in Asia, especially in Japan. By the 1970s, well over half of the state's wheat crop was exported, and new barge ports on the Snake River near Lewiston, Idaho, promised to ease the passage of grain to seaports on the north Pacific Coast.

Montana's cattle ranches have become far more sophisticated and specialized than most people suspect. Some ranchers specialize in breeding stock, but most produce calves and finished animals for market. There are cow-calf and cow-calf-yearling ranchers who sell their animals at under two years of age, others who market more mature steers and heifers, and still others who buy young stock and graze it for varying periods of time before sale. Many operators use some or all of these methods. Most Montana cattle are shipped for finishing to out-of-state feedlots, especially to the Midwest, but also to northern Colorado, north Texas, and California.

Since 1970, Montana agriculture, like American agriculture in general, has passed through a sharp cycle of boom and bust. During the early and mid-1970s, abundant rainfall coincided with enormous grain sales to the Soviet Union to achieve a remarkable prosperity of high yields and high prices. By the mid-1970s, Montana wheat farmers averaged around thirty bushels per acre and sold their harvests for over four dollars per bushel. Cattle inventories that had totalled just over two million a decade earlier, at a gross value of $388 million, had risen to 3.4 million by 1974, at a value of a billion dollars.

But the 1980s brought a return to hard times in agriculture, as severe droughts hit the state and, more important, as commodity prices skidded downward because of rising global productivity and crop surpluses. In constant dollars, the total cash receipts accruing to Montana agricultural producers fell from over $2 billion in the late 1970s to about $1.6 billion in the late 1980s. Montana land values fell from an average of $264 per acre in 1984 to $167 in 1989, and agriculture's share of the state's economic base declined spectacularly, from 43 percent in the early 1970s to 18 percent in the late 1980s. The number of farms and ranches continued to drop—to about twenty-four thousand in 1989, even fewer when one considers that many of these are noncommercial "hobby farms" whose owners derive most of their income elsewhere.

Agriculture is still Montana's number-one industry, as it has been since the early years of the twentieth century. Agricultural receipts in Montana for 1988 totalled nearly $1.8 billion, nearly twice those of its closest competitor, tourism. This continuing predominance of agriculture reflects Montana's failure to industrialize or otherwise diversify its economy, but it is also true that the state is a robust producer. In 1988, Montana farms yielded 59,970,000 bushels of wheat, ranking eleventh among the fifty states in output, and grazed 2,350,000 head of cattle, placing it thirteenth among states. Efforts to secure more agricultural "finishing" or "valued-added" industries, such as meatpacking plants or large-scale feedlots, are not likely to succeed. Montana is simply too far from the large markets. But the state will continue to be a major producer of high-protein wheat, and its vast rangelands, which are in better shape than those of warmer states that graze year-round, will always make it a prime cow-calf cattle producer. But if Montana wishes to maintain its position as an important producer of agricultural products, it will have to invest more in basic and applied research, such as molecular biology and marketing.

Beyond dispute, agriculture lies at the heart of Montana's economy, providing not only its largest cash income but also the marketing base for dozens of towns and cities. Yet, mechanization and concentration have robbed agriculture of both population and social influence. Gone are the tens of thousands of farm workers who once sacked wheat, pitched hay, or dug sugar beets. And gone are most of the small "family farms" that Jim Hill dreamed of. In 1920, 82,000 Montanans found employment in agriculture; by 1988, only 35,457 made their living working the state's farmlands.

These cold, heartless figures tell us a lot about what has happened to Montana over the past half century. Although agriculture has stabilized and generally prospered in the Treasure State, it has also lost population and strength. Agriculture is less the style-setter and pacesetter of Montana than it used to be. As families have left their farms, the small towns that served them inevitably have lost population. Following a trend that began in about 1920, rural Montanans still anxiously watch their people, especially their young people, move to the cities. That beautiful dream of building a rural commonwealth based on the small family farm has been lost forever, a victim of "progress."

THE DECLINING ROLE OF METAL MINING

Much like agriculture, metal mining also fell in employment and influence after 1920. Before that time, the mining of copper, the Anaconda Copper Mining Company, and the city of Butte dominated the economic, social, and political life of the state. The Anaconda, having crushed and absorbed most of its competition, controlled the "Richest Hill on Earth" and relied on Butte's underground mines as its main source of copper. Anaconda also had interests that reached well beyond Butte. It had smelters, refineries, and reduction works at Anaconda, East Helena, and Great Falls; hundreds of thousands of acres of western Montana timberland; lumber mills at Bonner; a powerful chain of newspapers; and many other investments. The Company also had a robust "Siamese twin," the Montana Power Company.

The Montana Power Company took shape in 1912 when John D. Ryan, president of the Amalgamated Copper Company (which became the Anaconda Copper Mining Company in 1915), merged several small hydroelectric plants, some of them located at the Great Falls of the Missouri, into one large firm. Ryan, a capable and hardboiled man, wanted to sell power both to his giant Anaconda Company and to the Milwaukee Railroad, of which he was a director. Although the energetic Ryan served as president of both Anaconda and Montana Power until his death in 1933, the utility was never an Anaconda subsidiary. In 1928, the ownership of Montana Power passed to an eastern holding company, American Power and Light, and in 1950 to individual stockholders. Despite this loose corporate connection, Montanans often referred to Anaconda–Montana Power as simply "the Company"—and with good reason. For twenty years, the two firms were joined under Ryan's presidency, and for many years they shared the same legal, political, and publicity staffs. Combined, the two corporations had awesome strength and influence.

During its heyday, from 1900 until the 1940s, the Anaconda Company wielded such enormous power in the state that Montana gained the unenviable reputation of being little more than a corporate asset. In the mid-1940s, for instance, John Gunther wrote these famous, if overstated, words in his *Inside U.S.A.*: "Anaconda, a company aptly named, certainly has a constrictorlike grip on much that goes on, and Montana is the nearest to a 'colony' of any American state, Delaware alone possibly excepted." But for all its naked power and its heavy-handed manipulation of state politics, Anaconda never ran Montana. It shared and contested power with other interest groups, and, like any other corporation, it changed with the times.

Beginning in the 1920s, Anaconda's role in Montana began a subtle transformation. Under the ambitious direction of John Ryan and his close associate Cornelius "Con" Kelley, Anaconda, like so many American corporations of the 1920s, launched a major program of expansion. In 1922, the Company bought control of the Connecticut-based American Brass Company, the world's greatest producer of brass, a copper alloy. The purchase made Anaconda, which was already the world's leading copper producer, the world's leading copper fabricator as well. The all-important acquisition of American Brass allowed Anaconda to stabilize copper sales and production. In 1929-30, the firm created another fabricating subsidiary, the Anaconda Wire and Cable Company, with plants at Great Falls and at other locations outside the state.

The Company's move into brass increased its appetite for copper. Because Butte's complex and deepening underground mines required high labor and operating costs, Ryan and Kelley began a search for new, cheaper sources of the red metal. The mining industry had been turning heavily toward the open-pit removal of low-grade ores using enormous earth-moving equipment, a much less expensive method than working high-grade deposits in underground tunnels. In 1923, Anaconda negotiated the purchase of the world's greatest copper ore bodies, the holdings of the Guggenheim family in the Andes Mountains of Chile. Anaconda paid $77 million for the mines, which included the fabulously rich open pit at Chuquicamata. It was the largest cash transfer that Wall Street had ever seen. Chuquicamata and Anaconda's other mines in Chile soon became the Company's most important source of copper. They produced two-thirds of Anaconda's primary copper and three-fourths of its earnings. The Company expanded in other areas, too. It bought up the remaining Montana properties of the late W. A. Clark in 1928 and completed its acquisition of the valuable Green Cananea Copper Company of northern Mexico in 1929.

Anaconda's spectacular expansion had a profound impact on Montana, which became only a province in the Company's far-flung corporate empire. Often, when storm clouds gathered on the political horizon in Montana, rumors would circulate that the Company might shut down its Butte operation and turn exclusively to its more profitable Latin American mines. Fears of an Anaconda pullout lifted dramatically in 1947, however, when Con Kelley announced his "Greater Butte Project," a multi-million-dollar program aimed at extracting low-grade ores by using a method of underground blasting called "block-caving." In the judgment of *Forbes* magazine, however, the project turned out to be a "costly bust." Within a few years, it gave way to open-pit mining, a method that had always seemed impossible because it meant blasting away large parts of the city.

Beginning in the early 1950s, open-pit mining literally transformed the city of Butte. As the Berkeley Pit relentlessly deepened and widened, it ate constantly away at the old uptown area of the city. Residents and businesses fled toward the "Flats," south of town. Steadily, the expensive underground mines closed down, and the hardrock miners and smeltermen became a vanishing breed. Open-pit mining is highly automated and requires far fewer employees than underground mining does. As the underground mines closed, Butte, once the economic and political center of the state, saw its population and political power steadily crumble away. Gradually, almost imperceptibly, the Company's shadow over Montana grew smaller and smaller. Anaconda's only new commitment to the state after World War II was its aluminum operation, which opened at Columbia Falls and Great Falls in 1955.

Not surprisingly, as Anaconda diversified and expanded into a global corporation and as Marcus Daly's lieutenants passed from the scene, the Company began to inch away from the iron-fisted political methods of the past. Even as early as the 1930s, younger executives like W. H. Hoover and the talented lobbyist and public relations man Al Wilkinson started urging the Company to take a more restrained approach. Following the retirement of Cornelius Kelley, who reportedly clung to the old ways until the end, changes came rapidly. Anaconda sold its newspapers in 1959 and drifted further and further away from its once intimate association with the Montana Power Company. By the late 1960s, Anaconda bore little resemblance to the fiery dragon it had once been. Instead, it behaved like most other extractive corporations in the western states— lobbying quietly in Helena, advertising to win public favor, and stewing about new anti-pollution standards. Anaconda had entered the twentieth century.

Then, with incredible abruptness, came the decline and fall. In 1971, Anaconda suffered a staggering blow when the leftist government of Chile seized and nationalized the Company's invaluable mines there. Anaconda declared a net loss of $357.3 million for 1971. As one observer put it, the corporation had passed "From Riches to Rags" and was fighting for its very life. Loss of its Chilean properties forced Anaconda to rely more heavily on its domestic mines in Montana, Arizona, and Nevada. At the same time, however, the firm's critical need to cut expenses led to dramatic shutdowns of some costly operations in Montana, and the zinc operation, based at Great Falls and Anaconda, got the axe. In mid-1972, in a move of great importance, Anaconda sold its lumber operation, including 670,500 acres of Montana forestland, to Champion International for $117 million. The Company began making more sweeping cuts in the mid-1970s. In December 1974, Anaconda announced the termination of roughly seven hundred to a thousand jobs in Butte and Anaconda. In

The Berkeley Pit. As the concentration of copper in Butte ores diminished, the Anaconda Company employed a new methodology, open-pit mining, to keep the mines profitable during the 1950s.

February 1975, the even more devastating word arrived that fifteen hundred more layoffs would follow. These shattering job losses, amounting to nearly one-third of Anaconda's Montana payroll, resulted mainly from the Company phasing out the last of the underground mines, the old ore concentrator and foundry at Anaconda, and the recently begun Continental-East open-pit mine at Butte.

The depreciated Anaconda became a prime takeover target for eager conglomerates in a period when highly profitable energy companies were seeking ways to expand into metal mining. In 1977, the California-based oil giant ARCO (Atlantic Richfield) purchased Anaconda and made it into its Anaconda Minerals Division. Montanans welcomed this move, which seemed to promise a badly needed recapitalization of their old corporate behemoth. But copper markets continued to erode badly as South American and African producers flooded them and as satellite and fiber-optic communications displaced the red metal. So ARCO continued the slashing operation that Anaconda had begun. It closed down the old Anaconda smelter in 1980 and dismantled it. The Great Falls works was shut down, and the destruction of the old smokestack offered a traumatic and symbolic closing of a century of copper domination in the state. In 1983, ARCO suspended all of its mining operations in Butte and terminated the last seven hundred of its employees there. The population of Butte and Anaconda fell from 50,600 in 1980 to 43,200 in 1988. With its underground pumps shut down, the Berkeley Pit began to fill with toxic groundwater, a woeful residue of a once-great industry.

But when the Montana mining industry seemed to have all but died, it enjoyed a striking rebirth in the mid-1980s. The highly successful Missoula entrepreneur Dennis Washington bought up the old ARCO-Anaconda properties at Butte at bargain rates and soon had 330 employees profitably at work for his Montana Resources firm at the Continental Pit site. A number of other new mining firms, particularly gold operations, also began operations in Montana. The Spokane-based Pegasus Mining Company has several mines in production in the state, including their Zortman-Landusky operation with 160 employees and the Montana Tunnels project near Helena with 245 workers. ASARCO opened two major mining complexes, each with about 350 workers, at Troy and Rock Creek in western Montana; Placer Domes' Golden Sunlight Mine near Whitehall employs 250 people. The Chevron Resources-Manville Sales Corporation complex on the Stillwater River, which has 433 workers under contract, is the only source in the western hemisphere of the vital strategic metals platinum and palladium.

Montana mining, like a snake molting its skin, has passed through a major metamorphosis. What happened at Butte was an especially graphic instance of how the dynamic world economy affects a locality. The old Anaconda operation, sadly neglected and unimproved and heavily reliant on expensive union labor, could not compete with Chilean mines. In contrast, the Washington Corporations' Montana Resources employs state-of-the-art automation and a small, highly paid but nonunion work force. It and the other new technology mining firms compete well, and they are able to meet new, tough environmental laws. As the state of Montana passed its centennial year in 1989, mining still figured largely in its economy, generating nearly nine hundred million dollars in 1988. But it no longer dominates the state's economy or the political order as it once did, and surely that is for the best.

LABOR

Union labor and metal mining came of age together in Montana. For many years, the well-organized Butte-Anaconda miners and smeltermen, along with the scattered railroad brotherhoods, formed the hard core of union power in the state. By 1912, one local writer could describe Butte, with a semblance of truth, as "the strongest union town on earth." A two-member chimney-sweeps' union enjoyed recognition at Butte, and unions there once threatened to boycott the cemetery unless the lone gravedigger won his demands. But the turmoil surrounding World War I broke the power of the Butte Miners' Union, and from 1914 until 1934 the open shop prevailed at Butte and the unions stagnated.

The Roosevelt New Deal of the 1930s sparked a massive resurgence of union strength throughout the nation. Such New Deal laws as the National Labor Relations Act directly encouraged and supported unionization, and labor unions in Butte sprang back to life. During the summer of 1933, the Montana State Federation of Labor, led by its fiery president, Jimmy Graham, kicked off a high-geared organizational drive. The International Union of Mine, Mill and Smelter Workers, successor to the Western Federation of Miners, spearheaded a mighty effort to revitalize the nearly dormant Butte Miners' Union. In a July 9 rally at the Fox Theatre in Butte, organizers signed up twenty-three hundred miners; by July 20, they had forty-five hundred new members.

The main challenges facing the Mine, Mill organization, its Butte Miners' Union local, and the related smelting and crafts unions were to gain recognition and to win a favorable contract from the Anaconda Copper Mining Company. Negotiations between the Company and the unions dragged on until May 8, 1934, and then broke apart, leading to the most important strike in Montana's history. Over sixty-five hundred Mine, Mill and crafts unionists walked off the job. Tension polarized the mining city as company guards and labor organizers, some of them radicals, lined up against one another. Many predicted violence, but both sides worked to avoid it. The great strike of 1934 continued for four months and finally ended on September 17 in a major union victory. Anaconda granted the striking unions a wage increase, a forty-hour work week, and, most important of all, full recognition. After twenty years of impotence, Butte labor had regained the "closed shop."

After the 1934 strike, the American Federation of Labor locals in Montana steadily expanded their membership and political power. New unions, like the United Cannery Workers and the International Sheep Shearers, joined them. But the most important and powerful of all Montana unions was the Butte Miners' Union affiliate of the Mine, Mill and Smelter Workers. During 1937-38, Mine, Mill joined nine other nationwide unions to form the militant Congress of Industrial Organizations. Throughout the 1930s and into the 1940s, unions affiliated with both the American Federation of Labor and the Congress of Industrial Organizations rose to new heights of economic and political power in Montana.

The Montana miners and smeltermen fell on hard times after World War II. Cutbacks in underground mining cost them many jobs, and their union became embroiled in controversy. After determining that Communists had gained considerable influence among the leadership of the Mine, Mill and Smelter Workers Union, the CIO expelled that organization from its ranks in 1950. The CIO then gave jurisdiction over the metal miners, smeltermen, and refinery workers to one of its largest unions, the United Steelworkers of America. In Montana, however, the mine workers refused to part with their old union. The vast majority of them were not Communists, and they cared less about such charges than about loyalty to the union of their fathers. For years, the CIO and the Steelworkers hammered away at the Mine, Mill locals in Butte, Anaconda, East Helena, and Great Falls. Finally, through a 1967 merger agreement, the Steelworkers absorbed and took over the local affiliates of the once-mighty Mine, Mill and Smelter Workers Union.

After World War II, as the mining unions steadily declined in membership, a series of strikes periodically shut down Montana's mining industry, hitting Butte-Anaconda and the entire state with severe jolts. A major strike began in April 1946, calling out seven thousand men in four Montana cities. Violence erupted at Butte when bands of men, women, and children sacked the homes of nonunion "scab" workers. Strikes were also called in 1954, 1959-60, and 1962. The last major copper strike—the longest and costliest strike in the state's history—took place in 1967-68. The Steelworkers stayed out for eight and one-half months, and Montanans lost $34 million in wages alone.

Twelve-hundred-pound T-ingot being lifted from a casting station. During the postwar period, Montana's industrial economy included new factories that took advantage of another abundant natural resource—water power. (Columbia Falls Aluminum Co.)

The mine, smelter, and refinery workers' unions steadily eroded in membership and influence after World War II. So did Montana's other traditional blue-collar unions, suffering from automation and the determination of industry to avoid high-cost labor. For many years, two powerful unions, the Railroad Brotherhoods and the United Mine Workers, have wielded formidable strength in some parts of the state. Based in rail cities like Laurel, Livingston, Havre, and Missoula, the Railroad Brotherhoods, with enviable federally juried wages and hours, ranked among the aristocrats of organized labor. The Brotherhoods exercised potent political power, especially locally. But they, too, have suffered severely from road closures and cutbacks, such as the disastrous Burlington Northern closure of the Livingston shops in 1985 that cost 360 prime jobs. The UMW thrived for years at deep coal-mining centers like Red Lodge and Roundup, and Montanan Tony Boyle rose to the national presidency of the union before falling in scandal. But the new, open-pit coal mines either have no union or they employ less militant and more prosperous workers like Teamsters and Operating Engineers.

As the traditional blue-collar unions lost power in Montana, other labor organizations gained members. Some of these unions—such as the Teamsters, the Carpenters, Operating Engineers, the Lumber, Production and Industrial Workers, and the Pulp, Sulphite and Paper Millworkers—represented blue-collar workers. But Montana also mirrored a national trend as its organized work force became more white-collar and middle-class in its makeup. These unions, some of which are affiliated with the state AFL-CIO, are less wedded to old-fashioned ideological unionism and more attached to practical, bread-and-butter concerns. Among the most prominent white-collar unions in the Treasure State are the Retail Clerks, the Montana Federation of State Employees, the Montana Federation of Teachers, and the Montana Education Association. It is significant that the spokesmen for organized educators and other state employees are among the most influential people in the state.

Again following national trends since 1970, Montana has seen a sharp decrease in the share of its work force that is unionized. In the state's depressed economy, the trend has been to eliminate well-paid union jobs and replace them with lower paid service jobs and self-employment (in 1990, one in four working Montanans was self-employed). In 1989, the AFL-CIO had about forty thousand Montana members, and approximately fifteen thousand other workers belonged to other labor organizations. By any standard, Montana has traditionally been a strong union state. As AFL-CIO Executive Director Jim Murry, one of Montana's strongest political spokesmen, said: "We have a 100-year tradition of being tough as hell." And while labor has lost much of its membership, it is still one of the state's most potent political entities, as can be seen in its perennial strength in the Democratic party and its success in opposing some issues, such as the sales tax.

LUMBER, OIL, AND COAL

Three other extractive industries—lumber, oil, and coal—also have gained importance in Montana since 1920. Each of these industries has become a mainstay of the Montana economy, but each is also fluctuating and unsteady, wavering with the slightest shift in the national and world economy. And each industry, in its own way, poses a threat to Montana's fragile air, water, and land.

The lumber industry is as old as white settlement in Montana. Frontier lumbermen, serving mainly the scattered mining camps, cut timber wherever they found or needed it. Big-time lumbering arrived in Montana with the railroad and industrial mining booms of the 1880s. The Missoula-based firm of Eddy, Hammond and Company handled lucrative contracts for the Northern Pacific. In partnership with the railroad and with Marcus Daly, that powerful firm later formed the Montana Improvement Company to supply local rail and mining operations. But the Montana Improvement Company and its partners soon found themselves in difficult straits as a result of timber cutting on public lands. During the 1890s, the Great Northern Railroad completed its construction program, and Jim Hill's lowered freight rates allowed Montana lumber to penetrate markets in the Midwest and the East. To satisfy its voracious appetite for construction timber and fuel, the Anaconda Copper Mining Company went directly into the lumber business. By 1910, the Company had acquired over a million acres of timberland. With its operations centered at the company town of Bonner, located a few miles east of Missoula, Anaconda was the largest wood producer in Montana.

The state's lumber industry assumed its classic posture during the first four decades of the twentieth century. By national standards, production was irregular and small. The slower-growing Rocky Mountain forests could not match the productive forests on the West Coast and in the South, and Montana output usually totaled only 250 to 400 million board feet per year, roughly one percent of the nation's production. A few large concerns—mainly Anaconda at Bonner, the Great Northern's Somers Lumber Company near Kalispell, and the J. Neils Company at Libby—cut most of the timber logged in Montana, supplemented by a scattering of smaller outfits. In 1939, the lumber and wood products industry employed only 2,676 workers in Montana. The industry would show little growth until the end of World War II.

Until comparatively recent times, lumbering in Montana and elsewhere was a frightfully wasteful business. Today's hikers find reminders of that fact every time they come upon the abandoned burners, collapsing buildings, and ravaged hillsides where a "cut-out and get-out" logging camp once stood. Montanans, like most other westerners, were slow to grasp the need for forest conservation, and many of them howled in anger when President Theodore Roosevelt withdrew huge tracts of federal timberlands and placed them in National Forest reserves from 1901 through 1909. More than any other event, the terrible forest fire of August 1910 convinced local people of the environmental dangers they faced. The calamitous blaze, whipped by seventy-mile-per-hour winds, devastated northern Idaho and the country along the Idaho-Montana state line; killed eighty firefighters; destroyed much of Wallace, Idaho, and several small towns in Montana; and consumed three million acres of timberland. Smoke from the fire reddened the sun at Denver and Kansas City. In time, the local majority came to realize that the National Forests are an invaluable resource, where timber can be harvested as a renewable crop, watersheds and wildlife habitat can be protected, and recreation provided for a growing national population. The federal government now owns nearly 12 million of Montana's 17.3 million acres of forestland.

Montana's lumber industry grew dramatically during and especially after World War II. The nationwide demand for wood during the postwar building boom could not be fully supplied by the prime timber stands of the West Coast, Great Lakes, and South. Montana's forests of fir, spruce, and lodgepole and ponderosa pine, which had always been of generally marginal commercial value, began to attract more and more loggers. By 1948, there were 434 mills, most of them small, operating in the state. Employment in the wood products industry shot upward, to 5,374 in 1950 and 7,150 in 1955. The boom decreased during the late 1950s, and many of the smaller operators closed down. But by then, big-time investors had begun to develop a truly diversified wood products industry in Montana.

In 1957, the Hoerner Boxes and Waldorf Paper Products companies opened a large pulp mill west of Missoula. The operation steadily enlarged over the next several years, and in 1966 the owners merged into the Hoerner-Waldorf Company of Montana. Hoerner-Waldorf's pulp and paper enterprise brought hundreds of new jobs to the Missoula area and helped make that city the Montana boomtown of the 1960s. The company also helped stabilize operations for the dozens of mills that regularly supplied it with wood chips and fuel. Unfortunately, the plant also contributed to an air pollution problem in Missoula, which gained nationwide attention for that city and aroused many of its citizens to demonstrations of anger. Local women formed an organization known as GASP—Gals

Against Smog Pollution—and by the 1970s a major effort was underway to clean up Missoula's air.

Until the late 1960s, American lumbering continued to ride high on the wave of national prosperity. Based mainly at Missoula and Libby and in the Flathead Valley, the industry continued to expand and diversify. The manufacturing of particle board and formaldehyde began at Missoula; and veneer mills, new and larger plywood plants, and other finished or semi-finished products operations were established at various locations. Christmas tree growers prospered in the Flathead Valley, and pole producers increased their cutting and processing in the many areas of Montana where lodgepole pines grow.

Like other extractive industries, however, the wood products industry entered a long cycle of convolution in about 1970. After reaching a peak in productivity at 1.5 billion board feet in 1968, a faltering national construction economy hit the industry first in 1969-71 and then again even harder a decade later. The industry began to recover in 1983-84, but in a new form. Some mills closed and others were sold. In 1985, Champion International sold its pulp plant west of Missoula to Stone Container Corporation. The old-growth timber was disappearing, and the general trend was toward processing smaller logs in automated mills. So even as productivity surged in the late 1980s, with nearly nine hundred million dollars in receipts in 1988, employment fell from a high of 13,400 in 1978 to 11,130 in 1988.

The forest products industry remains a vital part of the Montana economy. As Charles Keegan concluded, "with the possible exception of the timber-producing regions in Oregon, there is no large region in the United States that is more dependent on the primary forest products industry than is the contiguous region encompassing western Montana and northern Idaho." Wood and paper products constitute Montana's major manufacturing industry and in 1990 claimed fully 15 percent of its economic base, up from less than 10 percent in the early 1970s. But perhaps more than any of Montana's other extractive industries, it is extremely vulnerable, not only to foreign competition, particularly from British Columbia, but also to problems of supply. Environmentalists and wilderness advocates have heavily criticized clear-cutting and below-cost timber sales on National Forest lands. As those groups have gained nationwide support, lumbermen have found that they are less able to secure adequate supplies of wood for their mills. The issue of whether Montana's forests will harbor more wilderness or supply more timber hovers like a great question mark over not only the wood products industry, but also over Montana itself.

Oil production began in Montana during the second and third decades of the twentieth century, when the increasing use of automobiles sent petroleum explorers in search of new deposits. Although there had been earlier discoveries in northwestern and south-central Montana, the first significant oil field in the state was opened in 1915 at Elk Basin, along the Wyoming-Montana line in Carbon County. In 1919, wells were drilled at Devil's Basin near Roundup and at Cat Creek on the lower Musselshell River. In 1922, Gordon Campbell, the developer of Devil's Basin and the key figure in Montana's fast-growing oil industry, made an important find on the Miller Ranch, north of Shelby. That strike opened the rich Kevin-Sunburst Field, one of the greatest in Montana's history.

Throughout the 1920s, Montana's first oil boom was centered in the state's north-central region, and the Kevin-Sunburst Field held the limelight. Oil money flowed into the nearby towns of Cut Bank and Shelby. In a burst of unrestrained optimism, a group of Shelby promoters tried to put their town on the map in 1923 by staging a world's heavyweight boxing championship between Jack Dempsey and Tommy Gibbons. They lost their shirts in the biggest flop in the history of world boxing when fewer than eight thousand people paid to attend.

Drilling activities steadily expanded in the region. In 1927, the Pondera Field opened near Conrad, and the highly important Cut Bank Field began to produce in 1931-32. Independents like R. C. Tarrent and Tip O'Neil first developed the Cut Bank deposits, and soon larger companies like Texaco and Montana Power moved in to process its high quality crude oil and natural gas. By 1936, the Cut Bank Field was the largest producer in Montana. Although a number of small refineries were built to work Montana's oil, the Great Depression of the 1930s dampened prospecting and production and blighted the boom of 1922-32.

Compared to big producers like Texas, Oklahoma, and California, Montana's oil production, like its lumber production, remained on a small scale until after World War II. Most of the state's oil continued to flow from the north-central fields and from the revived Elk Basin operations. As postwar prosperity increased the demand for petroleum, exploration and refining activities mounted in the Treasure State. Union Oil, Standard Oil, and the Farmers Union Central Exchange made heavy investments in Montana, and Continental Oil and Carter Oil built elaborate new refineries at Billings in the late 1940s. The most important breakthrough came in 1951, when major discoveries in the Williston Basin launched Montana's second oil boom.

The Williston Basin is a deep oil field lying beneath western North Dakota, southern Saskatchewan, and eastern Montana. Following initial strikes in North Dakota and in Dawson County, Montana, a frenzied race for oil leases set in across eastern Montana. One field came in after another throughout the early and middle 1950s—at Cabin Creek and East Poplar and at Glendive, Sidney, Wibaux, and Baker. Montana oil production doubled as a result of the Williston Basin boom, and Billings emerged as the center of the state's petroleum industry. More large oil companies moved into Billings, and refineries hurriedly expanded their operations. In 1954, the $20.5 million Yellowstone Pipeline was completed from Billings to Spokane. Billings boomed in population throughout the 1950s and took on the appearance of an Oklahoma-style oil town. By 1970, Billings' refineries handled over 85 percent of all the oil processed in the state.

As oil gained importance in Montana, so too did natural gas. Following the initial discoveries in the Baker-Glendive area in 1915, the Montana-Dakota Utilities Company began marketing natural gas to industrial and residential customers in far eastern Montana. Kevin-Sunburst, Cut Bank, and other old north-central fields yielded gas as well as oil. Beginning in the 1920s and 1930s, pipelines carried the gas to towns in west-central Montana, and Montana Power went into the business in a big way. By the 1950s Montana was producing over twenty billion cubic feet of natural gas a year, and many homes and businesses had come to rely on the inexpensive and efficient fuel for heating and power. Both Montana Power and Montana-Dakota Utilities made increasingly large investments in natural gas, and Montana Power imported sizable quantities from Canada and Wyoming to serve its local customers.

The late 1950s and 1960s saw a leveling trend in the Montana oil and gas business. Employment declined, and the future of the industry was in doubt. But 1967 brought new hopes for oil and the gas developers. In Blaine County, the Tiger Ridge natural gas field opened and proved to be the greatest discovery in nearly forty years. At almost the same time, Denver oilman Sam Gary brought in the mammoth Bell Creek oil field in Powder River County near Broadus. The shallow Bell Creek Field sent tremors of excitement through the Montana oil industry and offered hopes of a great new boom.

Montana petroleum production peaked at about the same time that the wood products industry did—oil in 1968 at 48.5 million barrels and natural gas in 1973 at 58.9 billion cubic feet. The industry then entered a hectic period of ups and downs that was driven by the fast-changing and rapidly integrating world economy. During the early to mid-1970s, and again during the years before 1984, world energy shortages dramatically drove up prices. This led to high profits, increased exploration and drilling, and handsome tax yields. Montana's petroleum receipts crested in 1981 at $1.45 billion. But then rising worldwide productivity and conservation turned the energy shortage into a glut, and prices plummeted. By 1987, the value of wellhead oil and gas production had fallen by two-thirds to only $500 million.

The oil and gas industry remains depressed in Montana, having made only a partial recovery and facing an uncertain future. Many wells are still capped, waiting for price increases that seem chimerical. Only twenty-five hundred employees worked in oil and gas exploration and production in 1987, about the same number as a decade earlier and nearly two-thirds fewer than in 1981. In 1987, petroleum's share of Montana's nonfarm economic base was only 7 percent, down from 17 percent in the boom year of 1981. The oil and gas industry, it would seem, will continue to figure in the state's future as it has in the past—marginally, with a relatively high value of product and potential tax yield, and with few jobs, although high wages for those few. Unless there is another energy crisis like that of the early 1970s and unless the complex and deep-lying "overthrust belt" in western Montana delivers a new bonanza, oil and gas will continue to lie at the periphery of the state's economic order.

Montana's premier energy resource is not oil but coal. Montana leads all other states in coal reserves. According to estimates of the United States Geological Survey, the Treasure State has roughly 108 billion tons of minable coal, far more than its closest contenders, Illinois (66 billion tons) and Wyoming (51 billion tons). Most of that coal, the Fort Union Formation, lies in shallow, easily strip-mined seams in southeastern and east-central Montana. Generally speaking, the coal is subbituminous and lignite, which is low in heating quality but also low in polluting sulfur content. How, when, where, how much, by whom, and whether this coal will be mined are serious questions for Montana.

Small coal mines were first opened in western Montana during the 1860s mining rushes, but significant development came only with the coal-fired, steam-powered railroads of the 1880s and 1890s. The Northern Pacific played a major role in developing Montana's first important mines in the vicinity of Bozeman Pass. Along the Yellowstone-Gallatin divide, several small towns were built by miners who worked the rich seams of bituminous coal, among them Chestnut, Timberline, Cokedale, and the Anaconda's company town of Storrs. The Bozeman area coal towns, and those nearby on the upper Yellowstone, such as Electric and Aldridge, prospered during the 1890s and then lost population and faded into ghost towns after World War I, after the centers of production had moved elsewhere.

Cascade County took over the lead in Montana coal output when the Great Northern Railway and the Anaconda Copper Mining Company began developing deposits near Great Falls. The Great Northern relied especially on the coal towns of Stockett and Sand Coulee, and the Anaconda concentrated on the mines at Belt, later shifting its emphasis to Sand Coulee. Following its 1906-9 expansion through Montana, the Milwaukee Railroad spurred development of the coal-rich Bull Mountains north of Billings. Roundup and Klein became important mining towns, and production in that area remained important until past mid-century.

By the 1890s, the Northern Pacific had shifted its base of operations from the Bozeman area to the much richer coal veins near Red Lodge. The Northwestern Improvement Company, a Northern Pacific subsidiary, led in the development of these mines; and by the early twentieth century, the Red Lodge district dominated Montana coal production. Boasting nearly five thousand inhabitants by 1910, Red Lodge was one of the most fascinating cities in the state, with a polyglot population of Welshmen, Slavs, Scandinavians, Germans, and Irish. The high-employment underground mines of the Red Lodge–Bearcreek area continued to produce for many years, but high labor costs and strikes after World War I persuaded the Northwestern Improvement Company to shift from underground to open-pit mining. By that time, surface mining of lower grade coal could be done with large shovels, and with only a fraction of the work force needed for underground mining. In 1924, the Northern Pacific–Northwestern Improvement Company, through a contract with the Minnesota-based Foley Brothers, began strip mining coal at Colstrip, south of Forsyth. By the mid-1930s, 40 percent of the coal produced in Montana came from the Colstrip pits.

In Montana, as in the rest of the nation, the coal industry fell on hard times during the 1920s and 1930s. The demand for coal declined sharply as the railroads converted to diesel and as more and more homes and businesses turned to fuel oil, natural gas, or electricity for heat and power. Production at all of Montana's underground mines—in Red Lodge, Roundup, and Cascade County—dropped lower and lower. World War II momentarily rekindled the demand for coal, and some of the state's underground mines came back to life. Montana's worst coal-mining disaster occurred at this time, in 1943, when seventy miners lost their lives at the Smith Mine near Red Lodge. After the war, the coal industry stagnated once again, and by the 1960s Montana was producing under five hundred thousand tons a year. In 1968, fewer than one hundred employees worked at coal mining in the state.

As Montana's coal industry faded into insignificance, knowledgeable people predicted that it would emerge again. Montana holds 13 percent of the nation's coal reserves, and it was only a matter of time until the more desirable fossil fuels became more scarce and expensive. When that happened, the easily stripped coal seams of southeastern Montana would once again attract developers. The visible recovery of Montana's coal industry began in 1968. Through its subsidiary Western Energy Company, Montana Power had earlier secured a long-term lease arrangement at Colstrip from the Northern Pacific. In 1968, Montana Power began stripping coal there and carrying it to a new steam-generating plant at Billings. At the same time, the Peabody Coal Company started shipping coal from the Colstrip area on large "unit trains" to Minnesota for use by electric utilities.

In October 1971, Montanans suddenly realized the full impact that a corporate coal boom might have on them when the Bureau of Reclamation, in cooperation with a number of energy and mineral companies, released the North Central Power Study. The study, anticipating the energy crisis that would soon follow, projected the construction of forty-two coal-powered generating plants, each of them to produce a whopping 10,000 megawatts annually. Twenty-one of the proposed plants were designated for eastern Montana, with the others to be located in the Dakotas and Wyoming. It was estimated that 2.6 million acre-feet of water from the Yellowstone River system might be needed each year to cool the gargantuan coal plants. Although the study never became working policy, it did call Montanans' attention to the rush for coal leases that was already underway, and it fueled the environmentalist crusade that had been mounting for several years. Fearful of a scarred landscape, damaged river systems, air pollution, and social dislocations that such massive development might bring, many Montanans reacted with alarm. The legislature passed tough environmental protection laws in 1971, culminating in a sweeping and controversial 30 percent coal severance tax in 1975, and environmentalist groups like the Northern Plains Resource Council launched vigorous anti-strip-mining campaigns (see Chapter 15).

While the controversy mounted, so did the mining of coal. Tonnage mined increased from seven million in 1971, to twenty-two million in 1975, to thirty million in 1980. In partnership with Pacific Northwest utilities, Montana Power stepped up its Colstrip mining and built two 350-megawatt generating plants there, with two more to follow, shipping electricity to the Northwest via huge transmission lines. Westmoreland Resources, a creature of several energy-related corporations, began operations at Sarpy Creek. Peabody Coal, a subsidiary of Kennecott Copper, opened its Big Sky Mine near Colstrip in 1969. In 1972, the Decker Coal Company started mass coal shipments to Chicago and later to Detroit utilities. Montana coal, 60 percent of it from federally owned land, was marketed west to the Columbia Basin, east to the upper Midwest, and South to Texas by way of a long Burlington Northern tendril.

The prospect of a massive energy boom, pleasing to developers and horrifying to environmentalists who feared the ruination of air, land, and water systems, soon began to ebb. During the 1980s, the same energy glut that sapped oil profits also affected coal. Wyoming, whose severance tax on coal was only half of Montana's, provided tough competition. And Midwest consumers, who valued the low-sulfur, low-polluting coal, began to shift toward short-term, more flexible and competitive contracts. Thus, futuristic strategies, such as slurry pipelines and turning the Powder River Basin into a "National Sacrifice Area," stayed on the shelf. Treasure State coal output leveled off in the 1980s at between thirty and forty million tons a year. Unless a technological breakthrough in coal utilization changes conditions, it seems unlikely that coal will ever revolutionize Montana and its economy, but the resource remains a huge blue chip for the state, whose intelligent exploitation and marketing could bring in badly needed revenues.

THE BROADER VIEW

Beyond lumber, oil, and coal, few other growth industries have arisen in Montana during modern times. One promising industry, however, is tourism, which showed dynamic growth during the 1980s. Tourism dates from Montana's earliest days, but we can chart the formal beginnings of tourism as a business from the later nineteenth century. The creation of Yellowstone National Park in 1872 and Glacier National Park in 1910 drew a continual flow of sightseers, visitors, and sportsmen to the state. So did the later preservation of national forests and pristine environments like the Bob Marshall Wilderness.

The railroads played a key role in developing Montana's early tourist industry. The Northern Pacific heavily promoted Yellowstone Park, basing its entry point at the city of Livingston. The Milwaukee Road developed a Yellowstone tourist route through the West Gallatin Canyon, and the Great Northern had a large interest in transportation and accommodations in Glacier National Park. During the later years of the nineteenth century, several elaborate resorts and spas appeared in the state, some of them advertising the benefits of hot springs and mineral waters. The most elaborate of these was the Broadwater Hotel and Natatorium, which transportation magnate C. A. Broadwater built west of Helena in 1889. Dude ranchers and outfitters developed another type of tourism during the early years of the twentieth century. By 1930, over a hundred dude ranches welcomed outdoor enthusiasts to Montana, most of them in the mountains and valleys north of Yellowstone Park. Rail-based tourism brought valuable dollars into the state, with tourists spending five hundred thousand dollars a year in Montana from 1900 through 1910.

Beginning in 1910, automobiles worked a revolution in American tour-

Among the identifying structures in Montana's wheat-growing region are grain elevators at trackside, where area farmers store and ship their produce to market. This photograph was taken near Dutton.

ism. As roads improved and as middle-class families acquired dependable cars, roadside "motels," camping spots, and restaurants began to challenge the old downtown hotels and railroad resorts. In 1915, Yellowstone Park authorities bowed to the inevitable and allowed cars to enter that wonderland through West Yellowstone. The Depression and the war years depressed the industry, but postwar prosperity brought an enormous boost to western tourism. By automobiles, airplanes, trains, and campers, affluent tourists came in ever increasing numbers. Most came for outdoor recreation—hunting and fishing, hiking and sightseeing, skiing and snowmobiling. Along the state's major highways, cities and towns sprouted new motels, restaurants, and gas stations to serve the tourists.

By the mid-1960s, out-of-state tourists were spending around $72 million a year in Montana. Tourism had become a mainstay of the state's economy, but Montana still had no large, multipurpose resorts that drew tourists to states like Colorado. In 1970, the Chrysler Realty Corporation, in partnership with newsman Chet Huntley and other investors, announced that it would construct a multi-million-dollar resort complex on the West Fork of the Gallatin River. Big Sky of Montana has continued to expand, although never to the extent initially projected, and so have other skiing and resort facilities at Whitefish, Red Lodge, and elsewhere in the state. But the industry in Montana remains lightly capitalized, unconcentrated, and heavily reliant on the simple amenities of an untrammeled environment.

Despite its obvious advantages, Montana has made little effort to build its tourist industry, or to tax it, although in 1987 it did initiate a "bed tax" whose revenues would be spent on promotion. But nonresident travel continued to grow anyhow. By 1989 travelers from out of state were spending about $650 million in Montana each year. Tourism's share of the economic base doubled from the early 1970s to the late 1980s, amounting to nearly 9 percent of the total in 1990. The industry employs over twelve thousand Montanans directly, another ten thousand indirectly. In terms of receipts generated—a billion dollars in 1988—the industry ranks second only to agriculture in the state. Some conservative Montanans dislike the tourist intrusions, and critics note that the industry pays only low-end, "service" wages and that the state's remote location makes it vulnerable to rising gasoline prices. But tourism is one facet of the state's economy that offers great growth potential and also potential new tax incomes, if Montana ever decides to enact the sales tax.

The closely related transportation industry is also vitally important to a state as large and as lightly populated as Montana is. In terms of Gross State Product—that is, the sum of all economic activity—the transportation–public utilities sector commanded a full 12.2 percent of the state total in 1986, far more than either agriculture or mining. But even though transportation generates considerable income and jobs for the state, it also presents severe problems. As elsewhere, railroads have made sharp cutbacks in Montana, particularly in rural spur lines, in passenger service, and in employment. Since its merger of the old Northern Pacific, Great Northern, and Burlington lines in 1969-70, the Burlington Northern Railroad has held a heavy preponderance in the Treasure State, especially after the closure of the tottering Milwaukee Road in the early 1980s. The Union Pacific still serves southwestern Montana, and the Soo Line the far northeast, offering some competition for agricultural marketing. And Dennis Washington's Montana Rail-Link prospers on the Laurel-Sandpoint (Idaho) line through southern Montana, which Burlington Northern divested in the mid-1980s. But high rail rates present a continuing problem for the Treasure State.

While rail transportation remains vital to Montana, air and highway traffic have steadily gained importance. Several major airlines serve the state—Continental, Delta, and Northwest Orient—and smaller lines like Big Sky attempt to work the in-state, rural sector. But federal deregulation has disadvantaged underpopulated states like Montana; and if rural carriers do not receive federal subsidies, the state's small cities and their hinterlands will lose much of the limited economic competitiveness they now have. Meanwhile, highways continue overwhelmingly to serve Montana's transportation needs. Interstate Highway 15, running north-south, and Interstates 90-94, on an east-west axis, have been completed. Those highways continue to be improved, as well as the two-lane systems, many of which badly need maintenance and repair.

Montana's transportation sector relies heavily on yet another major source of employment and income, government. The federal government pays 95 percent of the cost of constructing interstate highways in sparsely populated states like Montana and much of the cost of other national roadways as well. In terms of Gross State Product, state and local government claims nearly 9 percent of the Montana total for activities as diverse as elementary and secondary education, police, and firefighting—a greater share than that of either agriculture or mining. The federal government claims just under 4 percent, or about half that of agriculture.

Like all western states, Montana relies heavily on the federal government. Uncle Sam owns 29.6 percent of the Montana land mass, the least of any state in the Far West (that is, the Montana-New Mexico tier westward, but not including Alaska or Hawaii) because it was so heavily homesteaded. These huge federal acreages force Montana to deal intensively with custodial agencies like the Bureau of Land Management, the U.S. Forest Service, and the National Park Service. Such interactions breed

The growth of small and medium-sized cities after the construction of paved highways in Montana is reflected in this aerial view of Glasgow, taken in November 1960.

both frustration with bureaucracy and in-lieu-of-tax federal reimbursement benefits. Although Montana is not a major reclamation state like Arizona, Idaho, or California, the Bureau of Reclamation still plays a major role with giant dams like Canyon Ferry and Yellowtail. And although Montana is not the beneficiary of the enormous defense outlays enjoyed by California, Texas, Washington, or Utah, it does garner important economic benefits from Malmstrom Air Force Base at Great Falls and from the ICBM missile complexes of north-central Montana. Federal farm subsidies constitute a major share of Montana agricultural income, and the state is becoming more and more dependent on federal "transfer payments," such as Social Security and Medicare. Since 1950, the federal government has filled the void left by the decline of the old corporate domination.

Setting the lens more broadly, it becomes clear that Montana continues to lag far behind the nation in economic development. For obvious reasons—distance from markets, high transportation costs, and the absence of large urban areas—it has never attracted much in the way of manufacturing, or "value-added" industry, and it probably never will. Manufacturing makes up only 7.24 percent of Montana's GSP. But the state has followed the national trend of growth in the personal services sector. Wholesale trade constitutes 5.45 percent of Montana's GSP; retail trade 8.6 percent; combined finance, insurance, and real estate 16.51 percent; and other services 13.1 percent.

Montana's problem lies not in its failure to attract manufacturers, many of which are languishing throughout the nation, but in two interrelated facts. One is the heavy loss of high-paying, union jobs in traditional extractive industries, whose victims either leave the state or retreat to lower-paying service work or self-employment. The other is the failure to attract the modern high-technology, high-level service industries that have formed the major growth components of those states that prospered during the 1970s and 1980s. The Treasure State has attracted some small "high-tech" firms, such as Ribi Immunochem at Hamilton and Skyland Scientific Services and ILX Lightwave at Bozeman. But Montana has not attracted very many of those companies, and it has attracted no larger operations. The state has, in fact, made little effort to do so. Unlike many other states, such as Ohio or New Jersey, that have invested heavily to rebuild deteriorating economies, Montana has not attempted in any meaningful way to enter the tough and expensive race among states to attract the desirable new industries. And by allowing its system of higher education to deteriorate, Montana has to a large extent taken itself out of the race entirely.

As a result of all this, Montana entered the closing decade of the twentieth century farther out of the national mainstream than it had been at midcentury. In 1950, the state's per capita income had stood at a healthy 8 percent *above* the national average. By 1970, its per capita income had fallen to 12 percent below the national average and by 1988 to *22 percent below* the national average. This has meant a deteriorating standard of living for Montanans and a severe threat to their future. Although Montanans indisputably enjoyed a higher standard of living in 1990 than they did in 1920, they have also indisputably failed to share in the new era of national economic evolution. If the state continues to follow its old-fashioned "low-tax, low-service" approach to its political economy, thereby failing to invest in order to build and compete in a global economy, the deterioration will continue to deepen.

CHAPTER 14

A Social and Cultural Profile

Montana is a more complex and cosmopolitan place than most people assume. Outside observers often depict the state as an extension of the upper Midwest, mainly rural and Protestant in background and population. But in addition to midwestern farmers, a fascinating diversity of peoples have immigrated to Montana, and they continue to move there. Descendants of Montana's ethnic populations continue their traditions in many parts of the state alongside other ethnic groups that have chosen to live in Big Sky country since World War II. And we must remember that urban centers, in the peculiar form of mining camps, were established in Montana long before most of the wide-open areas began to attract a rural population. Despite the problems that have faced the small population of such a large and challenging area, Montanans have always displayed a genuine commitment to education and cultural achievement. The state developed a comprehensive educational system and a far-flung network of public universities and colleges. It also evolved a vigorous journalistic tradition that, after being blighted for years by the Anaconda Company's ownership of most of the major daily newspapers, has begun to resurface. Most impressive of all, Montanans have made surprisingly large contributions to American art and literature.

THE PEOPLE

The census of 1870, Montana's first, revealed that the new territory contained fewer than twenty-one thousand people. By 1990, roughly eight hundred thousand people lived in the state. This 120-year increase occurred unevenly, following the rises and declines of economic opportunity in Montana. The boom decade of the 1880s produced a whopping 265

347

percent population increase, and the homestead invasion of 1909-18 brought tens of thousands of people to northern and eastern Montana. Then the depressed 1920s witnessed a population decline of 2.1 percent. Thereafter, in a pattern that generally reflected economic trends, Montana's population underwent spurts of growth and sluggishness. During the prosperous 1950s, the population increased by 14.2 percent, but the economy flattened out during the 1960s, as more and more young people left the state in search of better opportunities. During the 1970s, prosperity returned, and the population jumped by more than 13 percent. But preliminary figures from the 1990 census indicate little growth during the depressed 1980s—so little, in fact, that it did not even keep up with the natural growth of reproduction.

Montana's slow growth rate has caused it to slip steadily downward on the ladder of state ranking. In 1920, it stood thirty-ninth among the states in population; by 1970 it had fallen to forty-third and by 1980 to forty-fourth. With its large land area—Montana is the fourth largest state—and its few people, Montana's population density is unbelievably low. The 1970 census found that there were 57.5 persons for each square mile in the nation at large. Montana had only 4.8 people per square mile in 1970 and 5.4 in 1980. Such figures are somewhat misleading, because the Treasure State has joined in the nationwide trend toward urbanization. The 1960 census recorded for the first time that more Montanans lived in cities than in rural areas. By 1980, about 53 percent of Montanans lived in urban areas, compared to 74 percent nationally. Ever since the collapse of homesteading in 1920, the state's rural areas have sadly watched their populations melt away. Between 1960 and 1970, forty of the state's fifty-six counties lost population. During the 1980s, many eastern Montana counties continued to lose population, while Gallatin, Ravalli, and Lake counties in the west attracted sizable new populations. Well over half of Montana's residents now live in seven counties: Yellowstone, Cascade, Missoula, Silver Bow, Flathead, Lewis and Clark, and Gallatin. A line drawn from Havre south through Lewistown to Billings divides the state into a western portion that continues to grow and an eastern section that continues to lose population. Many Montanans who still live in the eastern counties experience a degree of isolation that most other Americans can hardly imagine. For example, Garfield County High School in Jordan is one of the few places in the United States that still operate a public boarding school.

From the beginning, Montana attracted a wide variety of peoples. The fur trade attracted adventurers from France and Scotland, and the placer gold camps housed people from many different countries, especially Ireland, England, Germany, and Scandinavia. There was a small population

In mining communities, one of the most popular sports events was prize fighting. On May 18, 1884, in Butte, Duncan McDonald fought Peter McCoy for two hours and thirteen minutes for the middleweight championship of the world.

of African Americans, and many Chinese followed the gold frontier. The Chinese worked as miners; established businesses, such as laundries and catering; and generally supplied services to the whites in the mining towns. The gold camps also attracted Jewish merchants, some of whom were drummers and itinerant peddlers but others who established permanent businesses, especially in Helena and Butte. In Helena, Jewish merchants dominated dry goods and clothing enterprises during the 1860s and early 1870s.

The rise of industrial mining and the railroad industry added greatly to the population mix. More and more African Americans moved to Montana, some to work on the railroads and others to work as porters, servants, and laborers. Most of them followed family members who had migrated from the border states after the Civil War. By the 1890s, sizable African American populations had been established in Helena and Butte, where they established churches and other community organizations. The railroads hired Italian and Japanese laborers as maintenance workers. Marcus Daly imported thousands of Irish to Butte, and many "Cousin Jacks" from Cornwall, experienced and capable hardrock miners— immigrated too. The Irish and the Cousin Jacks dominated Butte society. They had their religious differences and sometimes had terrible fights, but they usually got along and even helped each other celebrate their respective holidays, St. Patrick's Day and St. George's Day. In its prime, Butte was one of America's most colorful polyglot cities, where more than thirty languages could be heard in its streets and homes.

By 1910, slightly over one-fourth of Montana's population was foreign born. Although government figures show that Canada, Ireland, Germany, and Scotland still supplied the largest numbers of immigrants, such gross census data clearly distort true national origins. "Canada," for example, included Canadian nationals and all who had lived there for even a brief time before coming to the United States, and until World War I "Austria" referred to several national and ethnic groups who lived within the Austro-Hungarian Empire.

By the early twentieth century, more and more newcomers were arriving in Montana from central and southern Europe. The railroads and the Butte mines employed Greeks, Bulgarians, Rumanians, Serbs, Croatians, Poles, Czechs, and large numbers of Finns and Italians. For years the state's largest Italian community was the Butte suburb of Meaderville, one of the liveliest gambling centers in the West. Most of the Butte Italians worked as hardrock miners; but some, like Dominic Bertoglio and Vincent Truzzolino, went successfully into the restaurant business.

The in-pouring of immigrant peoples to Montana changed the complexions of communities other than just Butte. Large numbers of Irish,

Ethnic communities maintained close relationships through religious affiliations, clubs and organizations, and social events, such as this formal dinner party at the Leopold Marks residence in Helena in 1890.

Welsh, Slavic peoples, Italians, and Finns immigrated to Red Lodge, Roundup, and other coal towns. South Slav stonemasons settled in Lewistown and helped build its businesses and public buildings. Slavs also worked in smelters in Anaconda and Great Falls. Norwegians, Swedes, Danes, and Finns gravitated heavily toward lumbering communities, such as Bonner-Milltown and Libby. After 1910, the homestead invasion drew thousands of Scandinavian and German farmers across the northern High Line and into east-central Montana. Those farm families left their imprint on the state in towns named Lothair and Opheim, in the liberal politics of the Farmers' Union, and in the prevalence of the Lutheran religion.

Some of the immigrants arrived in community groups. Dutch settlers moved to the Gallatin Valley during the 1890s as agricultural laborers. The tight-knit communities they established at the end of the nineteenth century relied on the strength of their Dutch Reformed faith, which continues to guide them in many of the traditional ways of life. Enough French-speaking people lived at Frenchtown near Missoula to require bilingual clerks in Missoula stores. Belgians settled near Valier, German-Russians moved into the Yellowstone Valley, and Danes established a religious colony near Dagmar. Strong religious bonds held the communities together. The state lost one such group during World War I when the Montana Council of Defense foolishly banned the use of the German language, driving hundreds of German Mennonite families into Canada.

During the final decades of the nineteenth century, the Anabaptist and German-speaking Hutterites migrated from Europe and established colonies in the American West, including Montana. Since the Reformation, the Hutterites have searched for sanctuaries where they could practice their religion and live in a communal style. Their numbers in Montana increased during the mid-twentieth century when discriminatory legislation in Canada forced many to migrate. The Hutterites are superb agriculturalists, and they have prospered in Montana. There are now more than forty Hutterite communities in the state, most of them east of the Divide near small agricultural cities.

Large-scale immigration to Montana ended in about 1920, but the state has continued to attract foreign immigrants. Hispanic people from Mexico and Latin America came in increasing numbers beginning in the 1920s, many to work in the beet fields in eastern Montana. Among the state's cities, Billings has the largest Hispanic population. During the early 1970s, Vietnamese, Hmong, and other Southeast Asian immigrants settled in Montana, particularly in the Missoula area. Because of these recent migrations and the endurance of older ethnic communities, Montana's ethnic cultures have continued to flourish, supported by traditions that

Black women in Montana organized statewide during the first half of the twentieth century. This photograph shows the first convention of the Montana Federation of Negro Women's Clubs in Butte.

continue to be important facets of cultural life. Cornish meat pies called "pasties" are still a Butte delicacy, and St. Patrick's Day is still a raucous occasion at Butte, Helena, and Great Falls. Until recently, Slavic groups in Montana continued to celebrate a pre-Lenten festival called "Mesopust," which included the trial of "Slarko Veljacic," an effigy that symbolized the previous year's misfortunes. Slarko was always found guilty and was stabbed and burned at the stake. The state's famous Welsh, Cornish, and German singing groups have persisted into modern times, and so have such fraternal groups as the Ancient Order of Hibernians, the Sons of Hermann, Sons of Norway, and the Narodjini Dom and Trobjnica lodges. And Scandinavian families still loyally savor their lutefisk and lefse.

National origins had a lot to do with religious preferences. The Roman Catholics, the Methodists, and the Episcopalians were especially active on the Montana gold frontier. Catholic priests, who were already at work as missionaries among the Indians, began saying mass at Virginia City in 1863. In that same year, Father Urban Grassi built the first church for whites at Hell Gate. Methodist missionaries first arrived in the gold camps during 1864, but really effective organization came in the 1870s with the work of F. A. Riggin and W. W. Van Orsdel. For many years the Reverend Van Orsdel, affectionately known as "Brother Van," was the best known Protestant missionary on the Montana frontier. Bishop Daniel S. Tuttle launched the Episcopal church in Montana when he came to Virginia City in 1867. By 1880, when Leigh R. Brewer was consecrated as Bishop of Montana, the Episcopalians had built up an impressive organization throughout the territory.

Other denominations were slower in getting started. Following preliminary work by Reverend Sheldon Jackson, the Presbyterians became an influence in Montana in 1872, when a small group of Princeton men founded seven churches in sixteen days and canvassed the entire territory. Baptist, Lutheran, and Congregationalist groups began to appear during the 1880s. The Lutherans, bolstered by German and Scandinavian immigration, came mostly during the post-1900 homestead rush and settled in large numbers in northern and far eastern Montana. The Congregationalists, fewer in number and heavily German, concentrated in the Yellowstone Valley, and many of them fled the state in the post-1918 depression.

Roman Catholicism has always been Montana's dominant religion. In 1906, a major census of religions by the federal government found that about 74 percent of all regular communicants in the state were Catholics, exactly twice the national percentage. The heavy concentration of Irish in western Montana largely explains the high number. In the same year, the largest Protestant groups were the Methodist, Presbyterian, Episcopal, and Lutheran churches. During the decade following 1906, homesteading swelled the ranks of Lutherans, until by 1916 Lutheranism ranked as Montana's second largest religion, a position it has maintained. By the early 1970s, homogenizing population trends had worked some changes. The Catholics remained in first place, but with fewer than 50 percent of churchgoers, even though Hispanic migration had added significantly to the total number of communicants. The Methodists continued to rank third, but the Episcopal church had slipped dramatically from fourth to eighth place. Replacing it as number four among Montana denominations was the fast rising Mormon church, which was especially strong in the southwestern part of the state. Various Baptist groups have grown markedly over recent years, as have a number of small, fundamentalist sects.

In contrast to Montana's slowly growing white population, its Indian population has increased dramatically. Only 11,343 Indians lived in Montana at the turn of the twentieth century. By 1990, there were approximately forty thousand Indians in Montana, a nearly four-fold increase in ninety years that is due in large part to improved health care and living conditions. Most of the Indians live on or near one of Montana's seven reservations. Although the reservations vary greatly in size, wealth, land-ownership patterns, and population, they share one enormous fact of life—an overwhelming dependence on the federal government.

The all-important Dawes Act of 1887 had attempted to guarantee the assimilation of the Indians into white society by allotting reservation lands to individual Indians. Allotment, the reformers wrongly assumed, would make the reservation Indians into happy, self-sufficient farmers. The extent to which the allotment process was used varied from reservation to reservation. The tiny Rocky Boy's Reservation, created in 1916, long after the others, was never allotted, and the land remains completely in tribal hands. On the other six reserves, allotment produced complex patterns of landownership. At the Blackfeet, Crow, and Fort Belknap reservations, more than half the land belongs to individual Indians. Roughly 45 percent of the large Flathead (Salish-Kutenai) Reservation consists of tribal lands, but individual Indians own little of the remaining 55 percent. Most of it belongs to whites, who bought up the allotted lands years ago. The extent of actual tribal ownership varies widely, from 100 percent at Rocky Boy's to about 60 percent on the Northern Cheyenne, to 25 percent or less on the Blackfeet, Crow, Fort Belknap, and Fort Peck reservations. Except for Rocky Boy's, the Montana reservations are checkerboards of lands owned by the tribes, individual Indians, whites, and the state and federal governments.

In 1924, Congress passed the Snyder Act, which conferred citizenship on all Indians. Although Indians are no longer wards of the federal government, they are still dependent on Uncle Sam in some special ways. The federal government acts as trustee for Indian lands and other resources and for some of their funds. Because trust lands and some other kinds of Indian property are exempt from state taxation, the federal government supplies some services on the reservations that would otherwise be supplied by the state. It is clear that citizenship did nothing directly to improve the Indians' lot. During the 1920s, while Indian Bureau agents were still trying to turn them into farmers and herdsmen, Native Americans suffered dreadfully from poverty, malnutrition, and such diseases as tuberculosis and trachoma. Slowly, the federal government began to realize that the philosophy behind the Dawes Act could never work.

Ironically, the Great Depression of the 1930s led to improvements on the reservations. New Deal agencies provided relief, employment at comparatively high wages, improved health care, and new roads and public buildings. More important, the New Deal also brought to fruition a basic reorientation of government policy with the passage in 1934 of the Indian Reorganization (Wheeler-Howard) Act, which was guided through the Senate by Montana Senator B. K. Wheeler. The Wheeler-Howard Act ended the allotment of lands to individual Indians and encouraged them to preserve their native cultures and develop tribal self-government. It authorized each tribe to organize as a federal corporation, to adopt a constitution, and to create a tribal council. Except for the Crows and the Fort Peck tribes, all of the Montana Indians quickly incorporated under the Wheeler-Howard Act, formed constitutions, and turned the management of their affairs over to elected tribal councils. The Fort Peck residents continued under an earlier constitution, and the Crows deliberate all important matters in a general council, composed of all adult members of the tribe, and delegate administration and lesser subjects to special executive committees.

World War II changed the lives of many Indians, as some men and women served in the armed forces and others took jobs in war plants. Those who returned to Montana after the war showed a new interest in self-government and demanded better education, an improved standard of living, and a tighter administration of reservation affairs. In 1946, Congress established the Indian Claims Commission to investigate charges that the federal government had taken Indian lands either in violation of treaty rights or with inadequate compensation. During the 1960s and early 1970s, the Crows, Northern Cheyennes, and Salish-Kutenais won major settlements through the commission.

Generally speaking, though, Washington, D.C., showed little sympathy for Native Americans during the postwar period. Tiring once again of the "Indian Problem," Congress drifted back toward the thinking that led to the Dawes Act—quick assimilation into white society. Two important measures in 1953 reflected this attitude. The states were allowed to assume civil and criminal jurisdiction over the reservations and, more significantly, Congress approved the controversial policy of "termination," which totally cut off federal supervision of the tribes. In line with this philosophy, the Bureau of Indian Affairs launched a "relocation" program during the 1950s, aimed at removing Indians from the reservations and placing them in areas of greater employment opportunity. Luckily for Montana's tribes, these disastrous programs affected them less than many Indians elsewhere.

Since the early 1960s, the termination policy has been abandoned in all but name. Replacing it, especially through the Great Society programs of the Johnson administration, have been renewed efforts to improve life on the reservations. Conditions on the state's seven reservations are varied. Generally, population growth has surpassed the capacities of the reservations to support their people. Predictably, the result is high unemployment, heavy welfare loads, and other social problems. In most cases, even those Indians who are employed in farming and ranching need supplemental wages. The problem is that the reservations are located in isolated rural areas where there are few employment opportunities, especially for those with limited job skills.

The Salish-Kutenai Reservation is Montana's most prosperous, mainly because of its favored location in the northwestern part of the state. Only about half of the enrolled Salish-Kutenai people live on the reserve. Much of the land was allotted and passed into white hands, but most of the land remaining under Indian control is tribal land that produces valuable stands of timber. The tribe profits from timber and Christmas tree sales, from valuable grazing leases, from annual payments by Montana Power for rental rights on Kerr Dam, and from employment opportunities in the lumber industry. Recreational possibilities are endless in the Flathead Valley, and the tribes own a resort at Blue Bay on Flathead Lake.

The story on the other reserves is generally one of poverty and substandard living conditions. Traditionally, agriculture has offered the largest nonfederal source of income. Roughly half of the Blackfeet families, for instance, receive some income from agriculture. The Blackfeet also rely on logging, oil and gas leases, and the sale of Indian crafts at Browning and St. Mary. The Crows lease most of their farming and ranching lands, and the economic situations of the Crows and the Northern Cheyennes is drastically affected by changes in the coal-mining industry. At Rocky Boy's, Fort Belknap, and Fort Peck, the outlook seems the least promising, as the agricultural land there cannot begin to support the population. During the 1980s, the tribes have increasingly tried to improve conditions by attracting industry. The Crow, Blackfoot, and Fort Peck Indians have all established industrial parks and other initiatives, but so far with only limited success.

THE SCHOOLS

Montana has long boasted a literacy rate that is far above the national average, even with the large foreign-born element in its historical population base. In 1900, only 6.6 percent of Montana's population was illiterate, compared to 11.3 percent of the nation. By 1960, the state's illiteracy rate had fallen to a minuscule one percent, still less than half the national percentage of 2.4. This good showing is due in large part to the absence of either urban or rural poverty on a massive scale. It is also due to Montana's long-term commitment to public education.

Public schools were started in Montana soon after the territory was created in 1864. Like most frontier people, Montanans looked on common schools as vital agencies of civilization. In his 1865 address to the first territorial legislature, Governor Sidney Edgerton asked the lawmakers to establish a public school system in words that typified American ideals. In "a free government like ours," Edgerton argued,

> where public measures are submitted to the judgment of the people, it is of the highest importance that the people should be so educated as to understand the hearing of public measures. A self-ruling people must be an educated people, or prejudice and passion will assume power, and anarchy will soon usurp the authority of government.

The legislature responded to Edgerton's appeal with a law authorizing county commissioners to establish local school boards and school districts and to impose a one mill property tax to support public education. Montana's first public school opened at Virginia City in March 1866, and a second began holding classes at Bozeman during the following winter. But it was hard to keep schools going in the unstable mining camps, and early progress was disappointingly slow. By 1870, Montana reported only fifteen schools, employing twenty-seven teachers to handle approximately seven hundred students.

Using the California code as a model, the 1872 legislature passed a new school law that became the basis of Montana's modern educational system. The 1872 law provided increased financial support, clarified the powers of county superintendents and the duties of teachers, and placed sweeping powers in the hands of a territorial superintendent of public in-

Radio communication and entertainment revolutionized leisure time activities in Montana during the 1920s. The "Night Owl" show, hosted by Ed Craney and Emmett Burke, was popular in Butte during the 1930s.

Cultural activities have always maintained an important place in Montana, from art classes, such as this one at Helena High School during the 1890s, to music, dance, and artistic exhibitions.

struction. It also required that "education of children of African descent shall be provided for in separate schools." Wisely, Governor Potts appointed Cornelius Hedges to be superintendent of public instruction. With bachelor's and master's degrees from Yale and a law degree from Harvard, Hedges held impressive credentials for the job, and his capable performance in office earned him the title "Father of Education in Montana." During Hedges's three consecutive terms, which began in 1872 (he served a fourth in 1883-85), the number of schools increased dramatically, the school term expanded from three to five months, and mandatory teachers' institutes improved the quality of instruction. The first high schools in the territory also appeared during Hedges's tenure, at Helena in 1876, Deer Lodge and Bozeman in 1878, and Butte in 1879. By 1880, Montana had a firmly established public school system.

As the years went by, the legislature further revamped the school laws. In 1881, it set up a textbook commission to select uniform texts for all the schools. The state continued to use such a commission, in one form or another, until 1943. In 1883, the lawmakers enacted Montana's first compulsory school attendance law and, in the same measure, repealed that section of the 1872 law that required separate schools for African Americans. Statehood brought additional changes. The new state received its due when, in passing the Enabling Act of 1889, Congress set aside sections 16 and 36 in each Montana township as public school lands for the purpose of supporting education. Montana's 1889 constitution made the office of superintendent of public instruction elective and placed control of education in the hands of a State Board of Education, composed of the governor, the superintendent of public instruction, the attorney general, and eight citizen members appointed by the governor.

The problems confronting the state board changed little over the years—how to secure adequate funding, how to upgrade teacher certification requirements, how best to determine teaching and disciplinary methods. Curriculum content posed a major concern. The 1872 law provided for the usual fundamentals: reading, writing, spelling, arithmetic, geography, English, American history, bookkeeping, health, physical training, and morals. Most of the changes made in the basic curriculum over the years have turned it in a more "practical" direction. In 1911, the legislature authorized training in industrial and vocational skills; and in 1917, Congress passed the Smith-Hughes Act to provide federal aid for such programs. These programs, which aim less at real education than at job training, have been joined by a variety of others that emphasize patriotism, consumerism, or coping with such social problems as race prejudice, drugs, and alcohol.

By doubling the number of Montana schoolchildren, the great homestead boom of 1909-18 placed enormous strains on the state's educational system. Numerous little school districts were established to bring scattered farm children within reasonable traveling distance of a schoolhouse. But when the bottom fell out of farming industry, hundreds of these rural districts lost their tax bases. As roads improved and reliable buses became available, rural residents came to realize that consolidating school districts was the only answer to their problems. In 1929, there were still twenty-five hundred one- and two-room schools in Montana. By 1950, only 1,321 of them remained. By 1970, the state had cut back to 574 elementary districts and 166 high school districts; and by the 1989-1990 school year, the state had only 374 elementary districts. The trend continues, as more and more rural schools face the certain prospect of closure.

Closely related to the number of school districts is the problem of school finance. Prior to 1927, school districts depended mainly on the property taxes they could raise on their own. This simple arrangement caused great variations among school districts, both in tax burden and in quality of education. Attempting to improve schooling in the small, poorer districts, the 1927 legislature created a Common School Equalization Fund, supplied with revenues from taxes on inheritance, oil, and metals and distributed by the State Board of Education. In 1949, the legislature revised the system by enacting the landmark School Foundation Program Law, which is the basis of all modern Montana policy. The 1949 law sought to guarantee every Montana youngster a sound education by channeling state funds into those districts where local and county tax dollars were not adequate to meet minimal needs and standards. By passing the law, Montana committed itself to underwriting the education of all its needy children. The equalization of public school funding continued to move, in Montana and elsewhere, in a more progressive and expensive direction. In response to a Montana Supreme Court ruling that the state's educational system was inequitable and unconstitutional, the 1989 legislature increased foundation funding by nearly sixty million dollars between fiscal years 1990 and 1991, a striking 20 percent increase.

In addition to the public schools, parochial schools have also educated Montana youth. Most of them are operated by the Roman Catholic Church, with the remainder supported by the Lutheran, Hutterite, Seventh Day Adventist, Mennonite, and Christian Reformed churches. In more recent years, inflation and the cost squeeze have forced many parochial grade schools and high schools to close their doors.

HIGHER EDUCATION

In Montana, as in most states, the first colleges were privately endowed. Citizens in Deer Lodge took the initiative in the territory by founding the Montana Collegiate Institute in 1878. After faltering for a few years with tiny enrollments, the institute passed into the control of the Presbyterian Church, which renamed it the College of Montana. Aided by W. A. Clark, the college brought in graduates from the Columbia University School of Mines and established courses in mining engineering and metallurgy. Some of its young faculty, such as renowned humanist and literary critic Irving Babbitt, went on to distinguished careers. But the College of Montana never really prospered. It lost enrollment through the 1890s, closed and reopened, and then shut down permanently in 1916.

The Methodists started an educational institution of their own in 1890, when they opened Montana University in the Prickly Pear Valley north of Helena. The name of the school became a problem when the state created a public university system, so the Methodist institution was renamed Montana Wesleyan University and later Montana Wesleyan College. In 1898, the institution was moved to Helena. Montana Wesleyan merged in 1923 with the College of Montana under the name Intermountain Union College. After the Helena earthquake of 1935 damaged its campus, Intermountain Union College merged with the Billings Polytechnic Institute which had been founded back in 1908. The new institution, took the name Rocky Mountain College, and it continues to operate in Billings.

Montana has two Roman Catholic colleges. In 1909, Bishop John P. Carroll opened Mount St. Charles College as a boys' school supported by the Diocese of Western Montana at Helena. The campus was renamed Carroll College in 1932 to honor its founder. In that same depression year, the Diocese of Eastern Montana opened the Great Falls Junior College as a girls' school. The institution received four-year accreditation in 1939 and changed its name to the College of Great Falls. Both these colleges eventually became co-educational, Great Falls in 1937 and Carroll in 1946, and both operate today, the College of Great Falls at a new campus opened in 1960.

Montana was delayed several years in creating a state-supported system of higher education because of the intense jockeying among cities over which would become the capital. After that contest had narrowed to a battle between Helena and Anaconda, the 1893 legislature tackled the education question. In the tradition of frontier logrolling politics, the lawmakers unfortunately decided to create a multi-unit system that would gratify several ambitious cities and keep hard feelings to a minimum. They located a university in Missoula, an agricultural college in Bozeman, a school of mines at Butte, and a normal college at Dillon. In opting for an expensive, multi-unit university system, the legislators turned down a lucrative and sensible offer from Paris Gibson, the founder of Great Falls. Gibson offered the state a grant of land and a sizable cash endowment if it would locate a single-unit state university in his city. Impressed less by

Gibson's logic than by other cities' competition to secure state institutions in their towns and the argument that a decentralized system would bring higher education within easy travel of any family, the legislature turned him down.

Following that irreversible decision, four separate campuses slowly took shape. Because few Montana students had access to a high school education until early in the twentieth century, the campuses initially devoted much of their energy and resources to "preparatory departments" that prepared the students for college-level course work. High schools were soon established to serve most areas of the state, however, and the university units, especially those at Missoula and Bozeman, began to develop new courses and degree programs. Predictably, the state campuses increasingly competed with one another, lobbying the legislature for funds and beating the brush for students. With good reason, a Montana educator would later describe the university system's first two decades as "years of guerrilla warfare."

Competition between the university units was wasteful and expensive, as critics like Gibson had foreseen, and it led to a strong movement for "consolidation" of the four units into one central campus. But consolidation meant closing down campuses, and it proved then, as it would later, to be politically impossible. As an alternate solution, the 1913 legislature attempted to coordinate the four units, cut down duplication, and lower expenses by welding them into a single university system composed of four integrated parts. The legislature increased the supervisory powers of the State Board of Education and authorized it to employ a chancellor to oversee the entire university system.

In the meantime, the homestead movement brought thousands of new families to northern and eastern Montana, areas far removed from the four campuses in the state's southwestern corner. Those who favored consolidation now faced even stronger opposition from the newly settled regions, which wanted new colleges built to serve them. In the end, the consolidationists lost and the expansionists won. The voters turned down a 1914 initiative providing for consolidation, and the lawmakers turned in the opposite direction by authorizing two new campuses: Northern Montana College at Havre and Eastern Montana Normal College (now Eastern Montana College) at Billings. The two new colleges would not open their doors until the late 1920s, after the bottom had already dropped out of homesteading. Hard-pressed Montana taxpayers now found themselves with six, rather than four, campuses to support.

The failure of consolidation meant mounting demands for state revenue, which came mainly from the general fund raised by the statewide property tax. Beginning with voter approval of two initiative measures in

1920, the state turned to special mill levies for help in carrying the higher education tax load. Again in 1930, the electorate renewed the one-and-a-half-mill levy of ten years before, and in 1940 voters increased it to three and one-half mills. In Montana, as elsewhere, the end of World War II placed enormous strains on the university system as thousands of veterans knocked on college doors with federal funding under the GI Bill. The 1947 legislature responded by referring two referenda to the people, one raising the university levy to six mills and the other providing for a five-million-dollar building bond issue. Both were approved in the 1948 election. This all-important levy was renewed in 1958 and then perennially at ten-year intervals thereafter.

Adopting the chancellorship system in 1913 did little to satisfy critics of the far-flung university system. In fact, the first two chancellors, Edward C. Elliott and M. A. Brannon, were surrounded by political controversy. Legislators, hard hit by pleas for tax relief during the Great Depression, aimed their knives at the chancellor and the university system. During the 1933 session, the lawmakers turned back bills to close the Havre and Billings campuses and chose instead to make wholesale cuts throughout the system. They forced Chancellor Brannon to resign by refusing to appropriate any funds to pay him. The system-wide budget cuts of 1933 dealt a near lethal blow to the Montana system of higher education. Reporting to the State Board of Education in 1935, President Alfred Atkinson of Montana State College at Bozeman commented plaintively "that we have lost 25 faculty members since 1933 because they went to more remunerative positions. The aggregate of their beginning salaries in their new positions was an increase of 47.2 per cent."

The university system remained underfunded and without a chancellor for years. As part of his general effort to rationalize the operations of state government, Governor Sam Ford persuaded the 1943 legislature to reinstitute the chancellorship. The State Board of Education then appointed as chancellor University of Montana President Ernest O. Melby, who accepted with the stipulation that he be allowed to remain in Missoula. The arrangement led inevitably to trouble, for supporters of the other five units immediately accused Melby of bias. Melby and the Board of Education launched yet another campaign to tighten control over the six units. The chancellor wanted to convert the Dillon campus into a vocational school and to turn the Havre and Billings units into junior colleges. Predictably, the legislature turned him down flat.

Since Melby's day, Montana has re-examined its university system time and time again, but no major changes were made until the adoption of the 1972 constitution. Having proven to be ineffective, the chancellor's position was abandoned after 1950. In 1959, the legislature designated the Board of Education, when acting on university system matters, as the Board of Regents and created the position of executive secretary to handle its business. Student enrollment in the university system, following a steady increase through the 1950s, mushroomed during the prosperous 1960s. And the campuses, especially those at Missoula and Bozeman, expanded with new buildings and new faculty. Increasingly, the university system became a major arm of state government, investment, and employment.

The state made significant new commitments to higher education during those growth years. With federal assistance, Montana established vocational-technical education centers in Billings, Butte, Great Falls, Helena, and Missoula in 1969. In a highly important decision of 1971, the legislature provided partial state funding for Montana's three locally run community colleges in Glendive, Miles City, and Kalispell and placed them under the authority of the Board of Regents. In order to provide its students with specialized training that its own university system could not afford, Montana joined in two cooperative interstate programs. Through the Western Interstate Commission for Higher Education (WICHE), which began in 1950-51, students from Montana and twelve other states can enroll in out-of-state universities for specialized training in such areas as medicine, dentistry, and veterinary medicine. And through the WAMI (Washington, Alaska, Montana, Idaho) program, set up by the University of Washington Medical School in 1970, twenty Montana students each year begin their medical education at Montana State University and finish it at the University of Washington.

The great boom of the 1960s only compounded the problems of duplication and lack of coordination in the state's university system. Montanans tried once more to rationalize and reorder the system in their new Constitution of 1972. The new constitution separated the control of higher education from that of public education in general. It placed higher education under a distinct Board of Regents that "shall have full power, responsibility, and authority to supervise, coordinate, manage and control the Montana university system." The regents were directed to employ a commissioner of higher education to facilitate their control and coordination of the universities.

Over the next two decades, the newly empowered Board of Regents, which was truly constituted as an independent branch of state government, and the Office of the Commissioner of Higher Education that answered to it, extended their authority over the system. In 1987, the legislature also placed the five vocational-technical campuses under the board's authority. As before, however, the problems of a duplicative, multi-unit system—now numbering six four-year institutions, three community colleges, and five "vo-techs"—seemed intractable. In 1973, the legislature empowered a large Commission on Post-Secondary Education to look at the situation once again. But when the commission's staff recommended closing the Dillon campus and converting Montana Tech at Butte into a community college, the commission demurred and accepted the status quo. In 1989-90, Governor Stan Stephens created an Education Commission for the Nineties and Beyond, and once again this body, while decrying the severe underfunding of Montana's system of higher education, thumpingly defended the multi-unit system and placed the issue of "access" in the forefront.

As Montana entered the 1990s, the fact of its comparative lack of governmental commitment to higher education seemed undeniable. Following a period of "catch-up" funding during the boom times of 1977-83 came a long and dreary era of base cuts and, more important, funding freezes and failures to keep up with inflationary costs. By the late 1980s, the state's two universities ranked at or near last place in the nation in state support, more than 25 percent below their peer institutions in the region. Over 28 percent of Montana's high school graduates were leaving the state to pursue their college education elsewhere. All of the four-year units faced severe problems of deferred maintenance of facilities, underfunded libraries and laboratories, student tuition rates that rose while state support fell, and danger to accreditation. It spelled the increasingly real threat of both lost opportunity for Montanans and declining economic, social, and cultural competitiveness for the state.

THE MEDIA

Newspapers appeared early on the Montana frontier, with local editors serving as community boosters and usually outspoken partisans in their political views. From the appearance of the territory's first newspaper in 1864, the *Montana Post* of Virginia City, until well into the twentieth century, Montana supported an interesting, vigorous, and highly personal brand of journalism. Some of the best known early editors, such as Thomas Dimsdale of the *Montana Post* and Robert E. Fisk of the *Helena Herald*, were better known for their prejudices than for their talent. But others, like R. N. Sutherlin of the *Rocky Mountain Husbandman* in White Sulphur Springs and W. K. Harber of the Fort Benton *River Press*, were men of intelligence, honesty, and candor. Some of their editorials still make good reading today.

The War of the Copper Kings had a critical impact on Montana journalism. Each of the great copper magnates—Clark, Daly, and Heinze—used the press to further his own interests. The result of this partisan warfare was the Anaconda Company's control over most of the state's major daily newspapers. After being attacked by W. A. Clark's paper, the *Butte Miner*, Marcus Daly brought in a capable journalist named John H. Durston to create a paper of his own. A Yale graduate who held a doctorate in philology from the University of Heidelberg, Durston made Daly's *Anaconda Standard* into the state's best newspaper. By the early 1900s, the *Standard* appeared regularly on the newsstands of fourteen cities outside Montana, including New York, Chicago, and all major cities on the West Coast.

Not to be outdone by his elders, young F. A. Heinze founded the *Reveille* of Butte. Heinze's venomous editor, P. A. O'Farrell, specialized in broadsiding Standard Oil and the Amalgamated Copper Company. "The Standard Oil Trust," he proclaimed, "Will Ride Into Montana Much As Charles the Fifth Rode Into Antwerp." By 1900, the Butte press had become little more than a pawn of the warring copper kings. As veteran journalist Martin Hutchens later recalled, "The newspapers spouted mud in a manner to cause the Yellowstone geysers to look like toy fountains." Stung by Heinze's attacks and beaten in the 1900 campaign, Standard Oil-Amalgamated Copper ominously began buying up daily newspapers in order to bend statewide public opinion in its direction.

By 1929, Anaconda owned eight daily newspapers: the *Anaconda Standard*, the *Daily Post* and *Montana Standard* of Butte, the *Daily Missoulian* and *Sentinel* of Missoula, the *Billings Gazette*, the Helena *Independent Record*, and the Livingston *Enterprise*. The Company papers commanded 55 to 60 percent of the daily press circulation in the state. Furthermore, through its many statewide business connections and its ties with Montana Power, the Company also influenced weekly papers and such independent dailies as the *Great Falls Tribune*. Although Company officials denied that they controlled editorial or news policies, their denials were hardly convincing. As John M. Schiltz once remarked, the sameness of Company papers defied coincidence. Al Himsl, a veteran Montana journalist and one-time employee of the Company-owned *Billings Gazette*, stated categorically that "the individual papers enjoyed little autonomy. They were told what to do from the top." According to Himsl, Anaconda strongmen Cornelius Kelley and Dan Kelly always kept a close eye on the press. After Con Kelley's death in the mid-1950s, Himsl contended, the Company editors remained in the Company rut out of habit.

The Anaconda Company's press policy did change over the years. Until the late 1920s, Company editors continued the practice of free-swinging attacks on their enemies, such as B. K. Wheeler in 1920 and Joseph Dixon in 1924. During the 1928 gubernatorial campaign, for instance, the *Anaconda Standard* described anti-Company candidate Wellington Rankin as having "all the dignity of a baboon, all the self-restraint and poise of a tomcat, all the calm deliberation and judicial decision of a jack-ass, all the finer emotions and sentiments of a yellow dog, all the nobility and character of a snake."

Perhaps the Anaconda Company found such attacks to be self-defeating, for by the early 1930s it had completely changed its approach. Instead of attacking its foes, the Company press now simply ignored them, "blacking out" controversial candidates and issues. On their edito rial pages, Company papers largely avoided state affairs and dwelled in-stead on problems far from home—a tactic people in the trade called "Afghanistaning." Anaconda's papers became, in the words of Richard T. Ruetten, "monuments of indifference." Modern Montanans can only wince at the thought of what effect that policy must have had on the work-ing of democracy in the state. The March 1957 *Quill*, the magazine of Sigma Delta Chi, the journalism honorary society, ranked the states on the basis of news coverage of their legislatures. Montana stood forty-seventh among the forty-eight states.

After years of mounting criticism for its "captive press" policy, the Ana-conda Company announced in June 1959 that it was selling its entire press operation to Lee Newspapers, a midwestern chain. Almost immediately, the Lee management introduced sweeping changes that brightened up the drab old Anaconda papers and brought them out of the era of green eyeshades. It upgraded personnel policies and mechanical facilities, ex-panded and improved its news staffs, established a state news bureau in Helena, and supplemented its Associated Press coverage with the *New York Times* News Service. In order to improve the work of reporters and editors, Lee encouraged them to attend conventions and conferences, in-cluding the American Press Institute seminars at Columbia University. The newspaper employees responded positively to a new sense of free-dom. Veteran journalist Bert Gaskill later recalled that Lee's employees "did everything we could to show the public the Anaconda Company's copper collar was gone." At long last, Montanans had access to objective and professional news reporting.

Viewed in a broader perspective, the end of Anaconda Company jour-nalism was part of a nationwide trend of mergers and consolidation, re-sulting in fewer daily papers owned by fewer and larger firms. Lee News-papers combined the Butte *Daily Post* with the *Montana Standard* in 1961 and joined the *Missoula Sentinel* with an enlarged *Missoulian* in 1969. More significantly, in 1965 the Warden family announced the sale of the *Great Falls Tribune* to the Minneapolis Star and Tribune Company, which in turn sold the paper to the Gannett chain at the close of the 1980s. Montana has fully joined the trend in less populated states toward ownership of major papers by outside chains. An interesting exception is the Livingston-based Yellowstone Newspapers, which owns newspapers not only in that city but also in Miles City, Glendive, Terry, and Dillon.

While depending on the daily papers and on television and radio for broader news coverage, rural and small-town Montanans rely upon their weekly and semiweekly newspapers for local information. Most small-town editors have confined their focus to local horizons, but some have addressed larger issues in the best tradition of American journalism. In more recent years, a list of such able country editors would include Dan Whetstone of Cut Bank, Miles Romney of Hamilton, Tom Stout of Lewistown, Hal Stearns of Harlowton, and Mel Ruder of Columbia Falls. In 1965, Ruder won a Pulitzer Prize for his coverage in the *Hungry Horse News* of the terrible floods of 1964.

Like all other Americans, Montanans have become increasingly reliant on the electronic media since the 1920s. The *Great Falls Tribune* launched Montana's first licensed radio station, KDYS, in 1922, broadcasting to only fifteen receiving sets in the entire city. After eighteen months of service, which included remote coverage of the Dempsey-Gibbons fight at Shelby, KDYS quit the business. Montana's first permanent station was KFBB, which F. A. Buttrey began at Havre late in 1922 and moved to Great Falls in 1929. All of Montana's larger cities supported radio stations by the 1930s, and Ed Craney of Butte united a number of them into his XL Radio Network, one of the first regional networks in the nation. By mid-1972, fifty-four radio stations operated in the Treasure State.

Like the radio boom of thirty years earlier, the television craze came to rural areas like Montana in the early 1950s. Ed Craney, the state's most successful radio entrepreneur, set up Montana's first television station in 1953, KXLF-TV at Butte. Other cities followed suit until thirteen different commercial TV stations were operating in the state by 1990, and the newly formed KUSM station at Montana State University offered the hope of statewide public television offerings with local programming. Cable TV service brought a wide variety of program offerings to local viewers, primarily from Spokane and Salt Lake City stations. And by the 1980s, satellite television reception dishes made a range of offerings available to rural Montanans that networks could never provide. More than any other single influence, radio-television has shattered Montana's isolation and broadened the horizons of its people, drawing them more and more into the mainstream of American life.

MONTANA AND THE ARTS

Montana has made some striking contributions to the nation's visual arts and literature. The word "art" in Montana seems almost synonymous with the name of Charles M. Russell, that self-taught painter, illustrator,

Sumner Matteson took this photograph of Nancy and Charlie Russell at the Sun Dance ceremonies on the Fort Belknap Indian Reservation in 1905.

Joseph Kinsey Howard, 1948

sculptor, and writer whose statue represents Montana in the National Statuary Hall of the Capitol in Washington, D.C. A St. Louis native, Charlie Russell first came to Montana as a sixteen-year-old cowboy in 1880. To the amusement of his fellow cowhands, Russell's natural talent kept him constantly occupied painting, drawing, and modeling clay. His first published work appeared in *Harper's Weekly* in 1888, and during the 1890s his work gained in popularity. In 1896, Russell married Nancy Cooper, who forced him both to end his carousing and to think commercially about his art. Russell hit his prime during 1905-20. After his first one-man show in New York City in 1911, he staged a steady parade of showings in major cities, including London, Rome, Chicago, Minneapolis, and Los Angeles. The Prince of Wales bought one of Russell's paintings to hang in Buckingham Palace, and in 1925 the great Corcoran Gallery of Art in Washington, D.C., celebrated the cowboy artist in a special Russell exhibition.

Charlie Russell's works of art offer a panorama of the passing frontier. Part of Russell's power as an artist stems from his genius with colors, his incredible mastery of detail, and his ability to depict the spectacular Northern Plains environment and its remarkable people. But equally important was his romantic reaction to "progress," his melancholy attachment to the untrammeled Old West that he saw fading into oblivion. Russell's art stirs a love for the land and its native inhabitants. He lived among the Blackfoot Indians in Canada for a few months in 1888 and always identified strongly with them. "Those Indians have been living in heaven for a thousand years," he once told cowboy Teddy Blue Abbott, "and we took it away from 'em for forty dollars a month." Probably no other character of Montana's past can inspire the affection that this sentimental cowboy artist has received from later generations.

Although overshadowed by Russell, three other Montana artists also deserve special note. Edgar S. Paxson, an upstate New Yorker, immigrated to Montana in 1877 and worked for a time as a freighter, Indian fighter, and scout. He settled briefly in Deer Lodge and supported himself by painting signs, buildings, and theater scenery. Eventually, Paxson was able to devote all of his time to painting, first at a studio in Butte and later in Missoula. By the time of his death in 1919, he had completed over twenty-five hundred paintings, six of them now hanging in the state capitol and eight others in the Missoula County Courthouse. Paxson was a painstaking perfectionist who spent twenty years preparing his well-known mural *Custer's Last Stand*. He was a romantic like Russell, but his works deal less with cowboys than with trappers, Indians, and larger historic events.

Danish-born Olaf Carl Seltzer lived in Great Falls near his close friend Charlie Russell. Seltzer worked as a machinist for the Great Northern until the early 1920s, when he was finally able to rely on his artistic talents for a living. His earlier paintings touched many themes, but the West captured his full attention in his later work. Seltzer worked beautifully with oils, watercolors, and pen and ink, and his wildlife studies are popular masterpieces. Less famous but equally significant was German-born Winold Reiss, who first came west in 1919-20. Fascinated by the Blackfeet and by their history of buffalo hunting and intertribal warfare, Reiss produced many striking studies of Indian life and gained wide recognition when the Great Northern reproduced them on its calendars. Reiss opened an art school at St. Mary Lake during the 1930s, where several prominent artists, including Victor Pepion and Albert Racine, studied.

During more recent years, a striking number of professional and amateur Montana artists have risen to national prominence. Among the best are Elizabeth Lochrie, who specialized in interpreting Indian culture, woodcarver John Clarke, sculptor Bob Scriver, and the versatile Branson Stevenson. Stevenson, who is best known for his pottery and etchings, became one of Montana's truly outstanding artists. His work has been shown at New York's Metropolitan Museum, the Library of Congress, Pittsburgh's Carnegie Institute, the Denver Museum, and in the State Department's International Traveling Craft Exhibit. Montana artists have found many outlets for their creativity. In addition to such nationally famous art centers as the C. M. Russell Museum in Great Falls and the Montana Historical Society Museum in Helena, many other Montana cities take great pride in their collections and exhibits. The Montana Institute of the Arts, founded in 1948, offers support to many artists, and the Archie Bray Foundation, established in Helena in 1951, has done much to further local interest in ceramics.

Like their predecessors, most of Montana's modern-day artists employ a realistic style to depict the land, the wildlife, the people, and the dramatic events from Montana's colorful past. The tradition is alive in the work of such popular Montana painters as Irvin "Shorty" Shope, J. K. Ralston, and Ace Powell. In large part, the prevalence of realism can be ascribed to the influence of Russell and to the fascination of Montanans with their history. But the key element is the land itself and its overwhelming beauty and grandeur. Billings watercolorist James Haughey put it nicely:

> In Montana the country... almost dictates working in the direction of realism rather than abstraction, but if I were back in New York and living in that environment I'm inclined to think that I might become an abstract painter. Out here the relationship of man to the country, the land to the sky, suggests a more realistic way of working than would life in a metropolitan area.

Nontraditional western art has also thrived in Montana since 1960. Branson Stevenson was one of the precursors and encouragers of modern art in Montana, and his workshops and willingness to experiment in new media inspired others. Absarokee artist Isabelle Johnson, at Eastern Montana College, and ceramicist Frances Senska and painters Jesse Wilbur and Robert DeWeese, at Montana State University, contributed to the new trend. In Native American art, Neil Parsons at the College of Great Falls has expanded traditional artistic horizons.

A central event in the rise of modern art in Montana came in 1951 with the establishment of the Archie Bray Foundation near Helena. Using an old brickworks as a ceramics studio, Bray attracted great artists such as Peter Voulkos and Rudy Autio and began to receive international attention. The Foundation has continued to attract distinguished artists from around the world. Two Montana institutions, the Montana Historical Society in Helena and the Yellowstone Art Center in Billings, share a significant collection of modern art. The collection of art by abstract expressionists, put together by George Poindexter, a New York stockbroker and descendant of a prominent pioneer family, includes paintings by Jackson Pollock, Willem de Kooning, and Franz Kline. The artistic health of the state is vibrant and continues to impress knowledgeable people from around the nation.

Montana's contribution to regional writing may be even larger than its achievements in the visual arts. In 1984, writers William Kittredge and Annick Smith enlisted a group of scholars and writers to collaborate on an anthology of Montana literature. Published in 1988, *The Last Best Place* surprised even its editors with the richness, breadth, and depth of the state's literary past. The anthology reveals that Montana's writers have expressed the same fondness for depictions of the land, the wildlife, and the history of this area as have its painters and other artists.

Among the best of Montana's early writers were James Willard Schultz and Frank Bird Linderman. Both exploited the romance of the fading frontier days they had experienced as young men. Schultz came to the territory in 1877 and lived among the Blackfeet until his Indian wife died in 1903. During most of those years, he ranched in the Two Medicine River country and supplemented his income by guiding hunting parties and writing stories for popular magazines. After 1903 Schultz devoted all of his time to writing, mainly juvenile stories about Indians and the frontier. At his best and most serious, he wrote realistically and affectionately of the Indians he knew so well. Schultz eventually produced thirty-seven books, including *My Life as an Indian* (1907) and *Friends of My Life as an Indian* (1923).

Like Schultz, Frank Bird Linderman knew and loved the Indians, but he wrote about them with greater skill and precision. Linderman arrived in Montana in 1880 and pursued an active life as a woodsman, assayer, merchant, newspaperman, state legislator, and insurance salesman. His fascination with the Indians and their culture dominated his life. Linderman played a key role in creating the Rocky Boy's Reservation, and he devoted his later years to creating accurate portrayals of Indian life and legend. Among the best of his works are *Indian Why Stories* (1915) and *How It Came About Stories* (1921). His other important works include *American* (1930), the life of Crow Chief Plenty Coups; *Red Mother* (1932), a biography of the Crow woman Pretty Shield; and two novels of the fur trade era, *Lige Mounts: Free Trapper* (1922) and *Beyond Law* (1933).

Considering its remoteness from major publishing centers, Montana has attracted a surprising number of professional writers. The fiction writers have pursued various themes. Margaret Scherf of Kalispell, for instance, has produced over twenty mystery novels since 1940. Others have also written in this vein, including James Crumley, whose stories and novels, especially *The Wrong Case* (1975), have attracted wide readership. But in Montana, as elsewhere in the Rocky Mountain West, the western motif prevails. The first Montanan to take up western fiction in a big way was former schoolteacher Bertha Muzzey. Writing under the name B. M. Bower, she produced more than five dozen novels of the West between 1904 and 1952, the most famous being *Chip of the Flying U* (1904).

Writers Dan Cushman, Norman A. Fox, and Robert J. McCaig all grew up in Great Falls, which, has long been a center of western writing. Cushman is easily the most significant writer in this group. He wrote pulp westerns until the market dried up and then began to produce works of lasting merit. According to Vine Deloria Jr., Cushman's humorous study of impoverished Indians, *Stay Away, Joe* (1953), is "a favorite among Indian people," although his autobiographical story *Plenty of Room and Air* (1975) may be his best work. One of the founders of the Western Writers of America, Norman Fox produced vast quantities of western popular fiction. The circulation of Fox's books runs into the millions, and Hollywood turned four of them, including the original *Gunsmoke*, into movies. While not as well known as Fox, McCaig turned out western novels into the early 1980s and is highly regarded as a craftsman by fellow western writers.

Among the most important writers in Montana's recent history is Joseph Kinsey Howard, the most notable among a circle of Great Falls writers and the author of superb nonfiction on Montana and the West. Howard grew up in Great Falls and at a young age became a successful local journalist. During a tragically brief career—he died at the age of forty-five—he also wrote critical and controversial articles for national magazines, such as *Harper's*, and several major books. Howard's most significant book was *Montana: High, Wide, and Handsome* (1943), an impressionistic history of the state. When the book first appeared, many reviewers regarded it as one of the nation's best regional studies. It has never gone out of print and has probably affected people's thinking about Montana more than any other work. Howard's treatment of Montana history was heavily romantic and melodramatic, depicting the good land where the "sky is so big" as cruelly misused and despoiled by wave after wave of mindless or evil exploiters. Modern historians have rejected many of Howard's simplistic conclusions, but readers continue to return to his beautifully written pages. The success of *Montana: High, Wide, and Handsome* brought Howard the association of many influential people, including Northwestern University philosopher Baker Brownell, who employed Howard in a University of Montana study group on small-town life. Howard's second book, an anthology entitled *Montana Margins* (1940), was a product of that study. In 1952, he finished his last book, *Strange Empire*, a fascinating study of Louis Riel and the Metis.

While working at the University of Montana, Howard assumed an important role in Montana's cultural affairs by organizing conferences and conducting seminars. The university's emergence as a significant force in cultural enhancement was also due to the contributions of H. G. Merriam, long the dean of literary affairs in Montana. For most of his long and active life (1883-1980), Merriam had a profound influence on Montana's cultural climate. Merriam, a Rhodes Scholar, moved to Missoula in 1919, bringing with him a vision of how Northwest literature could speak to Montanans in ways that national literature could not. He established the second creative writing program in the United States and gave aspiring regional writers an outlet in two magazines *Frontier* (originally a student publication) and *Midland* (1933), which were merged and published as *Frontier and Midland* until 1939. In its pages, Wallace Stegner, William Saroyan, and Merriam's students Dorothy M. Johnson and A. B. Guthrie Jr. introduced themselves to readers.

Dorothy Johnson grew up in Great Falls and Whitefish. During the 1930s and 1940s, she worked as an editor, mostly in New York City, and wrote successfully on nonwestern themes. After the war, she turned to western fiction, and in 1950 she returned to Whitefish and worked for her hometown newspaper. Her western stories found quick success, and the first collection, *Indian Country* (1953), helped win her an appointment to teach creative writing at the University of Montana School of Journalism. Her second collection, *The Hanging Tree*, appeared in 1957, and Hollywood based a major movie on the title story, appropriately starring Montana actor Gary Cooper. Two more of Johnson's stories, "The Man Who Shot Liberty Valance" and "A Man Called Horse," were also made into successful motion pictures. As popular magazines stopped publishing over the years, Johnson devoted more of her attention to writing books for juveniles. During her last years, she returned to adult literature with two Indian novels, *Buffalo Woman* (1977) and *All the Buffalo Returning* (1979), and a delightfully humorous autobiographical account of her youth, *When You and I Were Young, Whitefish* (1982).

A. B. Guthrie Jr., who grew up in Choteau, where he lived until his death in April 1991, was not only the state's foremost author but was one of the finest novelists ever to emerge from or write about the American West. After studying with H. G. Merriam at Missoula, Guthrie worked twenty-seven years as a journalist in Kentucky. In the late 1930s, he tried his hand at fiction and produced his first book, *Trouble at Noon Dance* (1943), which Guthrie himself later called "trash." The great turning point in his career came in the mid-1940s, when he received a Nieman Fellowship for a year's study at Harvard, where Guthrie worked under the distinguished Theodore Morrison.

The main body of Guthrie's work consists of six novels, which collectively depict regional history from the early frontier to modern times. First in the series was his masterpiece, *The Big Sky* (1947), a study of the mountain men and one of the finest historical novels in all of American literature. *The Way West* (1949) recounted life on the Oregon Trail and won Guthrie a Pulitzer Prize in 1950. In 1953, after the success of his first two novels, Guthrie turned to Teton County as the setting for his subsequent historical novels. *These Thousand Hills* (1956) described life on the Montana cattlemen's frontier, and *Arfive* (1970) and *The Last Valley* (1975) depicted life in a small Montana town. In 1982, Guthrie wrote *Fair Land, Fair Land*, which played out the fates of Boone Caudill and Dick Sommers, two characters from his earlier novels. Both men come to violent ends in the novel, but more important is Guthrie's description of the despoiling of the land by the whites' enterprise. Guthrie's other books include a wide variety of fiction and nonfiction. In addition to *The Big It* (1960), a collection of short stories, and *The Blue Hen's Chick* (1965), an autobiography, Guthrie published five mysteries: *Wild Pitch* (1973), *The Genuine Article* (1977), *No Second Wind* (1980), *Playing Catch-Up* (1985), and *Murder in the Cotswolds* (1989). In his writings and in public appearances, Guthrie also became an outspoken and forceful supporter of Montana's conservation movement, arguing eloquently against a mindless form of development that threatens to destroy the environment. Guthrie's role as a spokesman for the environment was altogether appropriate, for an important theme of his historical novels is the encroachment of "civilization" and its destruction of the natural habitat.

Several worthy successors to H. G. Merriam at the University of Montana, including Richard Hugo and William Kittredge, have carried on the creative writing program there. In his all-too-brief life, Hugo published nationally recognized poetry, essays, and a mystery novel. Often set in Montana and other western landscapes, his poetry emphasizes the themes of land, places, and people and celebrates the triumph of the human spirit. After Hugo's death in 1982, his poems were gathered in a superb collection, *Making Certain It Goes On* (1984). Kittredge has written a wide variety of fiction and nonfiction, including three acclaimed volumes of short stories and essays. His *Owning It All* (1987) continues the tradition of Montana authors writing about and questioning the economic development of the American West.

Hugo and Kittredge have inspired an impressive group of Missoula writers. Among their students are novelist Ralph Beer, short-story writers Mary Clearman Blew and David Long, and the versatile Blackfeet–Gros Ventre poet-novelist James Welch. Welch's first two novels, *Winter in the Blood* (1972) and *The Death of Jim Loney* (1979), attracted national attention and shocked some white readers in their frank exposition of modern Native American life. His historically based novel *Fools Crow* (1986) examines with sympathetic understanding Indian life during the last of the buffalo days, and his *The Indian Lawyer* (1990) returns readers to modern times and the struggle of an Indian living in the white world.

Recent achievements by other writers demonstrate that Missoula is not the only seedbed for creative writing in Montana. Dude rancher Spike Van Cleve from Melville published several collections of essays, including *40 Years' Gatherin's* (1977), which proved that the bunkhouse tradition of storytelling is still vital. In 1976, retired University of Chicago professor Norman Maclean produced *A River Runs Through It*, which many consider to be the best example of all modern Montana fiction. Ivan Doig's magnificent, autobiographical *This House of Sky* (1979), about his growing up in central and northern Montana, was nominated for a National Book Award. Doig followed up with a trilogy about the first hundred years of Montana statehood. In *English Creek* (1984), *Dancing at the Rascal Fair* (1987), and *Ride With Me, Mariah Montana* (1990), he used the fictional McCaskill family of Scottish homesteaders to explore the realities and subtleties of life in Montana.

Montana has also attracted an impressive group of essayists, novelists, and magazine writers who appreciate the state's cultural community and natural environment. Novelists Thomas McGuane and Richard Ford, nature writer David Quammen, and essayist Tim Cahill have brought their experience to the state and added to its cultural distinction. Whether native-born or immigrant and wherever they live in Montana, these writers have eschewed the use of worn-out, romanticized frontier themes. The simple frontier nostalgia of previous generations has given way to a subtle reflection on the land and its people and their doubtful future in a society dominated by consumer individualism.

CHAPTER 15

Politics and Government in Modern Montana, 1945-1990

Since the end of World War II, Montana's political culture has changed in many ways, some dramatic and some subtle. These changes, naturally, have arisen from deeper-lying shifts in the state's basic economic-social order. On both the right and left of the political spectrum, the trend has been away from polarity and toward diversity and modernization. To the right of center, the once awesome power of the Anaconda Company declined, while the roles of other corporations and conservative interest groups increased. At the same time, the old left-wing coalition of small farmers and metal miners gave way to a more broadly based and less strident medley of liberal groupings based mainly in the small cities. Montana's political record since 1945 has reflected these changes. A broad range of conservative and liberal forces came to compete for political power in Montana. For years, they competed on fairly even terms, with a conservative era in the 1950s matched by a liberal one in the 1960s and 1970s. The 1980s have seen an unprecedented erosion of liberal power in Montana, as it has throughout the West. If this situation is less colorful than the wide-open political confrontations of the past, when the storms seemed to swirl around the hurricane's eye of Company domination, it is also much healthier and more openly democratic. Montana is a classically western state where open and direct democracy thrives. In a positive vein, this political culture produced one of America's most highly regarded constitutions in 1972. Less reassuring, two decades later it seems unable to cope with the clear danger of an outmoded system of taxation and a collapsing state infrastructure that threatens Montana's future.

THE CHANGING POLITICAL PROFILE

Like every other state and political community, Montana has a distinctive "political culture." This political culture has arisen from the needs, demands, desires, and prejudices of the people and interest groups that have lived within the state's borders. Although Montana is small in population, its political culture is surprisingly complex. No one interest group, no one ideology, no one political party prevails there. In contrast to the old Democratic South or the Republican Midwest, Montana's two major parties have been evenly matched since the 1880s. And compared to such conservative neighbors as Wyoming, Idaho, or Nebraska, Montana has had a strong liberal bent that usually balanced equally strong conservative tendencies. All of this has led to close and hard-fought political contests. Montana's political battles sometimes discourage its people, but they seldom bore them.

The key political factor in Montana, as in all other open societies, is the match of strength between conservative and liberal forces, between those who resist change and those who seek it. Conservatives in Montana are essentially like conservatives elsewhere in the nation. Most come from the more affluent elements of society, and they are basically opposed to big government, deficit spending, and social permissiveness and experimentation. They generally oppose the growth of the welfare state system that began with the New Deal of the 1930s.

Montana conservatives have powerful groups behind them, with the greatest financial and organizational support coming from corporations and big-time agriculture. Throughout Montana's modern history, ranchers and the more successful grain farmers have usually thrown their support behind conservative causes and candidates, whether Republican or Democrat. Tightly knit and determined groups like the Montana Stockgrowers Association, the Montana Wool Growers Association, and the Montana Farm Bureau Federation have always been active and alert, especially during election campaigns and legislative sessions. Although the erosion of rural population has eaten into their power base, these conservative organizations still wield great influence.

Corporations provide the key financial muscle for conservative efforts in Montana. The old corporate giant of Montana, the Anaconda Company, steadily retreated from its earlier political domination after World War II. The clearest signals of the retreat were the 1959 sale of the Company newspapers and the breakup of the firm's close union with the Montana Power Company, which Anaconda executives had helped create. The split between the "Montana Twins," which had become obvious by the early 1960s, apparently arose from executive rivalries and from conflicting attitudes toward public power, especially power from Hungry Horse Dam. Although the two firms continued to ally on specific issues, each increasingly went its own way. The Anaconda, for instance, continued to work selectively within both political parties, while Montana Power preferred the Republican party and almost always backed conservative candidates. According to many observers, Montana Power is today the most politically influential corporation in the state.

The Anaconda Company no longer stands alone as the center of corporate influence in Montana, nor does Montana Power. A variety of corporate interests always worked the Montana system, even in the days of Anaconda's domination, but they have become more varied over the years and less tied to one leader. Corporate interests in Montana no longer use heavy-handed methods to get their way. Even the Anaconda Company abandoned its notorious "watering holes" for legislators several decades ago; instead, they use the same methods of lobbying, campaign contributions, advertising, and community involvement that their counterparts do elsewhere. Some corporations, such as Burlington Northern, Champion International, Montana-Dakota Utilities, Plum Creek Lumber, Peabody Coal, the First Bank System, and Washington Corporations, are major political players on their own. But the trend has been more toward trade associations that work on behalf of entire industries, such as the Montana Automobile Dealers Association, the Montana Coal Council, the Montana Medical Association, the Montana Mining Association, the Montana Motor Carriers Association, the Montana Petroleum Association, and the Montana Wood Products Association. Looking after all of them is the Helena-based Montana Chamber of Commerce.

Many political observers, obsessed with the image of corporate domination, have overlooked the strong countervailing power held by liberals in Montana in their struggles with conservatives. Like the conservatives, Treasure State liberals have traditionally come from all levels of society, but especially from the laboring classes, the ranks of smaller farmers, the legal profession, and the students and faculties of the campuses. Also like the conservatives, Montana liberals draw on the support of powerful organizations. Union labor and smaller farmers, traditionally the bastions of local liberalism, are still vitally important in Montana. The AFL-CIO and the Farmers' Union are key elements in the old progressive wing of the Democratic party, and both organizations continue to voice the reformism and governmental activism that emerged out of the New Deal–Fair Deal eras of the 1930s and 1940s. Although both organizations have suffered severe losses of membership over the past half-century, they both remain highly organized and exercise great power in the Democratic party.

On the left, as on the right, the trend has been toward a dispersal of political power. Since the 1930s, the rural electrical cooperatives, created by the Rural Electrification Administration, have been a significant progressive force, strong enough to protect themselves from attacks by the state's investor-owned utilities. Liberal environmentalist groups, such as the Sierra Club, the Northern Plains Resource Council, and the Environmental Information Center, gained recognition during the 1970s, especially among young people, and became a significant political factor. They have been joined by a myriad of groups advocating wilderness preservation and public access to streams and forests. Probably the most important, and subtle, new base of progressive support is with the white-collar, middle-class employees of the urban areas. Many of them are unionized teachers and public employees, and they tend heavily toward the pragmatic progressivism that is articulated, for example, by the Montana Education Association.

Montana has an intricately balanced kaleidoscope of diverse interests, reaching from the far right to the far left, with an increasingly heavy concentration in the center, leaning more recently to the right-of-center. The political balance has traditionally been so delicately poised that Montana usually swung predictably, like a weather vane, with the shifting winds of national sentiment. The state has almost always offered a close reflection of the national mood. America entered the postwar era in a conservative frame of mind, and so did Montana. The "Eisenhower Equilibrium" of the 1950s found its local manifestation in the complacent political styles of J. Hugo Aronson and Mike Mansfield. Nationally and locally, politics became heated again from the mid-1960s into the 1970s, as voters reacted angrily and cynically to issues like the Vietnam War and Watergate, and the Democrats won support. Similarly, Montana produced a liberal-environmentalist and Democratic resurgence in the 1970s. As the nation at large entered the conservative cycle of the Reagan-Bush era in the 1980s, so did Montana with the centrist conservatism of Governor Ted Schwinden and Republican legislative leaders like Jack Ramirez and Bob Marks.

One of the most refreshing aspects of Montana politics is its open, breezy, grass-roots democratic atmosphere. The state's small and unpretentious population has ready access to political leaders and political power, and local people like their politics low keyed and down to earth. They expect their legislators and other public servants to respond to them personally and directly, and they more often than not applaud them when they behave more like mavericks than like members of any coherent political organization. To many Montanans, Senator Mansfield was simply "Mike"; homespun Governor Hugo Aronson won many votes because he appealed to people as the "Galloping Swede"; and national reporters were awestruck that Governor Schwinden's name appeared in the Helena telephone directory and that he occasionally answered calls himself. *New York Times* writer Tom Wicker captured the flavor of Montana politics in his description of a typical campaign gathering at Billings in 1966:

> ...there were the candidates up there on the truck bed, earnest and tongue tied, and there were the ladies serving potatoe salad under the trees and there were several hundred big, informal, sun-burned American men who were willing to eat chili burgers on a hot Sunday while listening to the speaking. The cry of the politician may be too much with us, but in places like Pioneer Park, where the process begins, it has the authentic ring of an authentic people that is all too seldom heard in Washington.

MONTANA IN WASHINGTON: THE LIBERAL TRADITION

Despite the many broadening changes in Montana's governmental order, the "political schizophrenia" that first appeared during the 1920s persisted long into the late 1980s. Montanans perennially preferred liberals in Washington and conservatives in Helena. Such behavior is not unique to Montana, but it is certainly pronounced there. One reason for this puzzling ambivalence was the fact that the liberal vote has always been heavily centered in a few urban areas. It could more easily sway statewide elections, especially primary elections, than localized legislative contests, where the more conservative rural interests usually held an edge. Another factor favoring liberals running for congressional office was the nationwide dominance of liberal Democrats, which meant that the Democrats the local voters sent to Washington would join the congressional majority. Then again, liberals who ran for national office usually faced less opposition from local corporations than liberals who ran for state office, where they might have caused those interest groups more direct problems.

Whatever the explanations, the fact of Montana's longtime preference for liberal representation in Washington is beyond dispute. This is particularly obvious in the state's choice of United State senators. Incredibly, from the inception of the popular election of senators in 1913 until 1989, Montana sent only one Republican to the U.S. Senate. Following the 1946 primary defeat of B. K. Wheeler, the state broke its normal pattern by choosing an archconservative Republican, Zales Ecton of Gallatin County, to join veteran liberal Democrat James E. Murray in the Senate. Ecton's Senate career was brief and unspectacular.

James E. Murray, who served in the Senate longer than any other Montanan (1935-61), first went to Washington during the heyday of the

New Deal. Although a man of great wealth, Murray was also a determined and outspoken liberal. He was a less than dynamic campaigner, but the loyal support of liberal farmer-labor groups carried him through a long string of re-election victories, some of them by hairline margins. In the Senate, Murray was a capable parliamentarian, an unwavering friend of organized labor, and one of the leading liberal lawmakers of the Roosevelt-Truman years. The list of key reform measures that he championed is an imposing one that includes the United Nations, legislation protecting small businesses during World War II, the Employment Act of 1946, and the unsuccessful efforts for national health insurance and a Missouri Valley Authority. By the later 1950s, old age had impaired Senator Murray's effectiveness, but his political career and record ranks as one of the most formidable in Montana's history.

In 1953, Murray was joined in the Senate by a low-keyed liberal Democrat named Mike Mansfield. Perhaps the most distinguished of all political figures in Montana's history, Mansfield made an amazing and unique rise to fame. He broke into politics in 1940-42 as a little-known history professor from the University of Montana at Missoula. Winning election to the western district congressional seat in 1942, Mansfield launched a ten-year career in the House of Representatives. Neither his political philosophy nor his style ever really changed over the years. A compromising New Deal Democrat, he built a solid reputation as a businesslike congressman who carefully looked after the needs and wants of his constituents. Mansfield gained national recognition for his expertise in foreign affairs, concentrating especially on the Far East. In home state politics, he carefully skirted the hot issues and factional fights that destroyed so many other ambitious young politicians.

Mansfield reached the crossroads of his political journey in 1952, when he challenged the re-election bid of conservative Republican Senator Zales Ecton. The campaign was close, hard-fought, and sometimes vicious. The Democrat ran largely on his successful record of fetching federal appropriations for his state, a record capped by the dedication of Hungry Horse Dam just before the election. Mansfield was wounded, however, by a clumsy smear campaign that certain extremist groups launched against him. The appalling attack on his character, drawing on the methods being used by Senator Joseph McCarthy in national politics, attempted to brand Mansfield as being soft on Communism. But the attack failed to persuade voters, and Mansfield pulled through to a close victory.

Following that narrow escape from defeat, Mike Mansfield coasted to easy Senate re-election three times and rose to a position of invincible strength. He won election as Senate Majority Leader in 1961 and held

Montana's "Three M's"—Congressman Lee Metcalf, Senator James E. Murray, and Senator Mike Mansfield—posed for this photograph in Washington, D.C., in 1956.

that prestigious post longer than any other man in American history. He remained the soft-spoken, pipe-puffing moderate, standing aloof from and above the fray. His shrewd nonpartisan stance frequently angered liberal Democrats, who wanted to see their leader more often on the front lines, but it allowed Mansfield to draw in thousands of Republican votes. Most Montanans seemed to regard him as a monument and certainly as an asset, for Mansfield's protection of the state's interests in Washington was legendary. He became so much a part of the state's political landscape that the names Mansfield and Montana seemed nearly inseparable. In his mid-seventies, Mansfield retired from the Senate in 1977, and President Jimmy Carter appointed him ambassador to Japan. He excelled in that post, which he held through the Reagan years to the great satisfaction of both the Japanese and the Americans.

Following Senator Murray's retirement in 1961, Lee Metcalf became Mansfield's junior partner in the Senate. Metcalf, a strong man who seemed consciously to avoid publicity, differed in many ways from his more famous colleague. Like Murray and unlike Mansfield, he was outspoken in his liberal views. He drew few conservative or Republican votes and relied heavily on farmer-labor support to stay in office. During his four terms in the House, from 1953 through 1961, he became known—perhaps better in Washington than in Montana—as one of the most determined liberals and conservationists in government. As a United States senator from 1961 until his death in office in 1978, Metcalf followed the same path. He was recognized as the Senate's leading critic of the giant electrical utilities industry, and his book *Overcharge* raised considerable controversy about utility rates and how they are set. In contrast to Mansfield, who usually faced only weak opposition, Metcalf had to run against tough conservative opponents in each of his three Senate races. Each time, tight organization and dedicated liberal support pulled him through.

The long-term Senate team of Mansfield and Metcalf finally gave way to yet another Democratic duo, John Melcher and Max Baucus, both of whom came to the Senate from Congress. A veterinarian from Forsyth, Melcher captured the traditionally Republican eastern district congressional seat in 1969 and went on to secure by a wide margin the Senate seat that Mansfield had vacated in the 1976 election. Melcher quickly became known as a national spokesman for agriculture and secured key assignments on the Agriculture, Nutrition and Forestry and the Energy and National Resources committees. He was not a liberal, but rather a centrist and even a conservative on some issues. His relationship with the progressive wing of the Democratic party was tenuous, and environmentalists treated him with suspicion. Melcher triumphed over a weak opponent in 1982; but in 1988, when the wilderness issue made compromise especially difficult, he lost to the amiable Republican Conrad Burns of Billings. For only the second time since 1913, the Democratic hold on Montana Senate positions was broken. Burns's victory, unlike Ecton's four decades earlier, seemed to portend a permanent shift. Montana seemed to be joining the general western trend toward conservatism and the Republican party.

Max Baucus, a descendant of the prominent Sieben ranching family based north of Helena, first went to Congress from the western district in 1974 and then won the Senate seat vacated by Metcalf in 1978. Over the years, Baucus has shown more interest in national and international issues than Melcher and has identified himself more with the predominant liberal wing of the Democratic party. He appeared to be vulnerable to Reaganite Republicans when he faced re-election in 1984, but a clumsy campaign that attempted to smear him as a "wimp" backfired badly. During his second term, Baucus has gone to greater lengths to defend home-state industries like agriculture and lumber and has gained considerable national publicity, particularly as a member of the Judiciary Committee. Still a young man, he has considerable potential to rise to the top of a Senate system based on seniority.

A glance at the occupants of Montana's two congressional seats since 1945 reveals a mixed liberal-conservative pattern. The First Congressional District—consisting generally of the western, mountainous counties—used to be known as the "safest Democratic district in the West," mainly because the labor-Democratic bastion of Butte-Anaconda dominated it. But in the Second District, which covers east-central Montana, the prevalence of conservative stockmen and large farmers and the relative absence of labor unions made for more conservative Republican voting patterns.

A long series of liberal Democrats have represented the western district: Mike Mansfield (1943-53), Lee Metcalf (1953-61), Arnold Olsen (1961-71), the aberrant Republican Dick Shoup (1971-75), and Max Baucus (1975-79). Conservative Republicans held a near monopoly over the eastern district seat. Wesley D'Ewart, a staunch conservative and a favorite of the stockgrowers, held sway from 1945 until 1955; and archconservative Orvin Fjare occupied the seat briefly in 1955-57. Democrat LeRoy Anderson took over during 1957-61, partly because of the unpopularity of President Eisenhower's farm policy and because of delays in starting construction of Yellowtail Dam. The eastern district returned to conservative hands, however, with the arrival of "Big Jim" Battin (1961-69), until centrist Democrat John Melcher broke the GOP hold on the east during 1969-77.

Since the mid-1970s, the old pattern of liberal Democratic representation in the western district and conservative Republican representation in the east has reasserted itself as strongly as ever. Pat Williams, an outspoken pro-labor, pro-education liberal, won the western district seat in 1978 and has held it ever since. Williams has risen to a prominent position in Congress, serving as one of seven majority whips in the House of Representatives and as a leading congressional spokesman on issues relating to education and the arts and humanities. He stands well to the left of his constituents on many issues, but his political acumen and oratorical abilities have enabled him to maintain his position. Ron Marlenee, who succeeded Melcher in the eastern district congressional seat in 1977, is Williams's polar opposite. His focus, like Melcher's, has been overwhelmingly on committees and issues relating to agriculture, the key livelihood of his district. When Marlenee does address mainstream issues, such as wilderness, it has been from a wholly conservative Republican position. The 1990 census indicated that it is likely that the two Montana congressional districts would be merged into one. This alarming prospect raised the interesting question of whether such a huge single district would lean more toward the liberalism of the west or the conservatism of the east.

TRENDS IN STATE GOVERNMENT: THE CONSERVATIVE TRADITION

However one tries to explain the situation—rural muscle at election time, the watchful eye of local corporate interests, or the voters' determination to keep down the costs of state government—there is no disputing the fact that the same Montana voters who have traditionally sent liberals to Washington have just as predictably chosen more conservative candidates to rule at home. A brief glance at the key political issues and personalities since 1945 reveals this peculiar voting pattern.

The major political issues of postwar Montana closely resemble those of other states, especially the neighboring states of the Intermountain West and Northern Plains. As in all states, the key questions center on the gut issues of how tax dollars are raised and how they are spent. By the early 1930s, Montana had come to rely on the traditional statewide property tax and the new income tax as its main sources of revenue. Unlike most states—including states similar to Montana, such as Colorado and Wyoming—Montana did not choose to employ a sales tax during the 1930s. By the 1940s, conservatives were pressing hard for a sales tax in order to take the pressure off the other two levies and to meet the ever-rising costs of government. But liberals opposed the tax, arguing that it was "regressive" and that it would place the main tax burden on middle and lower income groups. The sales tax issue has raised its head again and again since 1950, and each time liberal Democratic forces have beaten it down. Montana now belongs to a minority of only five states, constituting less than 3 percent of the American populace, that do not use the sales tax.

The taxation issue interlocks with that great bundle of questions concerning what services, and what level of services, can be expected from state government? Those services determine the size of the state budget and of the tax levy, and budgetary considerations, in turn, limit the breadth of state services. Ever since the great expansion of state government during the New Deal era, liberal Democrats have generally pushed for—and conservative Republicans have pushed against—a larger and more active government. The many departments of state government, each with its own clientele, grew side-by-side, competing with one another for available tax dollars. The multi-unit university system mushroomed into a huge bureaucracy as veterans from the war, followed by students of the affluent 1950s and 1960s, streamed onto the campuses. The Department of Highways boomed as both Montana and Uncle Sam committed millions to build and maintain broad, well-graded highways and controlled-access interstate freeways.

A multitude of other departments also clamored, with varying degrees of success, for their shares of the tax dollar. Among them were the Office of Public Instruction, the Public Service Commission, and the departments of Justice, Administration, Social and Rehabilitation Services, Fish, Wildlife & Parks, Lands, Commerce, Labor and Industry, Natural Resources and Conservation, and the sadly neglected custodial institutions at Boulder and Warm Springs. Each governor's term and each legislative session has rocked with claims and counterclaims regarding the needs and shortcomings of these agencies. One effort has rhythmically followed another in Montana's unending struggle to contain its expanding bureaucracy, to coordinate its administration, to eliminate waste and duplication, and eventually to pay the bills.

Yet another cluster of perennial issues arose from the ever-more-complex relationship between the state and federal governments. During the five decades following the New Deal, a number of different arms of the federal government increased their sway over resource-rich states like Montana. They included the departments of Agriculture, Interior, Health and Human Development, Education, Energy, Defense, and Transportation, and, more particularly, the Forest Service, the Federal Highway Administration, the bureaus of Reclamation and Indian Affairs, the Army Corps of Engineers, the Interstate Commerce Commission, and more recently the Environmental Protection Agency. The state always seems to be locked in angry quarrels with the federal government, including the river-oriented controversies over a Missouri Valley Authority, Paradise

Dam, and Yellowtail Dam; land-use questions like coal leases, clear cutting, and grazing permits; threats of funding cutbacks for farm price supports, highway construction, or crop storage facilities; and the real or threatened shutdowns of such Montana facilities as Glasgow Air Force Base, Anti-Ballistic Missile sites near Conrad, Forest Service offices at Missoula, the Veterans Administration hospital at Miles City, and the Federal Bureau of Investigation offices at Butte.

Looking back over the years since 1940, these issues have emerged time and again in shifting political contexts. As the war ended in 1945, conservative Republicans enjoyed a firm control of state government. Two-term GOP Governor Sam C. Ford (1941-49) sat in the governor's chair, and Republicans held comfortable majorities in both houses of the legislature. Ford, a capable administrator, was a veteran of the old progressive wing of the Republican party. By the 1940s, he had moved well to the right. Pointing to Ford's reliance on the support of Senator Wheeler and other conservative Democrats and to the power wielded by Ford's controversial ally Wellington Rankin, angry Republicans to the right and angry Democrats to the left complained of a "Wheeler-Ford-Rankin triumvirate" or "axis" that allegedly held the reins of government.

Debate during Governor Ford's years in office centered on issues that, in one form or another, would persist for years afterward: the sales tax; funding for public schools; the management of education, highway, and liquor bureaucracies; and Senator Murray's bill in Congress proposing massive federal resource development through a Missouri Valley Authority. Ford and the wartime state legislatures spent a lot of energy trying to reorganize and pare down the bureaucracy that had mushroomed during the 1930s. Hired by a Governor's Committee on Reorganization and Economy, the management consulting firm of Griffenhagen & Associates produced, in fifty-nine large reports, a massive list of recommendations for change in Montana. Many of these recommendations would eventually be adopted.

The same problems that plagued Ford also beset his Democratic successor, John Bonner. A former attorney general and popular veteran of World War II, Bonner defeated Ford in a rough 1948 gubernatorial contest. Bonner charged Ford with neglecting or abusing the highway and liquor operations and with allowing the state's custodial institutions to deteriorate. Ford cried smear and labeled anyone voicing such charges "a dirty, rotten, contemptible rat . . . a deliberate and willful liar." Bonner laid out a moderately liberal program, and the legislature generally cooperated with him. The most significant breakthrough of those years was the landmark School Foundation Program created by the 1949 legislature, which provided funds to equalize educational standards in Montana's many school districts. By 1951-52, however, Bonner and the Democrats were in trouble. Strong nationwide and statewide conservative trends aided the Republicans, and the Democrats were divided by factionalism and by accusations of personal misconduct against the governor.

In 1952, the nationwide triumph of Eisenhower Republicans was reflected in the sweeping victories of conservative Republicans in Montana. The Treasure State's version of Eisenhower was popular Governor J. Hugo Aronson (1953-61). Nicknamed the "Galloping Swede," Aronson rose to fame as a humble immigrant who had made it big as an oilman-rancher-businessman. The governor's popularity stemmed from a jovial, down-to-earth manner and from his legendary physical strength, stories of which still abound in Montana. As chief executive, Aronson struck a subdued pose, somewhat as Eisenhower did in the White House, and made little effort to change things or to crack the whip over lawmakers.

The Aronson years were a time of conservatism and outward calm. The powerful liberal forces unleashed by the New Deal had mellowed, and consensus seemed to prevail. Two major controversies that did break the calm arose over the questions of oil leases on state lands and the earmarking of gasoline taxes for highway construction. Both issues culminated in the 1956 election. By an overwhelming margin, the voters approved an "Anti-Diversion" amendment to the constitution that, in effect, gave the Department of Highways its own exclusive source of revenue—the highway fuel and users' taxes.

The important oil lease question became the focus of a bitter gubernatorial fight in 1956 between Aronson and his Democratic foe, Arnold Olsen, the attorney general who had captured liberal favor through his campaigns to lower utility rates and clean up illegal gambling. Olsen argued that the 12.5 percent maximum royalty that the state received from oil wells located on its school lands was so low as to constitute a "steal." Aronson countered that Olsen's obstruction of leasing as attorney general had cost the state millions of dollars in lost revenue. In the end, Aronson narrowly defeated Olsen, and the conservatives won on the oil lease issue. Following the Aronson-Olsen fight, the political waters quickly calmed and conservatives ruled at the executive, legislative, and judicial levels of government. A momentous change did occur in 1957, when the lawmakers created the Legislative Council, a key fact-finding body that would provide them with better intelligence and help free them from such a heavy reliance on lobbyists.

Montana's political pendulum swung even further to the right in 1960 with the election of Donald Nutter to the governorship. An archconservative from Sidney, Nutter soundly defeated liberal Democrat Paul Cannon by running on a platform that called for a better business climate, reduced taxes, major cuts in government services and payroll, and, if necessary, a sales tax. Governor Nutter proved, as anticipated, to be an extreme rightist once he was in office, even refusing to proclaim United Nations Day in Montana. The 1961 legislature, faced with a six million dollar deficit, followed Nutter's proposals and slashed expenditures for the custodial institutions, the university system, and other arms of government. It took many years for the state to outgrow the debilitating effects of those budget cuts.

Nutter never had a chance to pursue his retrenchment program, for he died in a terrible plane crash in January 1962. Replacing him was Lieutenant Governor Tim Babcock, a wealthy trucker from Billings whose conservative leanings approached those of his predecessor. Babcock, who would later get caught up in the fund-raising scandals during the Nixon administration, won election to a full term in 1964, and he governed the state from 1962 until 1969. The state payroll grew rapidly during those prosperous years, and the conservative calm of the 1950s continued.

Attempting to comply with the U.S. Supreme Court's "one man-one vote" ruling, the Montana legislature tried and failed to reapportion itself. The federal court did the job in 1965, as well it should have, since under the 1889 constitution each county was represented by one state senator. This meant that the 894 citizens of Petroleum County had the same representation as the 79,016 in Yellowstone County. Reapportionment meant the loss of legislative seats for rural areas and gains for the growing cities, and overall the conservatives lost and the liberals gained strength as a result of the important change.

Sixteen years of Republican rule finally came to an end in 1968, when Governor Babcock ran for re-election against Democrat Forrest Anderson. Anderson was a former legislator, supreme court justice, and attorney general and a seasoned political insider and veteran of Montana's political wars. Estimating that the state would need another fifty million dollars to fund mounting costs over the next biennium, Babcock campaigned for a 3 percent sales tax as the only solution. Anderson cagily responded by asserting that the sales tax could be avoided through reorganizing government, cutting costs, and increasing existing taxes. His slogan put it simply, too simply: "Pay More? What For!" Predictably, the sales tax issue allowed Anderson to defeat Babcock by a wide margin.

The Anderson administration (1969-73) brought Democrats back to the helm in Montana, but it did not mean a major shift to the left. Forrest Anderson was a conservative, establishment Democrat. On the stormiest issue of his term, the ballooning question of environmental protection, the governor generally sided with those who favored economic development against the environmentalists. He became embroiled in a marathon strug-

Governor J. Hugo Aronson at a bridge dedication ceremony in Forsyth in September 1958.

Governor Forrest Anderson with sponsors of legislation authorizing a Constitutional Convention in 1972.

gle with conservationist Fish and Game Director Frank Dunkle, threw his support behind the unsuccessful attempt by Anaconda to begin the open-pit mining of copper in the beautiful Lincoln area, and favored state construction of a controversial road to serve the Big Sky tourist development.

Government reorganization marked Anderson's major achievement. Following voter approval of an enabling constitutional amendment in 1970 and passage by the legislature of the Executive Reorganization Act in 1971, the Anderson administration began a major reshuffling of the bureaucracy, combining over a hundred state agencies into nineteen departments. Meanwhile, just as Babcock had forecast, the mounting demands and costs of government, intensified by sharp inflation, outpaced the appropriations made by the legislature. Funding failed to meet needs; and state agencies, especially the custodial institutions and the university system, found themselves in a crushing and destructive cost-price squeeze. The question "Pay More? What For!" seemed to have been answered.

BOOM AND BUST: THE 1970S AND 1980S

From the close perspective of the early 1990s, it seems clear that after a long period of relative quiet during the later 1950s and 1960s, a period of rapid social, economic, and political change set in around 1970-71. Sharp political changes, from liberalism in the 1970s to conservatism in the 1980s, closely reflected the boom-and-bust economic climate of the period. As usual, history warns us that the changes were not so abrupt as they seemed at the time. The forces of change built up slowly during the preceding two decades until their mounting pressure suddenly broke open the political landscape during and after the Anderson era.

The forces of change built slowly and subtly. The most important, overarching forces were nationalizing trends, which worked to break down local peculiarities and to draw the state closer into the main current of American life. No doubt the key long-term change was the slow and steady shift in the nature of the state's population. As farm population eroded, rural Montana gradually lost ground to the small but slowly expanding cities. Aided by reapportionment after 1965, the cities began to flex their muscles. From traditionally Democratic Butte, Great Falls, and Missoula to traditionally Republican Billings, Montana's cities became centers of moderate, middle-class, consensus politics, closely divided between the two parties and receptive to arguments for change. Meanwhile, the rural areas, having been hurt by change, tended to fear and resist it, and they moved in a more conservative direction. More and more, the growing urban middle class sang the state's political tune.

Other trends blended with urbanization. As the Anaconda Company's influence declined on the right and the mining unions' influence declined on the left, the political center expanded. Montanans, like other Americans, became less provincial and more cosmopolitan during the postwar decades. Travel, whether forced by the military or chosen because of business, employment, vacations, or education, broadened their horizons. And so did the revolution in communications. The Lee Newspapers brought an open and vastly improved news coverage to the state in the 1960s. Radio and television, both in network and local programing and via cable and satellite, brought global, national, and state developments into closer focus.

By the late 1960s, Montanans seemed to be changing their minds about their state and about themselves. Like most of their fellow countrymen, they were shocked by the crises of America's great cities, and they began to reassess what their state had to offer. Unlike previous generations, who had tended to see their future and the future of their children in leaving the state, the new generation of Montanans found appealing reasons for staying. This attitude expressed itself in a new concern for preserving the environment, a renewed pride in community, and a new interest in reforming and improving society and government. Not since the Progressive Era had Montana seen such widespread popular participation in politics as that which blossomed in the early 1970s.

The new activism surfaced dramatically in the legislature. The lawmakers of the 1970s tended to be younger, better educated, more environmentally aware, and more independent than their predecessors. They were less tied to party lines, harder to lobby, and more difficult for party leaders to discipline. Heralding these trends, the landmark legislature of 1971 passed tough environmental laws and provided for executive reorganization. It also passed the first minimum wage law in Montana's history, prepared a referendum to allow the voters to decide directly on the controversial sales tax issue, and made final preparations for an all-important constitutional convention.

No movement better captured the spirit of the times than did the drive for constitutional reform. The argument that the 1889 constitution was outdated and needed to be replaced reached back to before the days of Governor Dixon. Significantly, the argument began to find a strong reception in the late 1960s. In the November 1970 election, the voters approved Referendum 67, calling for a constitutional convention. In a special election of November 1971, they chose a hundred delegates to assemble for the purpose of drafting a new constitution. While choosing their "Con-Con" delegates, the people also gave their verdict on Referendum 68, which called for a sales tax. The voters rejected the Republican-sponsored sales tax by better than two to one, and this issue caused an anti-Republican backlash that helped explain the election of an exceptionally liberal-minded group of delegates to the constitutional convention.

Assembled at Helena under the chairmanship of Leo Graybill Jr. of Great Falls, the delegates did their work expeditiously. After fifty-four days they turned out a constitution—which at twelve thousand words long was less than half the length of its 1889 predecessor—that won plaudits for its progressivism. *Time Magazine* called it a "model document," and the federal government prepared a special film to portray it abroad as an example of grass-roots democracy in action. Among the most significant innovations in the new constitution were single-member legislative districts, annual (instead of biennial) legislative sessions (which the voters then rejected in a 1974 referendum vote, under a blitz of corporate lobbying), statewide property tax assessment, and major efforts to strengthen the powers of the legislature. After a hard-fought campaign that generally pitted urban interests that favored the constitution against rural interests in opposition, the document passed by the slender margin of 116,415 to 113,883. The Farm Bureau spearheaded a conservative drive to strike down the new constitution in court, arguing that technically a majority of voters in the election had not approved the document. But the Montana Supreme Court narrowly upheld the vote, and the new constitution brought the state a modernized framework of government beginning in 1973.

The progressive tide that carried in the new constitution during 1971-72 continued to flow during the years that followed. In the 1972 general election, Lee Metcalf won a third Senate term against tough Republican opposition. And Thomas Judge, a moderately liberal Democrat, replaced Governor Anderson, who had declined to run because of ill health. Both Judge's race against archconservative rancher "Big Ed" Smith and the fight over ratification of the constitution revealed a strikingly similar pattern. In both cases, a moderately liberal urban vote confronted a strongly conservative rural vote, and in each instance the liberals won. The liberal tide reached flood proportions in the midterm elections of 1974, boosted by the nationwide anti-Republican reaction to the Watergate scandals that brought down President Richard Nixon. Montana Democrats took overwhelming control of both houses of the legislature; and with Max Baucus's victory in the western district, Democrats gained complete sway over the state's congressional delegation. As historian Harry Fritz has argued, Montana passed through a major political metamorphosis during the late 1960s and early 1970s, a period of liberal activism featuring legislative reapportionment, a new constitution, a marked increase in participatory democracy, and especially the environmental protection movement that crested during the Judge administration.

Governor Tom Judge, a Helena advertising man and former legislator,

Governor Tim Babcock at the dedication of the Livingston airport in September 1962

Governor Thomas L. Judge at the signing of labor reform legislation in 1973.

had served as lieutenant governor under Anderson. A moderate progressive but no foe of the Democratic establishment, Judge enjoyed a two-fold advantage during his two terms (1973-81). First, Montana was experiencing prosperous years of bountiful harvests from the state's increasing reliance on the taxation of extractive industries. Second, the opposition Republican party suffered not only from the onus of Watergate nationally but also from the wounds of the state sales tax battle of 1971. No one epitomized those wounds more than influential GOP Miles City legislator Jim Lucas, who had pitched his bid for the governorship on tax reform and the sales tax—and had lost. Until late in the 1970s, Judge and the Democrats had things pretty much their way. They implemented the new constitution and the new bureaucracies it mandated, such as a centralized university system, and pressed forward with progressive legislation, such as consumer protection and right-to-know laws.

The key achievements of the Judge years lay in the realm of environmental protection, as Montana both responded to the threat of massive coal mining and displayed a new concern for its pristine lands. The new environmentalism surfaced with passage in 1971 of the Montana Environmental Policy Act and the 1972 constitution, which guaranteed citizens "the right to a clean and healthful environment." There followed a series of landmark laws that thrust the state into a position of national leadership in its tough stand toward environmental protection: the Montana Strip Mining and Reclamation Act (which forced a restoration of mined land), the Montana Water Use Act, the Montana Utility Siting Act, and the Strip Mine Coal Conservation Act, all passed in 1973, and the Major Facility Siting Act and the Coal Severance Tax, both enacted in 1975.

Governor Judge referred to the 30 percent Coal Severance Tax as "the most significant piece of legislation enacted in Montana in this century," and he may have been correct. The law set the highest severance tax rates in the country—Wyoming's was next highest, at 17.5 percent—and aimed to set aside permanent endowment funds for the future, when the coal was gone. By later amendment, a full 50 percent of the earnings from the tax would be set aside in a permanent trust fund; the legislature could routinely spend the interest, but the principle could be used only if a majority approved. Recalling the history of mine-out and get-out in the state, most Montanans applauded the tax. But coal consumers, particularly in the Midwest, attacked the tax as an unconstitutional interference with interstate commerce. Most of the coal was, after all, on federal lands. Critics referred to Montana and Wyoming residents as "blue-eyed Arabs" who were trying to enrich themselves at the expense of their fellow Americans. Finally, a coalition of utilities, mining firms, and congressional critics filed suit against Montana and its tax. In mid-1981, the U.S.

Supreme Court allowed the tax to stand, even while reserving the right of Congress to lower or even eliminate such levies in the future. The tax prevailed, a symbol of assertiveness in the new energy-rich West, and the Coal Trust Fund approached four hundred million dollars by the late 1980s.

In 1980, Judge gambled on renomination for a third gubernatorial term, but lost in the Democratic primary to his lieutenant governor, Ted Schwinden. A Wolf Point farmer and former legislator and land commissioner, Schwinden was a popular, moderate conservative, and he easily won the general election in 1980. In office, he staked out the middle of the road, holding the liberal wing of his party at bay while garnering GOP support. As one agricultural representative put it, he was a "hell of a politician. His budget out-Republicaned the Republicans." Like other Democratic governors in the region, Schwinden trimmed his sails to meet the rightist winds of the Reagan era, and he proved to be a fiscal conservative. Even his "Build Montana" program to lure new industry to the state was woefully underfunded compared to the incentive programs of most other states. But his consensual, folksy style of government was popular with the voters, who flocked to his "Capital for a Day" sessions around the state. In 1984, he easily won re-election to a second term.

During the first two years of his term, 1981-83, Schwinden enjoyed the continuation of 1970s prosperity; but then the state and region descended into severe depression, and the middle road grew bumpy. Montana—like Alaska, Wyoming, and other energy states—learned the danger of relying too much on natural resource taxes, which crested at $66.3 million in 1982 and fell to $28.3 million in collections by 1989. Meanwhile, anti-tax protests, modeled in part after California's Proposition 13, gained support in Montana. A bizarre and irresponsible drive to eliminate all property taxes failed an initiative vote in 1986, even as another initiative froze property taxes. With the dubious argument that Montana taxes were unendurably high in comparison to other states, the executive and legislative branches of government proceeded throughout the decade to hack away at the tax base in a piecemeal process of what some called "tax-tinkering." By so doing, without finding replacement revenue sources, they turned a dilapidated tax system into a disastrously inadequate one.

These changes in the state's system of taxation included income tax indexing and the elimination of the business inventory tax in 1981, the accelerated depreciation of business property in 1983, tax breaks for the oil industry in 1985, the rollback of the coal severance tax in 1987, and the reduction of property taxation of business equipment in 1989. Tax indexing could be justified to disallow income tax "bracket creep" due to inflation, but inflation costs continued to take their toll on government buying power anyway. During 1981-88, indexing cost the state $232.5 million in lost revenue. According to estimates, the total annual loss to the state from this melange of unstructured cuts is from seventy to eighty million dollars each year.

By the mid-1980s, Montana faced a deepening fiscal crisis, due to the downturn in its economy and to a tax system that had become increasingly arcane and inadequate in its reliance on a steep income tax and an inequitable patchwork quilt of property levies. Again, as twenty years before, critics pointed to the glaring absence of a sales tax, which most of America relies on to fund basic state services. But both the governor and the legislature resisted calls for tax reform and increased revenue. In 1981, the legislature had enjoyed a hundred million dollar revenue surplus, most of which had been generated by severance taxes on natural products. By 1985, there was no surplus and Montana faced future deficits. The result was not only a failure to keep up with inflation but a series of across-the-board cuts in state funding and services. In January 1986, Governor Schwinden ordered a 2 percent slashing of state budget bases, followed with another one in November. By the late 1980s, the funding shortfalls and the consequent erosion of state services had reached critical proportions. The salaries of state employees, from janitors to judges, ranked last or near-last in the nation. By fiscal year 1991, an entry-level grade 14 state employee had lost fully 20 percent of her or his buying power since 1979. The state's two universities were among the worst funded in the country, and increasing numbers of high school graduates were leaving the state for colleges elsewhere. And from public roads to public buildings, Montana's infrastructure was crumbling.

In 1988, the Republicans broke the twenty years of Democratic rule when conservative Havre businessman Stan Stephens defeated former Democratic Governor Tom Judge for the gubernatorial chair. And in 1989, the Treasure State celebrated its centennial of statehood. Neither event seemed to break the torpor into which Montana had fallen. The legislature, unlike its counterparts in the other "Centennial States" of the Northern Tier, elected not to invest any money in celebrating the state's hundredth birthday. If it had, there might have been more occasion to reflect on Montana's status as it entered its second century. If soberly undertaken, such reflection would not have been encouraging. Compared to the heady exuberance of the early 1970s, the state seemed stalemated politically and was declining in a national perspective. In 1889, the new state of Montana was entering the national mainstream in a mood of optimism and confidence. In 1989, in a mood of resignation and seemingly unable to face the hard issues, it appeared to be in real danger of leaving the national mainstream altogether.

That mood of resignation is all the more regrettable because, in so many ways, the state's prospects were brightening. As Montana entered the 1990s, its economy was visibly recovering, and its pristine environment and open lifestyle were, more than ever before, attracting retirees, vacationers, and seasonal residents. Across the nation, and even the world, Montana was becoming a byword for unspoiled nature and the good life. Montanans have always been resilient and ingenious survivors. The challenge facing the leadership generation of the 1990s loomed clearly as the decade began: to maintain the environmental and lifestyle heritage of their state while rebuilding a socio-economic-political structure that had fallen into dangerous disrepair.

Selected Bibliography

ABBREVIATIONS used below include: *Montana* [*Montana, the Magazine of Western History*]; *PHR* [*Pacific Historical Review*]; *PNQ* [*Pacific Northwest Quarterly*]; *WHQ* [*Western Historical Quarterly*].

Montana is blessed with a dynamic historiographical tradition and rich archival and documentary resources. In preparing this book, we have relied on our own primary research on selected topics, but we have also leaned heavily on that historiographical tradition and on archives throughout the state. These bibliographic essays, which complement the essays in the first edition of *Montana*, treat topics in each chapter, describe the best of the latest literature on each subject, and list relevant publications that should also be consulted.

ARCHIVES AND GENERAL WORKS

Archival repositories in Montana hold superb collections of manuscripts, photographs, and micromedia dealing with state, local, and regional history. Although outdated, Brian Cockhill and Dale Johnson's *Guide to Manuscripts in Montana Repositories* (Missoula: University of Montana Libraries, 1973) is the best source. *Not in Precious Metals Alone: A Manuscript History of Montana* (Helena: Montana Historical Society Press, 1976) is the only published manuscript history of the state.

The large holdings in the Montana Historical Society in Helena, which include nearly all of the newspapers published in the state, also feature collections that are strong in business, mining, banking, livestock raising, military, political, ethnic, Native American, oral, and photographic history. Especially significant are the Anaconda Company Collection, Sam-

401

uel T. Hauser Papers, T. C. Power Papers, F. Jay Haynes Photograph
Collection, and L. A. Huffman Photograph Collection. The Montana Historical Society also holds the records of Montana territorial and state government agencies, including the governor's office. The State Historic
Preservation Office in Helena has Historical and Archaeological Site Files
that include all nominations to the National Register of Historic Places
and extensive files containing cultural resource inventories from all
counties in the state.

The archives at the University of Montana in Missoula have special
holdings in natural resources, politics, business, literary, oral, and photo-
graphic history. Holdings include the Missoula Mercantile Collection,
James E. Murray Papers, Mike Mansfield Papers, Dorothy M. Johnson
Papers, Anaconda Forest Products Collection, and Western Montana
Oral History Collection. Montana State University's archival and mu-
seum collections in Bozeman include agricultural, scientific, technologi-
cal, and photographic history; archaeology; paleontology; and the WPA
Federal Writers Project history files. Of special note are the Burton K.
Wheeler Papers, F. Jay Haynes Yellowstone National Park Collection,
M. L. Wilson Collection, Matt Alderson Collection, and James Willard
Schultz Collection.

In addition to these major repositories, local and county historical societies and Indian reservation archives in Montana have important collections that document local and regional histories. Archival and reference
collections at Yellowstone National Park, Glacier National Park, Big Hole
Battlefield National Monument, and Custer Battlefield National Monument hold important documents in Native American and natural resource
history.

In addition to this volume, students of the state's history should turn to
other general source books, histories, and anthologies. Among the best
are Robert G. Athearn, *High Country Empire* (New York: McGraw-Hill,
1960); Merrill G. Burlingame, *The Montana Frontier* (1942; reprint,
Bozeman: Big Sky Books, 1979); Federal Writers Project, WPA,
Montana: A State Guide Book (New York: Viking Press, 1939, 1949);
Harry Fritz, *Montana: Land of Contrasts* (Woodland Hills, Calif.: Wind-
sor Publications, 1984); John W. Hakola, ed., *Frontier Omnibus* (Missoula and Helena: Montana State University and Montana Historical Society, 1962); James M. Hamilton, *History of Montana: From Wilderness to
Statehood* (Portland: Binfords & Mort, 1957, 1970); Joseph Kinsey Howard, *Montana: High, Wide, and Handsome* (1943; reprint, Lincoln: University of Nebraska Press, 1988); Howard, *Montana Margins* (New Haven: Yale University Press, 1946); William Kittredge and Annick Smith,
eds., *The Last Best Place: A Montana Anthology* (Helena: Montana His-

torical Society Press, 1988); William L. Lang, ed., *Centennial West: Essays on the History of the Northern Tier States* (Seattle: University of Washington Press, 1991); Michael P. Malone and Richard B. Roeder, eds., *The Montana Past: An Anthology* (1969; reprint, Missoula: University of Montana Press, 1973); William L. Lang and Rex C. Myers, *Montana: Our Land & People*, 2d ed. (Boulder, Colo.: Pruett Publishing, 1989); Rex C. Myers and Harry W. Fritz, eds., *Montana and the West: Essays in Honor of K. Ross Toole* (Boulder, Colo.: Pruett Publishing Company, 1984); Robert R. Swartout Jr., ed., *Montana Vistas: Selected Historical Essays* (Washington, D.C.: University Press of America, 1981); Robert Taylor et al., *Montana in Maps* (Bozeman: Big Sky Books, 1974); K. Ross Toole, *Montana: An Uncommon Land* (Norman: University of Oklahoma Press, 1959); Toole, *Montana: A State of Extremes* (Norman: University of Oklahoma Press, 1972); Carroll Van West, *A Traveler's Companion to Montana History* (Helena: Montana Historical Society Press, 1986).

Subscription, or "mug," histories contain valuable biographical and general information. The best and most recent is Merrill G. Burlingame and K. Ross Toole, eds., *A History of Montana*, 3 vols. (New York: Lewis Historical Publishing Co., 1957). Other subscription histories are Michael A. Leeson, ed., *History of Montana, 1739-1885* (Chicago: Warner, Beers and Company, 1885); Joaquin Miller, *An Illustrated History of the State of Montana* (Chicago: Lewis Publishing Company, 1894); *Progressive Men of the State of Montana* (Chicago: A. W. Bowen and Company, [1903]); Helen Fitzgerald Sanders, *A History of Montana*, 3 vols. (Chicago and New York: Lewis Publishing Company, 1913); Tom Stout, *Montana: Its Story and Biography*, 3 vols. (Chicago and New York: American Historical Society, 1921); Robert G. Raymer, *Montana: The Land and the People*, 3 vols. (Chicago and New York: Lewis Publishing Company, 1930). For local history, researchers should also consult the numerous community histories published during the territorial centennial (1964), the nation's Bicentennial celebration (1976), and the state centennial (1989).

General statistical information on Montana politics and economics can be found in *The Montana Almanac* (Missoula: University of Montana Press, 1958, 1960) and in its *Statistical Supplement* (1962-1963). For statistical information on a variety of agricultural topics, consult the Montana Agricultural Experiment Station *Bulletin*. For business conditions, see issues of the *Montana Business Quarterly*; and for information on mining resources, see the Montana Bureau of Mines and Geology *Bulletin*.

State and regional scholarly periodicals that publish articles on Montana and Northwest history are *Montana, the Magazine of Western His-*

tory, which has been published quarterly by the Montana Historical Society since 1951; *Pacific Historical Review*; *Pacific Northwest Quarterly*; and *Western Historical Quarterly*.

Chapter 1. Montana In Prehistory

Published studies of Montana and Northern Plains prehistoric sites appear regularly in two periodicals: *Archaeology in Montana* and *Plains Archaeologist*. For a summary of the latest theories on prehistory in the New World, see Brian M. Fagan, *The Great Journey* (New York: Thames & Hudson, 1987); Fagan, *The Journey from Eden* (New York: Thames & Hudson, 1991). The best general study of Montana and Northern Plains paleo-ecology and archaeology is George Frison, *Prehistoric Hunters of the High Plains* (New York: Academic Press, 1978). Also of value are Peter Farb, *Man's Rise to Civilization as Shown by the Indians of North America* (New York: Dutton, 1968); Leslie Davis, ed., *Lifeways of Intermontane and Plains Montana Indians* (Bozeman: Montana State University, 1979); Waldo R. Wedel, *Prehistoric Man on the Great Plains* (Norman: University of Oklahoma Press, 1961); W. Raymond Wood and Margot Liberty, eds., *Anthropology on the Great Plains* (Lincoln: University of Nebraska Press, 1980). For Montana's recent contributions to paleontology, see John R. Horner and James Gorman, *Digging Dinosaurs* (New York: Workman Publishers, 1988).

The literature on Indians in Montana and the Northern Plains is voluminous, ranging from nineteenth century ethnographic studies to biographies of well-known Indian personalities. The best general sources for North American Indians are John R. Swanton, *The Indian Tribes of North America* (Washington, D.C.: Smithsonian Institution, 1952); *The Handbook of Indians* (Washington, D.C.: Smithsonian Institution, 1945). For Indian populations, see Russell Thornton, *American Indian Holocaust and Survival: A Population History Since 1492* (Norman: University of Oklahoma Press, 1987). Francis Paul Prucha's *The Great Father: The United States Government and the American Indian*, 2 vols. (Lincoln: University of Nebraska Press, 1984), is a superb study of relationships between Indian peoples and the federal government. The best surveys of American Indian history are D'Arcy McNickle, *The Indian Tribes of the United States* (London: Oxford University Press, 1962); Alvin M. Josephy, *The Indian Heritage of America* (New York: Alfred A. Knopf, 1969); Harold E. Driver, *Indians of North America* (Chicago: University of Chicago Press, 1961, 1969); William T. Hagan, *American Indians* (Chicago: University of Chicago Press, 1961). See also Ruth M. Underhill, *Red Man's America* (Chicago: University of Chicago Press, 1953, 1971);

Clark Wissler, *Indians of the United States* (Garden City, N.Y.: Doubleday, 1940, 1966); William Brandon, *The Last Americans* (New York: McGraw-Hill, 1974); Wilcomb Washburn, *The Indian in America* (New York: Harper & Row, 1975).

In addition to the works on individual tribes, the traditional horse culture of the Plains Indians is covered in Reginald Laubin and Gladys Laubin, *The Indian Tipi: Its History, Construction, and Use* (Norman: University of Oklahoma Press, 1977); Ronald P. Koch, *Dress Clothing of the Plains Indians* (Norman: University of Oklahoma Press, 1977). On Native American art, see Ralph T. Coe, *Sacred Circles: Two Thousand Years of North American Indian Art* (Kansas City: Nelson Gallery of Art, 1977); Richard Conn, *Circles of the World: Traditional Art of the Plains Indians* (Denver: Denver Art Museum, 1982); John C. Ewers, *Plains Indian Sculpture* (Washington, D.C.: Smithsonian Institution Press, 1986); Norman Feder, *American Indian Art* (New York: Harrison House, 1982).

The history and culture of Salish and Kutenai Indians have drawn the attention of anthropologists and historians. The best works on the Salish are Olga W. Johnson, *Flathead and Kootenay* (Glendale, Calif.: Arthur H. Clark, 1969); John Fahey, *The Flathead Indians* (Norman: University of Oklahoma Press, 1974); James A. Teit, *The Salishan Peoples of the Western Plateau* (Washington, D.C.: Bureau of Ethnology, 1930); Peter Ronan, *History of the Flathead Indians* (1890; reprint, Minneapolis: Ross & Haines, 1965); H. H. Turney-High, *The Flathead Indians of Montana* (Menasha, Wisc.: American Anthropological Association, 1937). On the Kutenai, see Paul E. Baker, *The Forgotten Kutenai* (Boise: Mountain States Press, 1955); H. H. Turney-High, *Ethnography of the Kutenai* (Menasha, Wisc.: American Anthropological Association, 1941).

Basic to understanding the Blackfeet is John C. Ewers, *The Blackfeet: Raiders on the Northwestern Plains* (Norman: University of Oklahoma Press, 1958); Ewers, *The Horse in Blackfoot Indian Culture* (Washington, D.C.: Government Printing Office, 1955); Ewers, *Ethnological Report on the Blackfeet and Gros Ventre Tribes of Montana* (New York: Garland, 1974); Clark Wissler, *The Material Culture of the Blackfoot Indians* (New York: American Museum of Natural History, 1910). Two exceptional books on Blackfeet culture are Percy Bullchild, *The Sun Came Down: The History of the World as My Blackfeet Elders Told It* (San Francisco: Harper & Row, 1985); George Comes At Night, *Roaming Days* (Browning, Mont.: Blackfeet Heritage Program, 1978). Also important are Oscar Lewis, *The Effects of White Contact Upon Blackfoot Culture* (New York: J. J. Augustin, 1942); George Bird Grinnell, *Blackfoot Lodge Tales* (1892; reprint, Lincoln: University of Nebraska Press, 1962); Frank Bird Linderman, *Blackfeet Indians* (St. Paul: Brown & Bigelow, 1935); Walter

McClintock, *The Old North Trail* (Lincoln: University of Nebraska Press, 1968).

Recent books on the history and culture of the Crow Indians include Frederick Hoxie, *The Crow* (New York: Chelsea House, 1989); Rodney Frey, *The World of the Crow Indians* (Norman: University of Oklahoma Press, 1984); Fred W. Voget, *The Shoshoni-Crow Sun Dance* (Norman: University of Oklahoma Press, 1984); Peter Nabakov, ed., *Two Leggins: The Making of a Crow Warrior* (Lincoln: University of Nebraska Press, 1982). Readers should also consult the classic work of Frank Bird Linderman, *Plenty Coups, Chief of the Crows* (1930; reprint, Lincoln: University of Nebraska Press, 1962); Linderman, *Pretty-Shield, Medicine Woman of the Crows* (1935; reprint, New York: Harper and Row, 1960). The respected work of Robert H. Lowie, *The Crow Indians* (New York: Farrar and Rinehart, 1935) and *The Material Culture of the Crow Indians* (New York: American Museum of Natural History, 1922), remains insightful and valuable. Other useful volumes are Charles C. Bradley Jr., *A History of the Crow Indians* (Lodge Grass, Mont.: Lodge Grass Schools, 1971); Norman B. Plummer, *The Crow Indians* (New York: Garland Publishing Company, 1974). For Crows in the Yellowstone Valley, see Adrian Heidenreich, "The Native Americans' Yellowstone," *Montana* 35 (Autumn 1985): 2-17.

On the culture of the Gros Ventre and Assiniboine peoples of northern Montana, see George Horse Capture, ed., *The Seven Visions of Bull Lodge* (Ann Arbor, Mich.: Bear Claw Press, 1980); Loretta Fowler, *Shared Symbols, Contested Meanings: Gros Ventre Culture and History, 1778-1984* (Ithaca, N.Y.: Cornell University Press, 1987); *Assiniboine Memories: Legends of the Nakota People* (Harlem, Mont.: Fort Belknap Indian Community Association, 1983); and the WPA-produced *Land of Nakoda, the Story of the Assiniboine Indians* (Helena: State Publishing Company, 1942). Also valuable are Regina Flannery, *The Gros Ventres of Montana*, 2 vols. (Washington, D.C.: Catholic University of America Press, 1953-56); Alfred L. Kroeber, *Gros Ventre Myths and Tales* (New York: American Museum of Natural History, 1907); Kroeber, *Ethnology of the Gros Ventre* (New York: American Museum of Natural History, 1908); Edward E. Barry Jr., *The Fort Belknap Indian Reservation: The First One Hundred Years, 1855-1955* (Bozeman: Montana State University, 1974); David Rodnick, "The Fort Belknap Assiniboine of Montana ..." (Ph.D. diss., University of Pennsylvania, Philadelphia, 1936). On the Cree and Metis, see Jacqueline Peterson and Jennifer S. H. Brown, eds., *The New Peoples: Being and Becoming Metis in North America* (Lincoln: University of Nebraska Press, 1985); Verne Dusenberry, *The Montana Cree* (Stockholm: Almqvist and Wiksell, 1953); Carolissa Levi, *The*

Chippewa Indians of Yesterday and Today (New York: Pageant Press, 1956); Thomas R. Wessel, *A History of the Rocky Boy's Indian Reservation* (Bozeman: Montana State University, 1974).

The classic studies of the Cheyennes are by George B. Grinnell, *The Cheyenne Indians* (New Haven, Conn.: Yale University Press, 1923); Grinnell, *By Cheyenne Campfires* (New Haven, Conn.: Yale University Press, 1962). The best modern treatments of Cheyenne culture are Peter J. Powell's *The Cheyenne: Maheho's People, a Critical Bibliography* (Bloomington: Indiana University Press, 1980), *People of the Sacred Mountain* (New York: Harper & Row, 1979), and *Sweet Medicine*, 2 vols. (Norman: University of Oklahoma Press, 1969). See also John Stands in Timber and Margot Liberty, *Cheyenne Memories* (New Haven, Conn.: Yale University Press, 1967); John M. Moore, *The Cheyenne Nation: A Social and Demographic History* (Lincoln: University of Nebraska Press, 1980); Tom Weist, *A History of the Cheyenne People* (Billings: Montana Council for Indian Education, 1977). For the southern Cheyennes, see Donald J. Berthrong, *The Southern Cheyennes* (Norman: University of Oklahoma Press, 1963). The Shoshonis of Idaho and western Montana are covered in Virginia Trenholm and Maurine Carley, *The Shoshoni: Sentinels of the Rockies* (Norman: University of Oklahoma Press, 1964).

CHAPTER 2. EARLY EXPLORATIONS

The best general works on the science and the course of white exploration of Montana and the American West are two superb volumes by William H. Goetzmann, *Exploration and Empire* (New York: Alfred A. Knopf, 1966), and *New Lands, New Men: America and the Second Great Age of Discovery* (New York: Viking, 1986). Readers should also consult John Brebner, *The Explorers of North America, 1492-1806* (New York: Macmillan, 1933), and the best narrative treatment of exploration, Bernard DeVoto, *The Course of Empire* (Boston: Houghton, Mifflin, 1952).

The literature on imperial claims and conflicts in North America is large, but the best dealing with Montana and the West are Warren Cook, *Flood Tide of Empire: Spain and the Pacific Northwest, 1543-1819* (New Haven, Conn.: Yale University Press, 1973); Barry Gough, *Distant Dominion: Britain and the Northwest Coast of North America, 1579-1819* (Vancouver: University of British Columbia Press, 1980); Charles Gibson, *Spain in America* (New York: Harper and Row, 1966); W. J. Eccles, *France in America* (New York: Harper and Row, 1966). Helpful on the Russian advance on the Pacific Northwest are Derek Pethick, *The Nootka Connection: Europe and the Northwest Coast, 1790-1795* (Seattle: University of Washington Press, 1980); Howard I. Kushner, *Conflict on the*

Northwest Coast: American-Russian Rivalry in the Pacific Northwest, 1790-1867 (Westport, Conn.: Greenwood Press, 1975).

For pre-Lewis and Clark explorations in the Northern Plains, see A. P. Nasatir, *Before Lewis and Clark: Documents Illustrating the History of the Missouri, 1785-1804*, 2 vols. (St. Louis: St. Louis Historical Documents Foundation, 1952). The controversy about the Verendryes is covered in G. Hubert Smith, *The Exploration of the LaVerendryes in the Northern Plains, 1838-43*, ed. W. Raymond Wood (Lincoln: University of Nebraska Press, 1980). On the Verendryes, see also Lawrence J. Burpee, ed., *Journals and Letters of Pierre Gaultier de Varennes De La Verendrye and His Sons* (1927; reprint, New York: Greenwood Press, 1968); Nellis M. Crouse, *La Verendrye: Fur Trader and Explorer* (Ithaca, N.Y.: Cornell University Press, 1956); John W. Smurr, "A New Verendrye Theory," *PNQ* 43 (January 1952): 51-64.

There are many studies about the Louisiana Purchase, its importance to the United States, and the diplomacy that made it possible. Among the best are Alexander DeConde, *This Affair of Louisiana* (New York: Charles Scribner's Sons, 1976); John L. Allen, "Geographical Knowledge and American Images of the Louisiana Territory," *WHQ* 2 (April 1971): 151-70; Oscar Handlin, "The Louisiana Purchase: Chance or Destiny," *Atlantic Monthly* 195 (January 1955): 44-49; A. P. Whitaker, *The Mississippi Question, 1795-1803* (New York: D. Appleton, 1934).

Lewis and Clark historiography has increased enormously since 1970, illuminating the well-known story with new manuscript sources and interpretations. The most important advance is the University of Nebraska's new edition of the *Journals*, edited by Gary E. Moulton, which will be completed by the mid-1990s. On the history of the *Journals*, see Paul R. Cutright, *A History of the Lewis and Clark Journals* (Norman: University of Oklahoma Press, 1976). Foremost in new Lewis and Clark studies is the work by Donald Jackson, including *Letters of the Lewis and Clark Expedition, with Related Documents, 1783-1854*, 2d. ed., 2 vols. (Urbana: University of Illinois Press, 1978); *Thomas Jefferson and the Stony Mountains: Exploring the West from Monticello* (Urbana: University of Illinois Press, 1981); *Among the Sleeping Giants: Occasional Pieces on Lewis and Clark* (Urbana: University of Illinois Press, 1987). See also Ernest S. Osgood, ed., *The Field Notes of Captain William Clark, 1803-1805* (New Haven, Conn.: Yale University Press, 1964). Superb popular accounts of the expedition include David Lavender, *The Way to the Western Sea: Lewis and Clark Across the Continent* (New York: 1988); Bernard DeVoto, *The Course of Empire* (Boston: Houghton, Mifflin, 1952); John Bakeless, *Lewis and Clark: Partners in Discovery* (New York: W. Morrow, 1947).

Books on special subjects related to the expedition are James P. Ronda,

Lewis and Clark Among the Indians (Lincoln: University of Nebraska, 1984); Robert B. Betts, *In Search of York: The Slave Who Went to the Pacific with Lewis and Clark* (Boulder: Colorado Associated Press, 1985); John L. Allen, *Passage Through the Garden: Lewis and Clark and the Image of the American Northwest* (Urbana: University of Illinois Press, 1975); Eldon G. Chuinard, *Only One Man Died: The Medical Aspects of the Lewis and Clark Expedition* (Glendale, Calif.: Arthur H. Clark, 1979); Richard Dillon, *Meriwether Lewis* (New York: Coward McCann, 1965); Jerome O. Steffen, *William Clark: Jeffersonian Man on the Frontier* (Norman: University of Oklahoma Press, 1977).

Articles and books that treat special aspects of the expedition include Gary E. Moulton, "The Missing Journals of Meriwether Lewis," *Montana* 35 (Summer 1985): 29-39; W. Raymond Wood and Gary E. Moulton, "Prince Maximilian and New Maps of the Missouri and Yellowstone Rivers," *WHQ* 12 (October 1981): 373-86; William E. Foley and David Rice, "The Return of the Mandan Chief," *Montana* 29 (Summer 1979): 2-15; Brigham D. Madsen, *The Lemhi: Sacajawea's People* (Caldwell, Ida.: Caxton Printers, 1979); John E. Rees, "The Shoshoni Contribution to Lewis and Clark," *Idaho Yesterdays* 2 (Winter 1958): 2-13; John C. Ewers, "Plains Indians' Reactions to Lewis and Clark," *Montana* 16 (Winter 1966): 2-17; Donald Jackson, "The Public Image of Lewis and Clark," *PNQ* 57 (January 1966): 1-7. On Sacagawea, see Harold P. Howard, *Sacajawea* (Norman: University of Oklahoma Press, 1971); C. S. Kingston, "Sacajawea: The Evaluation of a Legend," *PNQ* 35 (January 1944): 2-18; Irving Anderson, "Probing the Riddle of the Bird Woman," *Montana* 23 (Autumn 1973): 2-17. For other specialized articles on Lewis and Clark, consult *We Proceeded On*, the quarterly journal of the Lewis and Clark Trail Heritage Foundation.

CHAPTER 3. THE ERA OF THE FUR TRADE

The study of the fur trade in the American West and Montana has increased dramatically since 1970. The best new general works are Theodore Karamanski, *Fur Trade and Exploration: Opening the Far Northwest, 1821-1852* (Norman: University of Oklahoma Press, 1983); David J. Wishart, *The Fur Trade of the American West* (Lincoln: University of Nebraska Press, 1979). Still comprehensive and valuable are Leroy R. Hafen and Ann Hafen, eds., *The Mountain Men and the Fur Trade of the Far West*, 10 vols. (Glendale, Calif.: Arthur H. Clark, 1965); Paul C. Phillips, *The Fur Trade*, 2 vols. (Norman: University of Oklahoma Press, 1961); Hiram M. Chittenden, *The American Fur Trade of the Far West*, 3 vols. (New York: Francis P. Harper, 1902).

The British-Canadian fur trade is documented and interpreted in E. E.

Rich, *The History of the Hudson's Bay Company, 1670-1870,* 2 vols. (London: Hudson's Bay Record Society, 1958-62); John S. Galbraith, *The Hudson's Bay Company as an Imperial Factor, 1821-1869* (Berkeley: University of California Press, 1957). A good popular history of the Hudson's Bay Company is Peter C. Newman, *Company of Adventurers* (New York: Viking Press, 1985), and Newman, *Caesars of the Wilderness* (New York: Viking Press, 1987). On David Thompson, see his *Narrative,* ed. Richard Glover (Toronto: The Champlain Society, 1962); M. Catherine White, ed., *David Thompson's Journals Relating to Montana, 1808-1812* (Missoula: University of Montana, 1950); Victor G. Hopwood, ed., *David Thompson: Travels in Western North America, 1784-1812* (Toronto: Macmillan, 1971). For information and interpretation of women in the Canadian-American fur trade, see Jennifer S. H. Brown, *Strangers in the Blood: Fur Trade Company Families in Indian Country* (Vancouver, B.C.: University of British Columbia Press, 1980); Sylvia Van Kirk, *Many Tender Ties: Women in Fur-Trade Society, 1670-1870* (Norman: Oklahoma University Press, 1980); William R. Swagerty, "Marriage and Settlement Patterns of Rocky Mountain Trappers and Traders," *WHQ* 11 (April 1981): 159-80. On Peter Skene Ogden, see Gloria G. Cline, *Peter Skene Ogden and the Hudson's Bay Company* (Norman: University of Oklahoma Press, 1974); Edgar I. Stewart, "Peter Skene Ogden in Montana, 1825," *Montana* 3 (Autumn 1953): 32-45; Albert J. Partoll, "Fort Connah: A Frontier Trading Post, 1847-1871," *PNQ* 30 (October 1939): 399-415.

For information on the upper Missouri River and Mandan trade, see W. Raymond Wood and Thomas D. Thiessen, eds., *Early Fur Trade on the Northern Plains: Canadian Traders Among the Mandan and Hidatsa Indians, 1738-1818* (Norman: University of Oklahoma Press, 1985); John Alwin, "Pelts, Provisions & Perceptions: The Hudson's Bay Company Mandan Trade, 1795-1812," *Montana* 29 (Summer 1979): 16-27; John C. Ewers, "The Indian Trade of the Upper Missouri before Lewis and Clark," *Bulletin of the Missouri Historical Society* 10 (Autumn 1954): 429-46; William E. Foley and C. David Rice, *The First Chouteaus: River Barons of Early St. Louis* (Urbana: University of Illinois Press, 1983); Richard M. Clokey, *William Ashley: Enterprise and Politics in the Trans-Mississippi West* (Norman: University of Oklahoma Press, 1980); Richard E. Oglesby, *Manuel Lisa and the Opening of the Missouri Fur Trade* (Norman: Oklahoma University Press, 1963); John E. Sunder, *Joshua Pilcher: Fur Trader and Indian Agent* (Norman: University of Oklahoma Press, 1968); Burton Harris, *John Colter: His Years in the Rockies* (New York: Scribner's Sons, 1952); David C. Rowe, "Government Relations with the Fur Trappers of the Upper Missouri, 1820-1840," *North Dakota History* 25 (Spring 1968): 481-505.

The era of the mountain men and the Rocky Mountain fur enterprise have generated more literature than any other phase of fur-trade history, much of it romantic. The best can be found in LeRoy R. Hafen and Ann Hafen, eds., *The Mountain Men and the Fur Trade of the Far West*, 10 vols. (Glendale, Calif.: A. H. Clark, 1965); Fred Gowans, *Rocky Mountain Rendezvous: A History of the Fur Trade Rendezvous* (Provo: Brigham University Press, 1975); Carl P. Russell, *Firearms, Traps, and Tools of the Mountain Men* (New York: Alfred A. Knopf, 1967); Lewis O. Saum, *The Fur Trader and the Indian* (Seattle: University of Washington Press, 1965); Keith Alger, "Robert Meldrum and the Crow Peltry Trade," *Montana* 36 (Summer 1986): 36-47; Dale L. Morgan, *Jedediah Smith and the Opening of the West* (Indianapolis: Bobbs-Merrill, 1953); J. Cecil Alter, *James Bridger* (Norman: University of Oklahoma Press, 1962).

The best book on John Jacob Astor and his bid for control of far western fur trading is James P. Ronda, *Astoria and Empire* (Lincoln: University of Nebraska Press, 1990). For the background on Astor's Missouri enterprise, see John D. Haeger, "Business Strategy and Practice in the Early Republic: John Jacob Astor and the American Fur Trade," *WHQ* 19 (May 1988): 183-202. The standard biography of Astor is Kenneth W. Porter, *John Jacob Astor, Business Man*, 2 vols. (New York: Russell and Russell, 1931). The best popular account is David Lavender, *Fist in the Wilderness* (Garden City, N.Y.: Doubleday, 1964). See also John E. Sunder, *The Fur Trade on the Upper Missouri, 1840-1865* (Norman: University of Oklahoma Press, 1965); Elliott Coues, ed., *Forty Years a Fur Trader on the Upper Missouri: The Journal of Charles Larpenteur*, 2 vols. (New York: F. P. Harper, 1898); David Smythe, "The Struggle for the Piegan Trade: The Saskatchewan Versus the Missouri," *Montana* 34 (Spring 1984): 2-15. On the American Fur Company's Fort Union, see Erwin N. Thompson, *Fort Union Trading Post: Fur Trade Empire on the Upper Missouri* (Medora, N.D.: Theodore Roosevelt Nature and History Association, 1986).

The role of the Jesuit missionaries during the fur-trade period is covered in William N. Bischoff, S.J., *The Jesuits in Old Oregon* (Caldwell, Ida.: Caxton Printers, 1945); Wilfred Schoenberg, S.J., *Jesuits in Montana, 1840-1960* (Portland: Oregon-Jesuit, 1960); Robert I. Burns, *The Jesuits and the Indian Wars in the Northwest* (New Haven, Conn.: Yale University Press, 1966). For Fr. Pierre-Jean DeSmet, see H. M. Chittenden and A. T. Richardson, eds., *Life, Letters, and Travels of Father Pierre-Jean de Smet, S.J.*, 4 vols. (New York: F. P. Harper, 1905); John U. Terrell, *Black Robe: The Life of Pierre-Jean de Smet . . .* (Garden City, N.Y.: Doubleday, 1964); William L. Davis, S.J., "Peter John DeSmet," *PNQ* 32 (April 1941): 167-96; 33 (April 1942): 123-52; 35 (January 1944): 29-43; 35 (April 1944): 121-42. Priests' memoirs include S. J. Point, *Wil-*

derness Kingdom: Indian Life in the Rocky Mountains, 1840-1847 (New York: Holt, Rinehart and Winston, 1967); Lawrence Palladino, S.J., *Indian and White in the Northwest: A History of Catholicity in Montana, 1831-1891*, 2d ed. (Lancaster, Penn.: Wickersham, 1922); A. B. Partoll, ed., *Mengarini's Narrative of the Rockies...and St. Mary's Mission*, Sources in Northwest History, no. 25 (Missoula: University of Montana, 1938). For the later history of the Jesuits in Montana, see Gerald McKevitt, S.J., "'The Jump That Saved the Rocky Mountain Mission': Jesuit Recruitment and the Pacific Northwest," *PHR* 55 (August 1986): 429-54. On the Helena Diocese, see Cornelia Flaherty, *Go with Haste into the Mountains: A History of the Helena Diocese* (Helena: Diocese Office, 1984). For St. Mary's Mission, see Lucylle H. Evans, *St. Mary's in the Rocky Mountains* (Stevensville, Mont.: Creative Historical Consultants, 1976). A superb fictional treatment of the missionary enterprise to the Indians in Montana is Mildred Walker, *If a Lion Could Talk* (New York: Harcourt, Brace, Jovanovich, 1970).

Chapter 4. The Mining Frontier

The best general treatments of mining in the Far West and in the Rockies are William J. Trimble, *The Mining Advance into the Inland Empire* (Madison: University of Wisconsin Press, 1914); T. A. Rickard, *A History of American Mining* (New York and London: McGraw-Hill, 1932); Rodman Paul, *Mining Frontier of the Far West, 1848-1880* (New York: Holt, Rinehart and Winston, 1963); Ronald C. Brown, *Hard-Rock Miners: The Intermountain West, 1860-1920* (College Station: Texas A&M University Press, 1979); Mark Wyman, *Hard Rock Epic: Western Miners and the Industrial Revolution* (Berkeley: University of California Press, 1979); Otis E. Young Jr., *Western Mining* (Norman: Oklahoma University Press, 1970); Young, *Black Powder and Hand Steel: Miners and Machines on the Old Western Frontier* (Norman: University of Oklahoma Press, 1976); William S. Greever, *The Bonanza West: The Story of the Western Mining Rushes, 1848-1900* (Norman: University of Oklahoma Press, 1963). See also older studies such as W. T. Mendenhall, *Gold and Silver Mining in Montana* (Boston: Collins Press, 1890); James A. Macknight, *The Mines of Montana* (Helena: C. K. Wells, 1892).

The best accounts of Montana's gold rushes are Muriel S. Wolle, *Montana Pay Dirt* (Chicago: Sage Books, 1963), on ghost towns and local gold rushes, and Larry S. Barsness, *Gold Camp: Alder Gulch and Virginia City, Montana* (New York: Hastings House, 1962). A lively popular history of the Montana gold rushes is Dan Cushman, *Montana: The Gold Frontier* (Great Falls: Stay Away Joe Publishing, 1973).

Revealing and instructive Montana goldfield memoirs and diaries include Andrew F. Rolle, ed., *The Road to Virginia City: The Diary of James Knox Polk Miller* (Norman: University of Oklahoma Press, 1960); L. Lyman Tyler, ed., *The Montana Gold Rush Diary of Kate Dunlap* (Denver: F. A. Rosenstock—Old West Publishing Company, 1969). Reminiscences published in *Contributions to the Historical Society of Montana* include Henry Edgar, "Journal of Henry Edgar—1963," vol. 3 (Helena: State Publishing Company, 1900): 124-42; Edgar, "Barney Hughes: An Appreciation," vol. 7 (Helena: Montana Historical and Miscellaneous Library, 1910): 197-8; Peter Ronan, "Discovery of Alder Gulch," vol. 3 (Helena: State Publishing Company, 1900): 143-52; James Fergus, "A Leaf from the Diary of James Fergus," vol. 2 (Helena: State Publishing Company, 1896): 252-4; David B. Weaver, "Early Days in Emigrant Gulch," vol. 7 (Helena: Montana Historical and Miscellaneous Library, 1910): 73-96.

For prospectors' methods, see Otis E. Young Jr., "The Prospectors: Some Considerations on their Craft," in *Reflections of Western Historians*, ed. John A. Carroll (Tucson: University of Arizona Press, 1969); Carroll, "The Craft of the Prospector," *Montana* 20 (Winter 1970): 28-39. For placer techniques, see Rodman W. Paul, *California Gold: The Beginning of Mining in the Far West* (Lincoln: University of Nebraska Press, 1965). On gold-rush boom psychology, see Grace Vance Erickson, "The Sun River Stampede," *Montana* 3 (January 1953): 73-78.

The best general studies of violence and vigilantism are Richard M. Brown, *Strain of Violence: Historical Studies of American Violence and Vigilantism* (New York: Oxford University Press, 1975); Wayne Gard, *Frontier Justice* (Norman: University of Oklahoma Press, 1949); W. Eugene Hollon, *Frontier Violence: Another Look* (New York: Oxford University Press, 1974). The classic accounts of Montana vigilantes include the first-hand account by Thomas Dimsdale, *The Vigilantes of Montana* (1866; reprint, Norman: Oklahoma University Press, 1953); Nathaniel P. Langford, *Vigilante Days and Ways* (1890; reprint, Missoula: University of Montana Press, 1957). Secondary accounts that tend to follow the apologetic tradition established by Dimsdale and Langford include Helen Fitzgerald Sanders and William H. Bertche Jr., eds., *X. Beidler, Vigilante* (Norman: University of Oklahoma Press, 1957); Hoffman Birney, *Vigilantes* (Philadelphia: Penn Publishing Company, 1929); Hubert H. Bancroft, *Popular Tribunals* (San Francisco: History Company, 1887). For modern reconsiderations, see Merrill G. Burlingame, "Montana's Righteous Hangmen: A Reconsideration," *Montana* 28 (October 1978): 36-49; Lew L. Callaway, *Montana's Righteous Hangmen: The Vigilantes in Action* (Norman: University of Oklahoma Press, 1982); R. E.

Mather and F. E. Boswell, *Hanging the Sheriff: A Biography of Henry Plummer* (Salt Lake City: University of Utah Press, 1987). See also Howard Temperley, *Guns, Gold and Vigilantes: Government on the Montana and British Columbia Mining Frontiers* (Norwich, England: University of Norwich, 1983); Rex C. Myers, "The Fateful Numbers 3-7-77: A Reexamination," *Montana* 24 (Autumn 1974): 67-70; J. W. Smurr, "Afterthoughts on the Vigilantes," *Montana* 8 (Spring 1958): 8-20; John W. Caughey, "Their Majesties the Mob," *PHR* 26 (August 1957): 217-34.

The best overviews of transportation in the West are Oscar O. Winther, *The Transportation Frontier: Trans-Mississippi West, 1865-1885* (New York: Holt, Rinehart and Winston, 1964); Winther, *Old Oregon Country: A History of Frontier Trade, Transportation, and Travel* (Bloomington: Indiana University Press, 1950); W. Turrentine Jackson, *Wagon Roads West* (Berkeley: University of California Press, 1950); Jackson, "Transportation in the American West," in *Historians and the American West*, ed. Michael P. Malone (Lincoln: University of Nebraska Press, 1983), pp. 123-47.

For discussions of Montana travel routes, see Oscar O. Winther, "Early Commercial Importance of the Mullan Road," *Oregon Historical Quarterly* 46 (March 1945): 22-35; Alton B. Oviatt, "Pacific Coast Competition for the Gold Camp Trade of Montana," *PNQ* 56 (October 1965): 168-76; Henry Talkington, "Mullan Road," *Washington Historical Quarterly* 7 (October 1916): 301-6; Alexander C. McGregor, "The Economic Impact of the Mullan Road on Walla Walla, 1860-1883," *PNQ* 65 (July 1974): 118-29. For the Wells Fargo operations in Montana, see W. Turrentine Jackson, *Wells Fargo Stagecoaching in Montana Territory* (Helena: Montana Historical Society Press, 1979).

Solid studies of the river routes to Montana's goldfields include William E. Lass, *A History of Steamboating on the Upper Missouri River* (Lincoln: University of Nebraska Press, 1962); Lass, "Steamboats on the Yellowstone," *Montana* 35 (Autumn 1985): 26-41; Hiram M. Chittenden, *History of Early Steamboat Navigation on the Missouri River*, 2 vols. (New York: Francis P. Harper, 1903); Alton B. Oviatt, "Steamboat Traffic on the Upper Missouri River, 1859-1869," *PNQ* 40 (April 1949): 93-105. For personal experiences on Montana-bound steamboats, see Lee Silliman, "'Up this Great River': Daniel Weston's Missouri River Steamboat Diary," *Montana* 30 (Summer 1980): 32-41; Rex C. Myers, ed., "'To the Dear Ones At Home': Elizabeth Fisk's Missouri River Trip, 1867," *Montana* 32 (Summer 1982): 40-49.

The classic study of the Whoop-Up Trail is Paul F. Sharp, *Whoop-Up Country: The Canadian American West, 1865-1885* (Norman: University of Oklahoma Press, 1973). Revisions to Sharp can be found in Henry C.

Klassen, "I. G. Baker and Company in Calgary, 1875-1884," *Montana* 35 (Summer 1985): 40-55; James M. Francis, "Montana Business and Canadian Regionalism in the 1870s and 1880s," *WHQ* 12 (July 1981): 291-304. On Fort Benton, see Joel Overholser, *Fort Benton: The World's Innermost Port* (Fort Benton: Privately published, 1987).

The Northern Overland Route is discussed in Helen McCann White, ed., *Ho! For the Gold Fields: Northern Overland Wagon Trains of the 1860's* (St. Paul: Minnesota Historical Society, 1966); W. M. Underhill, "The Northern Overland Route to Montana," *Washington Historical Quarterly* 23 (July 1932): 177-95; W. Turrentine Jackson, "The Fisk Expeditions to the Montana Gold Fields," *PNQ* 33 (July 1942): 265-82. The short-lived Carroll Trail is dealt with in Lee Silliman, "The Carroll Trail: Utopian Enterprise," *Montana* 24 (April 1974): 2-17. On the Salt Lake City connection, see Betty M. Madsen and Brigham D. Madsen, *North to Montana! Jehus, Bullwhackers, and Mule Skinners on the Montana Trail* (Salt Lake City: University of Utah Press, 1980). The history of the dangerous Bozeman Trail route is best detailed in Merrill G. Burlingame, *John M. Bozeman: Montana Trailmaker* (Bozeman: Gallatin County Tribune, 1971); Robert A. Murray, *The Bozeman Trail: Highway of History* (Boulder, Colo.: Pruett Publishing Company, 1988).

The mining camps as frontier urban areas have drawn increasing historical attention. The best recent studies include Duane A. Smith, *Rocky Mountain Mining Camps: The Urban Frontier* (Bloomington: Indiana University Press, 1967); Elliott West, *The Saloon on the Rocky Mountain Mining Frontier* (Lincoln: University of Nebraska Press, 1979); Paula Petrik, *No Step Backward: Women and Family on the Rocky Mountain Mining Frontier, Helena, Montana, 1865-1900* (Helena: Montana Historical Society Press, 1987). On African Americans on the frontier, see William L. Lang, "The Nearly Forgotten Blacks on Last Chance Gulch," *PNQ* 70 (April 1979): 50-57; J. W. Smurr, "Jim Crow Out West," in *Historical Essays on Montana and the Northwest*, ed. J. W. Smurr and K. R. Toole (Helena: Western Press, 1957), pp. 149-203. The Chinese in the gold rush are covered in Robert R. Swartout Jr., "From Kwantung to Big Sky: The Chinese Experience in Frontier Montana," *Montana* 38 (Winter 1988): 42-53; Randall E. Rohe, "After the Gold Rush: Chinese Mining in the Far West, 1850-1890," *Montana* 32 (Autumn 1982): 2-19. Anti-Chinese attitudes are discussed in Larry D. Quinn, "Chink, Chink, Chinaman: The Beginnings of Nativism in Montana," *PNQ* 58 (April 1967): 82-89.

For other mining camp conditions and problems, see Alice Cochran, "The Gold Dust Trail: Jack Langrishe's Mining Town Theaters," *Montana* 20 (Spring 1970): 58-69; Harrison A. Trexler, *Flour and Wheat in Mon-*

tana Gold Camps (Missoula: Dunston Printing and Stationery, 1918); W. W. Alderson, "Gold Camp Tubers," *Montana* 3 (Autumn 1953): 46-49; Dorothy M. Johnson, "Flour Famine in Alder Gulch, 1864," *Montana* 7 (Winter 1957): 18-27.

CHAPTER 5. MONTANA TERRITORY

The best general study of western territories is Earl S. Pomeroy, *The Territories and the United States: 1861-1890*, 2d ed. (Seattle: University of Washington Press, 1969). Also important are Jack E. Eblen, *The First and Second United States Empires* (Pittsburgh: University of Pittsburgh Press, 1968); Kenneth N. Owens, "Pattern and Structure in Western Territorial Politics," *WHQ* 1 (October 1970): 373-92. An important study of Montana's territorial political pattern is Richard B. Roeder, "Electing Montana's Territorial Delegates: The Beginnings of a Political System," *Montana* 38 (Summer 1988): 58-67. For an especially insightful look at Montana's pioneer generation, see Clyde Milner II, "The Shared Memory of Montana's Pioneers," *Montana* 37 (Winter 1987): 2-13.

The best study of Montana's territorial period is Clark C. Spence, *Territorial Politics and Government in Montana, 1864-1889* (Urbana: University of Illinois Press, 1975). See also Spence, "The Territorial Officers of Montana," *PHR* 30 (May 1961): 123-60; Robert E. Albright, "The Relations of Montana with the Federal Government, 1864-1889" (Ph.D. diss., Stanford University, Stanford, Calif., 1933); Elinor E. Malic, "The Political Development of Montana, 1862-1889" (M.A. thesis, University of California, Berkeley, 1923). See also Robert G. Athearn, "Early Territorial Montana: A Problem in Colonial Administration," *Montana* 1 (July 1951): 15-21.

The creation and naming of Montana is the subject of Wilbur E. Sanders, "Montana Organization and Naming," *Contributions to the Historical Society of Montana*, vol. 7 (Helena: Montana Historical and Miscellaneous Library, 1910), pp. 15-60; Merle W. Wells, "Territorial Government in the Inland Empire: The Movement to Create Columbia Territory, 1864-69," *PNQ* 44 (April 1953): 80-87.

The Civil War political divisiveness and the role of Confederate sympathizers in Montana are discussed by Robert G. Athearn, "Civil War Days in Montana," *PHR* 29 (February 1960): 19-33; James L. Thane Jr., "The Myth of Confederate Sentiment in Montana," *Montana* 17 (April 1967): 14-19; Stanley R. Davison and Dale Tash, "Confederate Backwash in Montana Territory," *Montana* (October 1967): 50-58.

The best work on Thomas Francis Meagher is Robert G. Athearn, *Thomas Francis Meagher: An Irish Revolutionary in America* (Boulder: University of Colorado Press, 1949). For other discussions of Meagher in

Montana, see the writings of James L. Thane Jr., "Montana Territory: The Formative Years, 1862-1870" (Ph.D. diss., University of Iowa, Cedar Rapids, 1972); "Thomas Francis Meagher: The Acting-One" (M.A. thesis, University of Montana, Missoula, 1967); "The Montana 'Indian War' of 1867," *Arizona and the West* 8 (Summer 1968): 153-70; "An Active Acting-Governor: Thomas Francis Meagher's Administration in Montana Territory," *Journal of the West* 9 (October 1970): 537-51.

On other aspects of territorial politics and jurisprudence, see Clark C. Spence, "Spoilsmen in Montana: James M. Ashley," *Montana* 18 (Spring 1968): 24-35; Spence, "Beggars to Washington: Montana's Territorial Bench in Montana, 1864-1889," *Montana* 13 (Winter 1974): 3-13; Stanley R. Davison, "1871: Montana's Year of Political Fusion," *Montana* 21 (Spring 1971): 44-55. For commentary on territorial courts, see John D. W. Guice, *The Rocky Mountain Bench: The Territorial Supreme Courts of Colorado, Montana, and Wyoming, 1861-1890* (New Haven, Conn.: Yale University Press, 1972). See also two works by Gordon M. Bakken, *The Development of Law of the Rocky Mountain Frontier: Civil Law and Society, 1850-1912* (Westport, Conn.: Greenwood Press, 1983) and *Rocky Mountain Constitution Making, 1850-1912* (New York: Greenwood Press, 1987).

CHAPTER 6. INDIAN REMOVAL

The best one-volume treatment of the destruction of Indian land titles and the Indian wars in the West is Robert M. Utley, *The Indian Frontier of the American West, 1846-1890* (Albuquerque: University of New Mexico Press, 1984). For the military story, see Robert A. Wooster, *The Military and United States Indian Policy, 1865-1903* (New Haven, Conn.: Yale University Press, 1988); Robert M. Utley, *Frontier Regulars: The United States Army and the Indian, 1866-1891* (New York: Macmillan, 1973); Paul Andrew Hutton, *Phil Sheridan and His Army* (Lincoln: University of Nebraska Press, 1985); Robert G. Athearn, *William Tecumseh Sherman and the Settlement of the West* (Norman: University of Oklahoma Press, 1956); Thomas W. Dunlay, *Wolves for the Blue Soldiers: Indian Scouts and Auxiliaries with the United States Army, 1860-1890* (Lincoln: University of Nebraska Press, 1982); Don Rickey Jr., *Forty Miles a Day on Beans and Hay: The Enlisted Soldier Fighting the Indian Wars* (Norman: University of Oklahoma Press, 1963). For an anti-military viewpoint on the wars, see Ralph K. Andrist, *The Long Death* (New York: Macmillan, 1964). The best discussion of Indian removal in Montana is in Merrill G. Burlingame, *The Montana Frontier* (1942; reprint, Bozeman: Big Sky Books, 1974).

The Fort Laramie treaties are discussed in L. R. Hafen and F. M.

Young, *Fort Laramie and the Pageant of the West* (Glendale, Calif.: Arthur H. Clark, 1938). The Stevens treaties in Montana are covered in Kent Richards, *Isaac I. Stevens: Young Man in a Hurry* (Provo: Brigham Young University Press, 1979). For the several Crow treaties, see Burton M. Smith, "Politics and the Crow Indian Land Cessions, 1851-1904," *Montana* 36 (Autumn 1986): 24-37; A. Glen Humphreys, "The Crow Indian Treaties of 1868 . . . ," *Annals of Wyoming* 42 (Spring 1971): 73-89.

The Marias Massacre is treated apologetically in Robert J. Ege, *Strike Them Hard* (Bellevue, Neb.: Old Army Press, 1970). It is put into national perspective by Paul A. Hutton, "Phil Sheridan's Pyrrhic Victory: The Piegan Massacre, Army Politics, and the Transfer Debate," *Montana* 32 (Spring 1982): 32-43. The removal of the Flatheads is described in Michael Harrison, "Chief Charlot's Battle with Bureaucracy," *Montana* 10 (Autumn 1960): 27-33; Arthur L. Stone, "Charlot's Last March," in *Montana Margins: A State Anthology*, ed. Joseph Kinsey Howard (New Haven, Conn.: Yale University Press, 1946), pp. 8-15.

On the Indian attack on the Bozeman Trail, see Anthony McGinnis, "Strike and Retreat: Intertribal Warfare and the Powder River War, 1865-1868," *Montana* 30 (Autumn 1980): 30-43; Susan Badger Doyle, "Indian Perspectives of the Bozeman Trail, 1864-1868," *Montana* 40 (Winter 1990): 56-67.

The literature on the Sioux, the invasion of whites, and the military pressure on the Sioux is large. The best studies of the Indian background are James C. Olson, *Red Cloud and the Sioux Problem* (Lincoln: University of Nebraska Press, 1956); George E. Hyde, *Red Cloud's Folk: A History of the Oglala Sioux* (Norman: University of Oklahoma Press, 1937); Richard White, "The Winning of the West: The Expansion of the Western Sioux in the Eighteenth and Nineteenth Centuries," *Journal of American History* 45 (September 1978): 319-43. The military is covered best in Robert A. Murray, *Military Posts in the Powder River Country of Wyoming, 1865-1894* (Lincoln: University of Nebraska Press, 1968); Dee Brown, *Fort Phil Kearny: An American Saga* (New York: G. P. Putnam's Sons, 1962). A popular history of the Bozeman Trail is Dorothy M. Johnson, *The Bloody Bozeman* (New York: McGraw-Hill, 1971). See also Grace R. Hebard and E. A. Brininstool, *The Bozeman Trail*, 2 vols. (Cleveland: Arthur H. Clark, 1922). For the military situation on the Yellowstone, see Mark H. Brown, *The Plainsmen of the Yellowstone* (New York: G. P. Putnam's Sons, 1961); Robert M. Utley, "War Houses in the Sioux Country: The Military Occupation of the Lower Yellowstone," *Montana* 35 (Autumn 1985): 18-25.

The military-Indian conflict is described and analyzed in John C. Ewers, "Intertribal Warfare as the Precursor of Indian-White Warfare on the Great Plains," *WHQ* 6 (October 1975): 397-410; Richard Slotkin, *The Fatal Environment: The Myth of the Frontier in the Age of Industrialism* (New York: Atheneum, 1985); Richard Drinnon, *Facing West: The Metaphysics of Indian Hating and Empire Building* (1980; reprint, New York: Shocken Books, 1990).

The 1876-77 Sioux campaign has generated an enormous literature. For the military precursor, see Donald Jackson, *Custer's Gold: The United States Cavalry Expedition of 1874* (New Haven, Conn.: Yale University Press, 1966). The best accounts of the war are Edgar I. Stewart, *Custer's Luck* (Norman: University of Oklahoma Press, 1955); John S. Gray, *The Centennial Campaign: The Sioux War of 1876* (1976; reprint, Norman: University of Oklahoma Press, 1988). Other good studies include James H. Bradley, *The March of the Montana Column*, ed. E. I. Stewart (Norman: University of Oklahoma Press, 1961); Martin F. Schmitt, ed., *General George Crook: His Autobiography* (Norman: University of Oklahoma Press, 1960); C. C. Smith, "Crook and Crazy Horse," *Montana* 16 (April 1966): 14-26. On other aspects of the war, see Mary C. Gillett, "U.S. Army Surgeons and the Big Horn-Yellowstone Expedition of 1876," *Montana* 39 (Winter 1989): 16-27; Jerome A. Greene, *Slim Buttes, 1876: An Episode of the Great Sioux War* (Norman: University of Oklahoma Press, 1982); Paul L. Hedren, "An Infantry Company in the Sioux Campaign, 1876," *Montana* 33 (Winter 1983): 30-39.

Writings on George A. Custer, which are too numerous to list, are often partisan and should be read with care. A superb and balanced interpretation is Robert M. Utley, *Cavalier in Buckskin: George Armstrong Custer and the Western Military Frontier* (Norman: University of Oklahoma Press, 1988). See also Edgar I. Stewart, *Custer's Luck* (Norman: University of Oklahoma Press, 1955); Robert J. Ege, *Curse Not His Curls* (Fort Collins, Colo.: Old Army Press, 1974); Jay Monaghan, *Custer: The Life of General George Armstrong Custer* (Garden City, N.Y.: Doubleday, 1959). For the divergence of opinion on Custer, myths about the battle, and its place in American culture, see Robert M. Utley, *Custer and the Great Controversy: The Origin and Development of a Legend* (Los Angeles: Westernlore Press, 1962); Brian W. Dippie, *Custer's Last Stand: The Anatomy of an American Myth* (Missoula: University of Montana Press, 1976); Stephen E. Ambrose, *Crazy Horse and Custer* (Garden City, N.Y.: Doubleday, 1975). For an iconoclastic account of Custer, see Evan S. Connell, *Son of the Morning Star: Custer and the Little Bighorn* (San Francisco: North Point Press, 1984).

For treatments of the campaigns of Nelson A. Miles, see Brian Pohanka, ed., *Nelson A. Miles: A Documentary Biography of his Military Career, 1861-1903* (Glendale, Calif.: Arthur A. Clark, 1985); Virginia M.

Johnson, *The Unregimented General* (Boston: Houghton, Mifflin, 1962); Nelson A. Miles, *Personal Recollections and Observations* (Chicago: Warner, 1896); Milo M. Quaife, ed., *"Yellowstone Kelly": Memoirs of Luther S. Kelly* (New Haven, Conn.: Yale University Press, 1926); Don Rickey Jr., "The Battle of Wolf Mountain," *Montana* 13 (Spring 1963): 44-54.

The Nez Perce flight through Montana in 1877 is best described from the military viewpoint in Mark H. Brown, *The Flight of the Nez Perce* (New York: Putnam, 1967). For the Indian side, see Allen P. Slickpoo, *Noon Nee-Me-Poo (We, the Nez Perces) Culture and History of the Nez Perces* (Lapwai, Ida.: Nez Perce Tribe, 1973); Alvin M. Josephy Jr., *The Nez Perce Indians and the Opening of the Northwest* (New Haven, Conn.: Yale University Press, 1965); Merrill D. Beal, *"I Will Fight No More Forever," Chief Joseph and the Nez Perce War* (Seattle: University of Washington Press, 1963); L. V. McWhorter, *"Hear Me My Chiefs!": Nez Perce History and Legend* (Caldwell, Ida.: Caxton, 1952). For aspects of the Nez Perce flight, see William L. Lang, "Where Did the Nez Perces Go in Yellowstone in 1877?" *Montana* 40 (Winter 1990): 14-29; Rex C. Myers, "The Settlers and the Nez Perce," *Montana* 27 (Autumn 1977): 20-29; Stanley R. Davison, "A Century Ago: The Nez Perce and the Tortuous Pursuit," *Montana* 27 (Autumn 1977): 2-19. On the Bannock War, see George F. Brimlow, *The Bannock War of 1878* (Caldwell, Ida.: Caxton, 1938).

For the military frontier in Montana after 1877, consult Lewis O. Saum, "Stanley Huntley Interviews Sitting Bull: Event, Pseudo Event or Fabrication?" *Montana* 32 (Spring 1982): 2-15; Gary Pennanen, "Sitting Bull: Indian Without a Country," *Canadian Historical Review* 51 (June 1970): 123-40; Nicholas P. Hardeman, "Brick Stronghold of the Border: Fort Assinniboine, 1879-1911," *Montana* 29 (April 1979): 54-67; Donald Smythe, S.J., "John J. Pershing at Fort Assinniboine," *Montana* 18 (Winter 1968): 18-23. For the moving story of the Northern Cheyennes, see Gary L. Roberts, "The Shame of Little Wolf," *Montana* 28 (July 1978): 36-47; Mari Sandoz, *Cheyenne Autumn* (New York: McGraw-Hill, 1953).

The conditions on the reservations and relationships with whites is the subject of several studies. The best ones are Helen B. West, "Starvation Winter of the Blackfeet," *Montana* 9 (Winter 1959) 2-19; Orlan J. Svingen, "The Case of Spotted Hawk and Little Whirlwind: An American Indian Dreyfus Affair," *WHQ* 15 (July 1984): 281-98; Colin G. Calloway, "Sword Bearer and the 'Crow Outbreak' of 1887," *Montana* 36 (Autumn 1986): 38-51; Robert M. Utley, *The Last Days of the Sioux Nation* (New Haven, Conn.: Yale University Press, 1963). On the Dawes Act, see Janet A. McDonnell, *The Dispossession of the American Indian, 1887–1934* (Bloomington: Indiana University Press, 1991); Francis Paul Prucha, *The*

Great Father, 2 vols. (Lincoln: University of Nebraska Press, 1984); Leonard A. Carlson, *Indians, Bureaucrats, and Land: The Dawes Act and the Decline of Indian Farming* (Westport, Conn.: Greenwood, 1981); Frederick Hoxie, *A Final Promise: the Campaign to Assimilate the Indians, 1880-1920* (Lincoln: University of Nebraska Press, 1984); Loring B. Priest, *Uncle Sam's Stepchildren: The Reformation of United States Indian Policy, 1865-1887* (New York: Octagon, 1942); Henry E. Fritz, *The Movement for Indian Assimilation, 1860-1890* (Philadelphia: University of Pennsylvania Press, 1963); Wilcomb E. Washburn, *The Assault on Indian Tribalism: The General Allotment Law (Dawes Act) of 1887* (Philadelphia: J. B. Lippincott, 1975).

CHAPTER 7. STOCKMEN AND THE OPEN RANGE

The best overall treatment of the stockraising boom on the Montana frontier is Ernest S. Osgood, *The Day of the Cattleman* (1929; reprint, Chicago: University of Chicago Press, 1970). Other important books on the open-range cattle era are Louis Pelzer, *The Cattleman's Frontier* (Glendale, Calif.: Arthur H. Clark, 1936); Lewis Atherton, *The Cattle Kings* (Bloomington: Indiana University Press, 1961); C. W. Towne and E. N. Wentworth, *Cattle and Men* (Norman: University of Oklahoma Press, 1955); E. E. Dale, *The Range Cattle Industry . . . from 1865 to 1925*, 2d ed. (Norman: University of Oklahoma Press, 1960); E. S. Osgood, "The Cattleman in the Agricultural History of the Northwest," *Agricultural History* 3 (July 1929): 117-30; Louis Pelzer, "Financial Management of the Cattle Ranges," *Journal of Economic and Business History* 2 (August 1930): 723-41; Harold E. Briggs, "The Development and Decline of Open Range Ranching in the Northwest," *Mississippi Valley Historical Review* 20 (March 1934): 521-36. For 1880s statistics, see Joseph Nimmo Jr., *Report in Regard to the Range and Ranch Cattle Business in the United States* (Washington, D.C.: Government Printing Office, 1885). For the overall effect of cattle enterprises on the northern ranges, see Gene M. Gressley, *Bankers and Cattlemen* (New York: Alfred A. Knopf, 1966); W. Turrentine Jackson, *The Enterprising Scot: Investors in the American West after 1873* (Edinburgh: Edinburgh University Press, 1968); John Clay, *My Life on the Range* (New York: Antiquarian Press, 1924).

The open-range cattle business in Montana is chronicled in Robert S. Fletcher, *Organization of the Range Cattle Business in Eastern Montana*, Montana Agricultural Experiment Station Bulletin 265 (Bozeman, 1932); Fletcher, "The End of the Open Range in Eastern Montana," *Mississippi Valley Historical Review* 16 (September 1929): 188-211; Harold E. Briggs,

Frontiers of the Northwest: A History of the Upper Missouri Valley (New York: D. Appleton-Century Company, 1940). For descriptions of eastern Montana cattle ranching and photographs, see Mark H. Brown and W. R. Felton's volumes on the photography of L. A. Huffman of Miles City, *The Frontier Years* (New York: Holt, Rinehart and Winston, 1955), and *Before Barbed Wire* (New York: Holt, Rinehart and Winston, 1956). For articles in *Montana* on cattlemen, see Michael Kennedy's anthology, *Cowboys and Cattlemen* (New York: Hastings House, 1964).

The texture of Montana's ranching history is described in studies of individual ranchers and ranches. Some of the best include Lee M. Ford, "Bob Ford, Sun River Cowman," *Montana* 9 (January 1959): 30-43; William S. Reese, "Granville Stuart of the DHS Ranch, 1879-1887," *Montana* 31 (Summer 1981): 14-27; David Remley, "'To Struggle Against an Adverse Fate': Granville Stuart, Cowman," *Montana* 31 (Summer 1981): 28-41; Donald H. Welsh, "Cosmopolitan Cattle King: Pierre Wibaux and the W Bar Ranch," *Montana* 20 (Spring 1970): 50-57; J. Evetts Haley, *The XIT Ranch of Texas*, 2d ed. (Norman: University of Oklahoma Press, 1967); W. M. Pearce, *The Matador Land and Cattle Company* (Norman: University of Oklahoma Press, 1964). Robert H. Fletcher's *Free Grass to Fences: The Montana Cattle Range Story* (New York: University Publishers, 1960) is the best account of the Montana Stockgrowers Association. For an update, see Vivian A. Paladin, ed., *Montana Stockgrower: Special Centennial Edition*, vol. 55 (June 1984).

The best first-hand accounts are Paul C. Phillips, ed., *Forty Years on the Frontier, as Seen in the Journals and Reminiscences of Granville Stuart*, 2 vols. (Cleveland: Arthur H. Clark, 1925); John R. Barrows, *Ubet* (1934; Lincoln: University of Nebraska Press, 1987); E. C. Abbott and Helena H. Smith, *We Pointed Them North* (New York: Farrar and Rinehart, 1939); Nannie Alderson and Helena H. Smith, *A Bride Goes West* (New York: Farrar and Rinehart, 1942); Walt Coburn, *Pioneer Cattlemen in Montana: The Story of the Circle C Ranch* (Norman: University of Oklahoma Press, 1968); Isabelle Randall, *A Lady's Ranch Life in Montana* (London: W. H. Allen and Co., 1887); Robert Vaughan, *Then and Now; or, Thirty-Six Years in the Rockies* (Minneapolis: Tribune Printing Company, 1900).

On the problem of rustling and cattlemen-vigilantes, see Joan Bishop, "Vigorous Attempts to Prosecute: Pinkerton Men on Montana's Range, 1914," *Montana* 30 (Spring 1980): 2-15; Oscar O. Mueller, "The Central Montana Vigilante Raids of 1884," *Montana* 1 (January 1951): 23-35. For discussions on bison and their demise, see Larry Barsness, *Heads, Hides & Horns: The Compleat Buffalo Book* (Fort Worth: Texas Christian University, 1985); Francis Haines, *The Buffalo* (New York: Crowell, 1970);

James A. and C. Ivar Dolph, "The American Bison: His Annihilation and Preservation," *Montana* 26 (Summer 1976): 2-13; LeRoy Barnett, "The Ghastly Harvest: Montana's Buffalo Bone Trade," *Montana* 26 (Summer 1976): 14-25. For revision of the standard view of the bison's demise, see Rudolph W. Houchy, "The Buffalo Disaster of 1882," *North Dakota History* 50 (Winter 1983): 23-30; and Kenneth N. Owens and Sally L. Owens, "Buffalo and Bacteria," *Montana* 37 (Spring 1987): 65-67.

See J. Orin Oliphant on one source for Montana livestock in "The Cattle Trade from the Far Northwest to Montana," *Agricultural History* 6 (April 1932): 69-83. On the hard winter of 1886-87, see Leland E. Stuart's revisionist article, "The Winter of 1886-1887: The Last of Whose 5,000?" *Montana* 38 (Winter 1988): 32-41. For older interpretations of the hard winter, see Robert S. Fletcher, "That Hard Winter in Montana, 1886-1887," *Agricultural History* 4 (October 1930): 123-30; Ray H. Mattison, "The Hard Winter and the Range Cattle Business," *Montana* 1 (October 1951): 5-22.

Not much has been written on sheep raising in Montana. Edward Wentworth, *American Sheep Trails* (Ames: Iowa State College Press, 1948) is the best introduction. On Montana pioneer sheep operations, see Dick Pace, "Henry Sieben: Pioneer Montana Stockman," *Montana* 29 (Winter 1979): 2-15; John F. Bishop, "Beginnings of the Montana Sheep Industry," *Montana* 1 (April 1951): 5-8; Lee Rostad, "Charley Bair: King of Western Sheepmen," *Montana* 20 (Autumn 1970): 50-61. Jim Drummond, *Montana's Sheep Trails* (Helena: Montana Woolgrowers Association, 1983), presents an abbreviated history of sheep growing and the woolgrowers organization in Montana.

CHAPTER 8. RAILROADS, SILVER, AND STATEHOOD

There is no recent overall history of western railroads, but older studies give an adequate background. The best are John F. Stover, *The Life and Decline of the American Railroad* (New York: Oxford University Press, 1970); Robert E. Riegel, *The Story of Western Railroads* (New York: Macmillan, 1926); Julius Grodinsky, *Transcontinental Railway Strategy, 1869-1893* (Philadelphia: University of Pennsylvania Press, 1962). There is no general history of railroads and railroad-building in Montana, but Rex C. Myers, "Montana: A State and Its Relationship with Railroads, 1864-1970" (Ph.D. diss., University of Montana, Missoula, 1972), gives the best introduction to the subject. See also Thomas T. Taber, "Short Lines of the Treasure State: The Histories of the Independently Operated Railroads of Montana" (April 1960), ms., Montana Historical Society Library, Helena.

For discussions of the Utah & Northern, see Robert G. Athearn, "Railroad to a Far Off Country: The Utah and Northern," *Montana* 18 (Autumn 1968): 2-23; Athearn, *Union Pacific Country* (Chicago: Rand McNally, 1971); Merrill D. Beal, *Intermountain Railroads, Standard and Narrow Gauge* (Caldwell, Ida.: Caxton Printers, 1962). For the Milwaukee Railroad, see August Derleth, *The Milwaukee Road: Its First Hundred Years* (New York: Creative Age Press, 1948). On the Burlington Northern, see Richard C. Overton, *The Burlington Route* (New York: Alfred A. Knopf, 1965).

On the Northern Pacific Railroad, see Robert L. Peterson, "The Completion of the Northern Pacific Railroad System in Montana, 1883-1893," in *The Montana Past: An Anthology*, ed. Michael P. Malone and Richard B. Roeder (Missoula: University of Montana Press, 1970); E. V. Smalley, *History of the Northern Pacific Railroad* (New York: G. P. Putnam's Sons, 1883). See also a modern distillation of Smalley, Louis T. Renz, *The History of the Northern Pacific Railroad* (Fairfield, Wash.: Ye Galleon Press, 1980). Also see Edward W. Nolan, *Northern Pacific Views: The Railroad Photography of F. Jay Haynes, 1876-1905* (Helena: Montana Historical Society Press, 1983); James B. Hedges, *Henry Villard and the Railways of the Northwest* (New York: Russell and Russell, 1930).

For the land promotions and colonizing efforts of the Northern Pacific and other railroads in Montana, see two articles by Ross R. Cotroneo, "Selling Land on the Montana Plains, 1905-1915: Northern Pacific Railway's Land-Grant Sales Policies," *Montana* 37 (Spring 1987): 40-49; and "Western Land Marketings by the Northern Pacific Railway," *PHR* 27 (August 1968): 299-320. See also Theodore Schwinden, "The Northern Pacific Land Grants in Congress," (M.A. thesis, University of Montana, Missoula, 1950); Thomas A. Clinch, "The Northern Pacific Railroad and Montana's Mineral Lands," *PHR* 34 (August 1965): 323-35.

For studies of the Great Northern Railway and James J. Hill, see Albro Martin, *James J. Hill and the Opening of the Northwest* (New York: Oxford University Press, 1976); Stewart H. Holbrook, *James J. Hill: A Great Life in Brief* (New York: Random House, 1955); J. G. Pyle, *The Life of James J. Hill*, 2 vols. (New York: P. Smith, 1916-17). See also William L. Lang, "Corporate Point Men and the Creation of the Montana Central Railroad, 1882-87," *Great Plains Quarterly* 10 (Summer 1990): 152-66; Howard Schonberger, "James J. Hill and the Orient," *Minnesota History* 41 (Winter 1968): 178-90; John B. Rae, "The Great Northern's Land Grant," *Journal of Economic History* 12 (Spring 1952): 140-5.

On railroads and town development, see W. Thomas White, "Paris Gibson, James J. Hill & the 'New Minneapolis': The Great Falls Water Power and Townsite Company, 1882-1908," *Montana* 33 (Summer 1983):

60-69; White, "Commonwealth or Colony? Montana and the Railroads in the First Decade of Statehood," *Montana* 38 (Autumn 1988): 12-33; John C. Hudson, "Railroads and Urban Development," in *Centennial West*, ed. William L. Lang (Seattle: University of Washington Press, 1991); Hudson, "Main Streets of the Yellowstone Valley: Town-Building along the Northern Pacific in Montana," *Montana* 35 (Autumn 1985): 56-67. For an excellent discussion of pre-railroad urban development, see Carroll Van West, "Coulson and the Clark's Fork Bottom: The Economic Structure of a Pre-Railroad Community, 1874-1881," *Montana* 35 (Autumn 1985): 42-55.

Mining conditions in the Helena area are covered in Adolph Knopf, *Ore Deposits of the Helena Mining Region, Montana*, U.S. Geological Survey Bulletin 527 (Washington, D.C.: Government Printing Office, 1913); J. T. Pardee and F. C. Schrader, *Metalliferous Deposits of the Greater Helena Mining Region, Montana*, U.S. Geological Survey Bulletin 842 (Washington, D.C.: Government Printing Office, 1933). On Marysville, see Charles W. Goodale, "The Drumlummon Mine, Marysville, Montana," *Transactions of the American Institute of Mining Engineers* 49 (1915): 258-79; W. Turrentine Jackson, "The Irish Fox and the British Lion," *Montana* 9 (April 1959): 28-42; Clark C. Spence, "The Montana Company, Limited: A Case Study of Anglo-American Mining Investment," *Business History Review* 33 (Summer 1959): 190-203.

The best brief discussion of the development of silver mining in Montana is Robert A. Chadwick, "Montana's Silver Mining Era: Great Boom and Great Bust," *Montana* 32 (Spring 1982): 16-31. On the Philipsburg area, see S. F. Emmons and E. C. Eckel, *Contributions to Economic Geology 1906*, Geological Survey Bulletin 315 (Washington, D.C.: Government Printing Office, 1907); Donald L. Sorte, "The Hope Mining Company of Philipsburg" (M.A. thesis, University of Montana, Missoula, 1960). See also Dan Cushman, "Cordova Lode Comstock," *Montana* 9 (October 1959): 12-21; A. C. McMillan, "Granite's Glittering Glory," *Montana* 14 (July 1964): 62-73. Other mining districts are covered in Walter H. Weed and Louis V. Pirsson, *Geology of the Castle Mountain Mining District*, U.S. Geological Survey Bulletin 139 (Washington, D.C.: Government Printing Office, 1896); Alexander N. Winchell, *Mining Districts of the Dillon Quadrangle, Montana and Adjacent Areas*, U.S. Geological Survey Bulletin 574 (Washington, D.C.: Government Printing Office, 1914).

Clark C. Spence's *British Investments and the American Mining Frontier* (Ithaca, N.Y.: Cornell University Press, 1958), outlines foreign ownership of Montana mines, as does Patrick H. McLatchy, "A Collection of Data on Foreign Corporate Activity in the Territory of Montana,

1864-1889" (M.A. thesis, University of Montana, Missoula, 1961). See also Clark C. Spence, *Mining Engineers and the American West: The Lace-Boot Brigade, 1849-1933* (New Haven, Conn.: Yale University Press, 1970); Lewis Atherton, "Structure and Balance in Western Mining History," *Huntington Library Quarterly* 30 (November 1966): 55-84; Atherton, "The Mining Promoter in the Trans-Mississippi West," *WHQ* 1 (January 1970): 35-50.

For social conditions in the late territorial and early statehood periods, see Paula Petrik, *No Step Backward: Women and Family on the Rocky Mountain Mining Frontier, Helena, Montana, 1865-1900* (Helena: Montana Historical Society Press, 1987); Elliott West, *Growing Up with the Country: Childhood on the Far Western Frontier* (Albuquerque: University of New Mexico Press, 1989); Rex C. Myers, ed., *Lizzie: The Letters of Elizabeth Chester Fisk, 1864-1893* (Missoula: Mountain Press, 1989); Paula Petrik, "If She Be Content: The Development of Montana Divorce Law, 1865-1907," *WHQ* 18 (July 1987): 261-92. For discussions of urban politics, see Paula Petrik, "Strange Bedfellows: Prostitution, Politicians, and Moral Reform in Helena, Montana, 1885-1887," *Montana* 35 (Spring 1985): 2-13. On women's experiences, see Glenda Riley, *The Female Frontier: A Comparative View of Women on the Prairie and the Plains* (Lawrence: University Press of Kansas, 1988).

The movement toward statehood is covered in Clark Spence, *Territorial Politics and Government in Montana, 1864-1889* (Urbana: University of Illinois Press, 1975); Spence, *Montana: A History* (New York: W. W. Norton and Company, 1978); James M. Hamilton, *History of Montana: From Wilderness to Statehood* (1957; reprint, Portland: Binfords & Mort, 1970); Dave Walter, "'The Right Kind of Nail': Reactions to J. K. Toole's Montana Statehood Speech," *Montana* 37 (Autumn 1987): 46-57. On the woman's suffrage issue, see Leslie Wheeler, "Henry B. Blackwell, Woman Suffrage's Gray-Bearded Champion Comes to Montana, 1889," *Montana* 31 (Summer 1981): 2-13. For the political effects of statehood, see William L. Lang, "Spoils of Statehood: Montana Communities in Conflict, 1888-1894," *Montana* 37 (Autumn 1987): 34-45.

CHAPTER 9. COPPER AND POLITICS

The best treatment of the corporate disputes over Butte's copper mines is Michael P. Malone, *The Battle for Butte: Mining and Politics on the Northern Frontier, 1864-1906* (Seattle: University of Washington Press, 1981). The best first-hand description is C. P. Connolly's series of muckraking articles in *McClure's Magazine* 27-29 (August 1906-July 1907), later published as *The Devil Learns to Vote* (New York: Covici Friede,

1938). See also C. B. Glasscock, *The War of the Copper Kings* (New York: Bobbs Merrill, 1935); K. Ross Toole, "A History of the Anaconda Copper Mining Company: A Study in the Relationships Between a State and Its People and a Corporation, 1880-1950" (Ph.D. diss., University of California at Los Angeles, 1954); Toole, "When Big Money Came to Butte," *PNQ* 44 (January 1953): 23-29. On the power of the Anaconda Company in state politics, see Michael P. Malone, "Montana as a Corporate Bailiwick: An Image in History," in *Montana: Past and Present* (Los Angeles: William Andrews Clark Memorial Library, 1976), pp. 57-76.

On the rise of the copper industry and related industries, see Robert G. Raymer, *A History of Copper Mining in Montana* (Chicago: American Historical Publishing Company, 1930); Isaac Marcosson, *Anaconda* (New York: Dodd, Mead, 1957); K. Ross Toole, "The Anaconda Copper Mining Company: A Price War and a Copper Corner," *PNQ* 41 (October 1950): 312-29. On the relationship of copper and electrical power, see Carrie Johnson, "Electrical Power, Copper, and John D. Ryan," *Montana* 38 (Autumn 1988): 24-37. For an economic analysis of Anaconda into the 1930s, see "Anaconda Copper," *Fortune* (December 1936), pp. 83-94; "Anaconda II," *Fortune* (January 1937), pp. 71-77. An insider's view of the Amalgamated is Thomas W. Lawson, *The Crime of Amalgamated*, vol. 1 of *Frenzied Finance* (New York: Ridgeway-Thayer, 1905).

The best discussions of unionism in Butte are Jerry Calvert, *The Gibraltar: Socialism and Labor in Butte, Montana, 1895-1920* (Helena: Montana Historical Society Press, 1988); Vernon H. Jensen, *Heritage of Conflict* (Ithaca, N.Y.: Cornell University Press, 1954); Richard E. Lingenfelter, *The Hardrock Miners* (Berkeley: University of California Press, 1974); Ronald C. Brown, *Hard-Rock Miners* (College Station: Texas A&M Press, 1979). For the folklore of Butte and Butte mining, see the WPA Writers' Program, *Copper Camp* (New York: Hastings House, 1943).

For the impact of industrialism on Montana's miners, see David M. Emmons, "Immigrant Workers and Industrial Hazards: The Irish Miners of Butte, 1880-1919," *Journal of Ethnic History* 5 (Winter 1985): 41-64; Brian Shovers, "The Perils of Working in the Butte Underground: Industrial Fatalities in the Copper Mines, 1880-1920," *Montana* 37 (Spring 1987): 26-39.

There is no adequate biography of William Andrews Clark or Marcus Daly. The best short treatment of Clark is Michael P. Malone, "Midas of the West: The Incredible Career of William Andrews Clark," *Montana* 33 (Autumn 1983): 2-17. See also William D. Mangam, *The Clarks of Montana* (Washington, D.C.: Service Printing, 1939); Mangam, *The Clarks: An American Phenomenon* (New York: Silver Bow Press, 1941);

Forrest L. Foor, "The Senatorial Aspirations of William A. Clark" (Ph.D. diss., University of California, Berkeley, 1941). For political and economic results of copper barons' activities, see David M. Emmons, "The Orange and the Green in Montana: A Reconsideration of the Origins of the Clark-Daly Feud," *Arizona and the West* 28 (Summer 1986): 225-45; K. Ross Toole, "The Genesis of the Clark-Daly Feud," *Montana* 1 (April 1951): 21-33; Toole and Edward Butcher, "Timber Depredations on the Montana Public Domain, 1885-1918," *Journal of the West* 7 (July 1968): 351-62.

Montana's Populist movement is documented in Thomas A. Clinch, *Urban Populism and Free Silver in Montana* (Missoula: University of Montana Press, 1970); Clinch, "Coxey's Army in Montana," *Montana* 15 (Autumn 1965): 2-11. For other aspects of Populism in Montana, see Richard B. Roeder, "Crossing the Gender Line: Ella L. Knowles, Montana's First Woman Lawyer," *Montana* 32 (Summer 1982): 64-75; William L. Lang, "One Path to Populism: Will Kennedy and the People's Party of Montana," *PNQ* 74 (April 1983): 77-86.

On Fred Whiteside and his exposure of graft, see Dorothy M. Johnson, ed., "The Graft That Failed," *Montana* 9 (Autumn 1959): 2-11; 9 (Winter 1959): 40-50. On Heinze, see Sarah McNelis's favorable *Copper King at War: The Biography of F. Augustus Heinze* (Missoula: University of Montana Press, 1968); Daniel J. LaGrande, "Voice of a Copper King: A Study of the *Reveille*, 1903-1906" (M.A. thesis, University of Montana, Missoula, 1971). For a caustic look at the copper feuds and battles, see Jerre C. Murphy, *The Comical History of Montana* (San Diego: E. L. Scofield, 1912).

CHAPTER 10. THE HOMESTEAD BOOM

The most important study of homesteading on the Northern Plains is Mary Wilma Hargreaves, *Dry Farming in the Northern Great Plains, 1900-1925* (Cambridge, Mass.: Harvard University Press, 1957). See also Joseph Kinsey Howard, *Montana: High, Wide, and Handsome* (1943; reprint, Lincoln: University of Nebraska Press, 1985); K. Ross Toole, *Twentieth-Century Montana: A State of Extremes* (Norman: University of Oklahoma Press, 1972).

For regional developments, see Walter P. Webb, *The Great Plains*, 2d ed. (Waltham, Mass.: Blaisdell, 1959); Carl F. Kraenzel, *The Great Plains in Transition* (Norman: University of Oklahoma Press, 1955); Gilbert C. Fite, *The Farmers' Frontier: 1865-1900* (New York: Holt, Rinehart and Winston, 1966).

Montana's agricultural development is discussed in Merrill G. Burlingame, *The Montana Frontier* (1942; reprint, Bozeman: Big Sky Books, 1974); M. L. Wilson, "The Evolution of Montana Agriculture in Its Early Period," *Proceedings of the Mississippi Valley Historical Association* 9, pt. 3 (1917-18); Frank R. Grant, "To Husband the Land: Robert Sutherlin and the Irrigation-Dry Farming Controversy," in *Montana and the West*, ed. Rex C. Myers and Harry Fritz (Boulder, Colo.: Pruett Publishing Co., 1984), pp. 87-104; J. Bruce Putnam, "The Evolution of a Frontier Town: Bozeman, Montana, and Its Search for Economic Stability, 1864-1877" (M.A. thesis, Montana State University, Bozeman, 1973). On reclamationists, see Stanley R. Davison, "Hopes and Fancies of Early Reclamationists," in *Historical Essays on Montana and the Northwest*, ed. J. W. Smurr and K. R. Toole (Helena: Western Press, 1957), pp. 204-23.

For studies of land policies, see Everett N. Dick, *The Lure of the Land: A Social History of the Public Lands* (Lincoln: University of Nebraska Press, 1970). See especially William S. Peters and Maxine C. Johnson, *Public Lands in Montana: Their History and Current Significance* (Missoula: University of Montana Press, 1959). On promotion, consult Charles A. Dalich, "Dry Farming Promotion in Eastern Montana (1907-1916)" (M.A. thesis, University of Montana, Missoula, 1968); James G. Handford, "Paris Gibson: Montana Yankee" (M.A. thesis, University of Montana, Missoula, 1952).

Two valuable studies of who the homesteaders were and the nature of their experience are M. L. Wilson, *Dry Farming in the North Central Montana "Triangle,"* Montana State College Extension Service Bulletin 66 (Bozeman, 1923); Marie P. McDonald, *After Barbed Wire* (Glendive, Mont.: Frontier Gateway Museum, 1963). Rex C. Myers, "Homestead on the Range: The Emergence of Community in Eastern Montana 1900-1925," *Great Plains Quarterly* 10 (Fall 1990): 218-27, discusses an important and overlooked aspect of the homestead experience. See also Daniel N. Vichorek, *Montana's Homestad Era* (Helena: American Geographic Publishing, 1987). For local histories of homestead regions, see Harold J. Stearns, *A History of the Upper Musselshell Valley of Montana (to 1920)* (Harlowton and Ryegate, Mont.: Times-Clarion Publishers, 1966); Janet S. Allison, *Trial and Triumph: 101 Years in North Central Montana* (Chinook, Mont.: North Central Montana Cowbelles, 1968); Albie Gordon et al., *Dawn in Golden Valley* (n.p., 1971). A superb reminiscence is Orland E. Esval, *Prairie Tales* (Banner Elk, N.C.: Landmark House, 1979).

The experiences of homesteaders are reflected in Beth LaDow, "Chinook, Montana, and the Myth of Progressive Adaptation," *Montana* 39 (Autumn 1989): 10-21; Paul W. Gates, "Homesteading in the High

Plains," *Agricultural History* 51 (January 1977): 180-99; Dan Whetstone, *Frontier Editor* (New York: Hastings House, 1956); Edward J. Bell Jr., *Homesteading in Montana: Life in the Blue Mountain Country, 1911-1923* (Bozeman, Mont.: Big Sky Books, 1975); Paul T. DeVore, "Dry Farming Broke My Dad," *The Pacific Northwesterner* 18 (Winter 1974): 1-11. See also John T. Graham, "The Last of the Homesteaders," *Montana* 18 (Spring 1968): 62-75; Marie Snedecor, "The Homesteaders: Their Dreams Held No Shadows," *Montana* 19 (Spring 1969): 10-27; Anna Zellick, "Immigrant Homesteader in Montana, Anna Pipinich," *Environmental Review* 4 (1977): 2-16. For homestead locators, see William E. Farr, "Sollid Wants to See You: George Sollid, Homestead Locator," *Montana* 29 (Spring 1979): 16-27. For homestead communities and institutions, see J. Wheeler Barger, *Rural Community Halls in Montana*, Montana Agricultural Experiment Station Bulletin 221 (Bozeman, 1929); Jesse E. Richardson and J. Wheeler Barger, *Public School Dormitories for Rural Children in Montana*, Montana Agricultural Experiment Station Bulletin 201 (Bozeman, 1927).

The bulletins of the Montana Agricultural Experiment Station at Montana State University in Bozeman are extremely valuable sources of information on this and later farming eras. See, for example, F. B. Linfield and Alfred Atkinson, *Dry Farming in Montana*, Bulletin 63 (1907); Atkinson and J. B. Nelson, *Dry Farming Investigations in Montana*, Bulletin 74 (1908); G. W. Morgan and A. S. Seamans, *Dry Farming in the Plains Area of Montana*, Bulletin 89 (1920); Marion Clawson et al., *Farm Adjustments in Montana . . .*, Bulletin 377 (1940); E. A. Starch, *Economic Changes in Montana's Wheat Area . . .*, Bulletin 295 (1935); Carl F. Kraenzel, *Farm Population Mobility in Selected Montana Communities*, Bulletin 371 (1939).

CHAPTER 11. THE PROGRESSIVE ERA AND WORLD WAR I

Historians have given too little attention to Montana progressivism. Richard B. Roeder's "Montana in the Early Years of the Progressive Period" (Ph.D. diss., University of Pennsylvania, Philadelphia, 1971) is the best and most completed discussion. See also Jules Karlin's essay, "Progressive Politics in Montana," in *A History of Montana*, ed. M. G. Burlingame and K. R. Toole, 3 vols. (New York: Lewis Historical Publishing Co., 1957), 1:247-80. See also K. Ross Toole, *Montana: An Uncommon Land* (Norman: University of Oklahoma Press, 1959). Richard B. Roeder challenges Toole's interpretation in "Montana Progressivism: Sound and Fury and One Small Tax Reform," *Montana* 20 (October 1970): 18-26.

Jules Karlin discusses Joseph Dixon's career in *Joseph M. Dixon of Montana*, Part 1: *Senator and Bull Moose Manager, 1867-1917*, and Part

2: *Governor versus the Anaconda, 1917-1934* (Missoula: University of
Montana Publications in History, 1974); "Congressman Joseph M. Dixon
and the Miles City Land Office, 1903: A Study in Political Patronage," in
Historical Essays on Montana and the Northwest, ed. J. W. Smurr and
K. R. Toole (Helena: Western Press, 1957), pp. 231-49; and in "Young Joe
Dixon in the Flathead Country," *Montana* 27 (Winter 1967): 12-19.

J. Leonard Bates has written extensively on the career of Thomas J.
Walsh in "Senator Walsh of Montana, 1918-1924: A Liberal under Pressure" (Ph.D. diss., University of North Carolina, 1952); *Tom Walsh in
Dakota Territory* (Urbana: University of Illinois Press, 1966); "T. J.
Walsh: Foundations of a Senatorial Career," *Montana* 1 (Autumn 1951):
23-34; "Walsh of Montana in Dakota Territory: Political Beginnings,
1884-1890," *PNQ* 56 (July 1965): 114-24; and "Thomas J. Walsh: His Genius for Controversy," *Montana* 29 (Autumn 1969): 2-15. See also Jose-
phine O'Keane's uncritical treatment, *Thomas J. Walsh: A Senator from
Montana* (Francestown, N.H.: M. Jones Co., 1955), and Clarence L.
Brammer, "Thomas J. Walsh" (Ph.D. diss., University of Missouri, 1972).

On woman's suffrage, see Doris B. Ward, "The Winning of Woman
Suffrage in Montana" (M.A. thesis, Montana State University, Bozeman,
1974); T. A. Larson, "Montana Women and the Battle for the Ballot,"
Montana 23 (Winter 1973): 24-41; and the final chapters in Paula Petrik,
*No Step Backward: Women and Family on the Rocky Mountain Mining
Frontier, Helena, Montana, 1865-1900* (Helena: Montana Historical Soci-
ety Press, 1987). For other coverage of suffrage in Montana, see Ronald
Schaffer, "The Montana Woman Suffrage Campaign," *PNQ* 55 (January
1964): 9-15.

Jeannette Rankin does not have an adequate biography. The most recent are Kevin J. Giles, *Flight of the Dove: The Story of Jeannette Rankin*
(Beaverton, Ore.: Touchstone Press, 1980); Hannah Josephson, *Jeannette
Rankin: First Lady in Congress* (Indianapolis and New York: Bobbs-
Merrill, 1974). See also John C. Board, "Jeannette Rankin: The Lady
from Montana," *Montana* 17 (July 1967): 2-17; Board, "The Lady from
Montana: Jeannette Rankin" (M.A. thesis, University of Wyoming, Lara-
mie, 1964). On Jeannette Rankin's career and pacifism, see Joan Hoff Wil-
son's two articles, "'Peace is a Woman's Job . . .': Jeannette Rankin and
American Foreign Policy: The Origins of Her Pacifism," *Montana* 30
(Winter 1980): 28-41; and "'Peace is a Woman's Job . . .': Jeannette
Rankin and American Foreign Policy: Her Lifework as a Pacifist,"
Montana 30 (Spring 1980): 38-53. Also consult Ronald Schaffer, "Jean-
nette Rankin, Progressive-Isolationist" (Ph.D. diss., Princeton University, Princeton, N.J., 1959); Ted C. Harris, "Jeannette Rankin: Suffragist,
First Woman Elected to Congress, and Pacifist" (Ph.D. diss., University
of Georgia, Athens, 1972).

The history of labor movements and conditions during the Progressive period are documented in the biennial reports of the Montana Department of Labor and Industry, 1913-20, and in Vernon H. Jensen, *Heritage of Conflict: Labor Relations in the Nonferrous Metals Industry Up to 1930* (Ithaca, N.Y.: Cornell University Press, 1950). The best study of Butte unionism is Jerry Calvert, *The Gibraltar: Socialism and Labor in Butte, Montana, 1895-1920* (Helena: Montana Historical Society Press, 1988). See also Norma Smith, "The Rise and Fall of the Butte Miners Union, 1878-1914" (M.A. thesis, Montana State University, Bozeman, 1961); Arthur W. Thurner, "The Western Federation of Miners in Two Copper Camps: The Impact of the Michigan Copper Miners' Strike on Butte's Local No. 1," *Montana* 33 (Spring 1983): 30-45. For studies of railroad labor movements in Montana, see W. Thomas White, "Boycott: The Pullman Strike in Montana," *Montana* 29 (Autumn 1979): 2-13; White, "Protest Movements in the Pacific Northwest: A Comparative Look at Railway Workers in the Pullman Boycott of 1894 and the 1922 Shopmen's Strike," in *Centennial West*, ed. William L. Lang (Seattle: University of Washington Press, 1991).

The best studies of the IWW are Melvyn Dubofsky, *We Shall Be All: A History of the Industrial Workers of the World* (Chicago: Quadrangle Books, 1969); Joseph R. Conlin, *Bread and Roses, Too* (Westport, Conn.: Greenwood Publishing Co., 1969); Patrick Renshaw, *The Wobblies* (Garden City, N.Y.: Doubleday, 1967). Two studies of the radicals and their suppression are H. C. Peterson and Gilbert C. Fite, *Opponents of War, 1917-18* (1957; reprint, Seattle: University of Washington Press, 1968); and William Preston Jr., *Aliens and Dissenters: Federal Suppression of Radicals, 1903-1933* (Cambridge, Mass.: Harvard University Press, 1963). For studies of radical political action and socialism during the Progressive Era and World War I, see Jerry Calvert, "The Rise and Fall of Socialism in a Company Town: Anaconda, Montana, 1902-1905," *Montana* 36 (Autumn 1986): 2-13; George A. Venn, "The Wobblies and Montana's Garden City," *Montana* 21 (Autumn 1971): 18-30; Benjamin G. Rader, "The Montana Lumber Strike of 1917," *PHR* 36 (May 1967): 189-207. The Butte occupation of 1914 is discussed in Theodore Wiprud, "Butte: A Troubled Labor Paradise," *Montana* 21 (Autumn 1971): 31-38. On the Speculator Mine disaster, see Arnon Gutfeld, "The Speculator Disaster in 1917: Labor Resurgence at Butte, Montana," *Arizona and the West* 11 (Spring 1969): 27-38; Daniel Harrington, *Lessons from the Granite Mountain Shaft Fire, Butte* (Washington, D.C.: Government Printing Office, 1922). An interesting sidelight on IWW folklore is S. Page Stegner, "Protest Songs from the Butte Miners," *Western Folklore* 26 (April 1967): 157-67.

On the war hysteria in Montana and the Montana Council of Defense, see Arnon Gutfeld, *Montana's Agony: Years of War and Hysteria* (Gaines-ville: University of Florida Press, 1979); Anna Zellick, "Patriots on the Rampage: Mob Action in Lewistown, 1917-1918," *Montana* 31 (Winter 1981): 30-43; Nancy R. Fritz, "The Montana Council of Defense" (M.A. thesis, University of Montana, Missoula, 1966); Charles S. Johnson, "An Editor and a War: Will A. Campbell and the *Helena Independent*, 1914-1921" (M.A. thesis, University of Montana, Missoula, 1977); Robert E. Evans, "Montana's role in the Enactment of Legislation Designed to Sup-press the Industrial Workers of the World" (M.A. thesis, University of Montana, Missoula, 1964); Guy Halverson and William E. Ames, "The Butte *Bulletin*: Beginnings of a Labor Daily," *Montana Journalism Quarterly* 46 (Summer 1969): 260-6; Kurt Wetzel, "The Defeat of Bill Dunne: An Episode in the Montana Red Scare," *PNQ* 64 (January 1973): 12-20; K. Ross Toole, *Twentieth-Century Montana: A State of Extremes* (Norman: University of Oklahoma Press, 1972). For a first-person account of the repression, see Rufus M. Franz, "It Happened in Montana," *Men-nonite Life* 7 (October 1952): 181-84.

On Burton K. Wheeler, see Richard T. Ruetten's "Burton K. Wheeler, 1905-1925: An Independent Liberal under Fire" (M.A. thesis, University of Oregon, Eugene, 1957); "Burton K. Wheeler of Montana: A Progres-sive Between the Wars" (Ph.D. diss., University of Oregon, 1961). For Wheeler's viewpoint, see Burton K. Wheeler and Paul F. Healy, *Yankee from the West* (Garden City, N.Y.: Doubleday, 1962). For treatments of agricultural radicalism, see Theodore Saloutos, "The Montana Society of Equity," *PHR* 14 (December 1945): 393-408; Robert L. Morlan, *Political Prairie Fire: The Nonpartisan League, 1915-1922* (Minneapolis: Univer-sity of Minnesota Press, 1955); Rosemarie Fishburn, "The Montana Farmer: An Ideological Analysis, 1915-1922" (M.A. thesis, University of Montana, Missoula, 1971).

On the influenza outbreak, see Pierce C. Mullen and Michael L. Nel-son, "Montanans and 'The Most Peculiar Disease': The Influenza Epi-demic and Public Health, 1918-1919," *Montana* 37 (Spring 1987): 50-61. On urban problems and development, see Larry V. Bishop and Robert A. Harvie, "Law, Order & Reform in the Gallatin, 1893-1918," *Montana* 30 (Spring 1980): 16-25.

CHAPTER 12. DROUGHT, DEPRESSION, AND WAR

The best information and studies on the effects of the post-World War I drought and depression are in K. Ross Toole, *Twentieth-Century Mon-tana: A State of Extremes* (Norman: University of Oklahoma Press, 1972); Joseph Kinsey Howard, *Montana: High, Wide, and Handsome* (1943; re-print, Lincoln: University of Nebraska Press, 1985); M. L. Wilson, *Dry*

Farming in the North Central Montana "Triangle," Montana State College Extension Service Bulletin 66 (Bozeman, 1923), pp. 17-24; Donald J. Elliott, "Commercial Bank Failures in Montana, 1920-1926" (M.A. thesis, University of Montana, Missoula, 1967); Jeffrey L. Cunniff, "The Gilman State Bank: A Case Study of a Montana Bank Failure, 1910-1923" (M.A. thesis, University of Montana, Missoula, 1971).

The mine taxation issue and the 1920 campaign are described in Arnon Gutfeld, "The Levine Affair: A Case Study in Academic Freedom," *PHR* 39 (February 1970): 19-37; Louis Levine, *The Taxation of Mines in Montana* (New York: B. W. Huebsch, 1919); H. G. Merriam, *The University of Montana: A History* (Missoula: University of Montana Press, 1970), pp. 54-55; B. K. Wheeler and Paul F. Healy, *Yankee from the West* (Garden City, N.Y.: Doubleday, 1962), pp. 165-84; Mary L. Koessler, "The 1920 Gubernatorial Election in Montana" (M.A. thesis, University of Montana, Missoula, 1971). On a related subject, see Sheila M. Stearns, "The Arthur Fisher Case" (M.A. thesis, University of Montana, Missoula, 1969). Joseph Dixon's term as governor is covered in Jules Karlin, *Joseph Dixon of Montana* Part 2: *Governor versus the Anaconda, 1917-1934* (Missoula: University of Montana Publications in History, 1974).

The political trends during the 1920s and early 1930s are dealt with in J. Leonard Bates, *The Origins of Teapot Dome* (Urbana: University of Illinois Press, 1963); T. J. Walsh, "The True Story of Teapot Dome," *The Forum* 72 (July 1924): 1-12; Burl Noggle, *Teapot Dome* (New York: W. W. Norton, 1962); Paul A. Carter, "The Other Catholic Candidate: The 1928 Presidential Bid of Thomas J. Walsh," *PNQ* 55 (January 1964): 1-18; Richard T. Ruetten, "Senator Burton K. Wheeler and Insurgency in the 1920's," in *The American West: A Reorientation*, ed. Gene M Gressley (Laramie: University of Wyoming Press, 1968), pp. 111-31.

The effects of the Depression and the New Deal in Montana are the subjects of an increasing number of studies. For a gripping account of the agricultural depression in Montana, see Charles Vindex, "Survival on the High Plains, 1929-1934," *Montana* 28 (Autumn 1978): 2-11. Two studies present compelling statistics on the conditions in Montana during the early 1930s, *The People of the Drought States*, Research Bulletin, Vol. 2, Works Progress Administration (Washington, D.C.: Government Printing Office, 1937), and *Montana Drought Survey, 1934*, U.S. Division of Crop and Livestock Estimates (Helena, 1934).

Montana's place in the New Deal is dealt with in Leonard Arrington and Don C. Reading, "New Deal Programs in the Northern Tier States, 1933-1939," in *Centennial West: Essays on the History of the Northern Tier States*, ed. William L. Lang (Seattle: University of Washington Press, 1991); Arrington, "The New Deal in the West: A Preliminary Statistical Inquiry," *PHR* 38 (August 1969): 311-16; James T. Patterson, "The New Deal in the West," *PHR* 38 (August 1969): 317-27; Patterson, *The New Deal and the States: Federalism in Transition* (Princeton, N.J.: Princeton University Press, 1969). The change in Indian policy is discussed in Graham D. Taylor, *The New Deal and American Tribalism: The Administration of the Indian Reorganization Act, 1934-45* (Lincoln: University of Nebraska Press, 1980). The effects of New Deal policies on the Blackfeet Indian Reservation is covered in Anne Banks, "Jessie Donaldson Schultz and Blackfeet Crafts," *Montana* 33 (Autumn 1983): 18-35.

The best statistical description of relief efforts in Montana is Carl F. Kraenzel, *The Relief Problem in Montana*, Montana Agricultural Experiment Station Bulletin 343 (Bozeman, 1937). On agricultural planning, see Roy E. Huffman, "Montana's Contribution to New Deal Farm Policy," *Agricultural History* 33 (October 1959): 164-7. On the liquor issue, see Larry D. Quinn, *Politicians in Business: A History of the Liquor Control System in Montana* (Missoula: University of Montana Press, 1970). The important Fort Peck Dam project is the subject of Robert Saindon and Bunky Sullivan, "Taming the Missouri and Treating the Depression: Fort Peck Dam," *Montana* 27 (Summer 1977): 34-57. See also "10,000 Montana Relief Workers Make Whoopee on Saturday Night," *Life*, November 23, 1936, pp. 9-17; James Rorty, "Fort Peck: An American Siberia," *Nation*, September 11, 1935, pp. 300-1; John T. Ryan, "Chapters on the Fort Peck Development" (M.A. thesis, University of Montana, Missoula, 1961).

The political side of the New Deal is discussed in several articles by Michael P. Malone, including "The Montana New Dealers," in *The New Deal*, Vol. 2, *The State and Local Levels*, ed. John Braeman, Robert H. Bremmer, and David Brody, 2 vols. (Columbus: Ohio State University Press, 1975), pp. 240-68; "Montana Politics and the New Deal," *Montana* 21 (Winter 1971): 2-11; "Montana Politics at the Crossroads, 1932-1933," *PNQ* 69 (January 1978): 20-29. Among the many descriptions of Senator B. K. Wheeler's activities during these years, the best include Robert E. Burke, "A Friendship in Adversity: Burton K. Wheeler and Hiram W. Johnson," *Montana* 36 (Winter 1986): 12-25; Richard T. Ruetten, "Showdown in Montana, 1938: Burton Wheeler's Role in the Defeat of Jerry O'Connell," *PNQ* 54 (January 1963): 19-29; Ruetten, "Burton K. Wheeler and the Montana Connection," *Montana* 27 (Summer 1977): 2-19; Richard L. Neuberger, "Wheeler of Montana," *Harper's Magazine* (May 1940), pp. 609-18; Catherine C. Doherty, "The Court Plan, B. K. Wheeler and the Montana Press" (M.A. thesis, University of Montana, Missoula, 1954). Among the many assessments of why Wheeler lost in 1946, the fullest is Joseph P. Kelly, "A Study of the Defeat of Senator

Burton K. Wheeler in the 1946 Primary Election" (M.A. thesis, University of Montana, Missoula, 1959). On James E. Murray during the 1930s, see Forrest Davis, "Millionaire Moses," *Saturday Evening Post*, December 8, 1945, pp. 9-10.

The effects of World War II on Montana have not been studied much, but among the best studies are Robert D. Burhans, *The First Special Service Forces* (Washington, D.C.: Government Printing Office, 1947); Karen Fischer, "Training Sled Dogs at Camp Rimini, 1942-1944," *Montana* 34 (Winter 1984): 10-19; and "Golden River," *Harper's Magazine* (May 1945), pp. 511-23, on the Missouri Valley Authority. On the political trends, see "The Decline and Fall of Burton K. Wheeler," *Harper's Magazine* (March 1947), pp. 226-36; "The Montana Twins in Trouble," *Harper's Magazine* (September 1944), pp. 334-42; "Jim Murray's Chances," *Nation*, October 9, 1948, pp. 397-9.

CHAPTER 13. THE MODERN MONTANA ECONOMY

The best source for recent and current economic trends in Montana are the publications of the Bureau of Business and Economic Research at the University of Montana at Missoula. See especially *Entering the 1990s: 15th Annual Economic Outlook Seminar* (Missoula: Bureau of Business and Economic Research, 1990), and the six-volume *Montana Economic Study* (Missoula: Bureau of Business and Economic Research, 1970). See also issues of *Montana Business Quarterly*, which regularly publishes articles on Montana's economic trends. For the 1970s and 1980s, also consult publications of Montana Department of Intergovernmental Relations and Montana Department of Commerce. See also Montana Department of Agricultural and United States Department of Agriculture, Statistical Reporting Service, *Montana Agricultural Statistics*, Vol. 15: *County Statistics, 1972 and 1973* (Bozeman: Color World of Montana, 1974).

For very recent trends in Montana's economy, see Verne W. House and Douglas J. Young, *Trends in the Montana Economy and Taxation*, Montana Cooperative Extension Service Bulletin 1343 (Bozeman, 1986); "Montana: A State in Economic Crisis," *Billings Gazette*, June 8, 1986. Three recent publications of Montana State University's Burton K. Wheeler Center that address Montana's economy are Bruce R. Beattie and Douglas J. Young, *Montana Taxation and Expenditures: Issues and Options* (Bozeman: Montana State University, 1988); John M. Antle, *Montana in a Global Agriculture* (Bozeman: Montana State University, 1989); Gordon G. Brittan Jr. and Vanessa Brittan, *Public Lands and Federal Policies in Montana* (Bozeman: Montana State University, 1990).

There is no general history of Montana agriculture, but there are studies of specific agricultural developments. See John T. Schlebecker's *Whereby We Thrive: A History of American Farming, 1607-1972* (Ames: Iowa State University Press, 1975); *Cattle Raising on the Plains: 1900-1961* (Lincoln: University of Nebraska Press, 1963). Montana Agricultural Experiment Station bulletins contain much valuable information. See, for example, Roland R. Renne, *Montana Farm Foreclosures*, Bulletin 368 (February 1939); Renne, *Montana Farm Bankruptcies*, Bulletin 360 (June 1938); Layton S. Thompson, *Montana Cooperative Grazing Districts in Action*, Bulletin 481 (December 1951); Willard H. Godrey Jr. and Gail L. Cramer, *Costs and Returns of Producing Sugar Beets and Other Irrigated Crops in Montana*, Bulletin 635 (September 1969).

On M. L. Wilson and his associates, see William D. Rowley, *M. L. Wilson and the Campaign for the Domestic Allotment* (Lincoln: University of Nebraska Press, 1970); Thomas R. Wessel, "Wheat for the Masses: M. L. Wilson and the Montana Connection," *Montana* 31 (Spring 1981): 42-53; Harry McDean, "M. L. Wilson and the Origins of Federal Farm Policy in the Great Plains, 1909-1914," *Montana* 34 (Autumn 1984): 50-59; Mont H. Saunderson, "M. L. Wilson: A Man to Remember," *Montana* 34 (Autumn 1984): 60-63. See also Ronald L. Kenny, "The Fairway Farms: An Experiment in a New Agricultural Age" (M.A. thesis, Montana State University, Bozeman, 1969). For the Montana wheat culture, see Ralph E. Ward, "Wheat in Montana: Determined Adaptation," *Montana* 25 (Autumn 1975): 16-37. On women in Montana agriculture, see Laurie K. Mercier, "Women's Economic Role in Montana Agriculture: 'You Had to Make Every Minute Count'," *Montana* 38 (Autumn 1988): 50-61.

For the Anaconda Company and its changing role since 1920, see the works by Marcosson, Toole, and the editors of *Fortune Magazine* cited in Chapter 9. On the Montana Power Company, see Douglas F. Leighton, "The Corporate History of the Montana Power Company, 1882-1913" (M.A. thesis, University of Montana, Missoula, 1951); Michael P. Malone, "Montana as a Corporate Bailiwick: An Image in History," in *Montana: Past and Present* (Los Angeles: William Andrews Clark Memorial Library, 1976), pp. 57-76. For Anaconda during the 1960s and 1970s, see "Anaconda's 500-Year Plan," *Forbes*, December 15, 1968, pp. 22-32; "From Rags to Riches," *Forbes*, January 15, 1972, pp. 24-25; "A Neat Job," *Forbes*, December 1, 1972, pp. 40, 42; "An Ex-Banker Treats Copper's Sickest Giant," *Business Week*, February 19, 1972, pp. 52-55. Michael P. Malone discusses the demise of metal mining in "The Collapse of Western Metal Mining: An Historical Epitaph," *PHR* 55 (August 1986): 455-64. For the latest trends and forecasts, see Robin McCulloch, *Mining and Mineral Developments in Montana* (Butte: Montana Bureau of Mines and Geology, 1989). The recent purchase and operation of copper properties in Butte by Dennis Washington is covered in Richard L. Stern, "Denny's Always the Low-Cost Producer," *Forbes*, May 15, 1989, pp. 87-91. Duane A. Smith, *Mining America: The Industry and the Environment, 1800-1980* (Lawrence: University of Kansas Press, 1987), deals with the environmental costs of modern mining.

The modern history of Montana labor needs attention. The yearbooks of the AFL-CIO provide statistical information, while the "Montanans At Work" oral histories in the Montana Historical Society archival collections offer personal insights from Montana's workers. See also Laurie K. Mercier, "I Worked for the Railroad: Oral Histories of Montana Railroaders, 1910-1950," *Montana* 33 (Summer 1983): 34-59. Vernon Jensen's *Nonferrous Metals Industry Unionism, 1932-1954* (Ithaca, N.Y.: Cornell University Press, 1954) contains valuable information on Montana. On the 1934 strike, see Charles E. Sebold, "No Troops—No Violence," *Christian Century*, October 17, 1934, pp. 1310-11; Ward Kinney [Joseph K. Howard], "Montana Challenges the Tyranny of Copper," *Nation*, July 25, 1934, pp. 86-87, 98-99. For a discussion of women wartime workers, see Bob Vine, *Women of the Washoe* (Anaconda, Mont.: Robert Vine, 1989).

Montana's forest products industry has been neglected by historians. Delores Morrow surveys the lumber industry in "Our Sawdust Roots: A History of the Forest Products Industry in Montana," ms., Montana Historical Society Library, Helena. Edward B. Butcher in "An Analysis of Timber Depredations in Montana to 1900" (M.A. thesis, University of Montana, Missoula, 1967) and with K. Ross Toole, "Timber Depredations on the Montana Public Domain, 1885-1918," *Journal of the West* 7 (July 1968): 351-62, discusses corporate misuse of public forests. For a revision of that view, see Sherry H. Olson, *The Depletion Myth: A History of Railroad Use of Timber* (Cambridge, Mass.: Harvard University Press, 1971). For a description and discussion of cooperative fire protection, see William G. Robbins, *American Forestry: A History of National, State, and Private Cooperation* (Lincoln: University of Nebraska Press, 1985). John J. Little, "The 1910 Forest Fires in Montana and Idaho: Their Impact on Federal and State Legislation" (M.A. thesis, University of Montana, Missoula, 1968), discusses that great calamity. See also Maxine Johnson's discussion of "Wood Products in Montana," in the Spring 1972 issue of *Montana Business Quarterly*. Oil and natural gas trends are included in *Montana Oil Journal*. See also Don Douma, "The History of Oil and Gas in Montana," in *A History of Montana*, ed. M. G. Burlingame and K. R. Toole, 3 vols. (New York: Lewis Historical Publishing Co., 1957), 2:31-52; Eugene S. Perry, "Oil and Gas in Montana," *Memoir No. 35*, Montana Bureau of Mines and Geology (1953).

The beginnings of Montana's coal-mining industry are covered in Robert A. Chadwick, "Coal: Montana's Prosaic Treasure," *Montana* 23 (Autumn 1973): 18-31; Rita McDonald and Merrill G. Burlingame, "Montana's First Commercial Coal Mine," *PNQ* 47 (July 1956): 23-38. On the mining disaster at Red Lodge, see Paul Anderson, "'There Is Something Wrong Down Here': The Smith Mine Disaster, Bearcreek, Montana, 1943," *Montana* 38 (Spring 1988): 2-13.

The development of strip mining is the subject of William B. Evans and Robert L. Peterson, "Decision at Colstrip: The Northern Pacific Railway's Open Pit Mining Operation," *PNQ* 61 (April 1970): 129-36; William B. Evans, "Public Response to Strip Mining in Montana, 1920's to 1973," *Montana Business Quarterly* 11 (Summer 1973): 16-20. On the coal-mining controversy during the 1970s, see K. Ross Toole, *The Rape of the Great Plains* (Boston: Atlantic, Little, Brown, 1976); Richard L. Reese, ed., *Coal Forum* (Missoula: Montana Committee for the Humanities, 1974); Alvin M. Josephy Jr., "Plundered West: Coal Is the Prize," *Washington Post*, August 26, 1973, pp. C1, C4; James Conaway, "The Last of the West: Hell, Strip It!" *Atlantic* (September 1973), pp. 91-103; Louis D. Hayes, "Who Will Control Montana's Coal?" *Montana Business Quarterly* 13 (Spring 1975): 26-32. For statistics and an assessment of the impact of coal mining in eastern Montana, see Montana Energy Advisory Council, *Coal Development Information Packet* (Helena, 1974); Institute for Social Sciences Research, University of Montana, *A Comparative Case Study of the Impact of Coal Development on the Way of Life of People in the Coal Areas of Eastern Montana and Northeastern Wyoming: Final Report* (Missoula, 1974).

Historians have neglected the history of Montana tourism. The most recent overview is Robert F. Wallace and Daniel R. Blake, *Montana Travel Study* (Missoula: University of Montana, Bureau of Business and Economic Research, 1966). On special topics, see Robert G. Athearn, "The Tin Can Tourist's West," in *Montana and the West*, ed. Myers and Fritz, pp. 105-21. Michael P. Malone, "The Gallatin Canyon and the Tides of History," *Montana* 23 (Summer 1973): 2-17; Kenneth W. Karsmizki, "The Lewis and Clark Caverns: Politics and the Establishment of Montana's First State Park," *Montana* 31 (Autumn 1981): 32-45; Robert T. Smith, "The Big Sky Development: A Lesson for the Future," *American West* 12 (September 1975): 46-47. For descriptions of Montana's rodeos, see Liz Stiffler and Tona Blake, "Fannie Sperry-Steele: Montana's Champion Bronc Rider," *Montana* 32 (Spring 1982): 44-57. On Montana dude ranching, see Roberta Cheyney and Clyde Erskine, *Music, Saddles and Flapjacks: Dudes at the OTO Ranch* (Missoula: Mountain Press, 1978); Joel Bernstein, *Families That Took in Friends: An Informal History of Dude Ranching* (Stevensville, Mont.: Stoneydale Press, 1982); Spike

Van Cleve, *40 Years' Gatherin's* (Kansas City: The Lowell Press, 1977); Lawrence R. Borne, "Dude Ranching in the Rockies," *Montana* 38 (Summer 1988): 14-27.

CHAPTER 14. A SOCIAL AND CULTURAL PROFILE

There is no overall study of the general character, origins, and composition of Montana's population, but the publications of the U.S. Bureau of Census includes considerable data and should be consulted. There is also no ethnic history of Montana, but the subject is addressed in H. G. Merriam, "Ethnic Settlement of Montana," *PHR* 12 (June 1943): 157-68. Some of the best studies have appeared as articles in *Montana*, including Catherine Dowling, "Irish-American Nationalism in Butte, 1900-1916," 39 (Spring 1989): 50-63; Stacy A. Flaherty, "Boycott in Butte: Organized Labor and the Chinese Community, 1896-1897," 37 (Winter 1987): 34-47; Leona Lampi, "Red Lodge," 11 (Summer 1961): 20-31; Robert E. Levinson, "Julius Basinski: Jewish Merchant in Montana," 22 (Winter 1972): 60-68; Andrew F. Rolle, "The Italian Moves Westward," 16 (January 1966): 13-24; Robert R. Swartout Jr., "From Kwantung to Big Sky: The Chinese Experience in Frontier Montana," 38 (Winter 1988): 42-53; Monique Urza, "Catherine Etchart: A Montana Love Story," 31 (Winter 1981): 2-17; John R. Wunder, "Law and Chinese in Frontier Montana," 30 (Summer 1980): 18-31; Anna Zellick, "The Men from Bribir: The Croatian Stonemasons of Lewistown, Montana," 28 (Winter 1978): 44-55; Zellick, "'Fire in the Hole': Slovenians, Croatians, and Coal Mining on the Musselshell," 40 (Spring 1990): 16-31.

A model for other books on Montana ethnic groups is David M. Emmons, *The Butte Irish: Class and Ethnicity in an American Mining Town, 1875-1925* (Urbana: University of Illinois Press, 1989). The Cornish miners are covered in Arthur C. Todd, *The Cornish Miner in America* (Glendale, Calif.: Arthur H. Clark, 1967); A. L. Rowse, *The Cousin Jacks* (New York: Scribner, 1969); John Rowe, *The Hard-Rock Men: Cornish Immigrants and the North American Mining Frontier* (New York: Barnes and Noble, 1974). On the Jewish community in Helena, see Delores J. Morrow, "Jewish Merchants and the Commercial Emporium of Montana," in *Montana and the West*, ed. Rex C. Myers and Harry Fritz (Boulder, Colo.: Pruett Publishing Co., 1984), 17-36. For the Dutch, see Henry S. Lucas, *Netherlanders in America: Dutch Immigration to the United States and Canada, 1789-1950* (Ann Arbor: University of Michigan Press, 1955); Rob Kroes, "Windmills in Montana: Dutch Settlement in the Gallatin Valley," *Montana* 39 (Autumn 1989): 38-51.

There has been little published on Montana's religious life. Many

Christian denominations have published limited edition histories, but there is no overall study of Montana religious life (see citations in Chapter 3). On Montana's Hutterite populations, see John Hostetler, *Hutterite Society* (Baltimore: Johns Hopkins University Press, 1974); Dorothy Schweider, "Frontier Brethren: The Hutterite Experience in the American West," *Montana* 28 (Winter 1978): 2-15; Hans J. Peterson, "Hilldale: A Montana Hutterite Colony," *Rocky Mountain Social Science Journal* 7 (April 1970): 1-7; Hans D. Radtke, *The Hutterites in Montana: An Economic Description*, Montana Agricultural Experiment Station Bulletin 641 (Bozeman, 1971).

For studies of Montana's Indian tribes, see citations in chapters 1 and 6. An analysis of tribal self-government can be found in James Lopach, Margery H. Brown, and Richmond L. Clow, *Tribal Government Today: Politics on Montana Indian Reservations* (Boulder: Westview Press, 1990). For the difficult legal problems facing twentieth century Indians, see Charles F. Wilkinson, *American Indians, Time, and the Law* (New Haven, Conn.: Yale University Press, 1987). For white attitudes, see Brian W. Dippie, *The Vanishing American: White Attitudes and U.S. Indian Policy* (Middletown, Conn.: Wesleyan University Press, 1982). One of the best general works is Alvin M. Josephy Jr., *The Indian Heritage of America* (New York: Alfred A. Knopf, 1969). Verne Dusenberry published several valuable essays in *Montana*, including "The Rocky Boy Indians," 4 (Winter 1954): 1-15; "The Northern Cheyenne," 5 (Winter 1955): 23-40; and "Waiting for a Day That Never Comes," 8 (April 1958): 26-39.

Malcolm McFee, *Modern Blackfeet: Montanans on a Reservation* (New York: Holt, Rinehart and Winston, 1972), William Farr, *The Reservation Blackfeet, 1882-1945: A Photographic History of Cultural Survival* (Seattle: University of Washington Press, 1984), and Edward E. Barry Jr., *The Fort Belknap Indian Reservation: The First One Hundred Years, 1855-1955* (Bozeman: Montana State University, 1974), treat twentieth century life on Montana Indian reservations. See also Thomas R. Wessel, *A History of Rocky Boy's Indian Reservation* (Bozeman: Montana State University, 1974); and Charles C. Bradley Jr., *A History of the Crow Indians* (Lodge Grass, Mont.: Lodge Grass Schools, 1971). A popular history of Montana's Indians is William J. Bryan Jr., *Montana's Indians* (Helena: Montana Geographic, 1984).

General studies of the Montana public school system are James M. Hamilton, *History of Montana: From Wilderness to Statehood* (1957; reprint, Portland: Binfords & Mort, 1970); Emmet J. Riley, *Development of the Montana State Educational Organization, 1864-1930* (Washington, D.C.: Catholic University of America, 1931); Dale R. Tash, "The Development of the Montana Common School System, 1864-1884" (Ed.D. diss., Montana State University, Bozeman, 1968). On early educators, see George Lubick, "Cornelius Hedges: Frontier Educator," *Montana* 28 (Spring 1978): 26-35; Alice Cowan Coleman, "Miss Jacoby: 19th Century Educator, 20th Century Guardian of Excellence," *Montana* 28 (Spring 1978): 36-49.

On higher education, see M. A. Brannon, "The Montana System of Administering Higher Education," *School and Society* 35 (February 1932): 269-77; H. G. Merriam, *The University of Montana: A History* (Missoula: University of Montana Press, 1970); Merrill G. Burlingame, *A History of Montana State University* (Bozeman: Montana State University Office of Information, 1968); Edward Byron Chenette, "The Montana State Board of Education: A Study of Higher Education in Conflict, 1884-1959" (Ed.D. diss., University of Montana, Bozeman, 1972); Montana Commission on Post-secondary Education, *Review of Prior Studies of Post-secondary Education in Montana* (Helena, 1973).

Journalism in Montana is covered in *Montana Fourth Estate*, the trade journal of the Montana Press Association, and *Montana Journalism Review*, published by the University of Montana. Sam Gilluly's *The Press Gang: A Century of Montana Newspapers* (Great Falls: Montana Press Association, 1985) is full of anecdotes and historical vignettes. For Himsl quotes, see Steve L. Smith, "Profile of a Wire Editor," *Montana Journalism Review* 17 (1974): 47-52. Some useful studies are Rex C. Myers, "Montana's Colorful Press: From Crazyquilt to Great Gray Blanket," in *Montana and the West*, ed. Rex C. Myers and Harry Fritz (Boulder, Colo.: Pruett Publishing Co., 1984), pp. 71-86; Richard T. Ruetten, "Anaconda Journalism: The End of an Era," *Journalism Quarterly* 37 (Winter 1960): 3-12, 104; John M. Schiltz, "Montana's Captive Press," *Montana Opinion* 1 (June 1956): 1-11; Francis E. Walsh, "News Dissemination in the State Capital" (M.A. thesis, University of Montana, Missoula, 1972); William E. Larson, "News Management in the Company Press" (M.A. thesis, University of Montana, Missoula, 1971); Ruth J. Towe, "The Lee Newspapers of Montana: The First Three Years, 1959-1962" (M.A. thesis, University of Montana, Missoula, 1969).

Studies of Charles M. Russell and his art are numerous. The best recent studies are Peter H. Hassrick, *Charles M. Russell* (New York: Harry N. Abrams, 1989); Brian Dippie, *Looking at Russell* (Fort Worth, Texas: Amon Carter Museum, 1987); Dippie, *Remington and Russell: The Sid Richardson Collection* (Austin: University of Texas Press, 1982); Dippie, *"Paper Talk": Charlie Russell's American West* (New York: Alfred A. Knopf, 1979); Frank Bird Linderman, *Recollections of Charley Russell*, ed. H. G. Merriam (Norman: University of Oklahoma Press, 1963). See also "Charles M. Russell—Special Issue," *Montana* 34 (Summer 1984);

John C. Ewers, "Charlie Russell's Indians," *Montana* 37 (Summer 1987): 36-53; Hugh A. Dempsey, "Tracking C. M. Russell in Canada, 1888-1889," *Montana* 39 (Summer 1989): 2-15.

On other Montana artists, see Wesley M. Burnside, *Maynard Dixon: Artist of the West* (Provo: Brigham Young University Press, 1974); Forrest E. Fenn, *The Beat of the Drum and the Whoop of the Dance: A Biography of Joseph Henry Sharp* (Santa Fe: Fenn Publishing Company, 1983); William Gardner Bell, *Will James: The Life and Work of a Lone Cowboy* (Flagstaff, Ariz.: Northland Press, 1987).

Montana has published numerous articles on the history of Montana artists. On E. S. Paxson, see K. Ross Toole, "E.S. Paxson: Neglected Artist of the West," 4 (Spring 1954): 26-29; and Franz Stenzel, "E. S. Paxson: Montana Artist," 13 (Autumn 1963): 50-76. On O. C. Seltzer, see Michael Kennedy, "O. C. Seltzer: Meticulous Master of Western Art," 10 (Summer 1960): 2-21. See also John C. Ewers, "Weinold Reiss: His Portraits and Proteges," 21 (Summer 1971): 44-55; Dorys Crow Grover, "W. H. D. Koerner & Emerson Hough: A Western Collaboration," 29 (Spring 1979): 2-15; Bob Cooney and Sayre Cooney Dodgson, "Fanny Cory Cooney: Montana Mother and Artist," 30 (Summer 1980): 2-17.

On the history of photography and photographers in Montana, see Donna M. Lucey, *Photographing Montana, 1894-1928: The Life and Work of Evelyn Cameron* (New York: Alfred A. Knopf, 1990); Mark H. Brown and W. R. Felton, *The Frontier Years: L. A. Huffman, Photographer of the Plains* (New York: Henry Holt and Company, 1955); Brown and Felton, *Before Barbed Wire: L. A. Huffman, Photographer on Horseback* (New York: Henry Holt and Company, 1956); Edward Nolan, *Northern Pacific Views: The Railroad Photography of F. Jay Haynes, 1876-1905* (Helena: Montana Historical Society Press, 1983); Montana Historical Society, *F. Jay Haynes: Photographer* (Helena: Montana Historical Society Press, 1981); William L. Lang, "'At the Greatest Personal Peril to the Photographer': The Schwatka-Haynes Winter Expedition in Yellowstone, 1887," *Montana* 33 (Winter 1983): 14-29; Delores J. Morrow, "Female Photographers on the Frontier: Montana's Lady Photographic Artists, 1866-1900," *Montana* 33 (Winter 1983): 76-84.

Good introductions to western literature are Richard W. Etulain, *A Bibliographical Guide to the Study of Western American Literature* (Lincoln: University of Nebraska Press, 1982); Thomas J. Lyon et al., eds., *A Literary History of the American West* (Fort Worth: Texas Christian University Press, 1986). For an interpretation of Montana literature, see William Bevis, *Ten Tough Trips: Montana Writers and the West* (Seattle: University of Washington Press, 1990); and the several essays in William Kittredge and Annick Smith, eds., *The Last Best Place: A Montana Anthology* (Helena: Montana Historical Society Press, 1988). See also Rufus Coleman, "Creative Writing in the Northwest: Whence? Why? Whither?" in *Historical Essays in Montana and the Northwest*, ed. J. W. Smurr and K. R. Toole (Helena: Western Press, 1957), pp. 250-94. On Joseph Kinsey Howard, see Richard B. Roeder, "Joseph Kinsey Howard and His Vision of the West," *Montana* 30 (Winter 1980): 2-11; Jyl Hoyt, "Montana Writer Joseph Kinsey Howard: Crusader for the Worker, Land and Indian Community" (M.A. thesis, University of Montana, Missoula, 1988); Norman A. Fox, "Joseph Kinsey Howard: Writer," *Montana* 2 (April 1952): 41-44. On Schultz, see Warren H. Hanna, *The Life and Times of James Willard Schultz (Apikuni)* (Norman: University of Oklahoma Press, 1986); Jessie Donaldson Schultz, "Adventuresome, Amazing Apikuni," *Montana* 10 (October 1960): 2-18. On Linderman, see Celeste River, "A Mountain in His Memory: Frank Bird Linderman . . . " (M.A. thesis, University of Montana, Missoula, 1990); H. G. Merriam, "Sign-Talker with Straight Tongue," *Montana* 12 (July 1962): 2-20. On B. M. Bower, see Stanley R. Davison, "Chip of the Flying U: The Author Was a Lady," *Montana* 23 (April 1973): 2-15. On Butte's place in Montana writing, see Richard B. Roeder, "The Copper Pen: Butte in Fiction," in *Montana and the West*, ed. Myers and Fritz, pp. 144-66. For Johnson and Guthrie, consult Stephen L. Smith, "The Years and the Wind and the Rain: The Biography of Dorothy M. Johnson" (M.A. thesis, University of Montana, Missoula, 1969); and Charles E. Hood Jr., "Hard Work and Tough Dreaming: A Biography of A. B. Guthrie, Jr." (M.A. thesis, University of Montana, Missoula, 1969).

The Boise State University "Western Writers Series" includes the following volumes on Montana writers: Jay Boyer, *Richard Brautigan*; L. L. Lee, *Walter Van Tilburg Clark*; Peter Wild, *John Haines*; Donna Gerstenberger, *Richard Hugo*; Judy Alter, *Dorothy Johnson*; James Rupert, *D'Arcy McNickle*; Peter Wild, *James Welch*.

Montana published a series of reflective essays by Montana authors, including Mary Clearman Blew, "Myths, History, and the Precarious Margin of Fiction," 34 (Winter 1984): 2-9; Ivan Doig, "You Can't *Not* Go Home Again," 35 (Winter 1985): 2-15; William Kittredge, "New to the Country," 36 (Winter 1986): 2-11; David Long, "Testimony," 37 (Spring 1987): 2-11. For an interpretation of Ivan Doig's use of history, see William G. Robbins, "The Historian as Literary Craftsman: The West of Ivan Doig," *PNQ* 78 (October 1987): 134-40.

CHAPTER 15. THE RECENT POLITICAL SCENE

There is no study of Montana politics during the post-war period. A solid introduction to twentieth century politics in the American West is

Michael P. Malone and Richard Etulain, *The American West: A Twentieth-Century History* (Lincoln: University of Nebraska Press, 1989). See also Gerald D. Nash, *The American West in the Twentieth Century* (Englewood Cliffs, N.J.: Prentice-Hall, 1973); Nash, *The American West Transformed: The Impact of the Second World War* (Bloomington: Indiana University Press, 1985). Also consult the annual volumes of *The Almanac of American Politics*, published by the *National Journal* in Washington, D.C. For general trends, see Neal R. Peirce and Jerry Hagstrom, *The Book of America: Inside Fifty States Today* (New York: W. W. Norton, 1983); Jerry Hagstrom, *Beyond Reagan: The New Landscape of American Politics* (New York: W. W. Norton, 1988). James J. Lopatch et al., *We the People of Montana: The Workings of a Popular Government* (Missoula: Mountain Press Publishing, 1983), contains information on Montana's government and political process. On Montana's political development during the twentieth century, see Michael P. Malone and Dianne G. Dougherty, "Montana's Political Culture: A Century of Evolution," *Montana* 31 (Winter 1981): 44-58.

Valuable studies of recent Montana politics include Thomas Payne, "Montana: Politics Under the Copper Dome," in *Politics in the American West*, ed. Frank H. Jonas (Salt Lake City: University of Utah Press, 1969); Neil R. Peirce's astute look at Montana in *The Mountain States of America* (New York: W. W. Norton, 1972), pp. 99-119. See also Ellis Waldron, "Montana," in *Rocky Mountain Politics*, ed. JeDon Emenhiser (Logan: Utah State University Press, 1971), pp. 73-99.

To put Montana politics in perspective, see Ira Sharkansky, *The Maligned States* (New York: McGraw-Hill, 1972); Herbert Jacob and Kenneth N. Vines, eds., *Politics in the American States: A Comparative Analysis*, 2d. ed. (Boston: Little, Brown, 1971); Thomas R. Dye, *Politics in States and Communities*, 2d ed. (Englewood Cliffs, N.J.: Prentice-Hall, 1973).

For interest groups in Montana, see Daniel J. Foley's series in the *Billings Gazette* during August and September 1972, and articles in *The People's Voice* (Helena), October 4, 1957, May 29, 1959. See also Michael P. Malone, "Montana as a Corporate Bailiwick: An Image in History," in *Montana: Past and Present* (Los Angeles: William Andrews Clark Memorial Library, 1976), pp. 57-76. Political views of stockmen can be found in Robert H. Fletcher, *Free Grass to Fences: The Montana Cattle Range Story* (New York: University Publishers, 1960). On the Farmers Union, see John A. Crampton, *The National Farmers Union: Ideology of a Pressure Group* (Lincoln: University of Nebraska Press, 1965); Gladys T. Edwards, *This Is the Farmers Union* (Denver: National Farmers Union, 1951); Mildred K. Stoltz, *This Is Yours: The Montana Farmers Union and*

Its Cooperative Policies (Minneapolis: Lund Press, 1956). For the development of the REA and public power in Montana, see Frank J. Busch, *Power for the People: Montana's Cooperative Utilities* (Missoula: University of Montana, 1976).

None of Montana's postwar congressional figures has yet received extensive biographical treatment. Timothy J. Carman's "Senator Zales Ecton: A Product of Reaction" (M.A. thesis, Montana State University, Bozeman, 1971) focuses on Ecton's 1946 election campaign. On Lee Metcalf, see Robert Sherrill, "The Invisible Senator," *Nation*, May 10, 1971, pp. 584-9.

For an interesting characterization of James E. Murray, see Forrest Davis, "Millionaire Moses," *Saturday Evening Post*, December 8, 1945, pp. 9-10, 103-4, 106. See also Joseph K. Howard, "Jim Murray's Chances," *Nation*, October 9, 1948, pp. 397-9; George L. Bousilman, "The 1954 Campaign of Senator James E. Murray" (M.A. thesis, University of Montana, Missoula, 1964); Thomas H. Nilsen, "James E. Murray and Reconversion (1943-1945)" (M.A. thesis, University of Montana, Missoula, 1973). Also see William B. Evans, "Senator James E. Murray: A Voice of the People in Foreign Affairs," *Montana* 32 (Winter 1982); Donald E. Spritzer, "One River, One Problem: James Murray and the Missouri Valley Authority," in *Montana and the West*, ed. Rex C. Myers and Harry Fritz (Boulder, Colo.: Pruett Publishing Co., 1984), pp. 122-43; Spritzer, *The New Dealer from Montana: The Senate Career of James E. Murray* (New York: Garland Publishing, 1986).

Historians have just begun to research postwar state politics. For the election of 1952 and 1954, see William D. Miller's "Montana and the Specter of McCarthyism, 1952-1954" (M.A. thesis, Montana State University, Bozeman, 1969). J. Hugo Aronson and L. O. Brockmann, *The Galloping Swede* (Missoula: Mountain Press, 1970), is an entertaining autobiography, but it is nearly devoid of political content. Politics during the 1960s are covered in Judith B. Rollins, "Governor Donald G. Nutter and the Montana Daily Press" (M.A. thesis, University of Montana, Missoula, 1963); Jerry R. Holloron, "The Montana Daily Press and the 1964 Gubernatorial Campaign" (M.A. thesis, University of Montana, Missoula, 1965). On the movement for governmental reform that resulted in the 1972 constitution, see Richard B. Roeder, "Energy in the Executive," *Montana Law Review* 33 (Winter 1972): 1-13. An admiring look at the constitutional convention is "Fresh Chance Gulch," *Time*, April 10, 1972, p. 18.

Election statistics and maps can be found in Ellis Waldron's *Montana Politics Since 1864: An Atlas of Elections* (Missoula: University of Montana Press, 1958); Ellis Waldron and Paul B. Wilson, *Atlas of Montana*

Elections 1889-1976 (Missoula: University of Montana Publications in History, 1978). Ellis Waldron, *Montana Legislators 1864-1979, Profiles and Biographical Dictionary* (Missoula: Bureau of Government Research, University of Montana, 1980), is a valuable reference tool. For post-1976 data, look at the secretary of state's compilations. The 1972 Constitutional Convention is covered in "Constitutional Symposium '89," *Montana Law Review* 51 (Summer 1989). The most valuable commentaries on postwar political trends are found in the series of state-by-state analyses published in *Western Historical Quarterly* between 1949 and 1971. A dated but still useful bibliography is Thomas Payne, "Bibliography on Montana Politics," *Western Political Quarterly* 11 (December 1958): 65-72.

Index